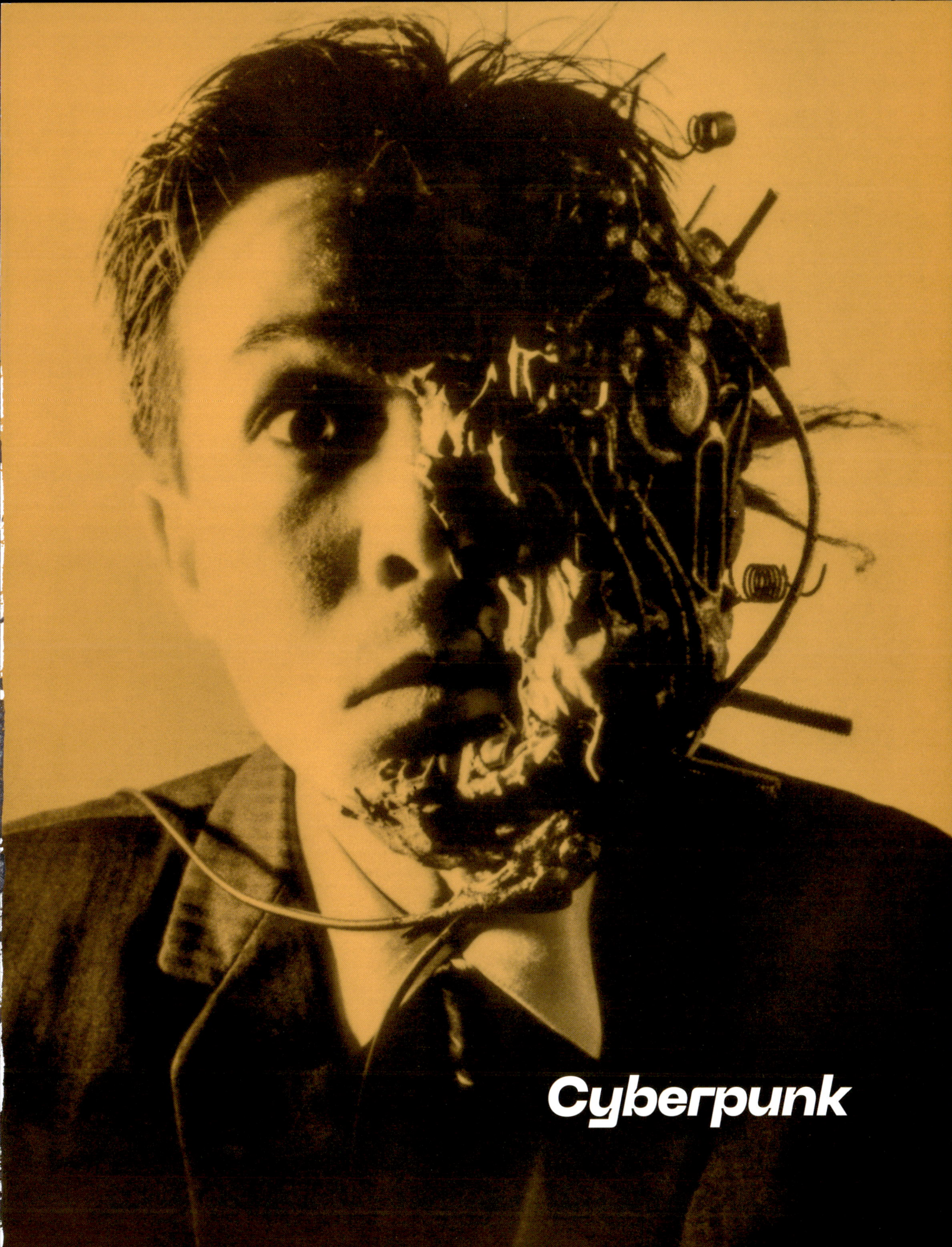

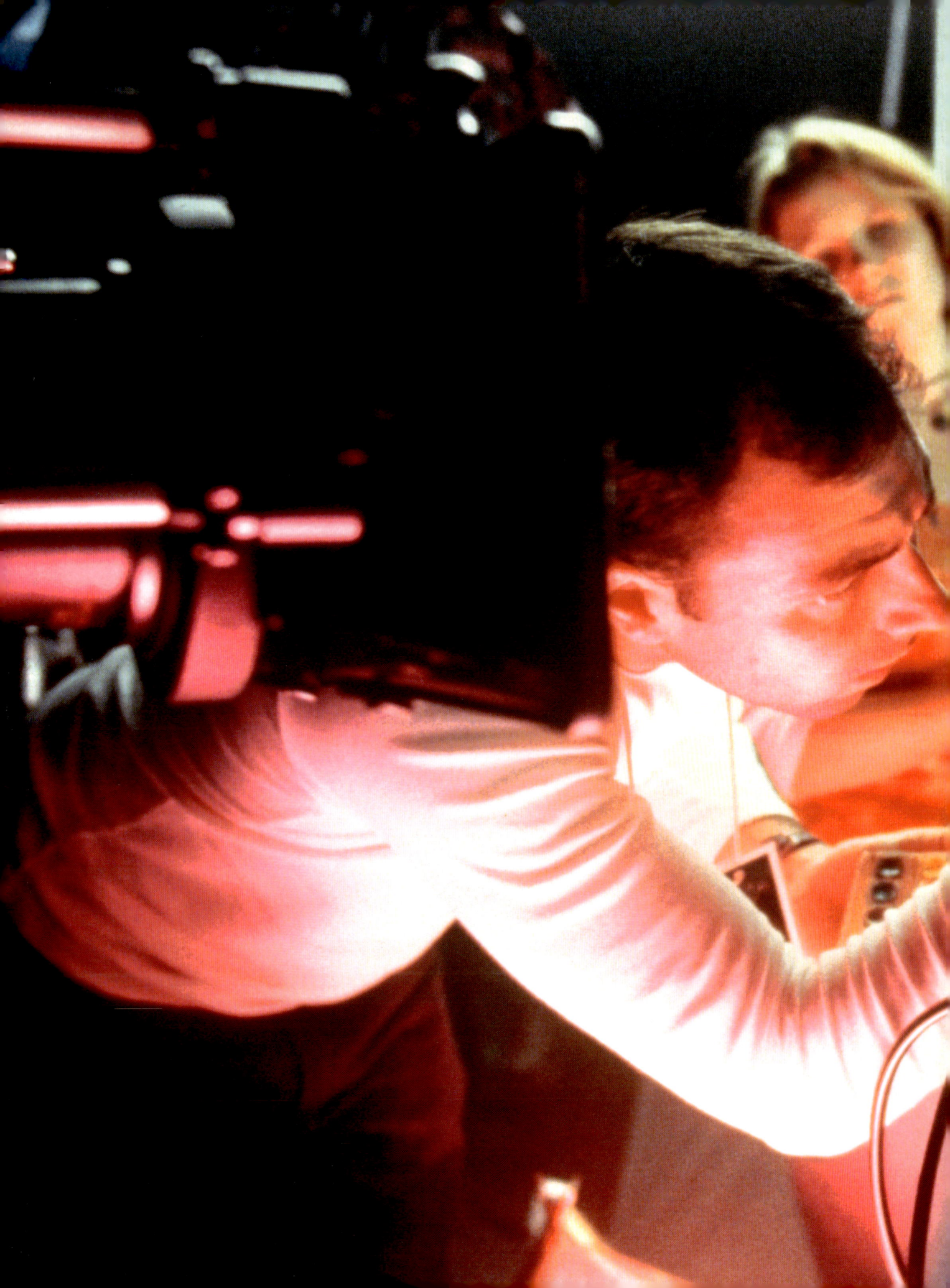

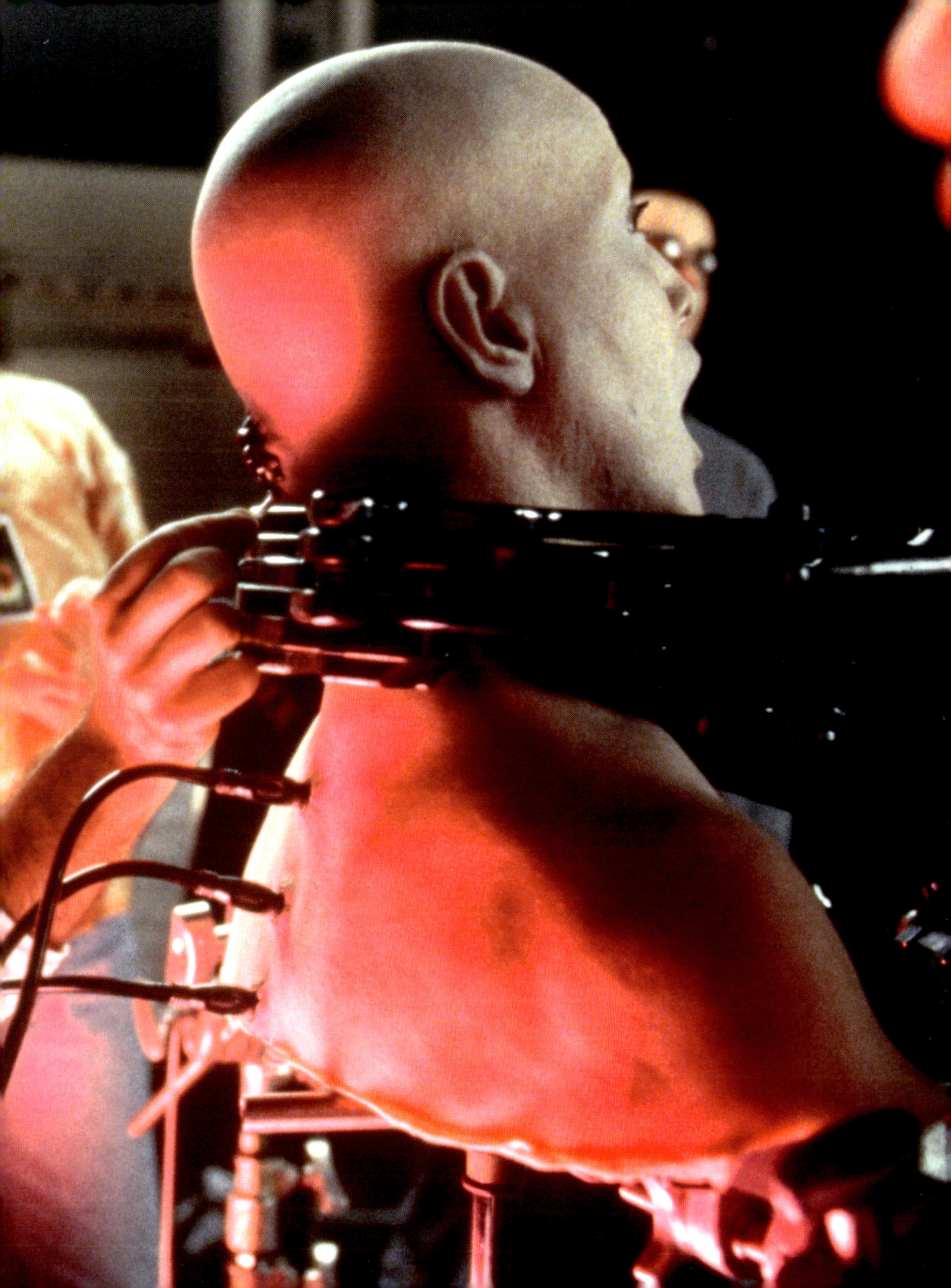

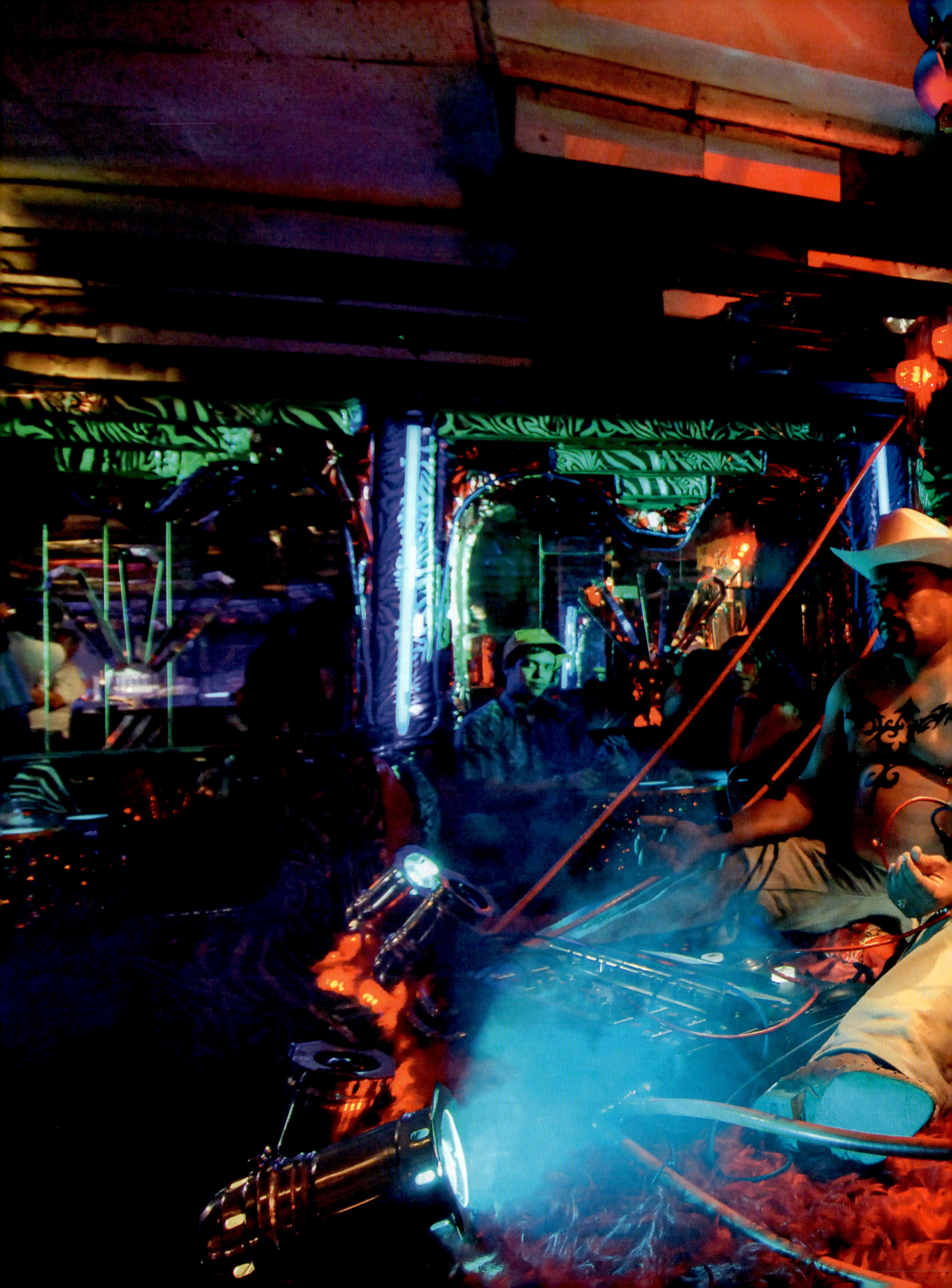

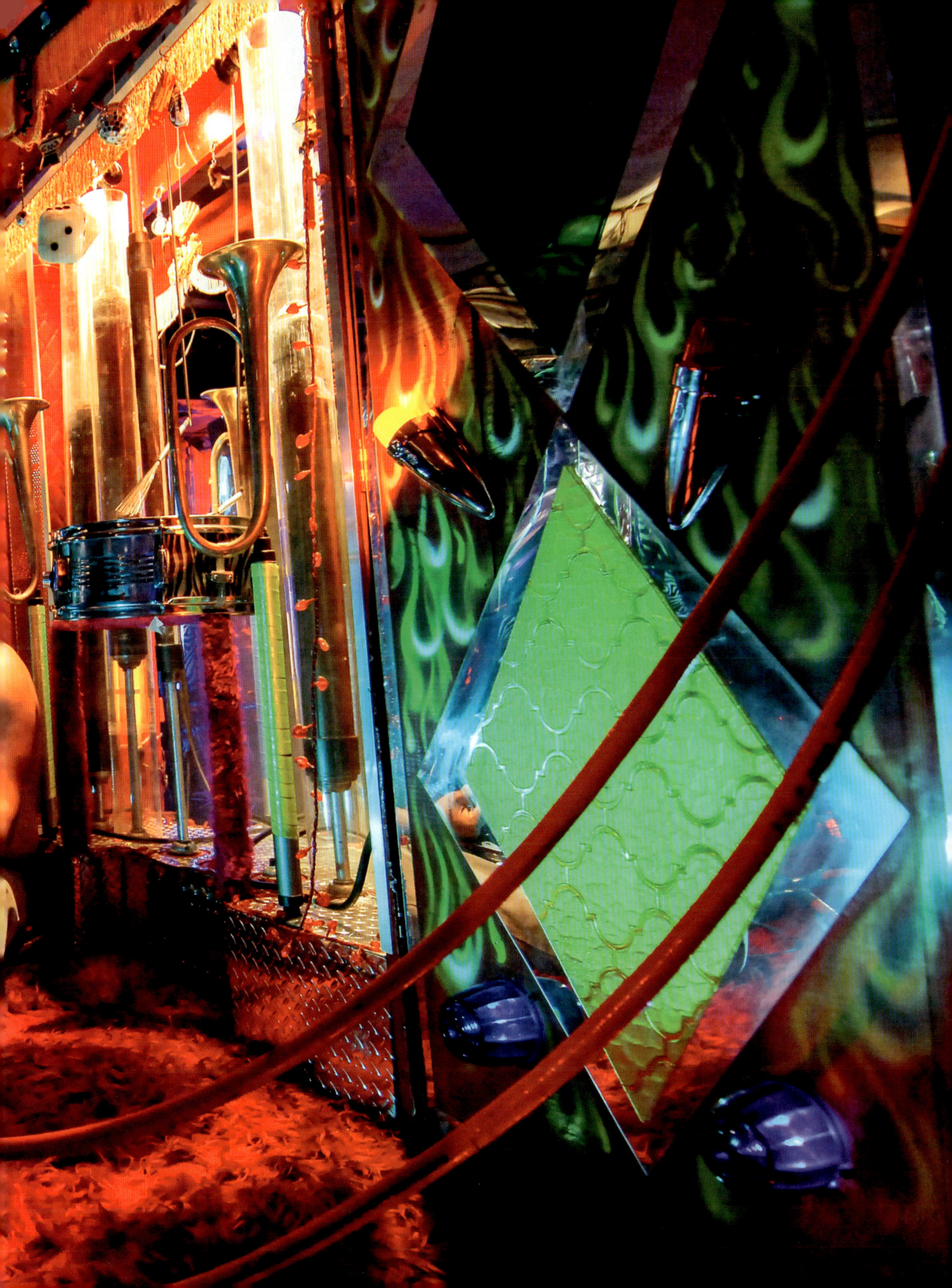

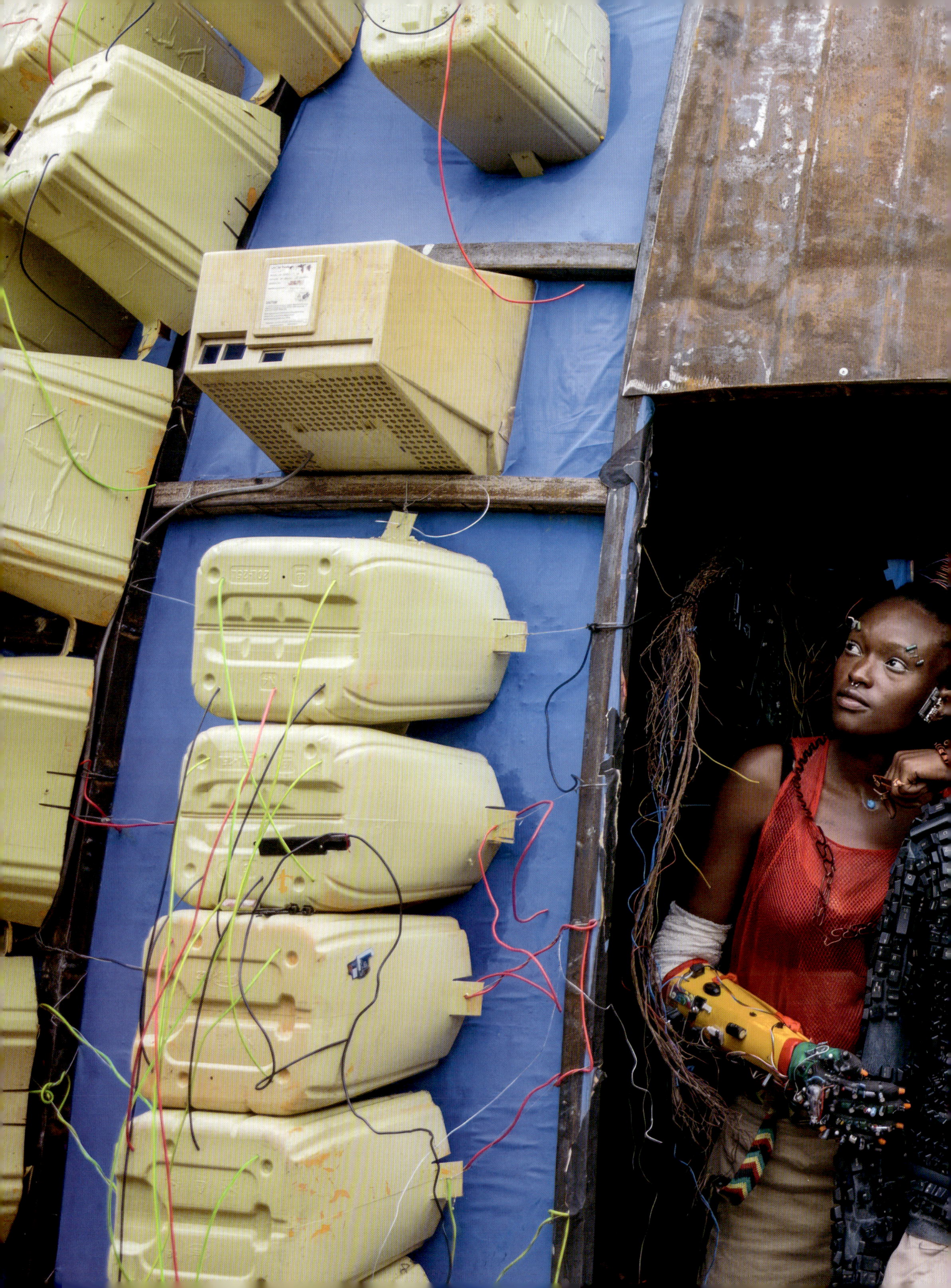

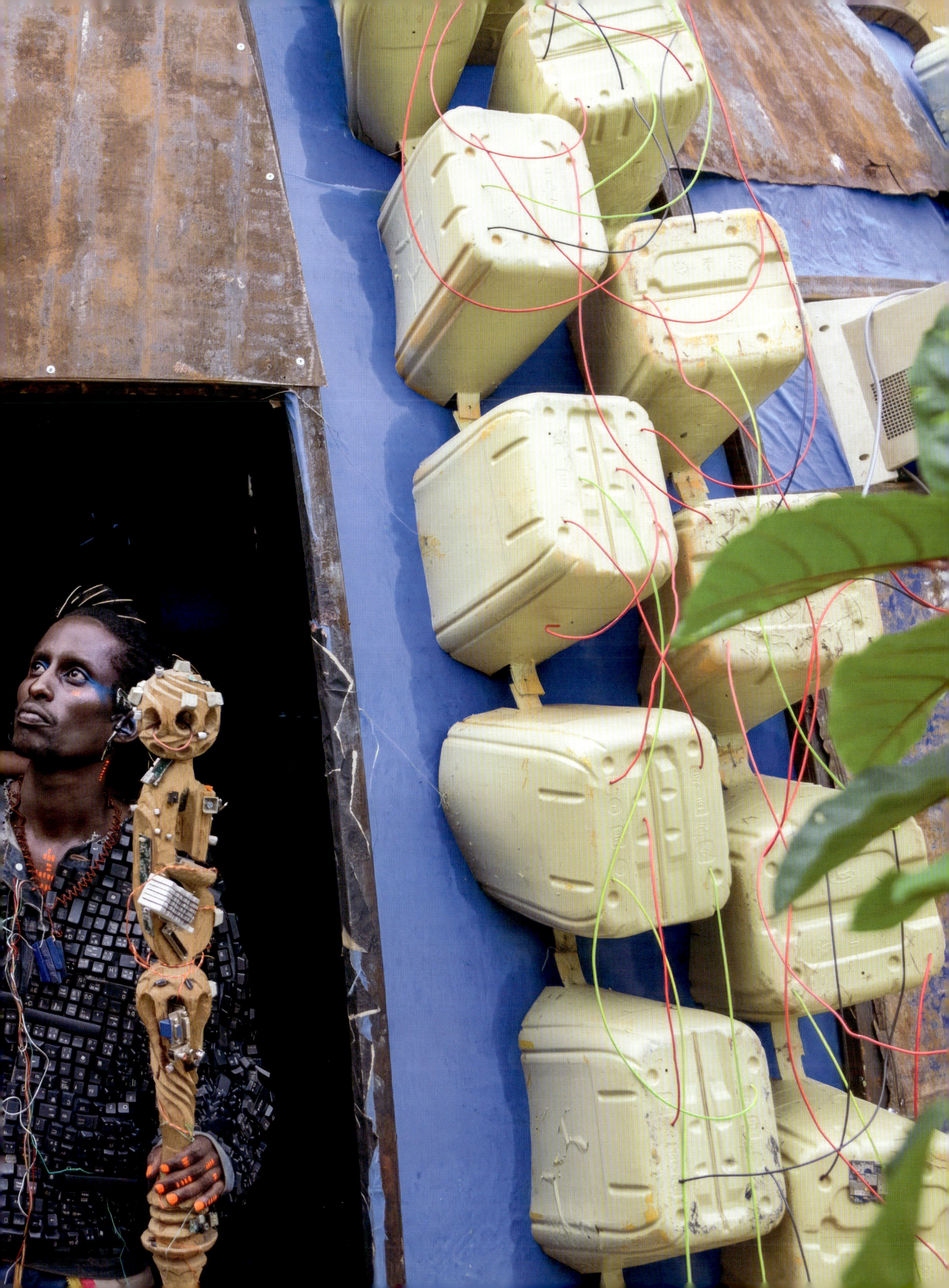

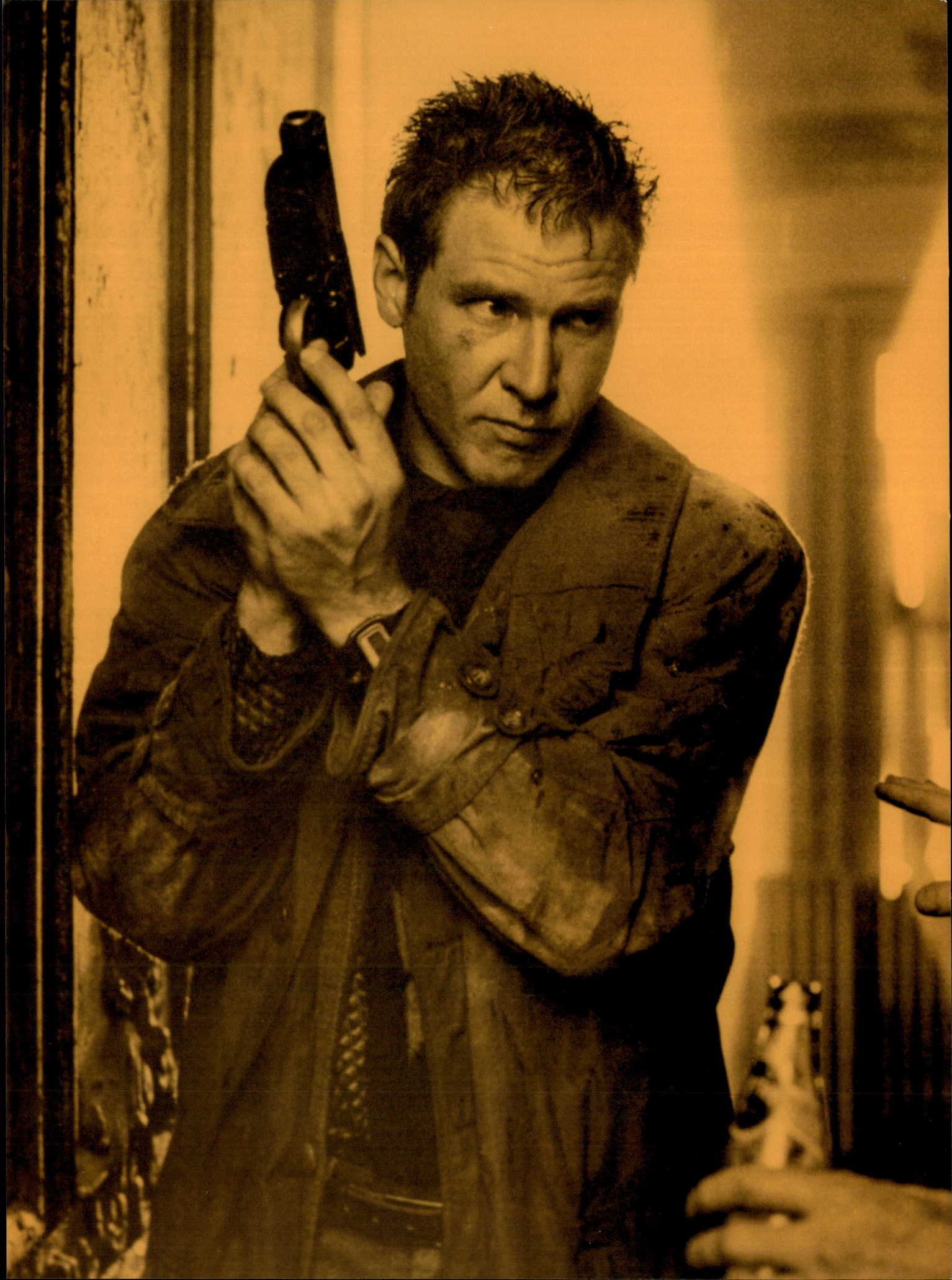

Cyberpunk

ENVISIONING
POSSIBLE
FUTURES
THROUGH
CINEMA

Edited by Doris Berger

Academy Museum of Motion Pictures, Los Angeles
DelMonico Books • D.A.P., New York

12
Foreword
Jacqueline Stewart

14
Acknowledgments
Doris Berger

16
Envisioning Possible Futures
Doris Berger

24
The Rise of Cyberpunk in Literature and Film
Carlen Lavigne

50
I, Cyberpunk
Alex Rivera

<u>Case Studies</u>

54
Westworld (1973)
Patrick B. Sharp

58
World on a Wire (1973)
David A. Kirby

64
Escape from New York (1981)
Emily Rauber Rodriguez

68
Blade Runner (1982)
Akira Mizuta Lippit

74
Tron (1982)
Nicholas Barlow

80
Videodrome (1983)
Millie De Chirico

86
The Terminator (1984)
Patrick B. Sharp

92
RoboCop (1987)
Emily Rauber Rodriguez

98
The Running Man (1987)
Craig Barron

102
Akira (1988)
Akira Mizuta Lippit

106
Tetsuo: The Iron Man (1989)
Nicholas Barlow

112
Ghost in the Shell (1995)
Akira Mizuta Lippit

118
Johnny Mnemonic (1995)
David A. Kirby

CONTENTS

124
Strange Days (1995)
Norman M. Klein

128
Welcome II the Terrordome (1995)
Ashley Clark

132
The Last Angel of History (1996)
DeForrest Brown Jr.

136
eXistenZ (1999)
K.J. Relth-Miller

142
The Matrix (1999)
Carlen Lavigne

148
Sleep Dealer (2008)
Emily Rauber Rodriguez

154
Pumzi (2009)
Maya S. Cade

158
Ex Machina (2015)
Carlen Lavigne

164
Neptune Frost (2021)
Shari Frilot

170
Night Raiders (2021)
Patrick B. Sharp

176
Futurisms: A Conversation with Danis Goulet and Wanuri Kahiu
Doris Berger and Nicholas Barlow

184
Selected Bibliography

188
Contributors

190
Credits

Foreword

I am excited to share *Cyberpunk: Envisioning Possible Futures Through Cinema*, made possible with support from Getty through its PST ART: *Art & Science Collide* initiative. The Academy Museum of Motion Pictures—with exhibitions and programs that give insight into the arts and sciences of movies—is an ideal institution to participate in this regional event that explores intersections of art and science, both past and present, familiar and unexpected. Cyberpunk, a subgenre of science fiction that focuses on technology and its impact on human life and earth's environment, is a fitting and particularly revelatory topic for this initiative.

Since the late nineteenth century, filmmakers have been creating and building upon technological innovations to invent new worlds on screen. As the sciences of motion pictures have evolved in this digital era, so too have the artistic visions presented so strikingly in cyberpunk films, which frequently explore fears about what new technologies might mean for us as a society. Today, the rapidly changing field of artificial intelligence is on the forefront of everyone's mind, making cyberpunk's visualizations of sentient machines gone awry—often against backdrops of social disorder, ecological crisis, and urban decay—more relevant than ever. The stories gain further significance when filmmakers from marginalized communities expand on these tropes with futuristic visions that reflect on generational trauma experienced in the wake of colonialism, enslavement, and labor exploitation. This project illustrates through a selection of Afrofuturist, Latinxfuturist, and Indigenous futurist films how these stories converse with themes and aspirations of cyberpunk, revealing the genre's wide-ranging influence.

I would like to express my deep gratitude to the exhibition's curatorial team—vice president of curatorial affairs Doris Berger, assistant curator Nicholas Barlow, and curatorial assistant Emily Rauber Rodriguez—for creating such engaging dialogues within the exhibition that explore new connections between and within film genres and cultures while also providing insight into the processes of filmmaking. I extend my deep appreciation to project advisors Danis Goulet, George Hull, Wanuri Kahiu, David A. Kirby, Carlen Lavigne, Akira Mizuta Lippit, and Patrick B. Sharp, who guided our curatorial team throughout this project, and to filmmaker Alex Rivera for his imaginative and inspiring collaboration on the exhibition's central montage.

Academy of Motion Picture Arts and Sciences CEO Bill Kramer was an early advocate of this project as my predecessor at the Academy Museum. I am deeply grateful to Bill and Academy chief operating officer and Academy Museum general counsel Brendan Connell, Jr., for their unwavering support throughout. I also thank Academy Museum chief audience officer Amy Homma for leading the efforts to share the fruits of this exhibition with the public, and particularly with educators and learners.

This exhibition showcases key holdings and new objects acquired for the Academy Museum and the Academy's Margaret Herrick Library. For their partnership, I extend my heartfelt thanks to executive vice president of the library, archive, and Science and Technology Council Randy Haberkamp, Margaret Herrick Library director Matt Severson, and Academy Film Archive director Michael Pogorzelski. I owe much to the members of the Academy Museum Board of Trustees, led by Ted Sarandos and vice-chair Miky Lee, as well as to Dominic Ng and Patricia Bellinger Balzer, who co-chair the Collections and Exhibitions Committee. Their governance, guidance, and support make all of our efforts possible.

I would like to express my immense gratitude to our funders and supporters, first and foremost the Getty Foundation, whose PST ART initiative has made such an impact on this city's artistic landscape. My thanks goes to Getty Foundation director Joan Weinstein and senior program officer Heather MacDonald for their incredible support. Thanks also to Katherine E. Fleming, Getty President and CEO, for her leadership in expanding PST ART into an ongoing initiative, in recognition of the crucial work it does to connect and convene Southern California cultural institutions with each other and the public so that we can look as a community at the critical issues we need to solve together. My thanks also to the Los Angeles County Board of Supervisors through the Los Angeles County Department of Arts and Culture led by director Kristin Sakoda.

Cyberpunk: Envisioning Possible Futures Through Cinema celebrates a genre that continues to create imaginative versions of the future. In today's ever-changing and uncertain world, these visions help us reflect on the past, interrogate the present, and engage in debates about possible tomorrows.

Jacqueline Stewart
Director and President

Acknowledgments

The exhibition *Cyberpunk: Envisioning Possible Futures Through Cinema* was developed as part of the Getty's PST ART: *Art & Science Collide* initiative. Conducting the archival research necessary to craft this exhibition during the COVID-19 pandemic was especially challenging. The team at the Getty Foundation was deeply supportive, and I would like to begin by thanking Joan Weinstein, Heather MacDonald, Zachary Kaplan, and Selene Preciado for their commitment to fostering intellectual exchange with various PST partners in such unprecedented times. PST ART presents more than sixty exhibitions across Southern California, and we were grateful for yet another opportunity to connect with our remarkable local museum communities.

This project would never have come to fruition without the committed and passionate efforts of assistant curator Nicholas Barlow and curatorial assistant Emily Rauber Rodriguez. I am indebted to them for their dedication and creativity. I would also like to acknowledge Manouchka Kelly Labouba and Ana Santiago for their invaluable contributions in the early phases of this project. A team of expert advisors, consisting of filmmakers Danis Goulet, George Hull, and Wanuri Kahiu, and scholars David A. Kirby, Carlen Lavigne, Akira Mizuta Lippit, and Patrick B. Sharp, acted as knowledgeable, engaged partners for us throughout the process. For the central montage illustrating cyberpunk's twentieth-century origins and the new global directions it has taken in the twenty-first century, we commissioned writer-director Alex Rivera to create a first-person script exploring key elements of the genre and its expansion into futurist cinemas. I am so thankful for his poetic contribution and the collaborative spirit he brought to creating this one-of-a-kind film montage with us.

I'd like to express my gratitude to our lenders for their generosity: the Toronto International Film Festival team, particularly Natania Sherman and Keith Bennie; Roger Servick and Michael Lund from the estate of Syd Mead; Jarett Hartman at the Walt Disney Archives; and Phoenix Alexander at the UC Riverside Library; as well as Paul Barkin, Danis Goulet, Tara Woodbury, Paul Haslinger, Patrick B. Sharp, and Alex Rivera for their major loans to this exhibition.

David Dryer and Gene Kozicki provided valuable background information and stories. The team from Magnopus, led by creative director Craig Barron with producer Daisy Leak and museum experience specialist Vince Beggs, contributed a special virtual reality experience connecting visitors to this exhibition and showcasing new VFX filmmaking tools. We also received great advice from Academy governor Brooke Breton and other members of the Academy's Visual Effects Branch Executive Committee.

Over the course of developing this exhibition, our access to images and objects was generously facilitated by: John Akomfrah and David Lawson at Smoking Dogs Films; Daniel Bosworth at A24; Patrick Boyd and Zach Martin at Samuel Goldwyn Films; Andy Bandit from Fox/Walt Disney Archives; Michael Buckhoff at the Walt Disney Company; Ashley Clark at Criterion Collection; Margarita Diaz, Dana Ellsworth, Gilbert Emralino, and Keith Kutscher at Sony Pictures Entertainment; Mark Greenhalgh, Julie Heath, Jeff Briggs, and George Feltenstein at Warner Bros.; Miranda Hambro and Barbara Miller at Museum of the Moving Image; Karla Nielsen at the Huntington Library; Rachel Parham at NBCUniversal Archives & Collections; and Rebecca Ruud at Paramount Pictures. Many thanks also to Kym Barrett, Stephen Dane, Lois DeArmond, Aaron Johnson, Tom Mes, Cedric Mizero, Simon Onwurah, Yûko Shiomaki, and Audrey Wolff as well as the talented filmmakers who helped with this project, including Ngozi Onwurah, Shinya Tsukamoto, Anisia Uzeyman, and Saul Williams.

At the Academy Museum, I am extremely thankful for the support of director and president Jacqueline Stewart, chief operating officer and general counsel Brendan Connell, Jr., and chief audience officer Amy Homma. A heartfelt thanks to vice president of advancement Matthew Youngner and his team, especially Dawn Mori and Sabira Parajuli, who worked diligently on the grants, for making our visions come true. My gratitude goes also to Academy CEO Bill Kramer for his support early on. I also thank Dilcia Barrera, the Academy's senior vice president for member relations, global outreach, and awards administration, for advising us throughout the project.

Cyberpunk: Envisioning Possible Futures Through Cinema includes key objects from the Academy Collections, in particular from the collection of the Academy Museum and the Margaret Herrick Library. At the museum, I'd like to thank curatorial consultant Nathalie Morris and collections curator Laura Mart for their research and guidance on acquiring new objects for our collection, as well as vice president of registration and collection management Sonja Wong Leaon and her team, in particular Bernie Sale, Jillian Griffith, and Renée Kiefer for managing the loans and acquisitions, and Sophie Hunter and Rio Lopez for their impeccable and creative conservation work. At the Margaret Herrick Library, I'd like to thank director Matt Severson as well as Russell Butner, Anne Coco, Laura Darlington, Meg de Waal, Rachel Rosenfeld, Warren Sherk, and Lea Whittington for their support in acquiring new objects, and Dawn Jaros and her team for conserving them diligently.

For our exhibition planning and production, my deep appreciation to executive vice president of exhibitions Shraddha Aryal and her team, especially Susan Jenkins, Daqian Cao, Lindsay Stavros, Laura Belevica, Kalani Mah, Kristy Jennings, Emily Tobias, Christopher Richmond, Bert Thomas, Will Slade, Josh Porro, Andrew Mueller, Phy Cottrell, Stephen Morrissey, and Jerry Buszek, for their creativity and collaborative spirit. Our digital content and strategy team, led by Agnes Stauber, was instrumental in creating meaningful digital interactions, including the recording of new oral histories with filmmakers John Carpenter, Mamoru Oshii, and Shinya Tsukamoto. A particular thank-you to Teague Schneiter, Franny Alfano, Yousef Assabahi, and Mae Woods, who worked thoughtfully on recording these voices. I am indebted to K.J. Relth-Miller and Christina Ybarra, who, with their teams, developed engaging film series and impactful educational initiatives and public programs. A warm thank-you to the communications team, especially Daniel Gomez and Stephanie Sykes, and the marketing team led by Adriana Fernandez. I would also like to express my gratitude to the legal team led by Lena Wong, especially Bria Grant and McKell Forbes for their diligent clearance work. I would like to thank former curatorial department coordinator Jaclyn Wu, who supported me in bringing everyone together throughout this project, and former project manager Cindy Ha for keeping us on schedule.

Last but not least, thank you to Stacey Allan and her publications team, especially Chelsea Bingham and Lars Eckstrom, for their work in realizing this catalogue. We found aesthetic kinship with graphic designer Michael Worthington, and I could not be happier with the look and feel of this book. I am additionally grateful to Nikki Bazar for her editorial finesse and Susan Richmond for her meticulous proofreading. And, of course, sincere gratitude to this publication's contributors: Nicholas Barlow, Craig Barron, DeForrest Brown Jr., Maya S. Cade, Ashley Clark, Millie De Chirico, Shari Frilot, David A. Kirby, Norman M. Klein, Carlen Lavigne, Akira Mizuta Lippit, Emily Rauber Rodriguez, K.J. Relth-Miller, and Patrick B. Sharp, as well as to Danis Goulet and Wanuri Kahiu, who shared insights into their processes and cultural backgrounds in an interview with Nicholas Barlow and myself.

I would like to end with some personal thanks, to my husband, Steven, and our dog, Pucci, both of whom spent innumerable hours with me watching exhilarating but also often challenging cinematic depictions of futures.

Doris Berger
Vice President of Curatorial Affairs

Envisioning Possible Futures
Doris Berger

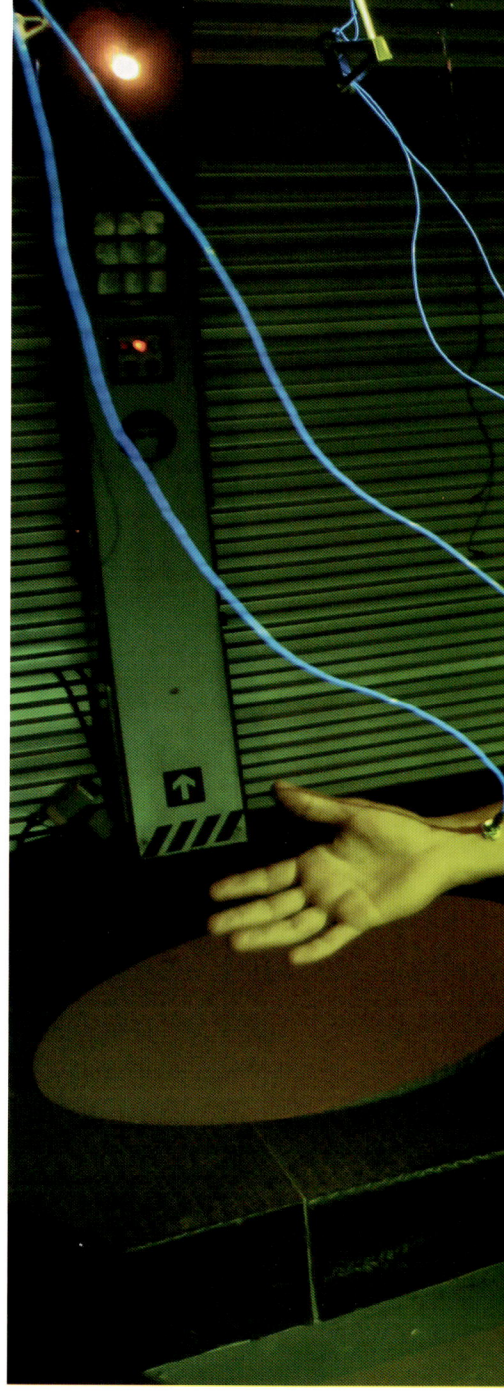

"We must engage with the future in order to make history."

WE ARE LIVING IN OUR IMAGINED FUTURE. The current debates about artificial general intelligence and cybersecurity, the fear of sentient machines harming humanity, and the destruction of our environment due to climate change connect our lived reality with cyberpunk narratives. These bleak scenarios—stable ingredients of futurist cinema since the late 1970s—feel so familiar now, as many of those imaginations have become real. Cyberpunk narratives combine cybernetics and digital culture with a punk attitude. They explore and reflect on topics such as new technologies, artificial intelligence, transhumanism, cyborgs, hacking culture, capitalism, colonialism, and race, gender, and class relations as well as climate change, often through a defiant approach toward established hierarchies. As these stories present visions of the future on our planet rather than in faraway galaxies, they also comment on our earthly past and present.

NOTES

Epigraph: See the homepage of the website for Deep Lab, "a collaborative group of cyberfeminist researchers, artists, writers, engineers, and cultural producers," accessed October 12, 2023, https://www.deeplab.net. Also quoted in Mindy Seu, *Cyberfeminism Index* (Los Angeles: Inventory Press, 2022), 266.

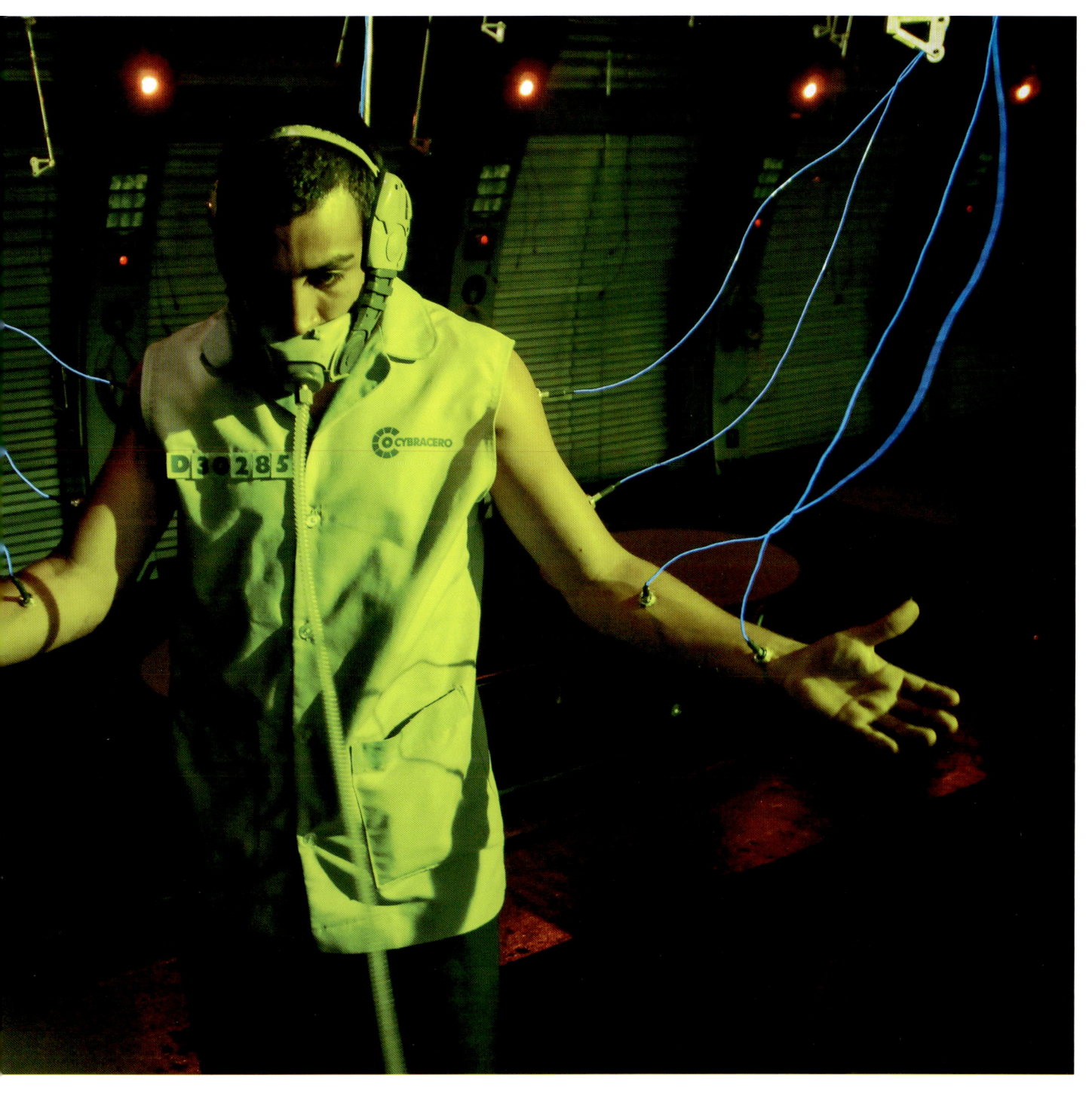

ABOVE: Luis Fernando Peña as Memo Cruz in *Sleep Dealer* (2008)

1./ Anna McFarlane, Graham J. Murphy, and Lars Schmeink, eds., *The Routledge Companion to Cyberpunk Culture* (New York: Routledge, 2020), 3.

Cyberpunk began as a subgenre of science fiction literature and cinema, eventually growing into a genre unto itself. Scholars emphasize "the importance of cyberpunk as a cultural formation, a means of engaging with our 21st-century technocultural age."[1] But who is imagining these futures and who plays an active part in them are key questions. While cyberpunk cinema in the United States during the 1980s and '90s was predominantly shaped by white male protagonists and filmmakers, international interest in this genre as well as the appeal for marginalized communities to create visions of the future broadened representations to include characters and stories about people of color, women, and members of the LGBTQ+ community.

How can we envision different futures when they are laden with the past? Futurist movements such as Afrofuturism, Indigenous futurism, Latinxfuturism, and Asian American futurism draw on what the scholar

Lesley Larkin calls "longstanding and distinct speculative traditions, as well as specific histories of oppression and exclusion, … articulat[ing] unique concerns and sensibilities while also sharing the goal of building more just worlds."[2] Common ground of most speculative fiction by marginalized communities is that the apocalypse has already happened by way of colonialism, enslavement, segregation, immigration laws, or environmental destruction, and that there is a need to visualize futures not fed by these oppressive pasts. Yet, in order to envision more just and equitable futures, it is important to imagine stories that are shaped not by generational trauma or destruction but rather by ancestral knowledge and practices. The collapse of a linear concept of time is a useful tool for these creative expressions. For example, the 1960s and '70s speculative fiction by the Black science fiction writers Samuel R. Delany and Octavia E. Butler, who composed narratives about fluid sexual identities

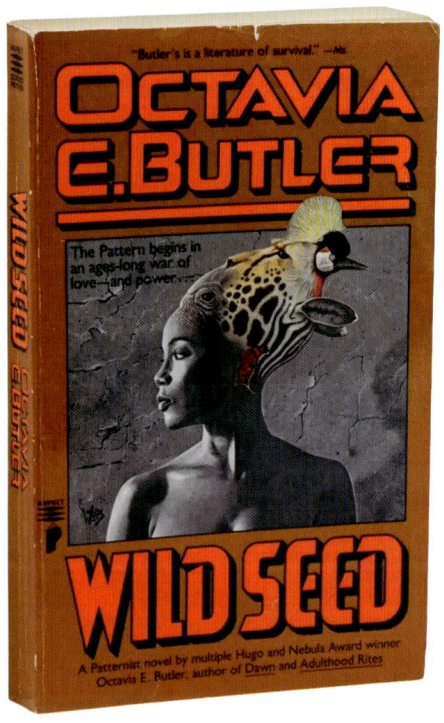

LEFT: Octavia E. Butler, *Wild Seed* (Doubleday & Company, 1980), Popular Library edition, 1988

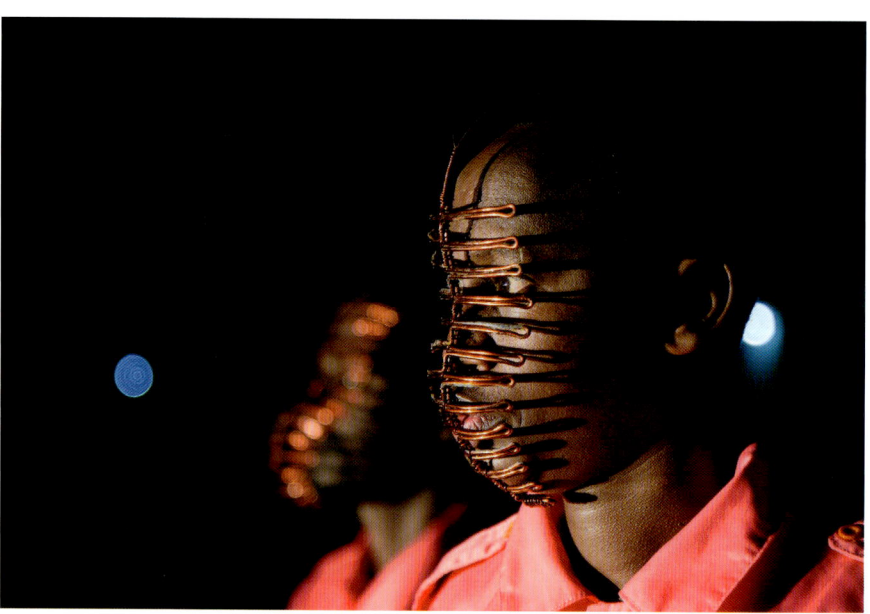

RIGHT: Scene from *Neptune Frost* (2021)

and ancestral knowledge and survival, respectively, had a major impact in shaping what would later be understood as Afrofuturism—a mode of expression that reaches across literature, music, film, fashion, and the visual and performative arts. The term *Afrofuturism* was coined by the critic Mark Dery in 1993,[3] and was expanded on by other authors, including Ytasha Womack, who defined it as "a way of looking at the future and alternate realities through a Black cultural lens" and as "a mode of self-healing and liberation." According to Womack, "Imagining oneself in the future creates agency, and also it's very significant because historically people of African descent were not always incorporated into many of the storylines about the future."[4]

In comparison, Indigenous futurist literature and film assert Native sovereignty and self-determination and forefront the idea of *survivance*.

2./ Lesley Larkin, "Afrofuturism," in *The Encyclopedia of Contemporary American Fiction: 1980–2020*, ed. Patrick O'Donnell, Stephen J. Burn, and Lesley Larkin, 2 vols. (Hoboken, NJ: Wiley, 2022), 8.

3./ Dery describes Afrofuturism as "speculative fiction that treats African-American themes and addresses African-American concerns in the context of twentieth-century technoculture." Mark Dery, "Black to the Future: Interviews with Samuel R. Delany, Greg Tate, and Tricia Rose," *South Atlantic Quarterly* 92, no. 4 (Fall 1993): 736.

4./ Ytasha Womack, "Afrofuturism: Imagination and Humanity," February 26, 2017, Sonic Acts, YouTube video, 25:10, https://www.youtube.com/watch?v=xlF9osXVfKk&t=3s; and Maiysha Kai, "Black History Meets Afrofuturism at Carnegie Hall," *TheGrio*, February 7, 2022, accessed

October 12, 2023, https://thegrio.com/2022/02/07/black-history-afrofuturism-carnegie-hall.

5./ Grace L. Dillon, "Introduction: Indigenous Futurisms, *Bimaashi Biidaas Mose, Flying* and *Walking towards You*," *Extrapolation* 57, nos. 1–2 (January 2016): 2. For more information on new Indigenous film projects, including Indigenous futurist movies, visit the imagineNATIVE website at https://imaginenative.org.

Indigenous futurist stories, writes American author Grace L. Dillon, "are not the product of a victimized people's wishful amelioration of their past, but instead a continuation of a spiritual and cultural path that remains unbroken by genocide and war."[5] While there is a need to be aware of the past in order to change the future, there is also a need to refuse being shaped by the past in order to envision more desirable futures.

Let's not forget the *punk* in *cyberpunk*. Punk first developed in music and fashion in the 1970s as a statement of rebellion and resistance against dominating social orders. It offered an ideological and aesthetic approach for people experiencing alienation and wanting to revolt against authority.[6] Cyberpunk narratives tend to have antiauthoritarian protagonists who rebel against established hierarchies, big corporations, or even nation-states, and often feature punk fashion elements, such as worn leather jackets, biker boots, bold makeup,

LEFT: Production design drawing for *The Running Man* (1987)

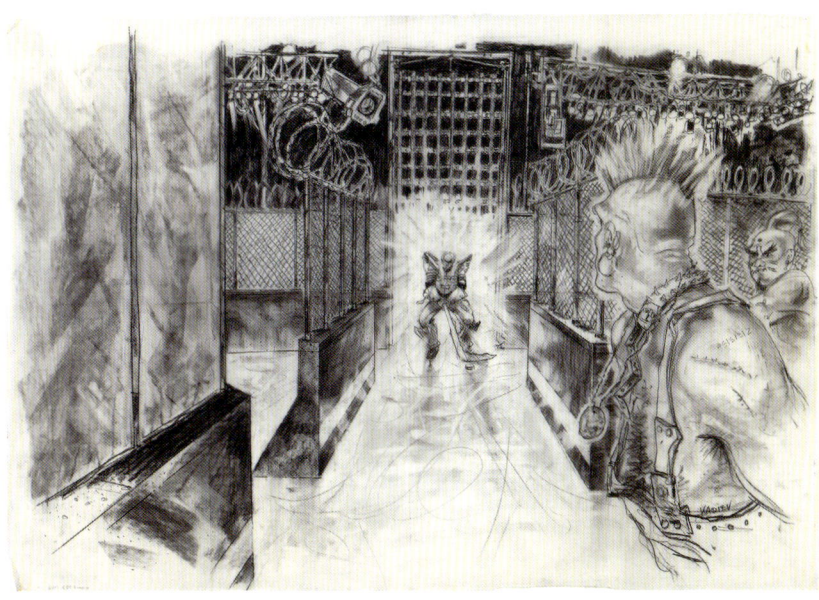

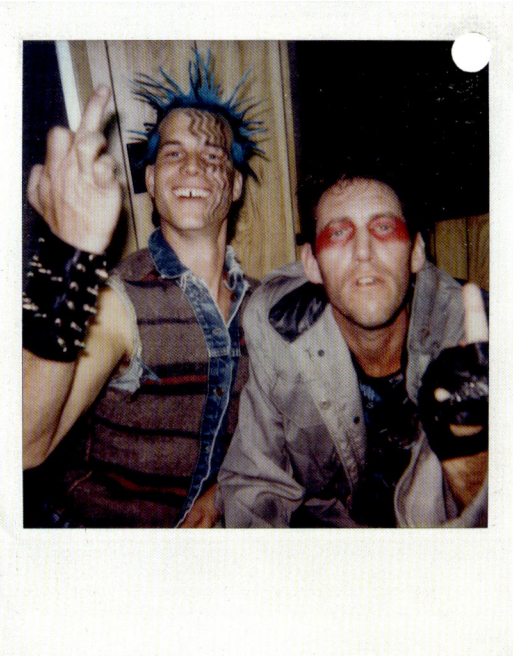

6./ See *Encyclopaedia Britannica Online*, s.v. "punk," accessed October 10, 2023, https://www.britannica.com/art/punk.

7./ Mendi and Keith Obadike, *The Sour Thunder: An Internet Opera*, 2002, quoted in Seu, *Cyberfeminism Index*, 107.

or spiky hairstyles. Punk's countercultural attitude is thus useful to filmmakers like the ones presented in this book, who wish to critique the status quo by questioning existing codes of conduct that often further systemic oppression. While hacking represents a rebellious practice toward technology, "Hacking is not simply about computer systems. It is also about other codes."[7]

The exhibition and its accompanying catalogue look at a multitude of cinematic practices that reflect on technoculture and on the state of our built and natural environments with a rebellious yet visionary mindset. Featuring near-future scenarios set in worlds that resemble our own, cyberpunk as well as many futurist films juxtapose technological advances with social upheaval, ecological crisis, and urban decay, often situated in dystopian wastelands, urban locales, or digital environments. Central to these stories are film-noir-like

ABOVE: Actors Bill Paxton (left) and David Kristin during production of *The Terminator* (1984)

antiheroes, yet these protagonists fight against technology gone haywire, oppressive political systems, or corrupt megacorporations. The movies frequently start with an exposition situating the viewer in a particular place and time in the near future, such as: "1997, NOW" (*Escape from New York*, USA, 1981), "Los Angeles, November, 2019" (*Blade Runner*, USA, 1982), "Los Angeles 2029 A.D." (*The Terminator*, USA, 1984), "31 Years after World War III: AD 2019 Neo Tokyo" (*Akira*, Japan, 1988), the "Maitu Community, East African Territory: 35 years after World War III—'The Water War'" (*Pumzi*, Kenya, 2009), or "Internet—2021" (*Johnny Mnemonic*, USA, 1995). In many cases, the settings are dystopian megacities—Los Angeles, Mexico City, Johannesburg, Tokyo—or devastated landscapes. The urban environments often feature spectacular aesthetic details that depict a tech-saturated world full of neon lights, modernist buildings, flying vehicles, and illuminated data highways.

8./ This film montage at the Academy Museum was a unique collaboration between the curatorial team, the exhibition's advisors, and Rivera, who was commissioned to write a script that presents an embodied perspective of the cyberpunk genre.

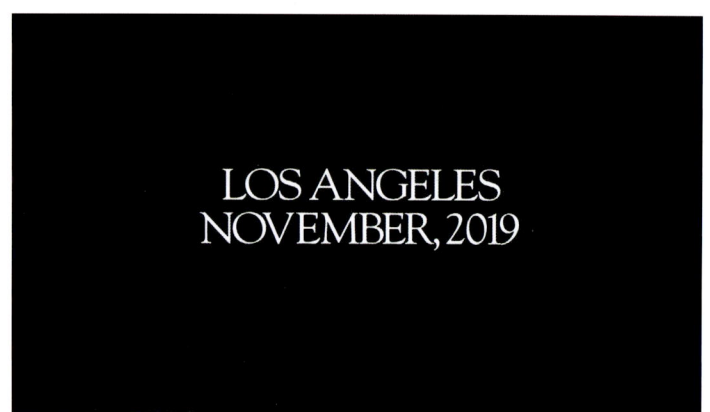

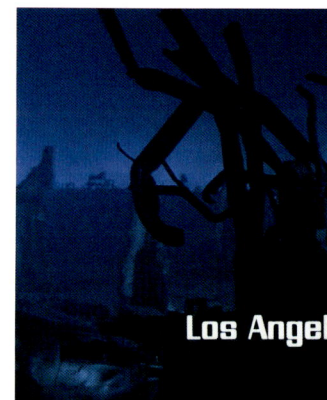

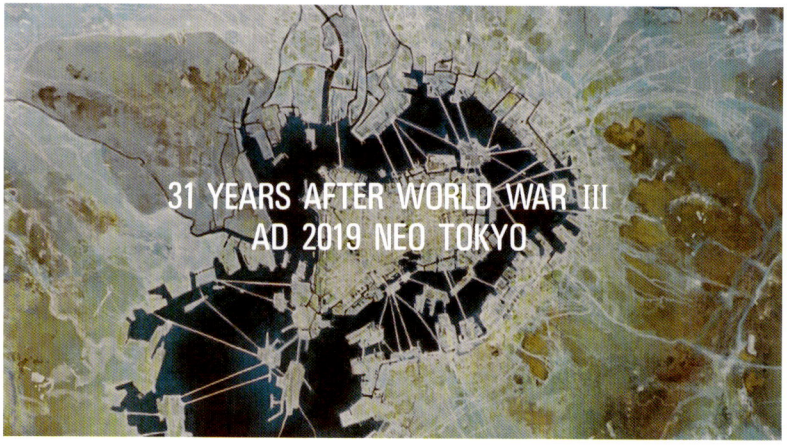

CLOCKWISE FROM TOP LEFT: *Blade Runner* (1982), *The Terminator* (1984), *Johnny Mnemonic* (1995), *Pumzi* (2009), and *Akira* (1988)

Cyberpunk: Envisioning Possible Futures Through Cinema explores the imaginative environments and tropes of cyberpunk and futurist cinema. The centerpiece of the exhibition is a large-scale montage of film clips that immerses viewers in futuristic scenarios, featuring a commissioned voice-over narrative by Alex Rivera, writer and director of *Sleep Dealer* (USA/Mexico, 2008).[8] The exhibition also includes original posters, costumes, props, and production design drawings from iconic cyberpunk and more recent futurist movies such as *Blade Runner*, *Tron* (USA, 1982), *Videodrome* (Canada, 1983), *The Terminator*, *The Running Man* (USA, 1987), *Akira*, *Strange Days* (USA, 1995), *The Matrix* (USA, 1999), *eXistenZ* (Canada, 1999), *Sleep Dealer*, *Ex Machina* (USA, 2015), *Alita: Battle Angel* (USA, 2019), *Night Raiders* (Canada/New Zealand, 2021), and *Neptune Frost* (Rwanda/USA, 2021).

9./ Jason Edward Lewis, "Terra Nullius, Terra Incognito," *BlackFlash* 21, no. 3 (June 2004): 16, quoted in Seu, *Cyberfeminism Index*, 206. To learn more about Lewis's work, visit https://jasonlewis.org.

This catalogue complements the experiential aspects of the exhibition by adding historical and scholarly context. In her essay "The Rise of Cyberpunk in Literature and Film," Carlen Lavigne examines the relationship between cyberpunk literary and cinematic works, and how both have changed over time to incorporate more diverse voices. The volume also includes short case studies of cyberpunk and futurist movies written by scholars, critics, and filmmakers that present a multitude of perspectives on this rich and international cinema culture. Accompanied by rarely seen behind-the-scenes photographs and other production materials, some of these texts offer insights into the creative processes of making these films, while others focus more on sociopolitical interpretations or express personal and poetic reflections. An interview with Canadian Cree-Métis filmmaker Danis Goulet and Kenyan Kikuyu filmmaker Wanuri Kahiu explores speculative fiction in relation to their respective

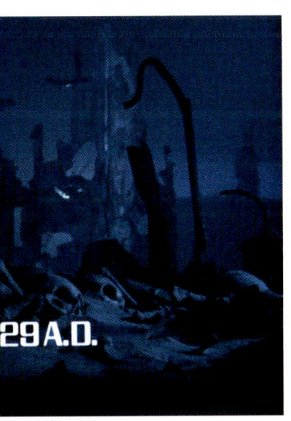

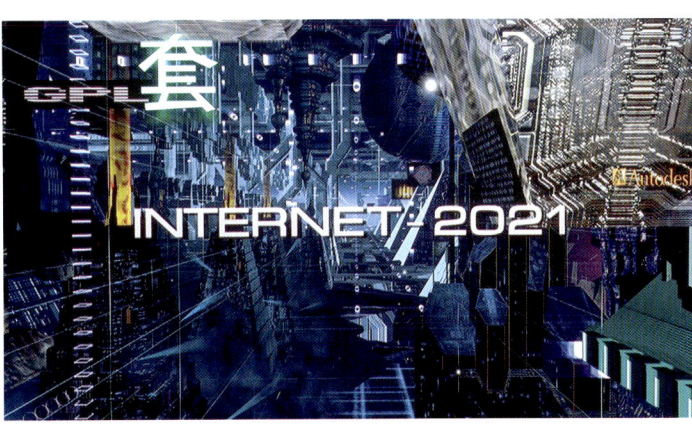

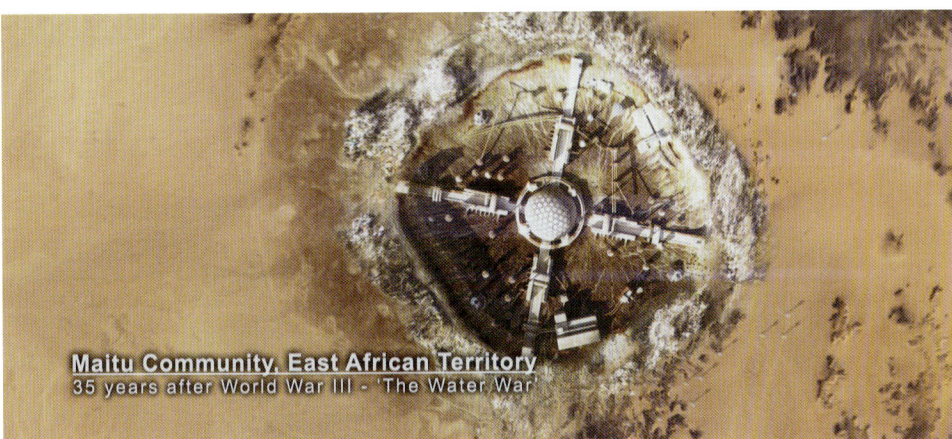

filmmaking practices, and a visual chapter spotlighting memorable cyberpunk film scenes, accompanied by Rivera's script, evokes the exhibition's central montage.

Cyberpunk: Envisioning Possible Futures Through Cinema highlights how cyberpunk and futurist films are international productions with devoted fans around the world, demonstrating that it is a fundamental human trait to imagine a future for one's community no matter where we are from or where we are going. As digital media theorist Jason Edward Lewis once stated, "We're all immigrants in cyberspace."[9]

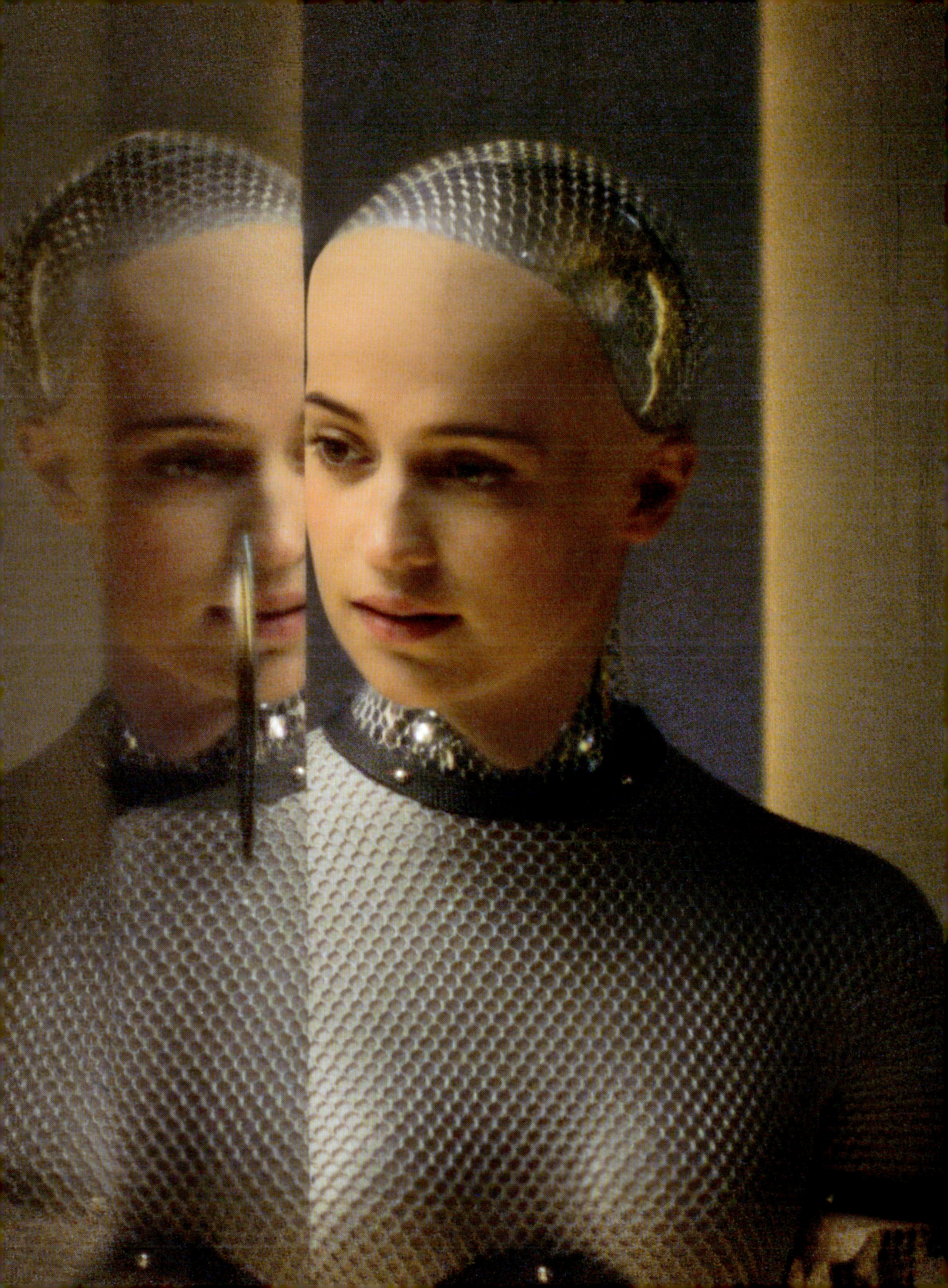

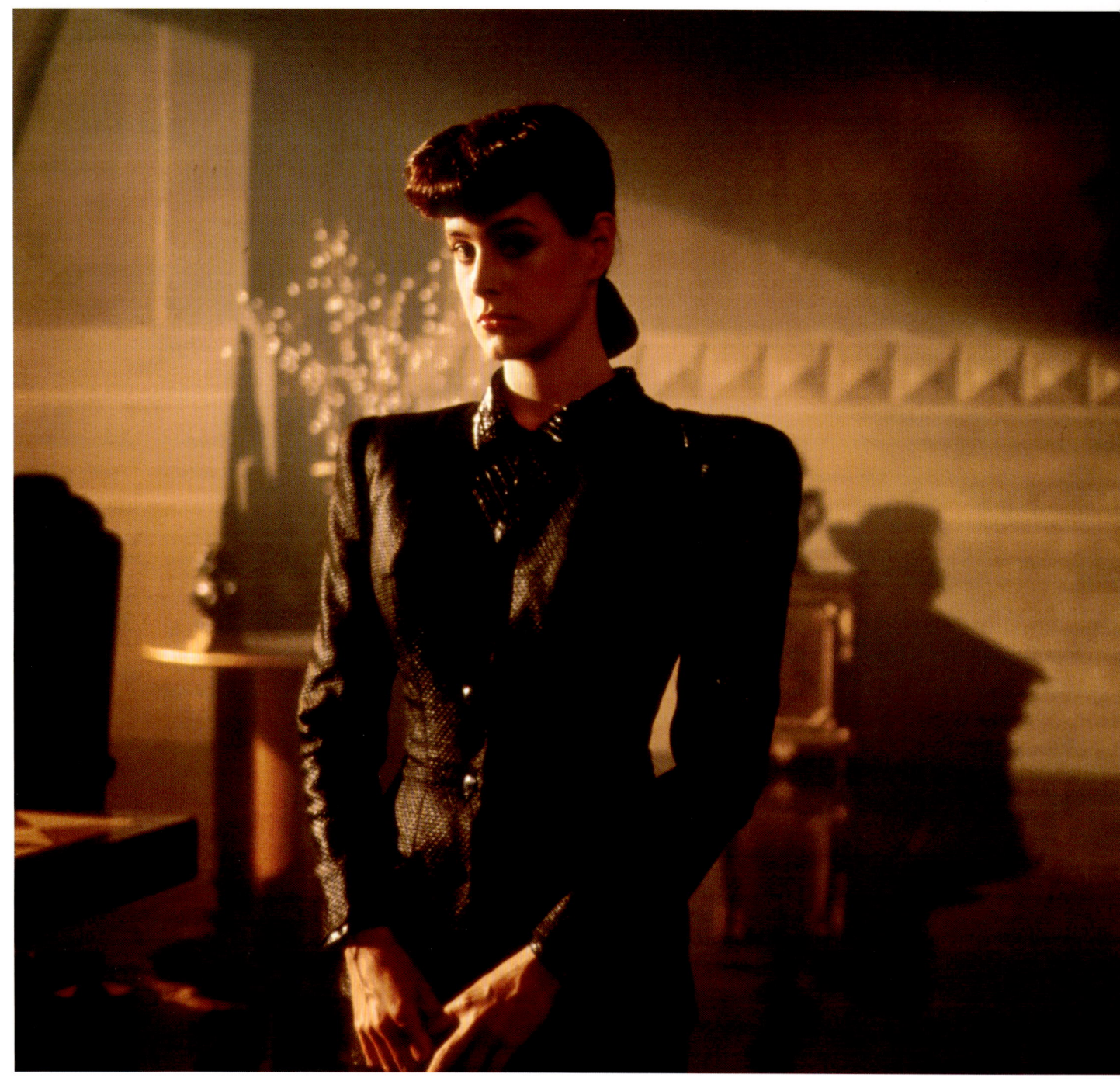

THE TERM *CYBERPUNK* ORIGINALLY COMES FROM LITERATURE. In 1983 the writer Bruce Bethke published a short story with that title in *Amazing Stories* magazine, about a group of teenage hackers.[1] A year later Gardner Dozois used the word in the *Washington Post* to describe a new wave of science fiction writers who were, as he put it, "purveyors of bizarre hard-edged, high-tech stuff," thus coining the name of the genre before many of its creators even knew they had formed one.[2] William Gibson, perhaps cyberpunk's best-known author today, has characterized the term as being primarily a "marketing strategy," but by 1986 there could be no doubt that something definitive was emerging in the cultural zeitgeist.[3]

Cyberpunk literature had materialized, seemingly organically, through the work of writers such as Gibson, Pat Cadigan, Rudy Rucker, Lewis Shiner, John Shirley, Bruce Sterling, and Vernor Vinge—many of them featured in

NOTES

1./ Bruce Bethke, "Cyberpunk," infinity plus (website), accessed August 16, 2023, http://www.infinityplus.co.uk/stories/cpunk.htm.

2./ Gardner Dozois, "Science Fiction in the Eighties," *Washington Post*, December 30, 1984.

3./ Larry McCaffery, "An Interview with William Gibson," in *Storming the Reality Studio*, ed. Larry McCaffery (Durham, NC:

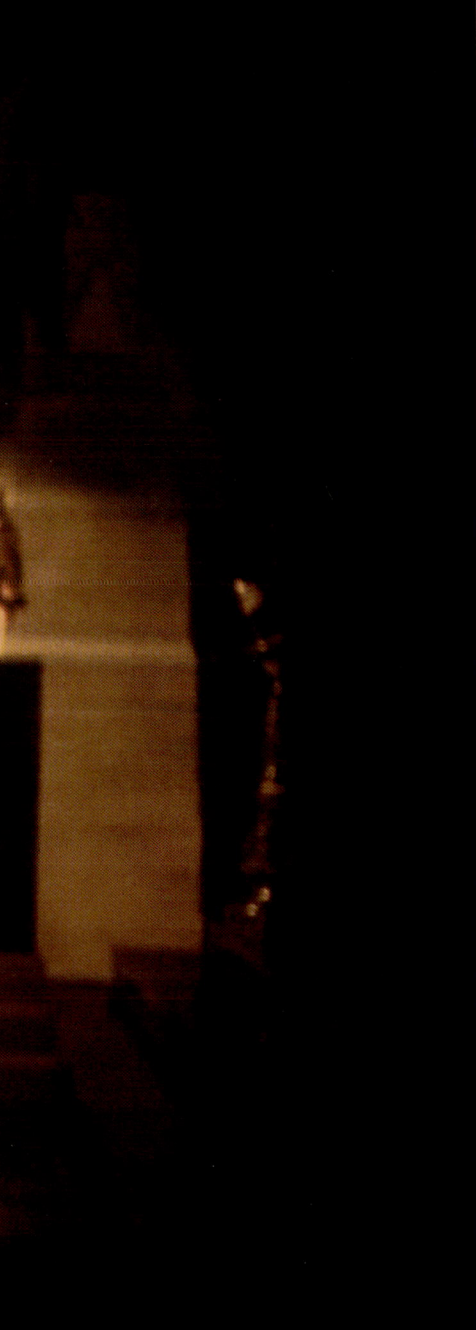

The Rise of Cyberpunk in Literature and Film
Carlen Lavigne

Duke University Press, 1991), 279.

4./ Bruce Sterling, ed., *Mirrorshades: The Cyberpunk Anthology* (New York: Arbor House, 1986).

5./ Stephen P. Brown, "Before the Lights Came On: Observations of a Synergy," in McCaffery, *Storming the Reality Studio*, 176.

Mirrorshades (1986), the first cyberpunk anthology, edited by Sterling.[4] As Stephen P. Brown, editor of the magazine *Science Fiction Eye*, argued: "The future was beginning to collect like dustballs in the corners and interstices of every home, every office, every street corner. It wasn't the lean, clean linear future of the mainstream science fiction writers, it was messy, disorganized, crowded and clamoring. It needed a new kind of fiction to describe it, dense, complex, jammed-to-the-gills fiction."[5]

    The development of cyberpunk in film is more difficult to trace. Many of the most influential cyberpunk literary works—such as Gibson's *Neuromancer* (1984), Sterling's *Schismatrix* (1985), and Neal Stephenson's *Snow Crash* (1992)—have yet to be translated to the screen. Nonetheless, literature and film seem to have maintained a symbiotic relationship in this ever-changing genre. At the same time that cyberpunk was becoming visible as a literary trend, "the

PREVIOUS SPREAD: Alicia Vikander as Ava in *Ex Machina* (2015)

ABOVE: Sean Young as Rachael in in *Blade Runner* (1982)

Movement," as Sterling termed it, was also emerging in American cinema.[6] Ridley Scott's *Blade Runner* (USA, 1982), arguably the foundational cyberpunk film, was released two years before Gibson's seminal novel. Though there were common themes, literature and film evolved distinctly throughout the first decade of cyberpunk's existence: literary works, like *Neuromancer*, Vinge's *True Names* (1981), Sterling's *Islands in the Net* (1988), and Cadigan's *Synners* (1991), tended to feature more hackers and virtual reality, while film—with some exceptions, like Steven Lisberger's *Tron* (USA, 1982) and John Badham's *WarGames* (USA, 1983)—often focused on cyborgs (beings composed of both organic and mechanical parts) fomenting spectacular violence, as can be seen in James Cameron's *The Terminator* (USA, 1984) and Paul Verhoeven's *RoboCop* (USA, 1987).[7] Still, there were striking similarities between *Blade Runner*'s and *Neuromancer*'s grim, sprawling cityscapes, tense tech futures, and anxieties about identity and "reality" in new digital and cybernetic worlds. As the flagship examples of cyberpunk in film and literature, both *Blade Runner* and *Neuromancer* set a tone for the aesthetic vibe and thematic approach of many cyberpunk works to come—a black-leather-and-neon future that replicated across literature, film, television, video games, fashion, home computing technologies, and the rapidly developing internet.

It is no surprise to find cyberpunk emerging independently across many cultural productions of the 1980s; these creations sprang from the same places, created by people who were influenced by similar experiences and ideas. Both *Blade Runner* and *Neuromancer* were closely tied to American literary science fiction. *Blade Runner* was a direct adaptation of Philip K. Dick's 1968 novel *Do Androids Dream of Electric Sheep?*[8] Dick, along with writers like Octavia E. Butler,

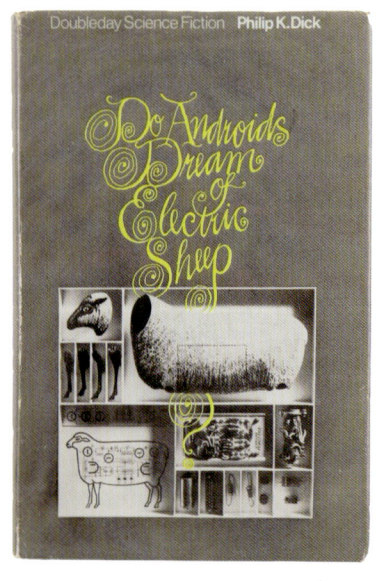

LEFT: Philip K. Dick, *Do Androids Dream of Electric Sheep?* (Doubleday & Company, 1968), first edition

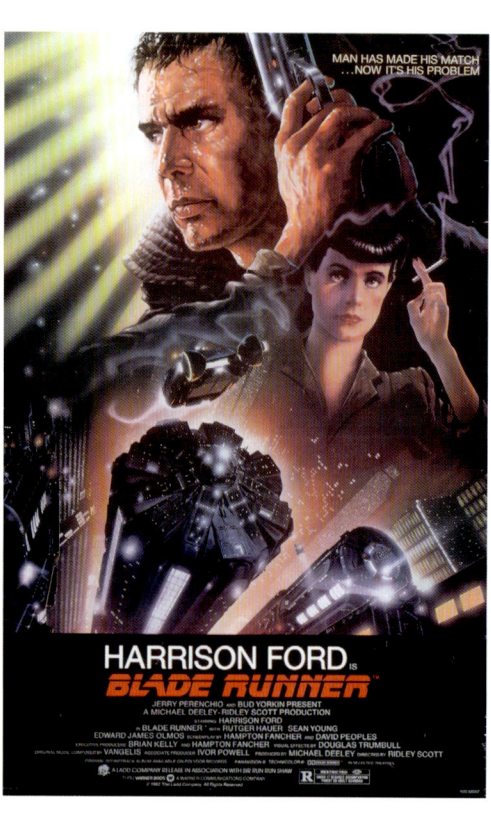

CENTER: Theatrical poster for *Blade Runner* (1982)

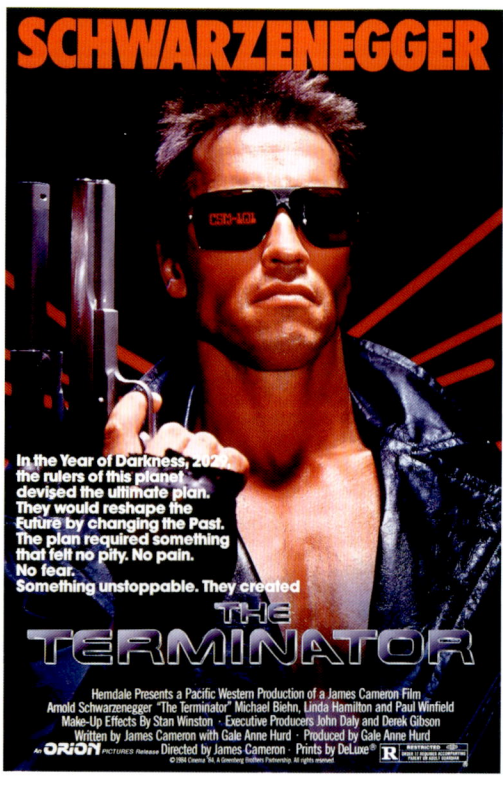

RIGHT: Theatrical poster for *The Terminator* (1984)

6./ Bruce Sterling, "Preface," in *Mirrorshades: The Cyberpunk Anthology*, ix–xvi.

7./ Andrew M. Butler, "Early Cyberpunk Film," in *The Routledge Companion to Cyberpunk Culture*, ed. Anna McFarlane, Graham J. Murphy, and Lars Schmeink (New York: Routledge, 2020), 119–27. For an extensive list of 1980s cyborg action films, see p. 123.

8./ Other Hollywood takes on Dick's work include Verhoeven's *Total Recall* (USA, 1990), Steven Spielberg's *Minority Report* (USA, 2002), Richard Linklater's *A Scanner Darkly* (USA, 2006), and George Nolfi's *The Adjustment Bureau* (USA, 2011) as well as the Amazon Prime series *The Man in the High Castle* (2015–19).

Philip José Farmer, Larry Niven, Thomas Pynchon, Joanna Russ, and John Varley, as well as H. G. Wells before them, was part of a well-established science fiction tradition that nurtured early cyberpunk novelists.[9] Many of the ideas that inspired cyberpunk both on- and off-screen can be traced to these earlier influences; cyberpunk was not the first science fiction to address cyborg bodies, corporate capitalism, or human identity in a technological age.

Cyberpunk as a genre deftly expressed the particular cultural anxieties of the 1980s. *Blade Runner* and *Neuromancer* are both postmodernist works concerned with ideas about reality, or what the French philosopher Jean Baudrillard called the "hyperreal": the difficulty of discerning what is "real" when the digital age has the potential to fool our every sense and when we don't know what or whom to trust because we are surrounded by a constantly changing pastiche of images and sounds that destabilize concepts of

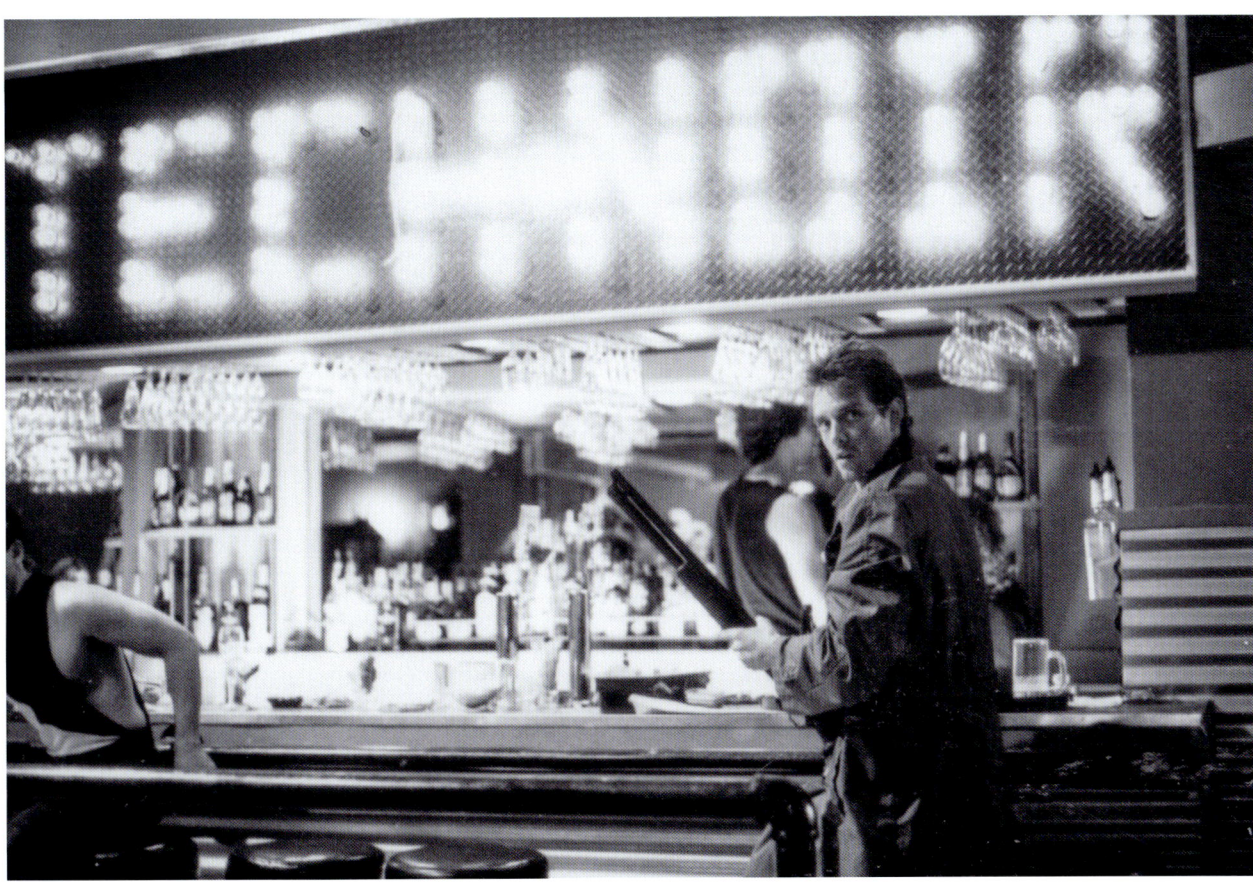

authenticity and meaning.[10] Today, we cannot tell if a video is legitimate or if a photograph has been altered, or even be certain whether we are speaking to an actual person, a scammer, or a chatbot; at cyberpunk's inception, the first whispers of digital uncertainty infiltrated both literature and film, inspired by rapid changes in personal computing and global communications systems.

The 1980s were also marked by Ronald Reagan's America, which brought the rise of free-market capitalism and empowered the exponential growth of global megacorporations. Cyberpunk works picked up on new anxieties about robotics, the dehumanization and devaluation of labor, and digital processes in which information became both product and currency.[11] As corporate workers sat interchangeably in front of increasingly powerful machines and more jobs became automated or remote, cyberpunk examined issues of technological

ABOVE: Michael Biehn as Kyle Reese in *The Terminator*

9./ Many of these authors are mentioned in Bruce Sterling's preface to *Mirrorshades* (see note 6)—though, notably, Sterling was criticized at the time for almost exclusively listing men.

10./ For more on hyperreality, see Jean Baudrillard, "Simulacra and Simulations," in *Jean Baudrillard: Selected Writings*, ed. Mark Poster (Cambridge: Polity Press, 2001), 169–87.

For more on postmodernism, see Fredric Jameson, "Postmodernism, or The Cultural Logic of Late Capitalism," *New Left Review* 1, no. 146 (July/August 1984): 53–92.

11./ Carlen Lavigne, *Cyberpunk Women, Feminism, and Science Fiction* (Jefferson, NC: McFarland, 2013).

12./ Roger Luckhurst, *Science Fiction* (Cambridge: Polity Press, 2005), 207. For more on these stereotypes in

exploitation, bodily autonomy, and the growing divide between the rich and the poor—and also linked these issues to cultural concerns about environmental decay and the loss of the natural world. In works like *Neuromancer* and *Blade Runner*, new dystopian economies were also marked by a fascination with Western stereotypes of Japanese culture, evoking concerns about global multinationals and the perceived specter of Japanese economic dominance.[12] Case, the hacker hero of *Neuromancer*, starts his journey beneath the light of a display of Japanese throwing stars, and at the beginning of *Blade Runner*, Rick Deckard (Harrison Ford) sits eating at a noodle stand, surrounded by a faux-Japanese cityscape—scenes emblematic of cultural angst about economic uncertainty and the perceived flagging of America's global influence.[13]

By the 1990s, ties between literary and cinematic cyberpunk had grown stronger, as Hollywood moved away from cyborg action and began to produce

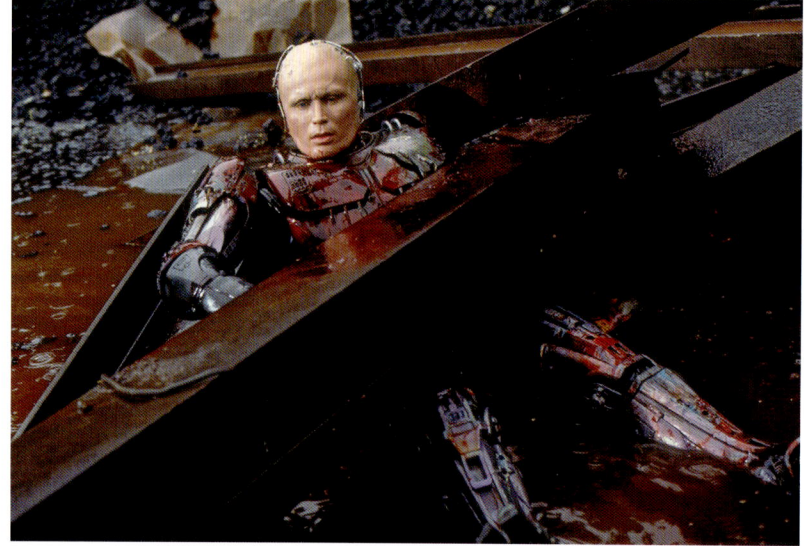

LEFT: Peter Weller as RoboCop in *RoboCop* (1987)

American and European cyberpunk and the relation to Japanese productions, see Kumiko Saito, "Anime," in McFarlane, Murphy, and Schmeink, *The Routledge Companion to Cyberpunk Culture*, 151–61.

13./ William Gibson, *Neuromancer* (New York: Ace Books, 1984), 12.

14./ Claudia Springer, "Psycho-cybernetics in Films of the 1990s," in *Alien Zone II: The Spaces of Science Fiction*

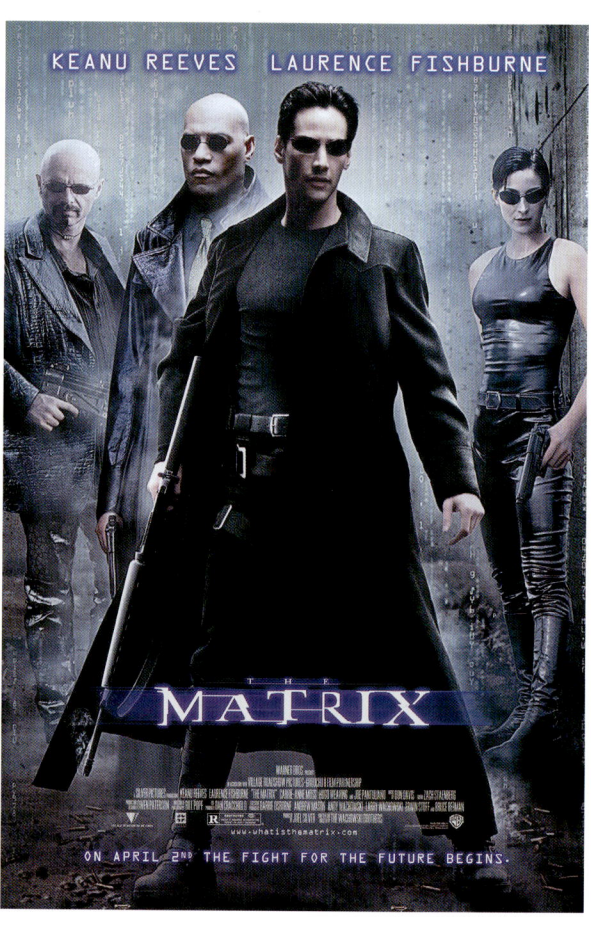

RIGHT: Theatrical poster for *The Matrix* (1999)

works that more directly reflected cyberpunk novelists' ideas about "slim young men and women jacked into cyberspace."[14] This change manifests in films like Irwin Winkler's *The Net* (USA, 1995), Iain Softley's *Hackers* (USA, 1995), Kathryn Bigelow's *Strange Days* (USA, 1995), and David Cronenberg's *eXistenZ* (Canada, 1999).[15] The black-leather-and-vinyl-clad, mirror-shaded code warriors of Lana and Lilly Wachowski's *The Matrix* (USA, 1999) clearly echo characters in *Neuromancer* and stories like it. Gibson's work also made it to screen in the form of Robert Longo's *Johnny Mnemonic* (USA, 1995), based on the 1981 short story of the same name. Cyberpunk had grown into an identifiable genre across media.[16]

The genre has never been static, however, and further change was already happening. Early cyberpunk was seen as somewhat monolithic and its major works, while expressing common anxieties about American life in the 1980s

Cinema, ed. Annette Kuhn (New York: Verso, 1999), 204; and also quoted in Butler, "Early Cyberpunk Film," 124.

15./ Butler, "Early Cyberpunk Film," 124.

16./ Cyberpunk's cross-media influences are too broad to detail here, but some select examples include the *Shadowrun* tabletop role-playing system (originally published by FASA, 1989), the video game *Deus Ex* (Eidos Interactive, 2000)

and its sequels, and the Fox television series *Dark Angel* (2000–02). Cyberpunk also had noted influences on fashion; for more on that topic, see Joseph Gleasure, "A Brief History of Cyberpunk on the Fashion Runway," *Shellzine*, June 9, 2022, https://shellzine.net/cyberpunk-fashion-runway. Furthermore, there has been a proliferation of cyberpunk terms like *cyberspace* (used in Gibson's *Neuromancer*) and *avatar* (popularized by Stephenson's *Snow Crash*), commonly used in describing real-world technologies. For an examination of broader cyberpunk culture in the mid-1990s, see Mark Dery, *Escape Velocity: Cyberculture at the End of the Century* (New York: Grove Press, 1996).

17./ Veronica Hollinger, "Cybernetic Deconstructions: Cyberpunk and Postmodernism," *Mosaic:*

and swiftly changing digital technologies and economic dynamics, were criticized as only representing the voices of a restrictive group. As scholar Veronica Hollinger noted, cyberpunk was "written for the most part by a small number of white middle-class men, many of whom, inexplicably, live in Texas."[17] Cyberpunk's prototypical works, in both literature and film, often followed a lone white male protagonist who seized power via his own initiative—a neoliberal version of the American Dream in which, despite cyberpunk's depictions of economic and technological oppression, those who fought hard could still achieve independence and success. This focus on white male heroes reflected a particularly narrow point of view that divorced cyberpunk narratives from movements and perspectives such as feminism, LGBTQ+ rights, and civil rights. According to critics, cyberpunk at its weakest offered reductive dreams of "creative mastery"[18] that served as "adolescent male fantasy."[19] The promise

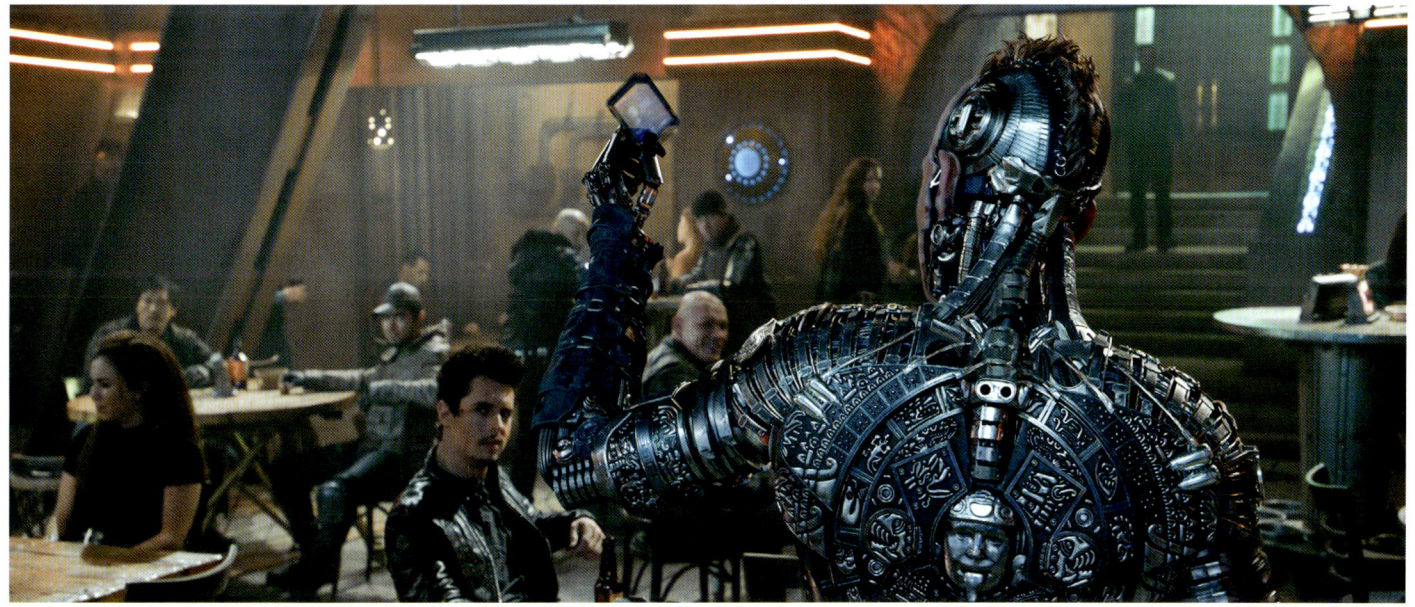

of disembodied digital domination was not a practicable or tempting prospect for marginalized people, whose identities and experiences had always been tied to the reality of their corporeal existences.[20] Likewise, the forces that oppress people socially and economically do not oppress everyone equally; works by authors from underrepresented groups often demonstrated deeper understandings of racism, sexism, homophobia, or ableism and the ways in which community resistance could work against white supremacy and patriarchy in addition to economic and technological alienation.

Cyberpunk had to change. New voices and perspectives were being acknowledged, and this shift took place most noticeably in literature. Women have a long history in science fiction, and though their contributions to cyberpunk were often overlooked, authors like C. L. Moore, James Tiptree Jr. (Alice

ABOVE: Aztec imagery worn by Ed Skrein as Zapan in *Alita: Battle Angel* (2019)

Sheldon), and Joanna Russ cast a long shadow over the genre's development; by the end of the twentieth century, they were joined by others, such as Kathleen Ann Goonan, Lisa Mason, Laura J. Mixon, Lyda Morehouse, Marge Piercy, Amy Thomson, and Sage Walker. LGBTQ+ writers began producing overtly queer narratives, including Melissa Scott's *Trouble and Her Friends* (1994), Cameron Reed's *The Fortunate Fall* (1996), and Edith Forbes's *Exit to Reality* (1997).[21] Additionally, although they were not counted as cyberpunk at the time, Afrofuturist works by authors such as Samuel R. Delany and Octavia E. Butler had been published since the 1960s, suggesting speculative new worlds in which white colonial forces were no longer dominant and exploring Black technological futures.[22] These themes were expanded upon in works like Nalo Hopkinson's *Midnight Robber* (2000) and Walter Mosley's *Futureland* (2001). Indigenous novels, such as Misha's *Red Spider White Web* (1990) and Daniel H. Wilson's *Robopocalypse* (2011), and short stories,

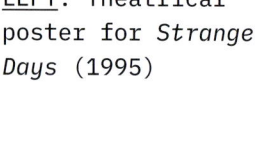

LEFT: Theatrical poster for *Strange Days* (1995)

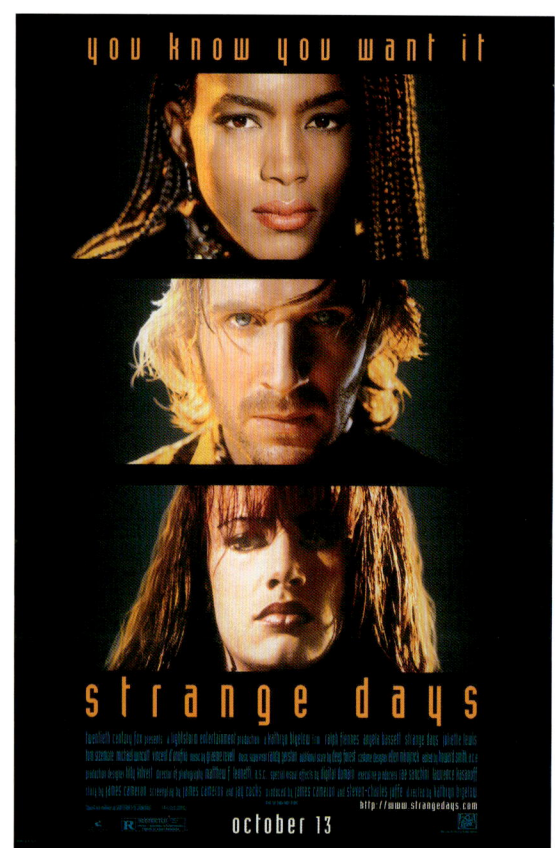

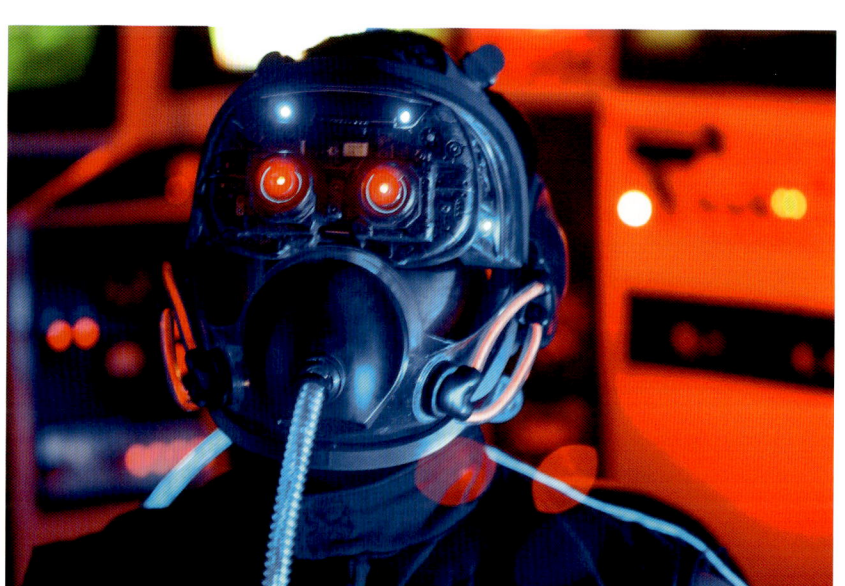

RIGHT: Jacob Vargas as Rudy Ramirez in *Sleep Dealer* (2008)

including Eden Robinson's "Terminal Avenue" (2004) and Brian K. Hudson's "Digital Medicine" (2016), likewise challenged cyberpunk's predominantly white male narratives.[23] Mexican American writers were producing what Lysa Rivera called "Chicanafuturist" works, including Alejandro Morales's *The Rag Doll Plagues* (1991) and Ernest Hogan's *High Aztech* (1992).[24] While classic cyberpunk also experienced a second wave, starting with Stephenson's *Snow Crash*, the 1990s saw the genre expand and thrive with a broad variety of new literary contributions.

Film has also been enhanced by these voices and perspectives. In addition to Bigelow's *Strange Days*—the first Hollywood cyberpunk film directed by a woman—cinematic offerings have grown to include Afrofuturist films like Ngozi Onwurah's *Welcome II the Terrordome* (UK, 1995), John Akomfrah's *The Last*

An Interdisciplinary Critical Journal 23, no. 2 (Spring 1990): 33. Cadigan was often dubbed the "Queen of Cyberpunk," singling out her status as one of the only female authors working in the genre.

18./ Kevin Robins, "Cyberspace and the World We Live In," in *Cyberspace/Cyberbodies/Cyberpunk: Cultures of Technological Embodiment*, ed. Mike Featherstone and Roger Burrows (London: Sage, 1995), 143.

19./ Lewis Shiner, "Inside the Movement: Past, Present, and Future," in *Fiction 2000: Cyberpunk and the Future of Narrative*, ed. George Slusser and Tom Shippey (Athens: University of Georgia Press, 1992), 23.

20./ For an in-depth examination of these issues in early cyberpunk, see Thomas Foster, *The Souls of Cyberfolk: Posthumanism as Vernacular Theory* (Minneapolis: University of Minnesota Press, 2005).

21./ Reed first published *The Fortunate Fall* under the name Raphael Carter.
22./ Consider Delany's *Nova* (1968) and *Stars in My Pocket Like Grains of Sand* (1984), or Butler's *Xenogenesis* trilogy (beginning with *Dawn* [1987]). See Isiah Lavender III and Graham J. Murphy, "Afrofuturism," in McFarlane, Murphy, and Schmeink, *The Routledge Companion to Cyberpunk Culture*, 353–61.

Angel of History (UK, 1996), and Wanuri Kahiu's short film *Pumzi* (Kenya, 2009) as well as Indigenous works such as Jeana Francis and Nigel R. Long Soldier's short film *Future Warrior* (USA, 2007), Jeff Barnaby's short film *File Under Miscellaneous* (Canada, 2010), and Danis Goulet's *Night Raiders* (Canada/New Zealand, 2021).[25] Cyberpunk continues to change, although its many creators seldom agree, and it can be difficult to define the borders of an increasingly slippery category. The genre has actually been declared dead multiple times at this point—a eulogy often repeated as personal computing, the internet, and global corporate capitalism have brought us to the point where we are already seen as living in a cyberpunk future; in many ways, the works of the 1980s are no longer groundbreaking or speculative. However, if we assume cyberpunk's time has ended, this leaves us, as the British writer Roger Luckhurst suggested, "only the problem of what to call the huge bulk of cyberpunk written long after

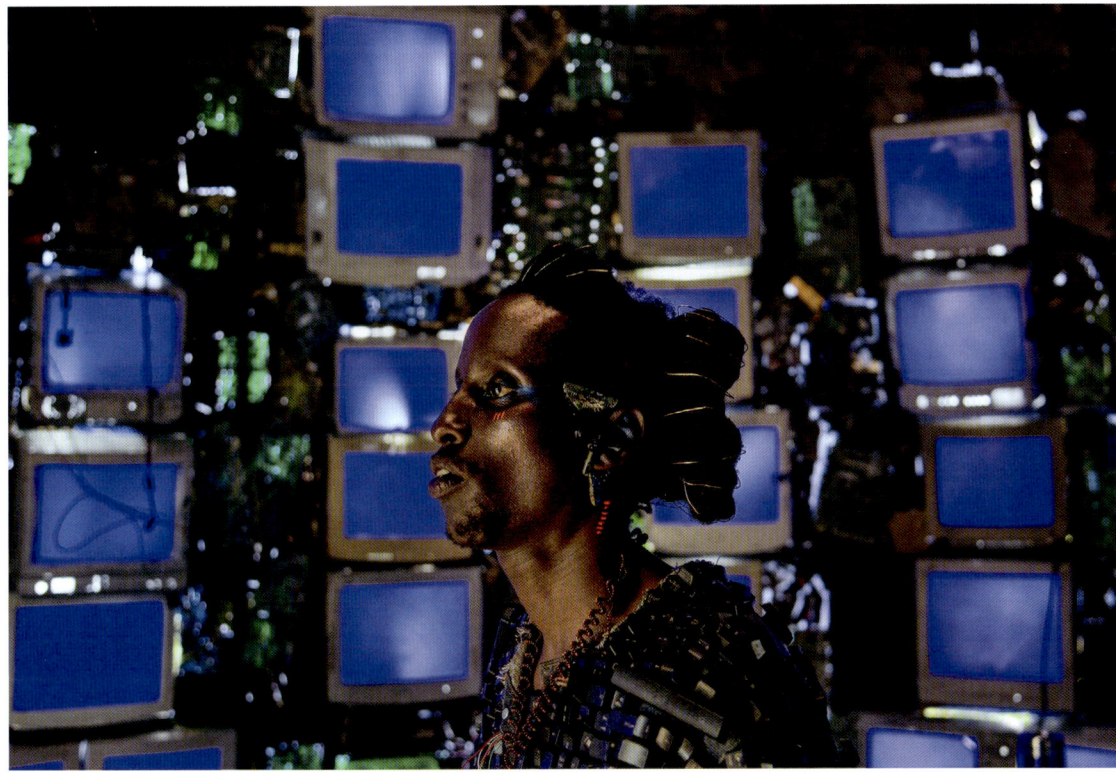

23./ Corinna Lenhardt, "Cyberpunk and Indigenous Futurisms," in McFarlane, Murphy, and Schmeink, *The Routledge Companion to Cyberpunk Culture*, 344–52.
24./ Lysa Rivera, "Chicana/o Cyberpunk after el Movimiento," *Aztlán: A Journal of Chicano Studies* 40, no. 2 (Fall 2015): 187–202.
25./ Lenhardt, "Cyberpunk and Indigenous Futurisms."
26./ Luckhurst, *Science Fiction*, 204.

this date."[26] There is so much more space into which cyberpunk can grow. In literature, it has fractured into a number of subgenres, like solarpunk—imagining environmentally sustainable technological futures in the face of global climate change—and hopepunk—envisioning positive, hopeful technological futures despite the ongoing threat of global catastrophe. In film, works like Denis Villeneuve's *Blade Runner 2049* (USA, 2017) and Lana Wachowski's *The Matrix Resurrections* (USA, 2021) assure us that Hollywood has not forgotten cyberpunk. As the genre evolves to explore more new voices and more new states of being, it only remains to be seen what will come next.

ABOVE: Bertrand Ninteretse as Matalusa in *Neptune Frost* (2021)

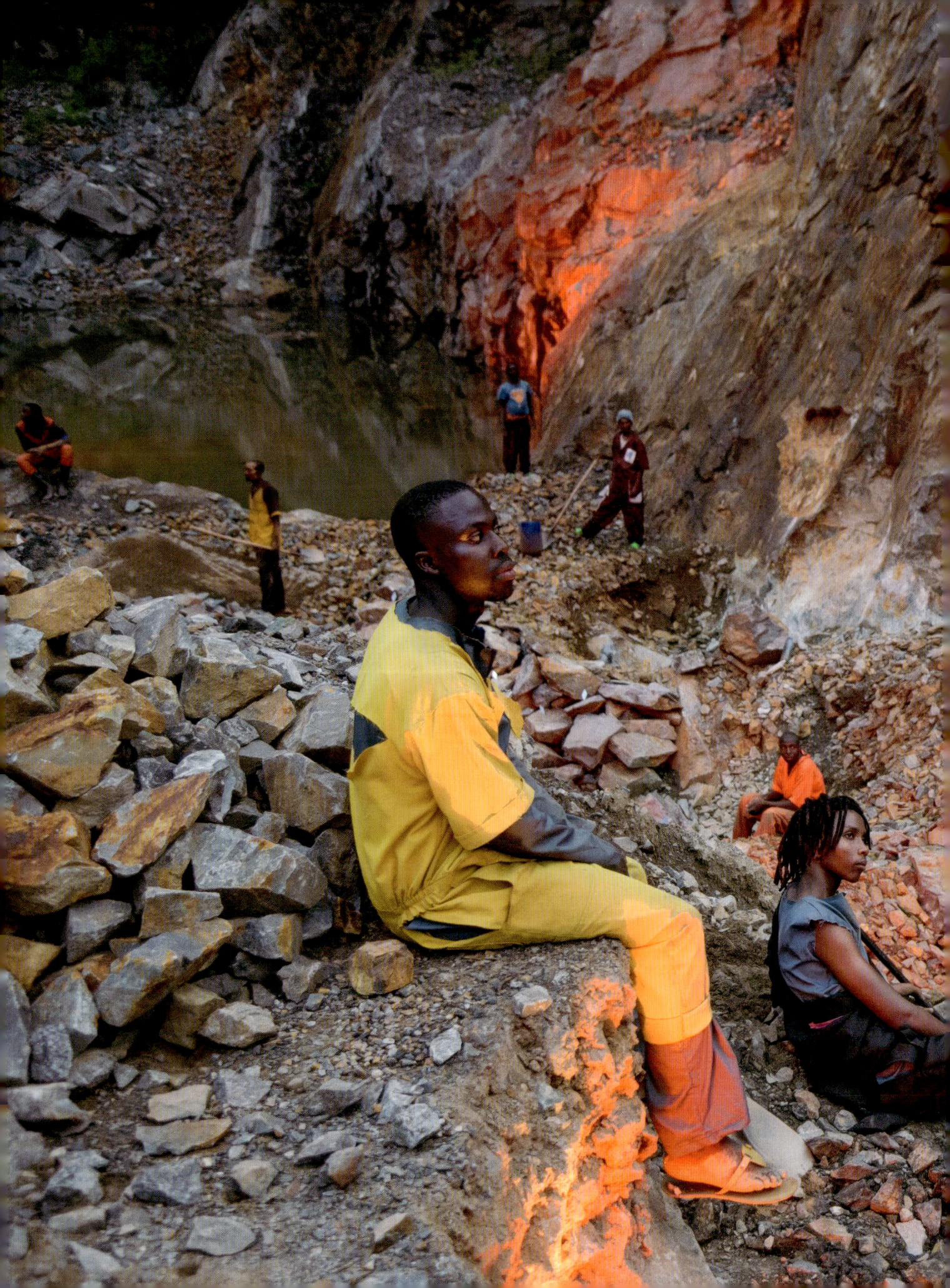

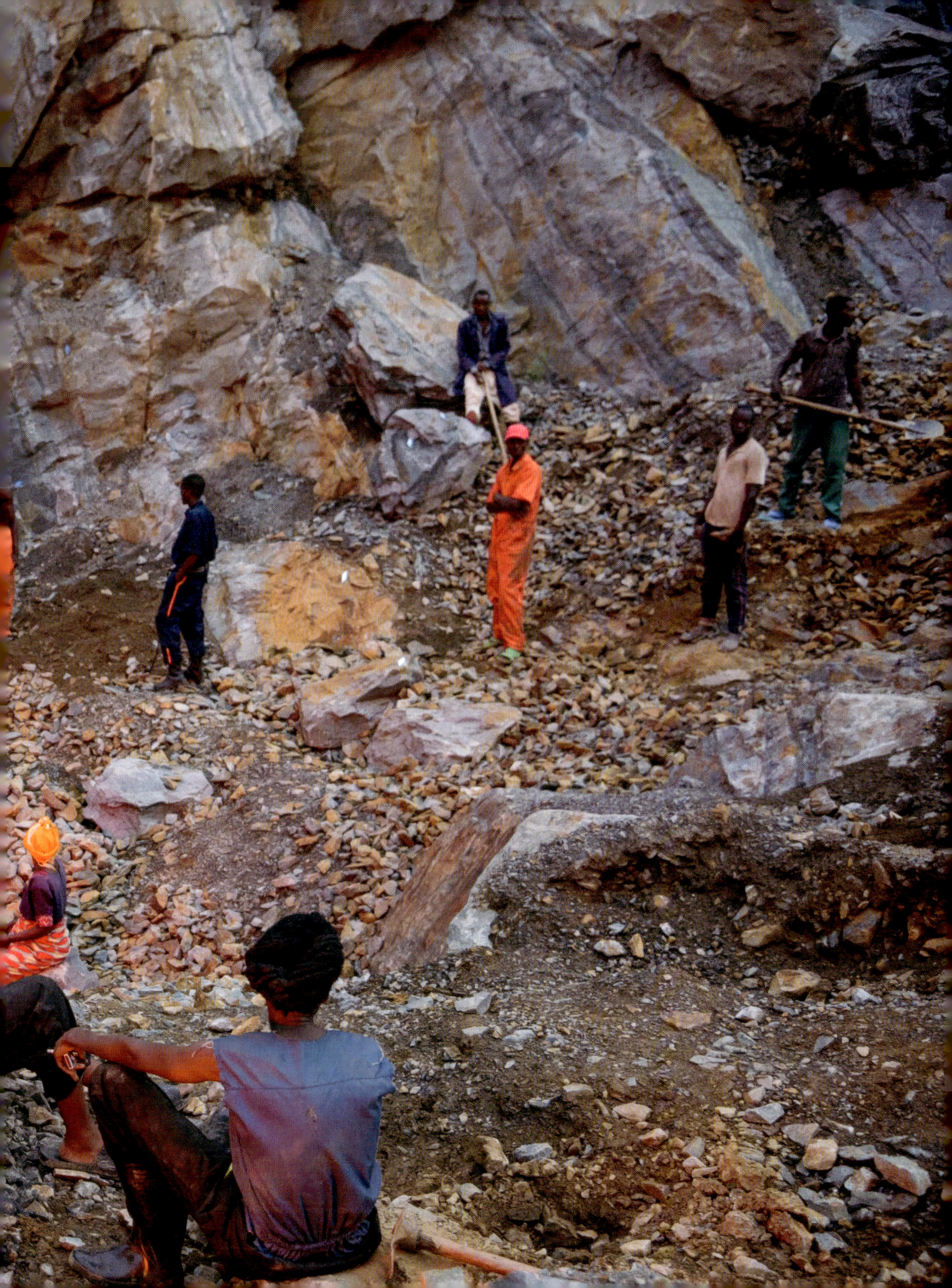

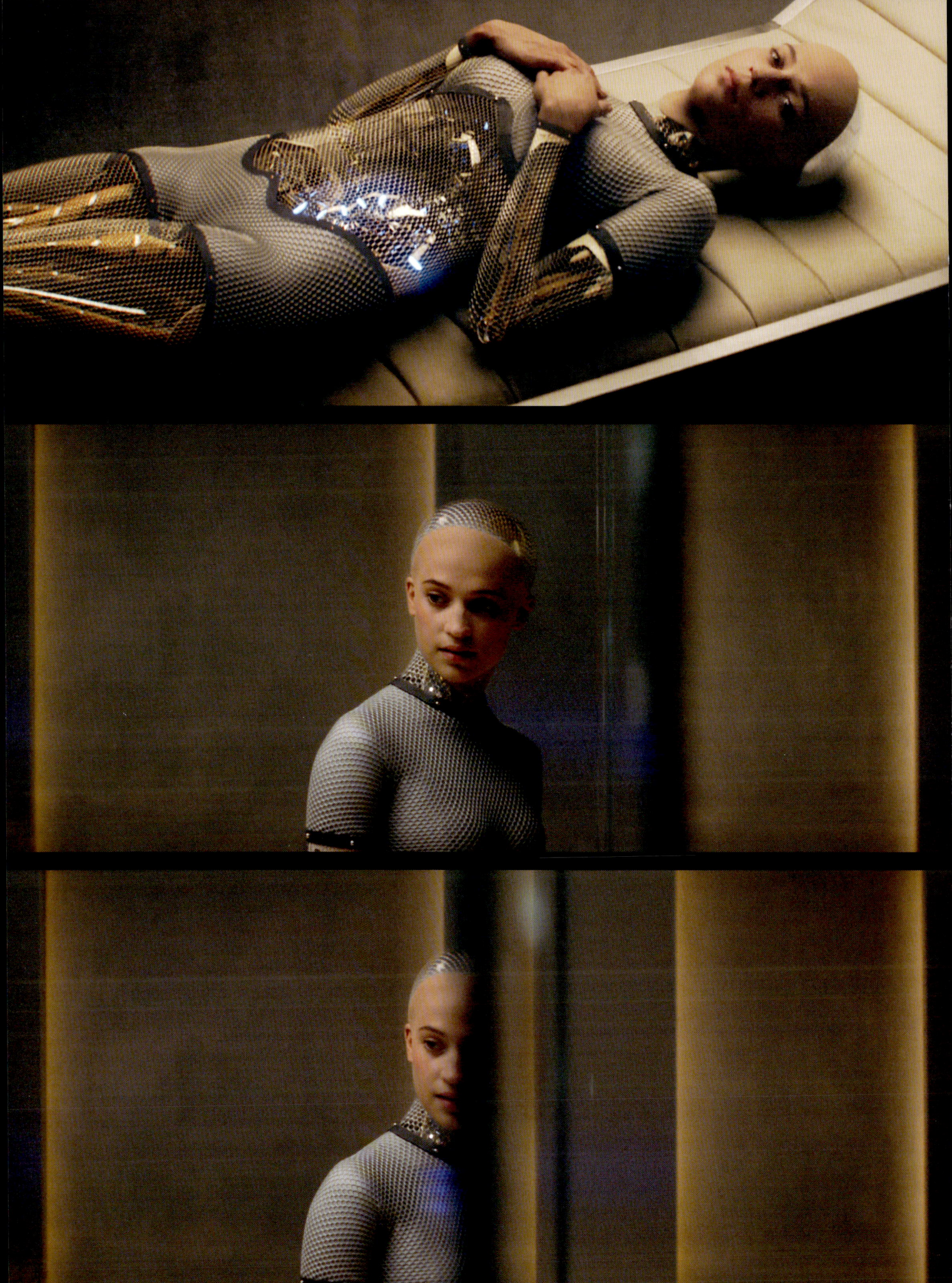

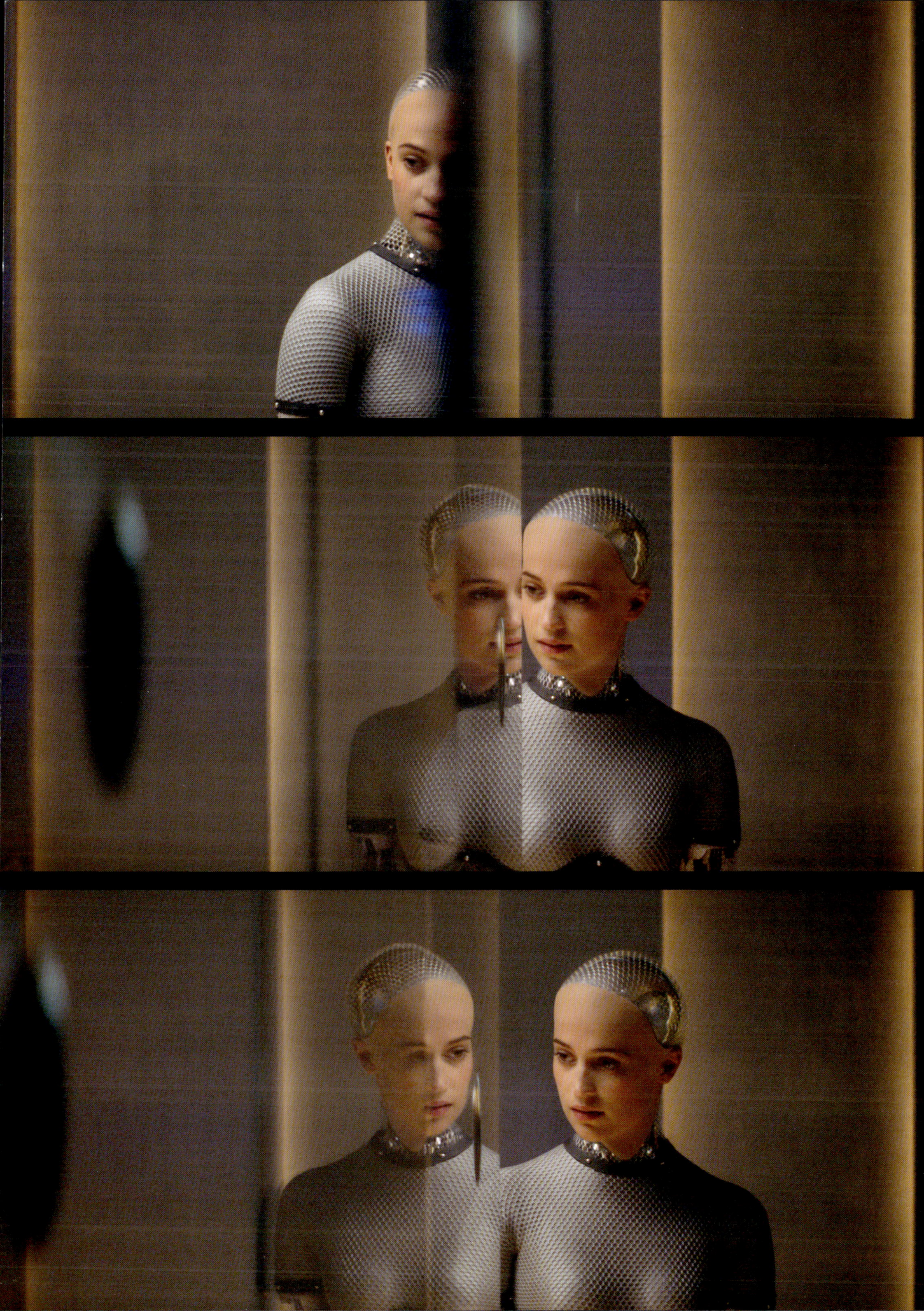

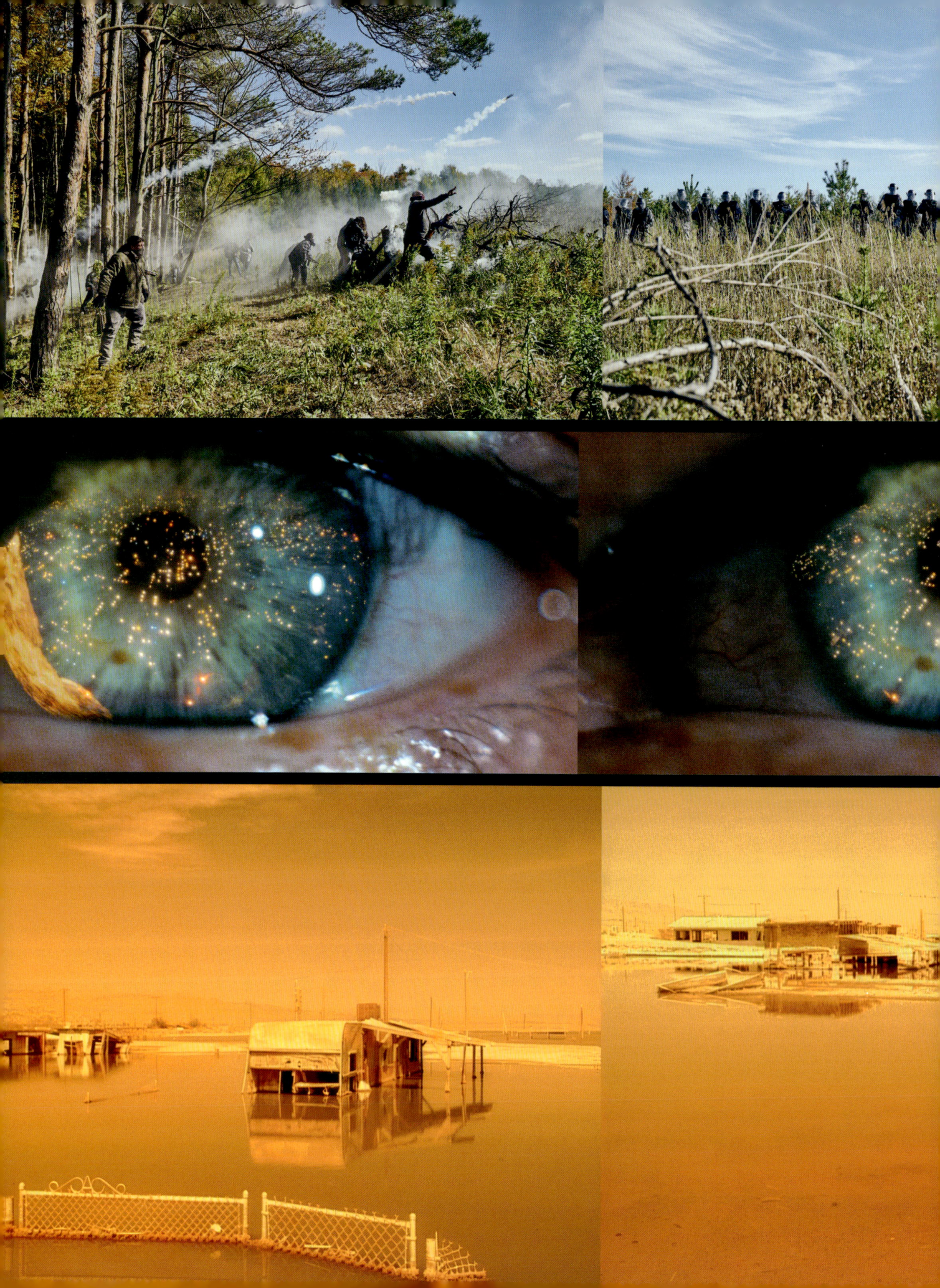

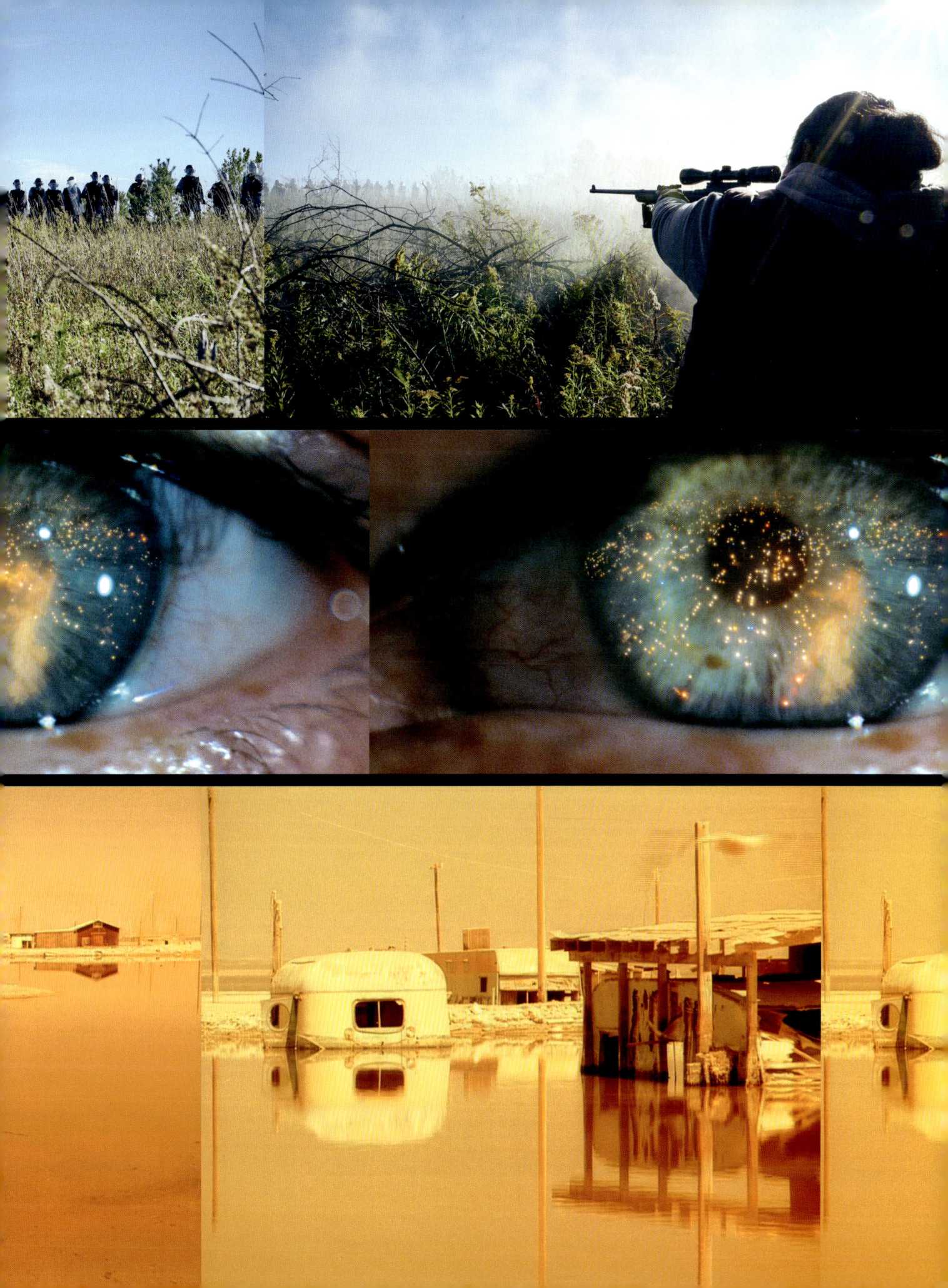

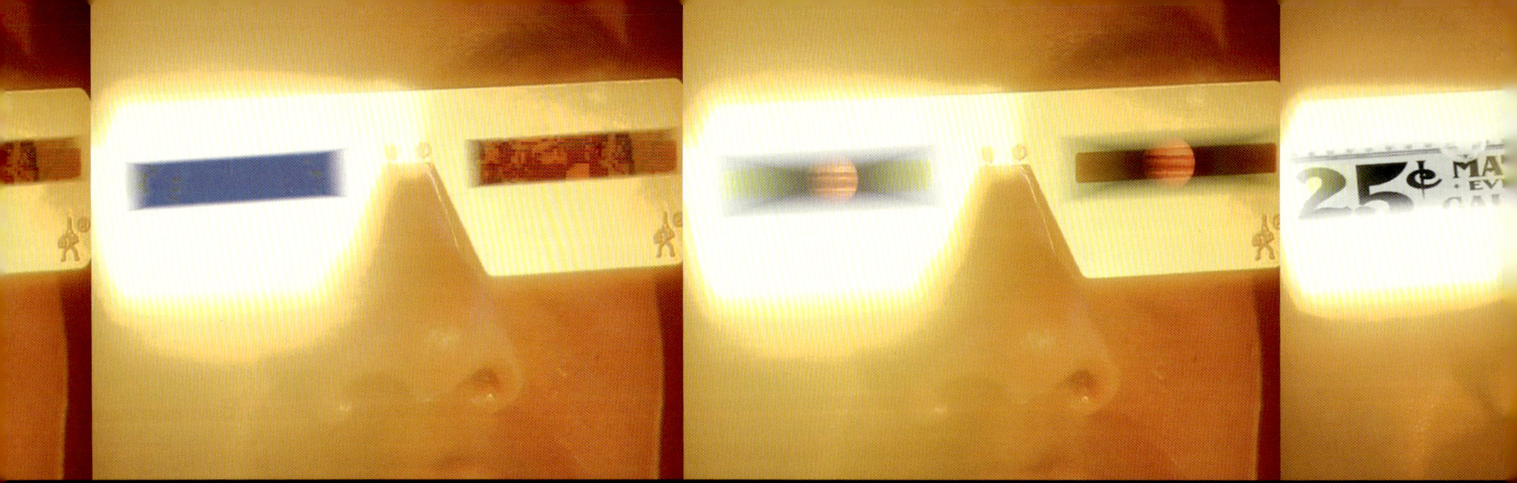

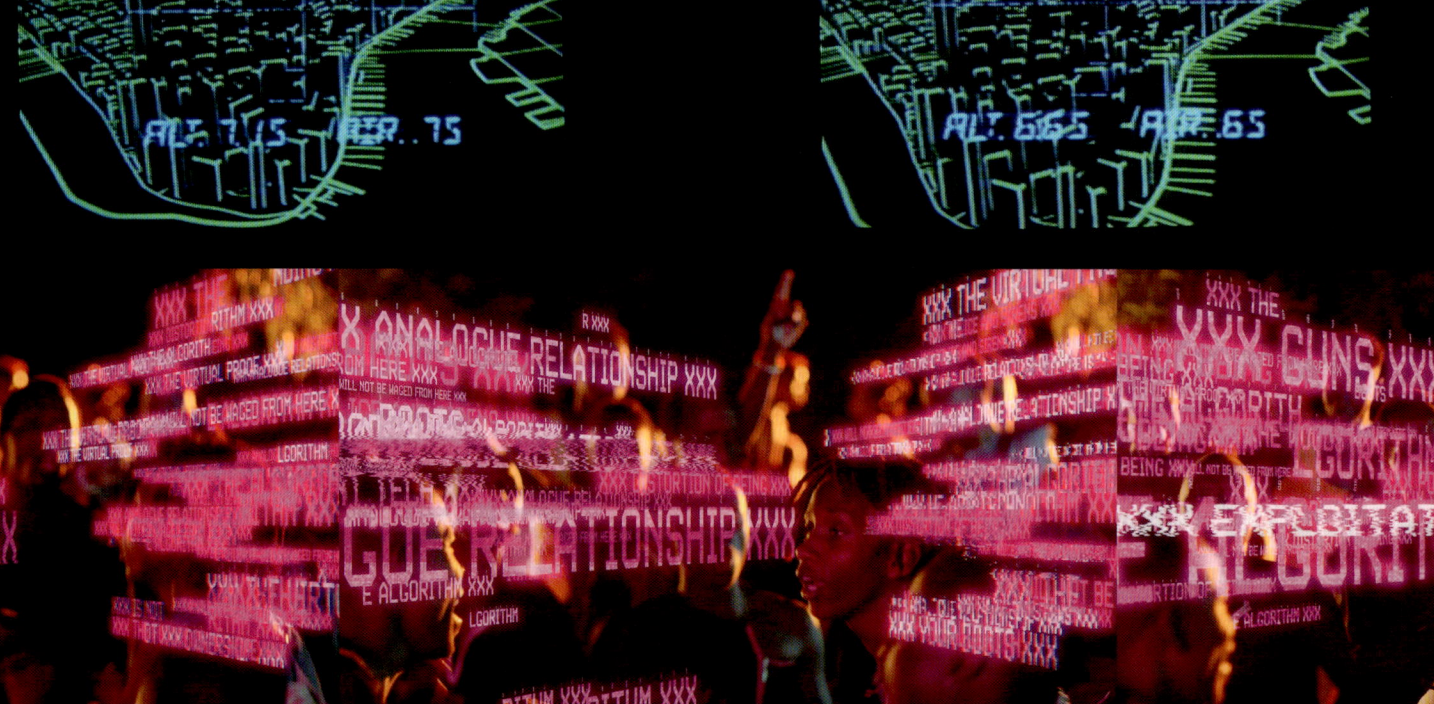

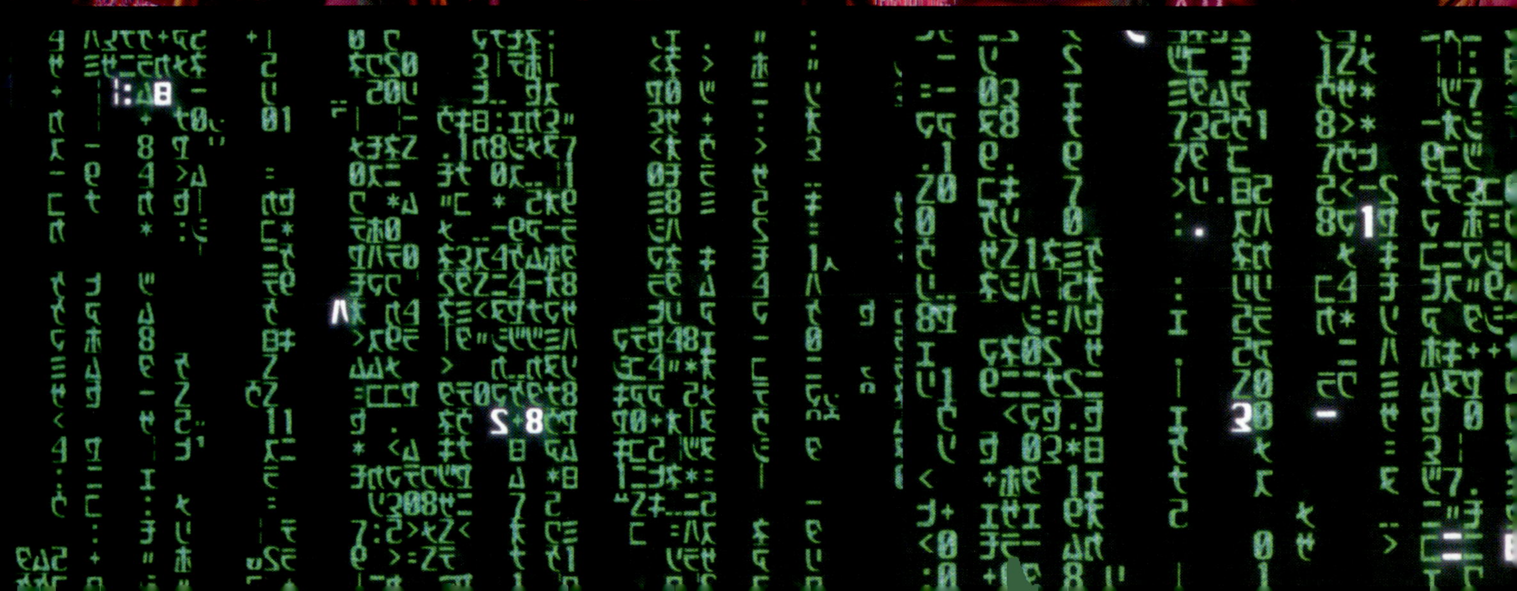

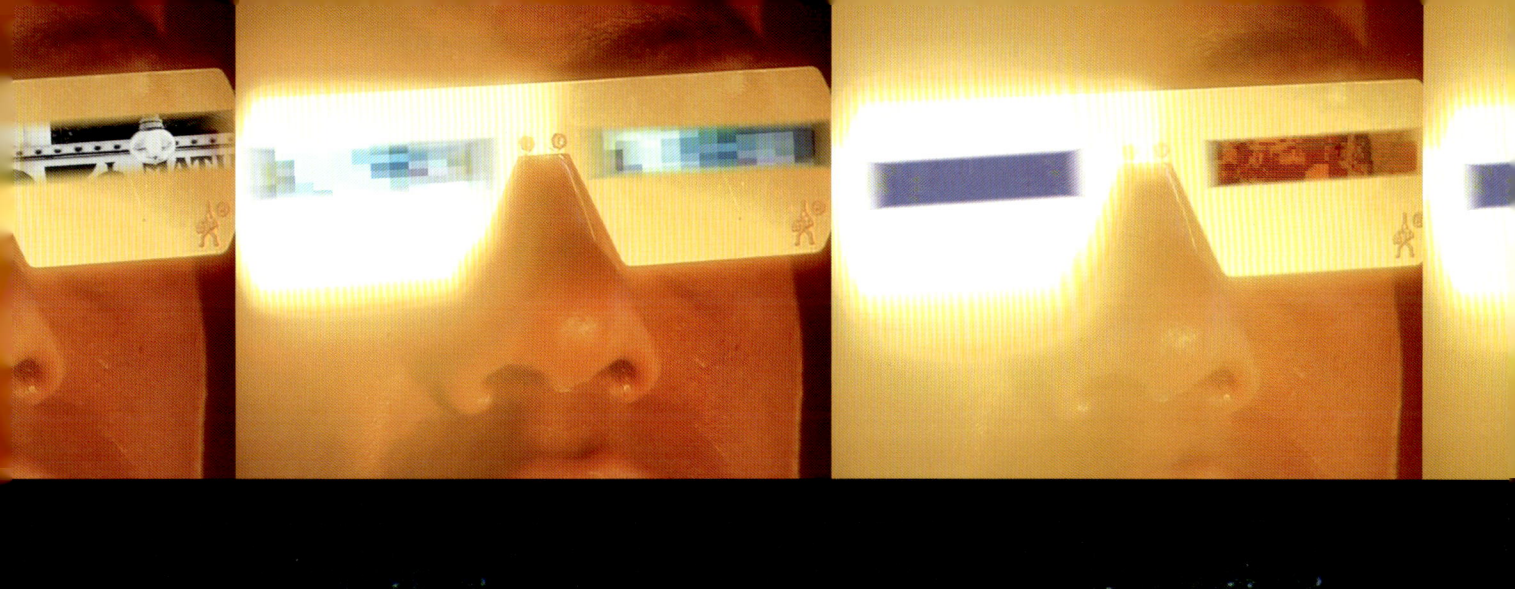
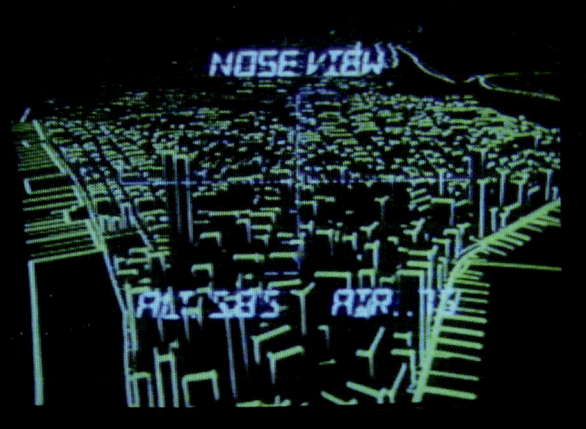
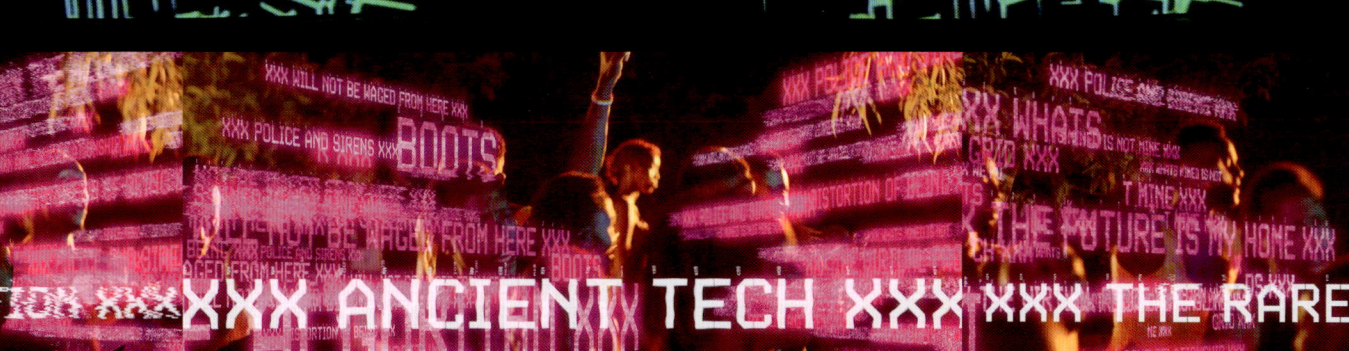

xxx ANCIENT TECH xxx xxx THE RARES

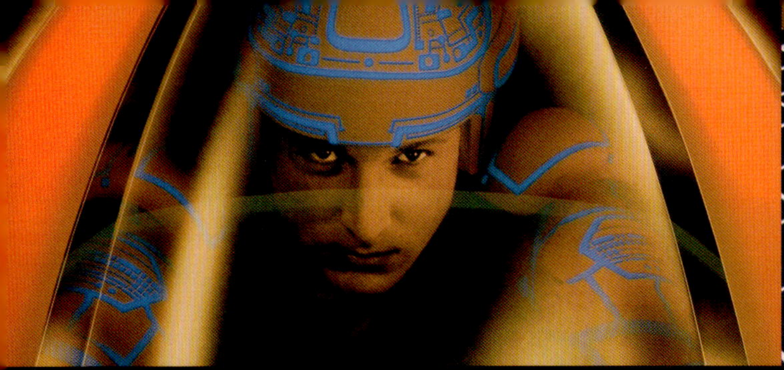

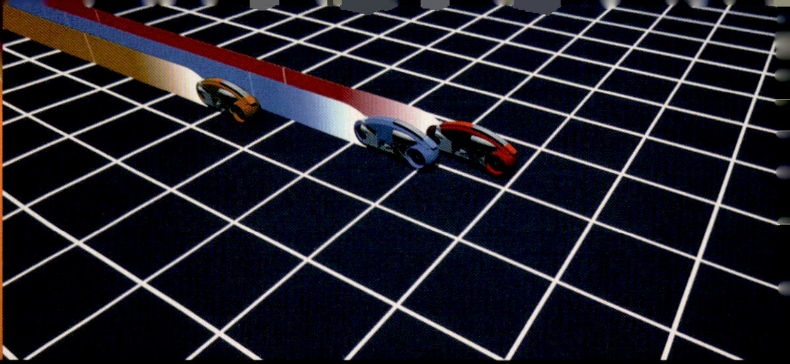

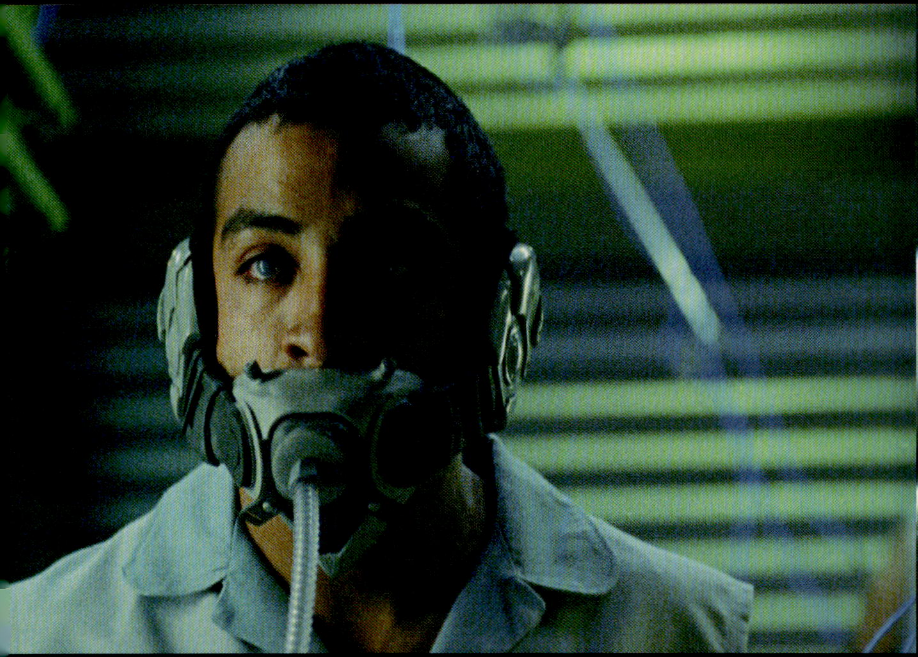

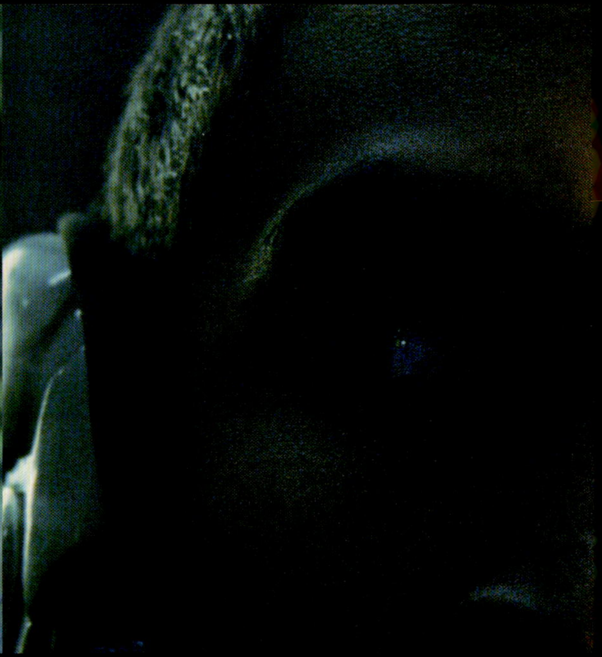

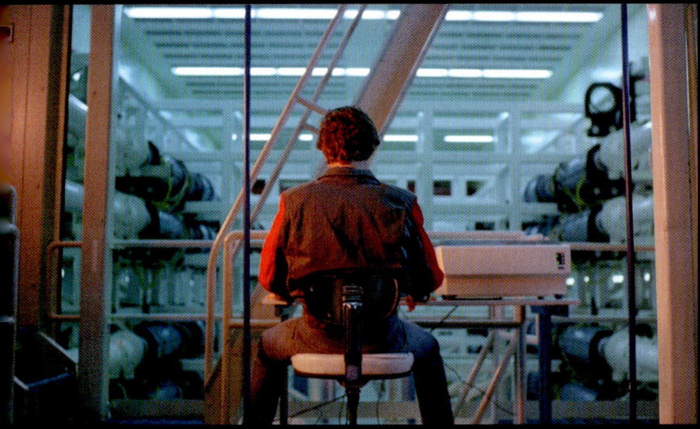

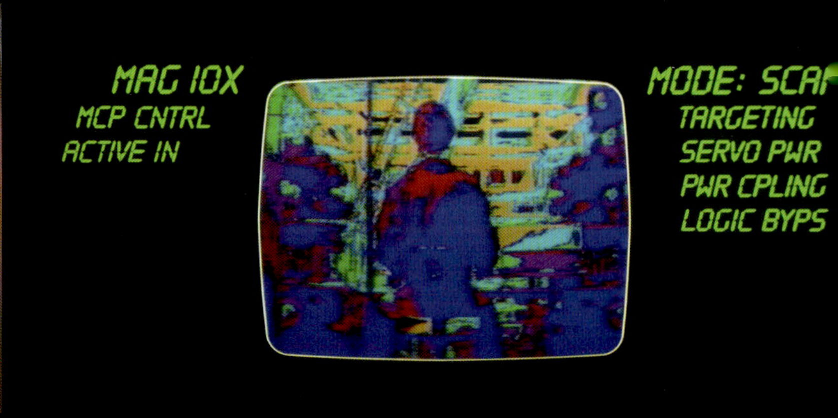

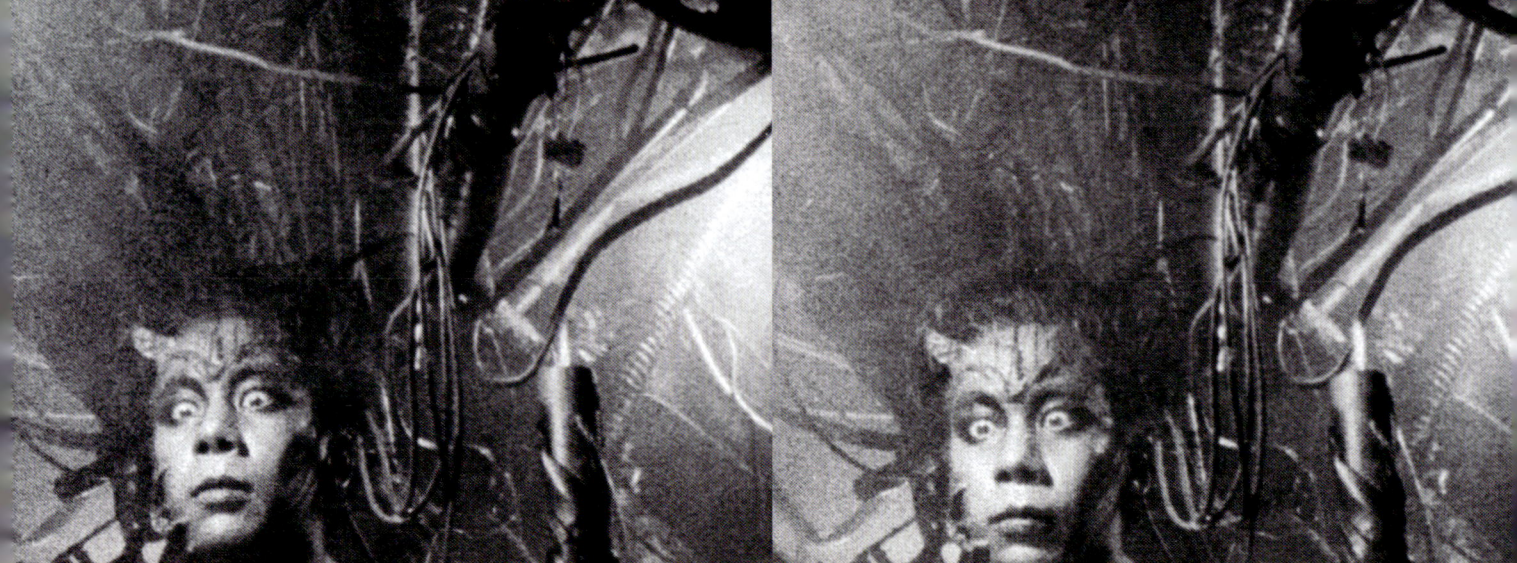

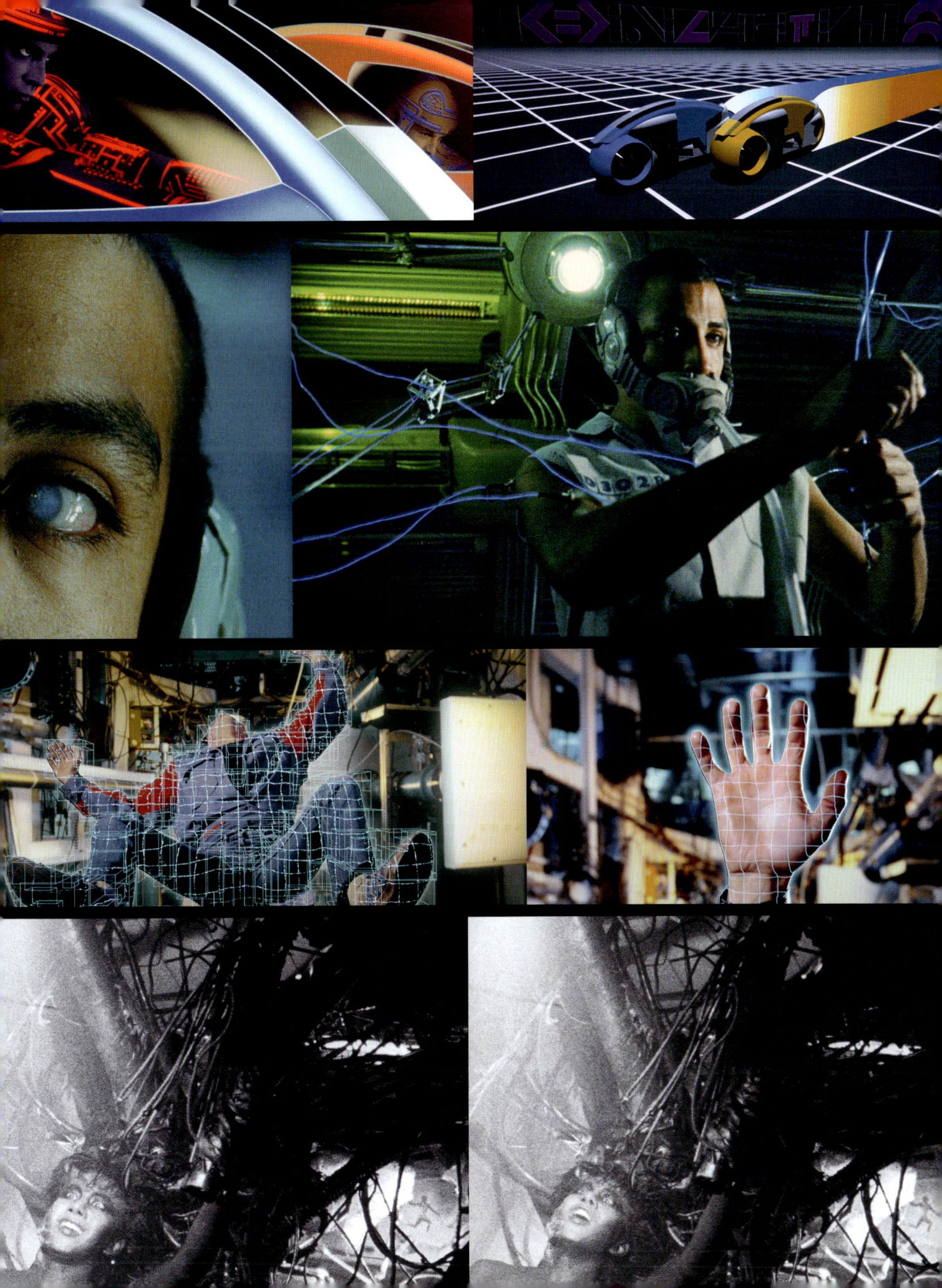

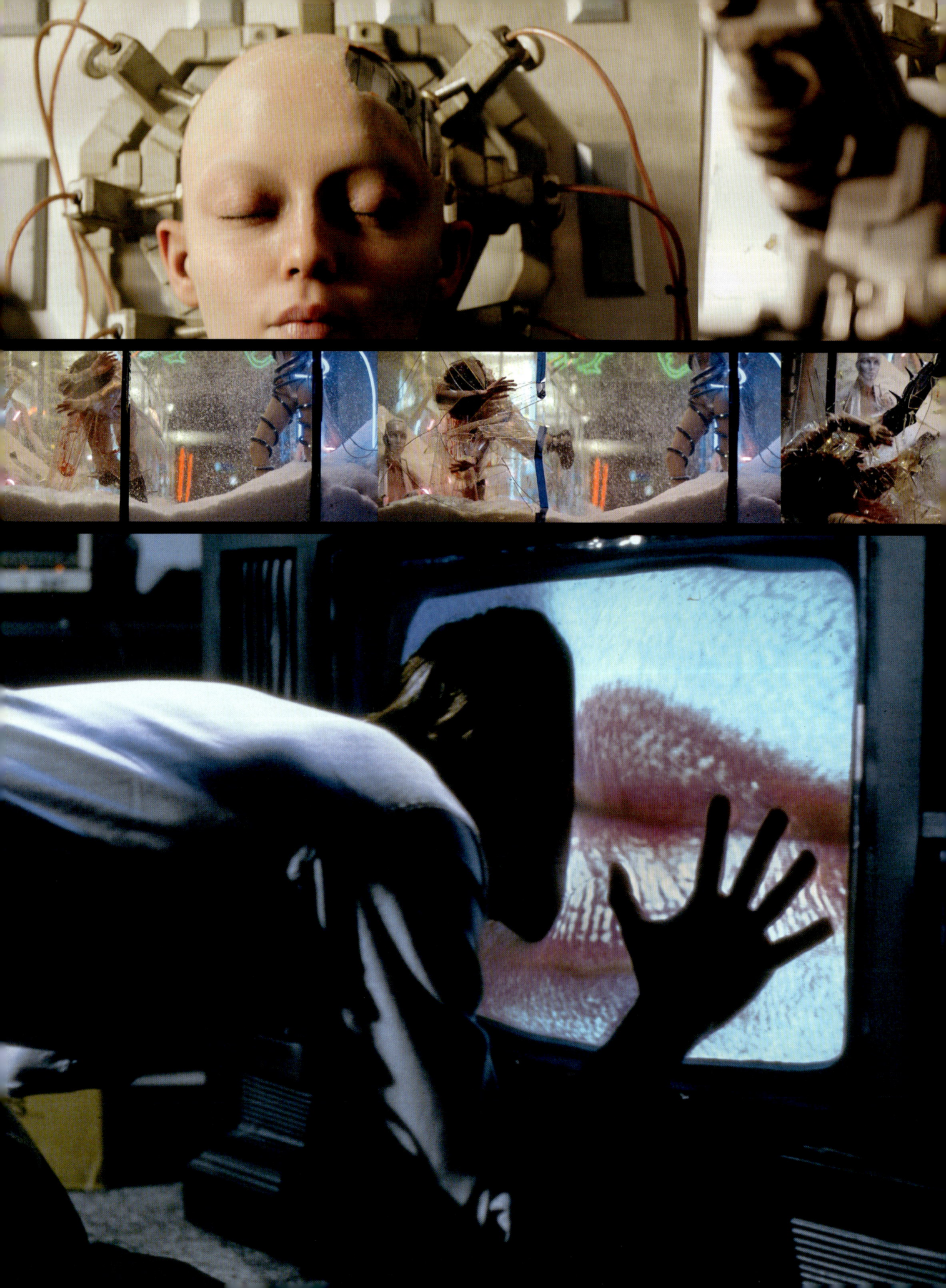

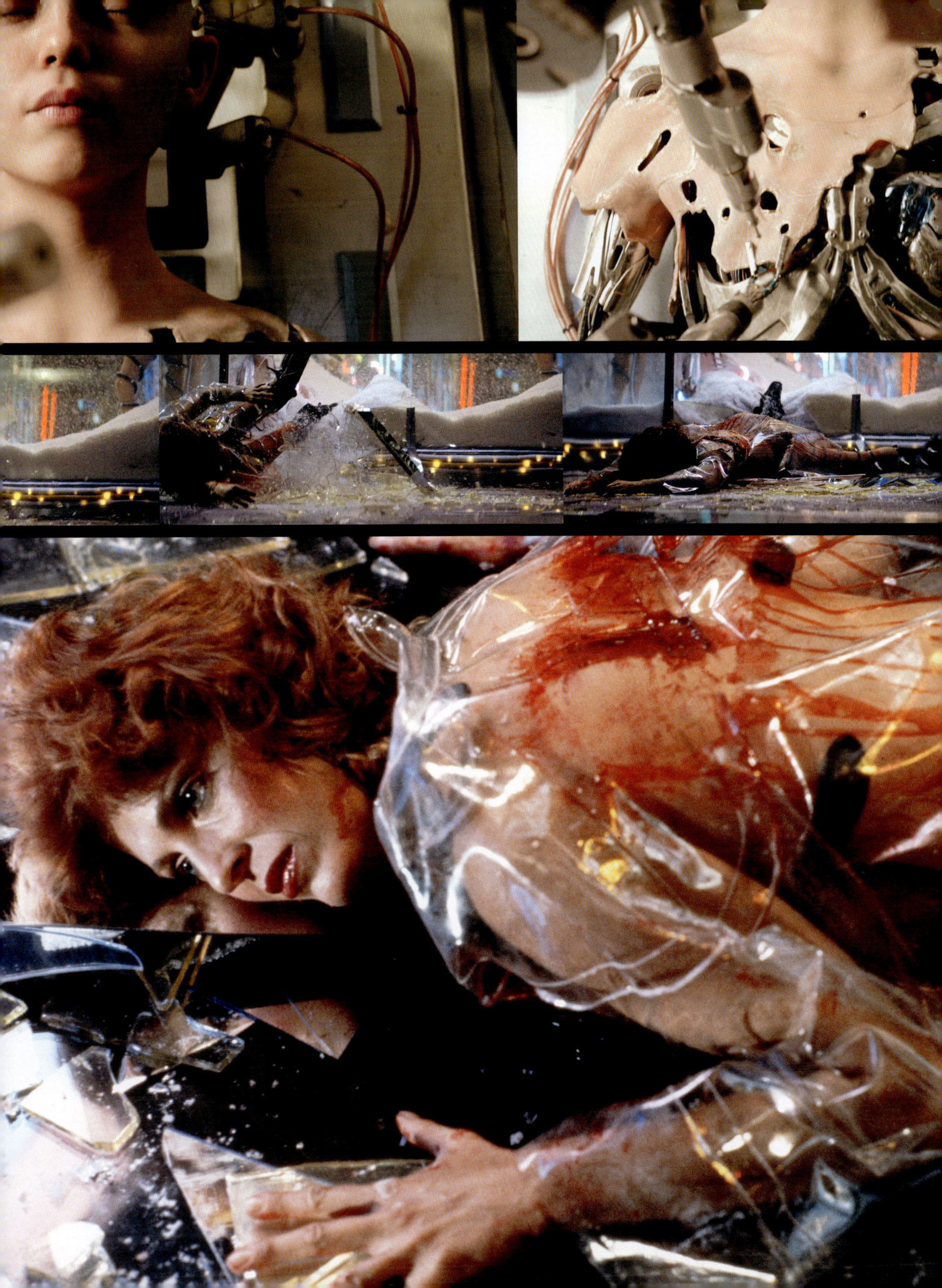

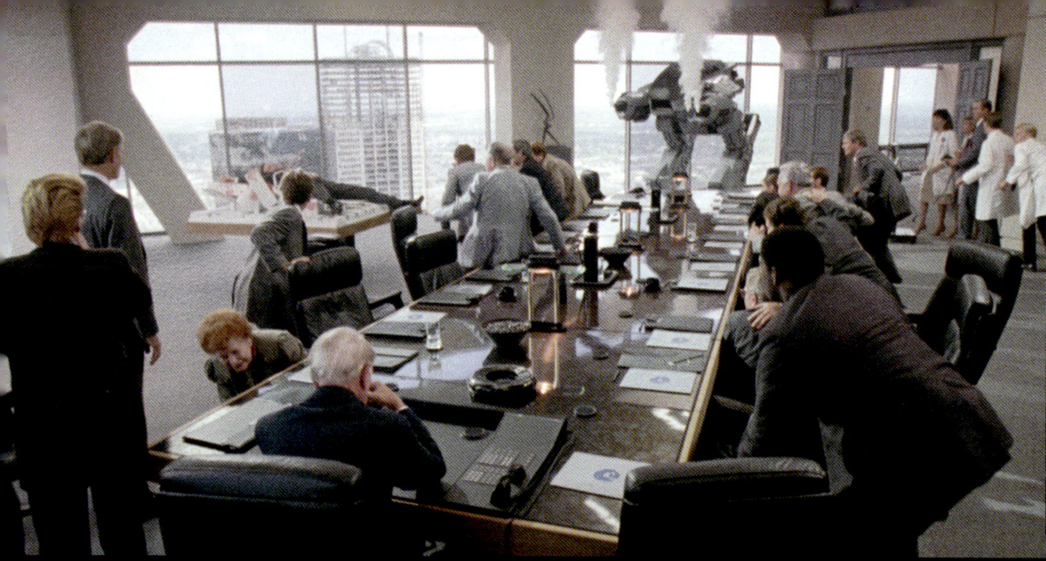

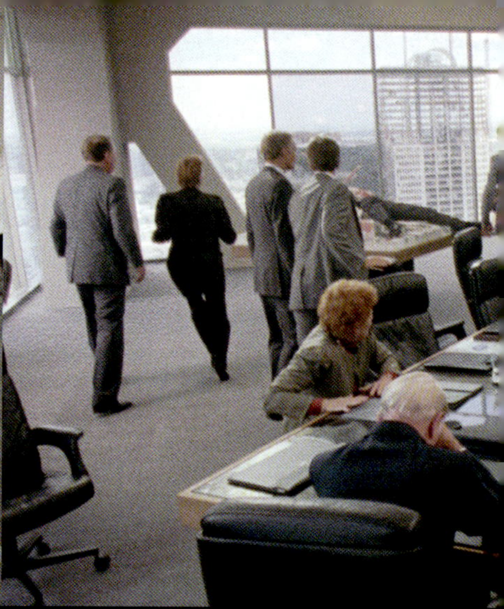

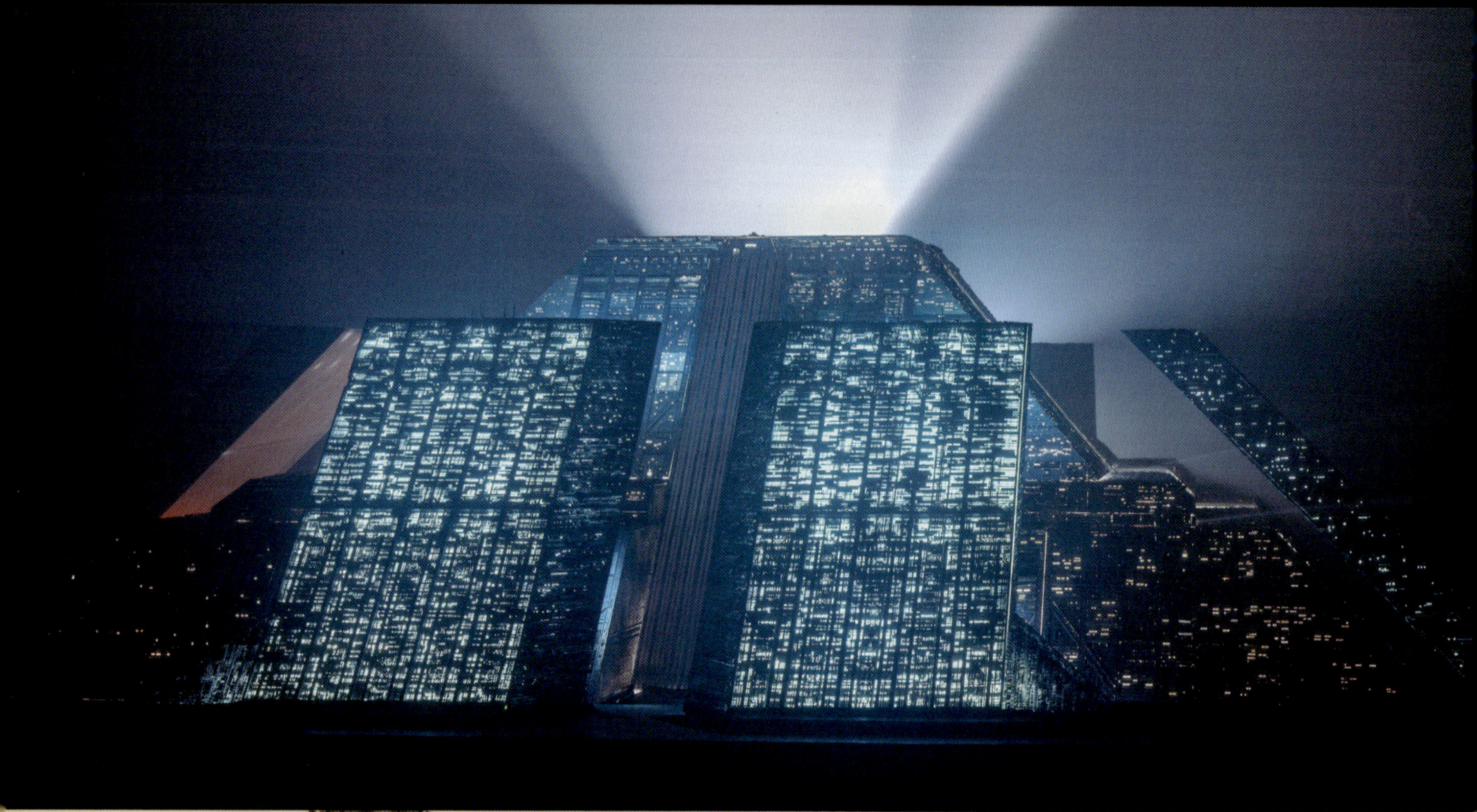

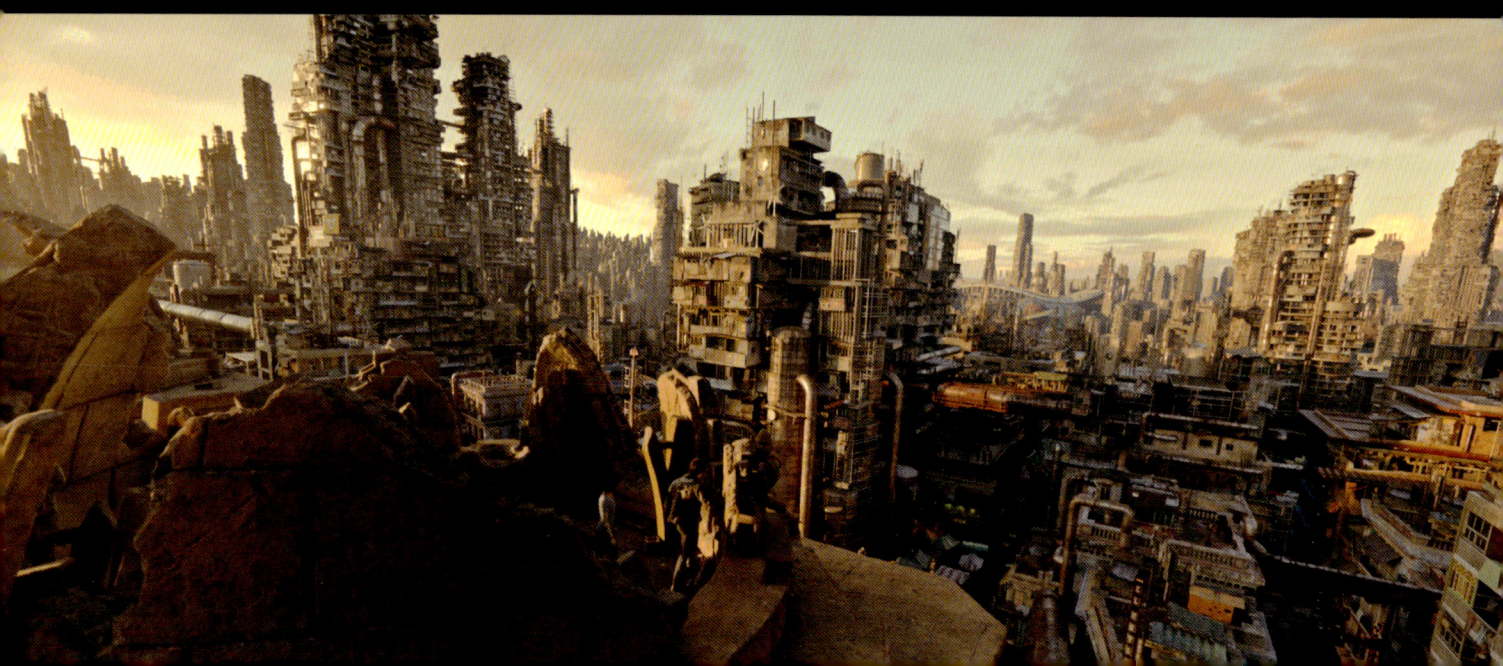

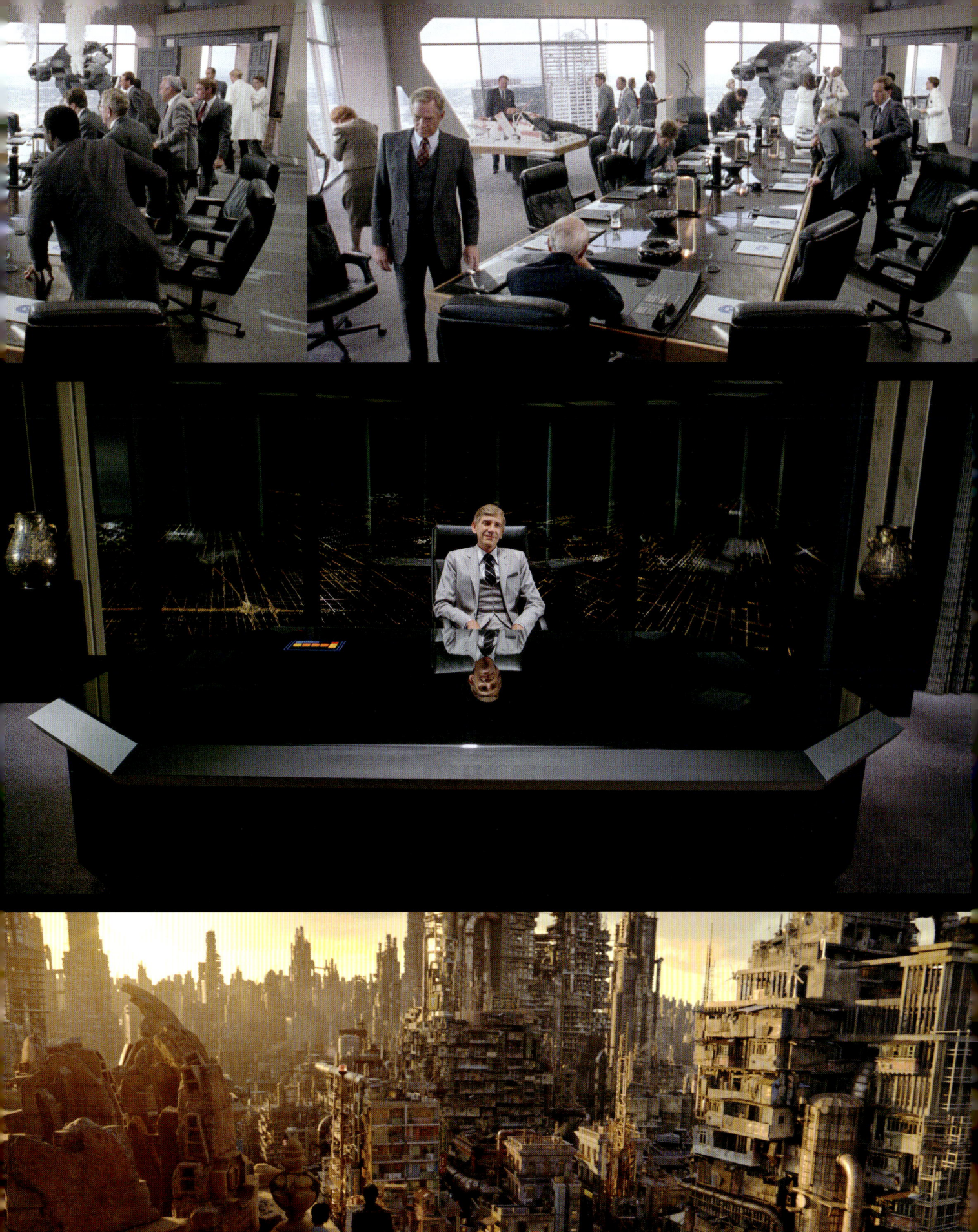

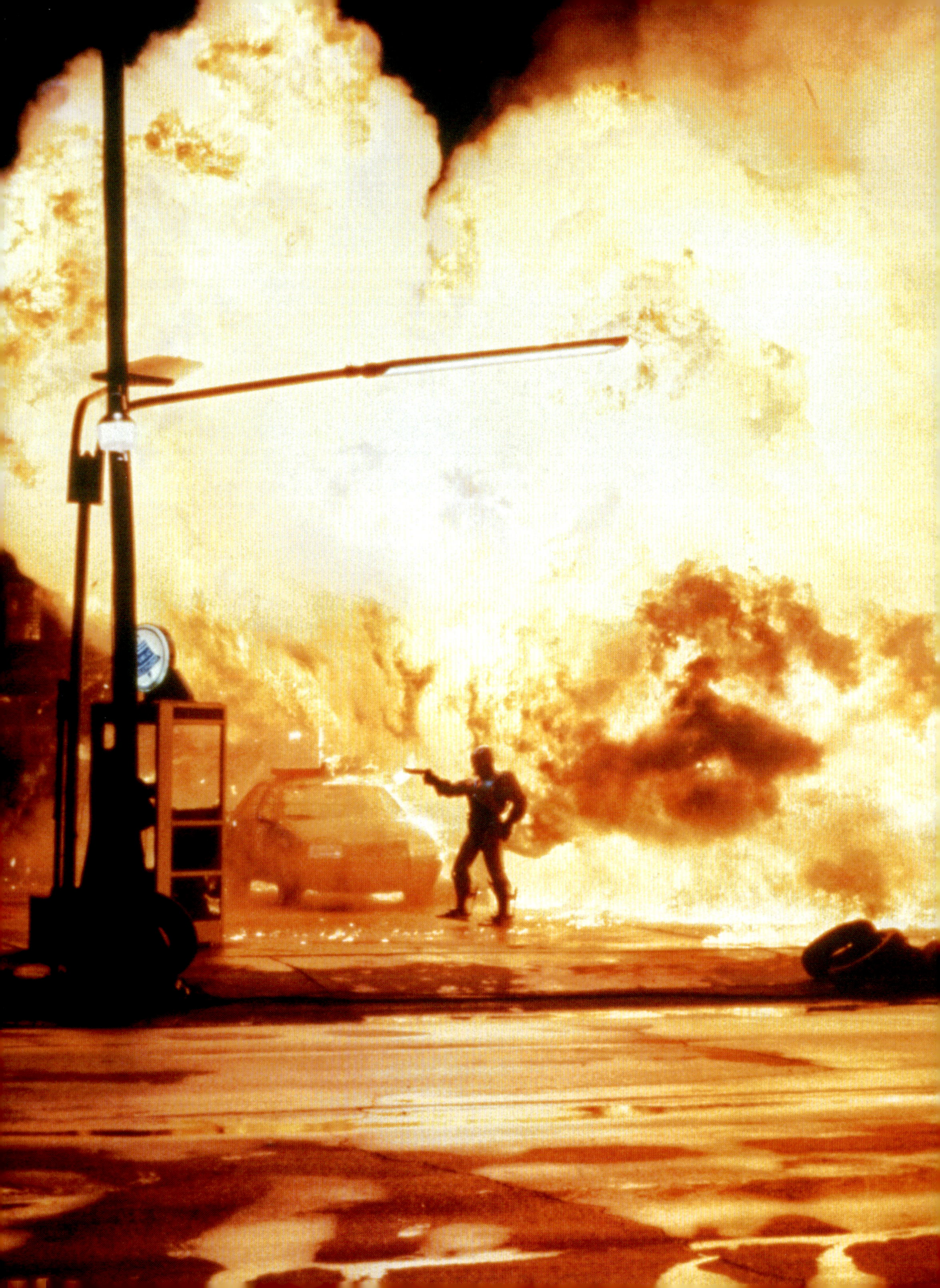

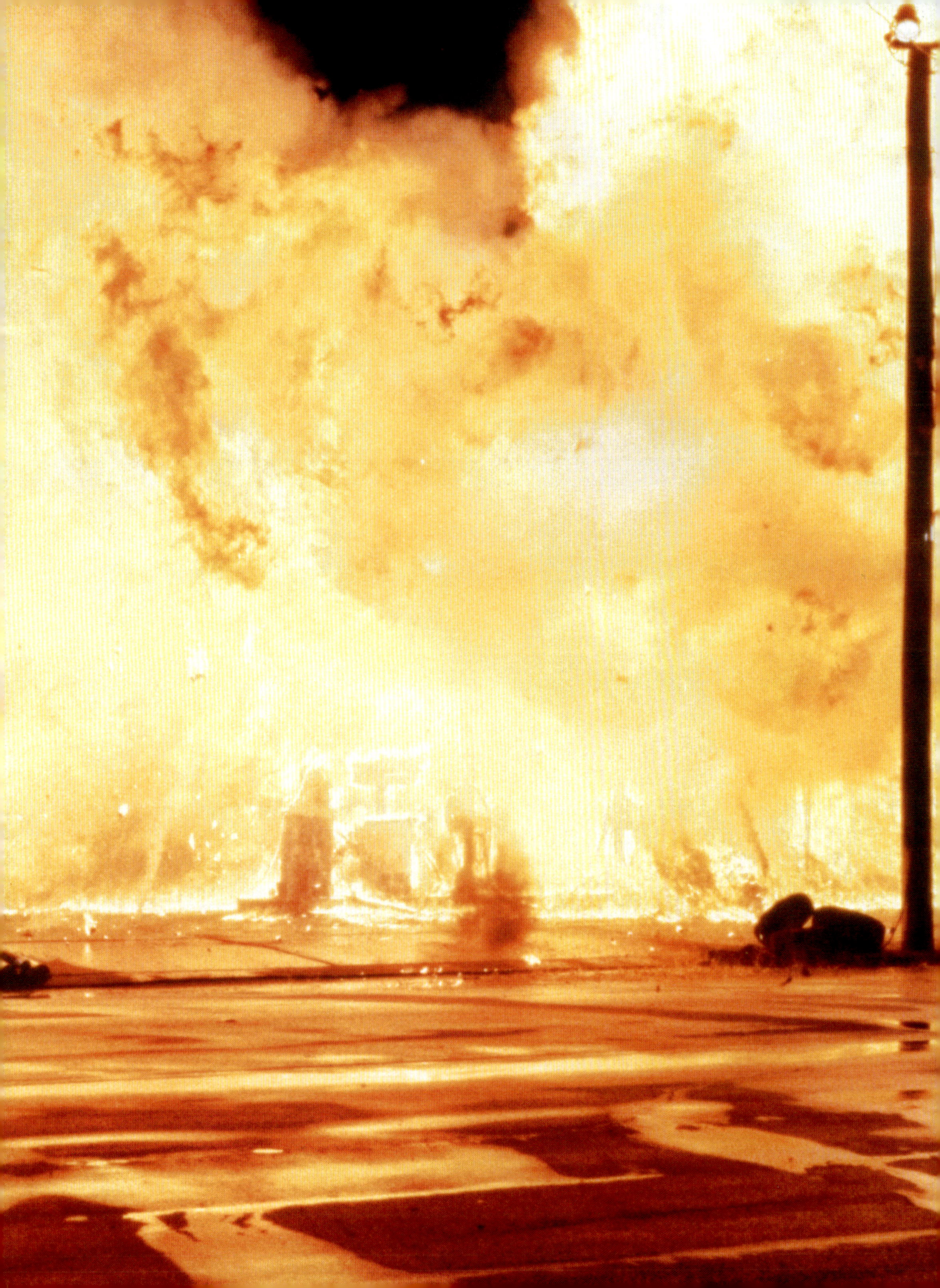

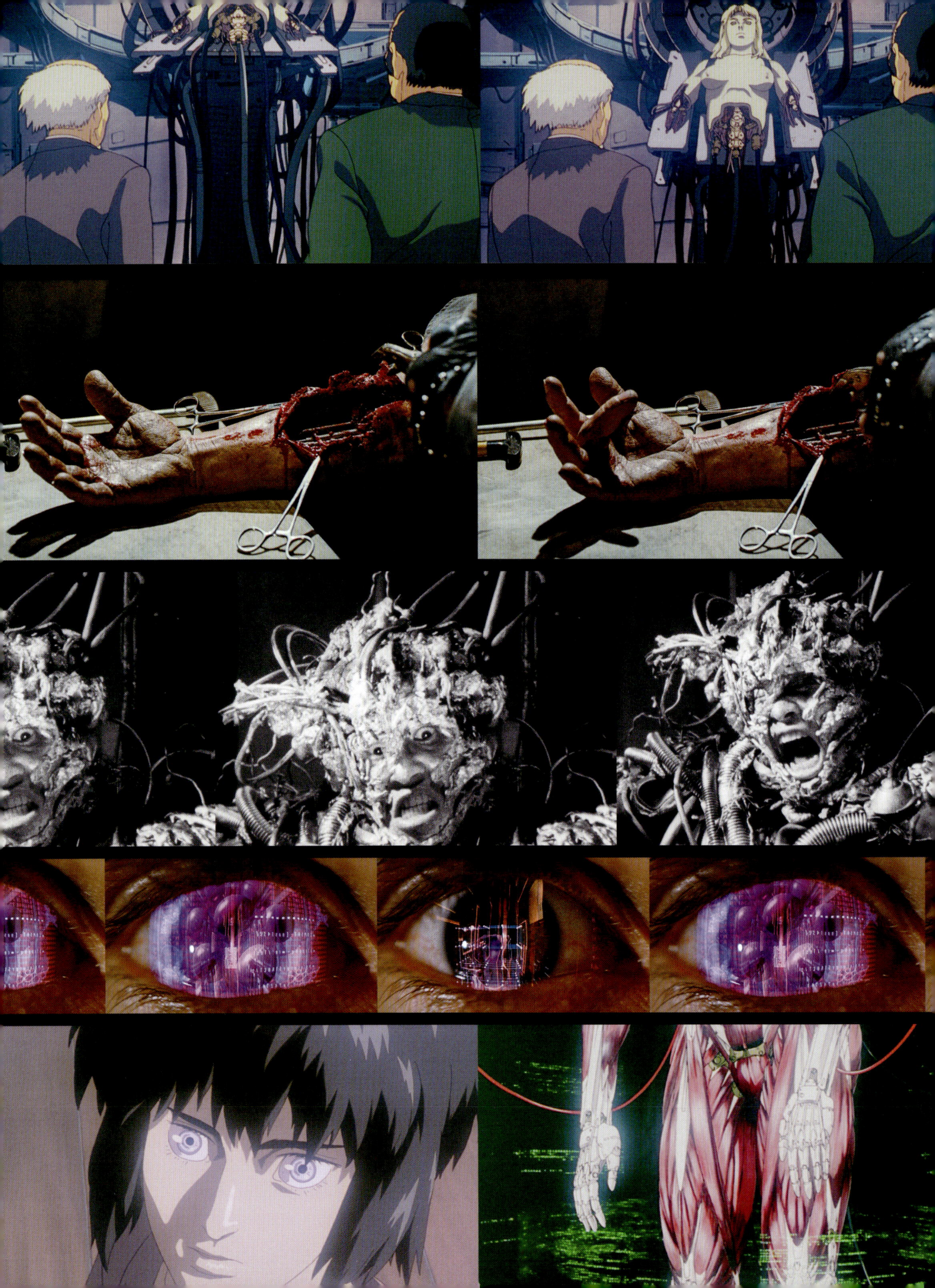

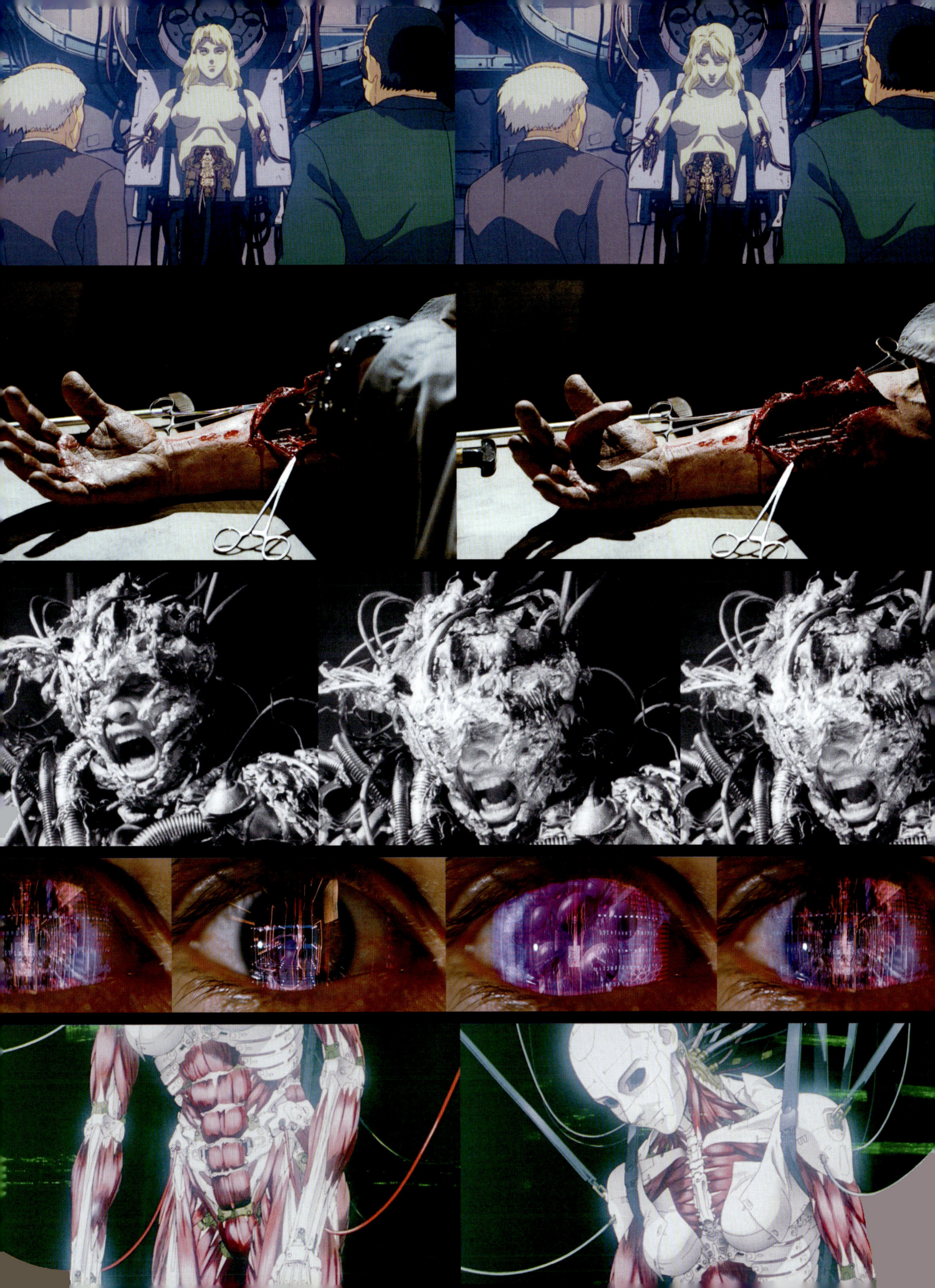

I, Cyberpunk
Alex Rivera

1.
I was born in the cobalt mines of Congo.
I was born in the high-tech factories of Tijuana.
I was born in a dark forest, under the gaze of a drone.
I was born in the mind of a hacker.
When I first opened my eyes,
I saw skyscrapers shimmering in cold rain.
Fortunes in the sky.
Hard streets, fluorescent lights, and digital exhaust down below.
I saw a world so connected. And divided.
As I was being born, computers were reproducing—networks blossoming—while something called 'nature' disappeared.
I encountered a world in which humans act like machines.
And machines hallucinate they are people.

2.
Everyone comes from somewhere.
I come from noir. From science-fiction. From punk and pulp and a bad string of code.
My ancestors dreamed of distant galaxies and of aliens close to home.
Of scientists, time travelers, and creatures who haunt the night.
But the alien terrain I explore is called 'Planet Earth: Tomorrow.'
In the stories I tell, the monsters are markets and circuits.
The villains are corporations and capitalism and ad-driven algorithms.
My heroes are outsiders who bend and break and survive the system.

3.
To understand people, I imagine machines.
Decades ago, I envisioned virtual realities, brain-machine interfaces.
Robots, cyborgs, and Artificial Intelligence.
Today's techno-realities first existed in my cinematic dreams.

4.
In me, you'll find legions.
Thieves. Hackers. Outcasts.
Cynical cops and warrior waitresses.
Tech titans who conspire in corporate castles,
And rebels who fight in forests and factories.

My characters visit tomorrow to bring back stories we need today.
They are canaries in the coal mine of your future.

5.
I've lived in many bodies.
At first, I knew where I was—who I was—and where the machines were.
It was us versus them.
But as I grew, my body changed. It became strange.
Alien, but not like a creature from outer space. No—my body became alien to *me*.
New openings appeared.
Portals.
Plugs.
Nodes.
Data entered my flesh—or was it the other way around?
One way or another, machines and I merged.
The boundaries and borders around my body began to disappear.
Gender itself, at times, fragmented like data on a broken hard drive.
Strangely, in a world of zeroes and ones, the binaries can break down.

To spy.
To kill.
And those who hack.
To subvert.
To find new ways to move.
To gamble and risk and find love and create circuits of liberation.
This is a story of a revolution-in-progress.

9.
And so, if you've ever wondered why this world gets more divided the more we get connected,
If you've ever wanted to press 'delete' on borders and barriers so people are as free as data,
If you've ever told a story about machines that serve people rather than profit,
If you've ever hacked the culture,
Then you are me.

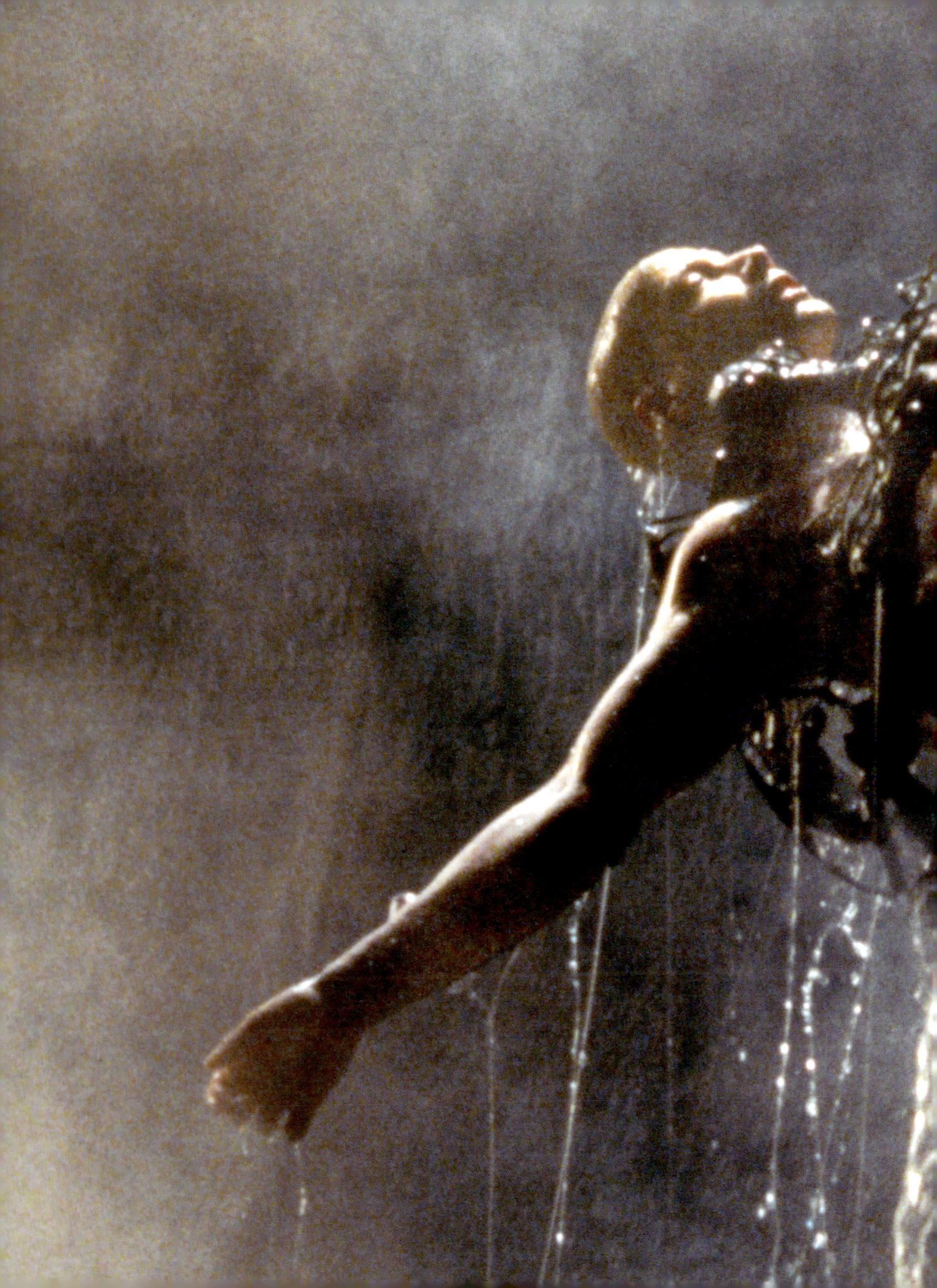

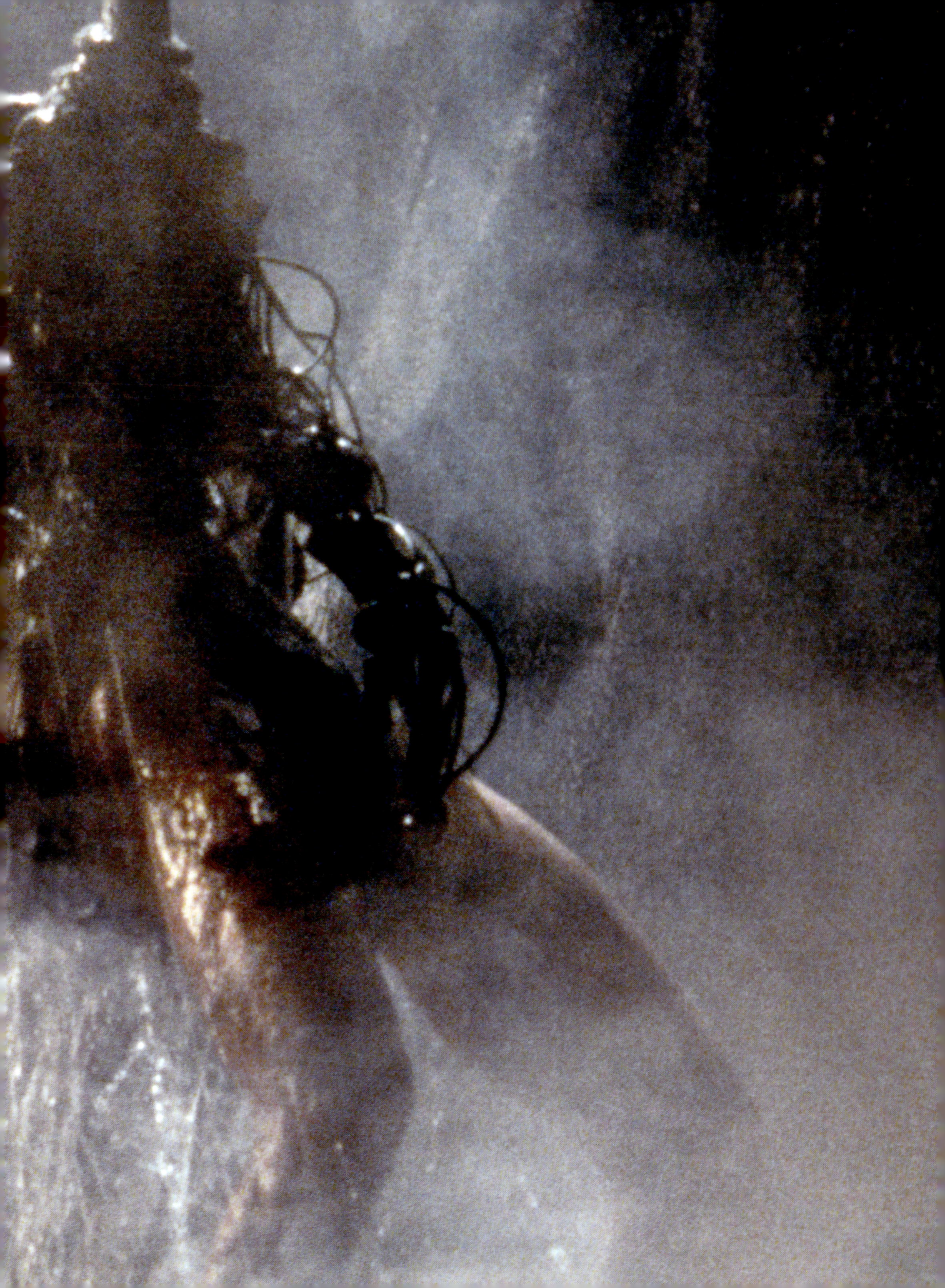

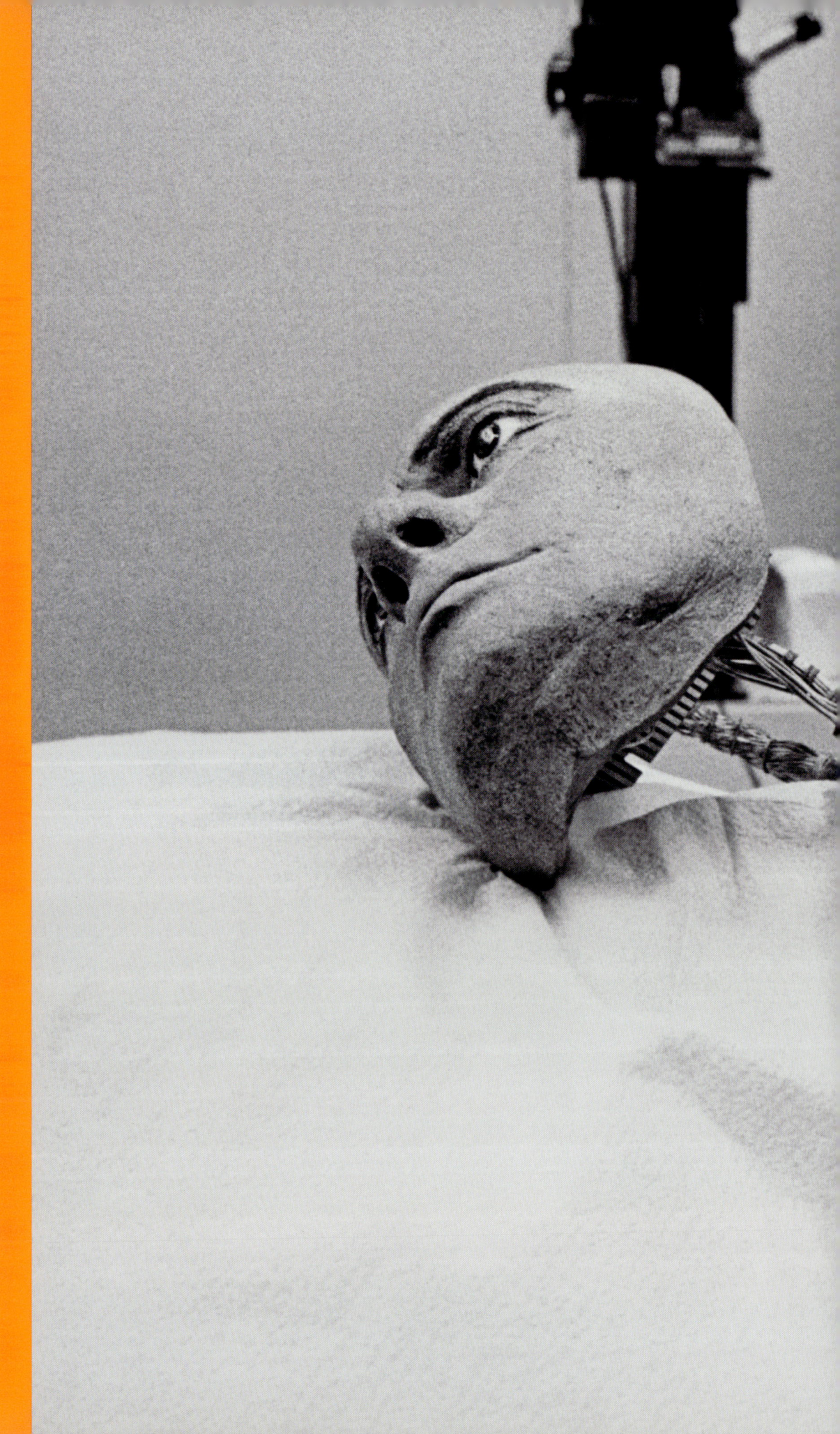

WESTWORLD

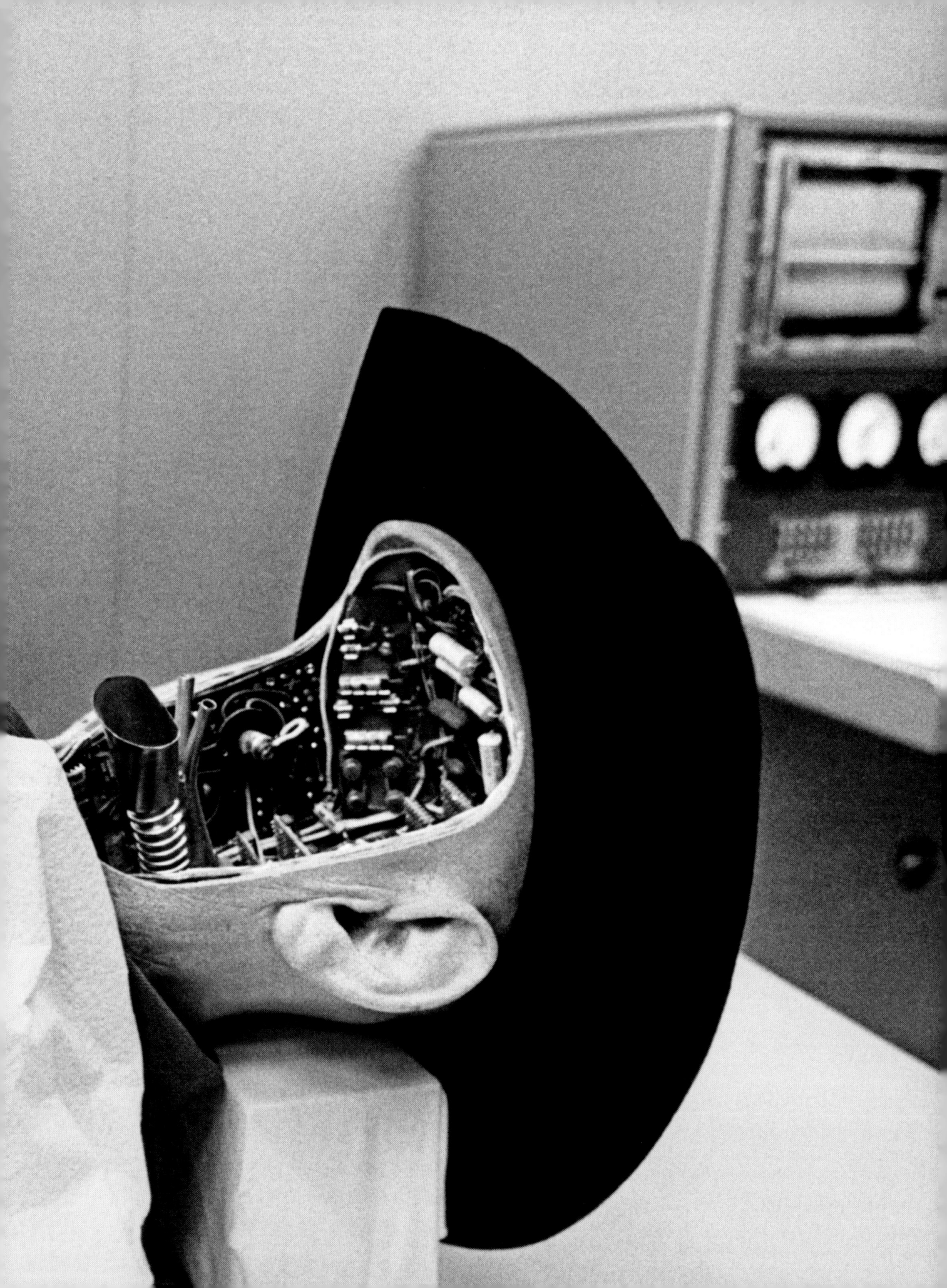

Westworld (USA, 1973)
Director: Michael Crichton

Film synopsis:
In a futuristic amusement park filled with humanlike androids, wealthy guests can indulge their wildest (and seediest) fantasies, role-playing as violent gunslingers or lecherous medieval knights. But when the robots malfunction, a deadly game of survival ensues as the androids turn against the visitors, sparking a battle for survival between humans and machines.

W ESTWORLD, WRITTEN AND DIRECTED BY Michael Crichton, is widely regarded as a proto-cyberpunk benchmark.[1] Notably, the film celebrates a cowboy style of male character that surfaces in various iterations in later cyberpunk films. This narrative device appears early on in *Westworld*, when the Gunslinger, a black-hatted robot played by Yul Brynner, heckles city slicker Peter Martin (Richard Benjamin) with the insult "He needs his mama."

The Western World area of the Delos theme park, where most of *Westworld* takes place, is a re-creation of the American Wild West. It is sold to visitors like Martin, a recently divorced lawyer from Chicago, as a space for men to recapture a form of frontier masculinity through combat with robot characters, such as the Gunslinger. However, activities throughout the park—which also includes the areas Medieval World and Roman World—reveal that the entire installation is just another playground for modern decadence that perpetuates the erosion of traditional concepts of masculinity.

At the heart of this decadent arena is the Delos corporation, a corrupt organization that has created a virtual world where technology allows people to express the worst parts of their nature. When the theme park's robots begin to malfunction and rebel, the very real violence that ensues allows Martin to emerge as the real hero of modernity: his intelligence and understanding of science enable him to outthink the machines, ultimately winning the battle with brains instead of guns or brawn. He does this while dressed as a cowboy, thus pioneering a style of male hero that was an important precursor to the cyber-cowboy hackers of William Gibson's

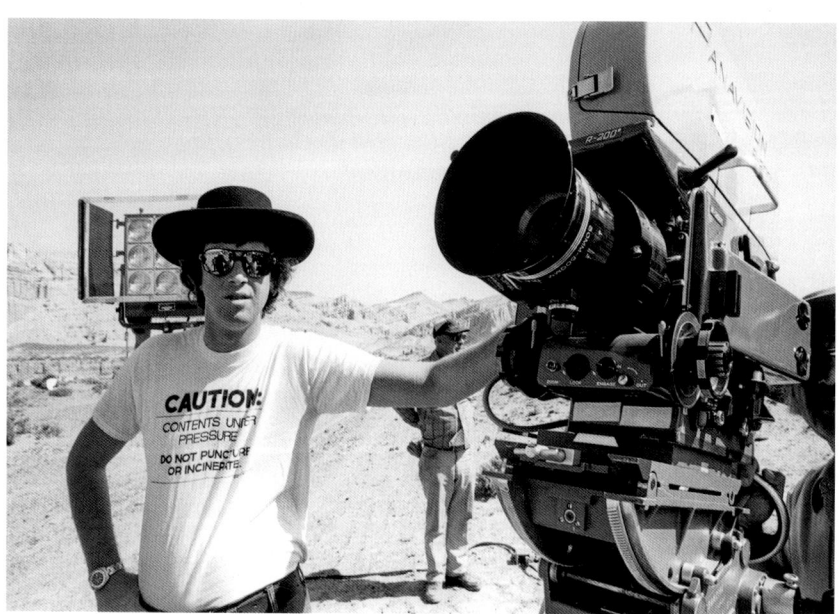

PREVIOUS SPREAD: Prop version of the Gunslinger, an android played by Yul Brynner

ABOVE: Director Michael Crichton on set

novel *Neuromancer* (1984) and the lead characters of films such as Paul Verhoeven's *RoboCop* (USA, 1987), featuring a gun-twirling cybercop, and Lana and Lilly Wachowski's *The Matrix* (USA, 1999), in which hacker Neo engages in a *High Noon*–style showdown with Agent Smith. The protagonists of these stories use their brains and techno-scientific skills instead of physical prowess to master machines and survive in dystopian scenarios.

Westworld's robot uprising recalls earlier science fiction works, including stories by 1960s authors such as Philip K. Dick and Harlan Ellison. Dick and Ellison rejected the naive optimism of Isaac Asimov and his "three laws of robotics,"[2] instead depicting the possible dangers of artificial intelligence and its potential to threaten human life and identity. In *Westworld*, Crichton includes an additional layer: a somewhat

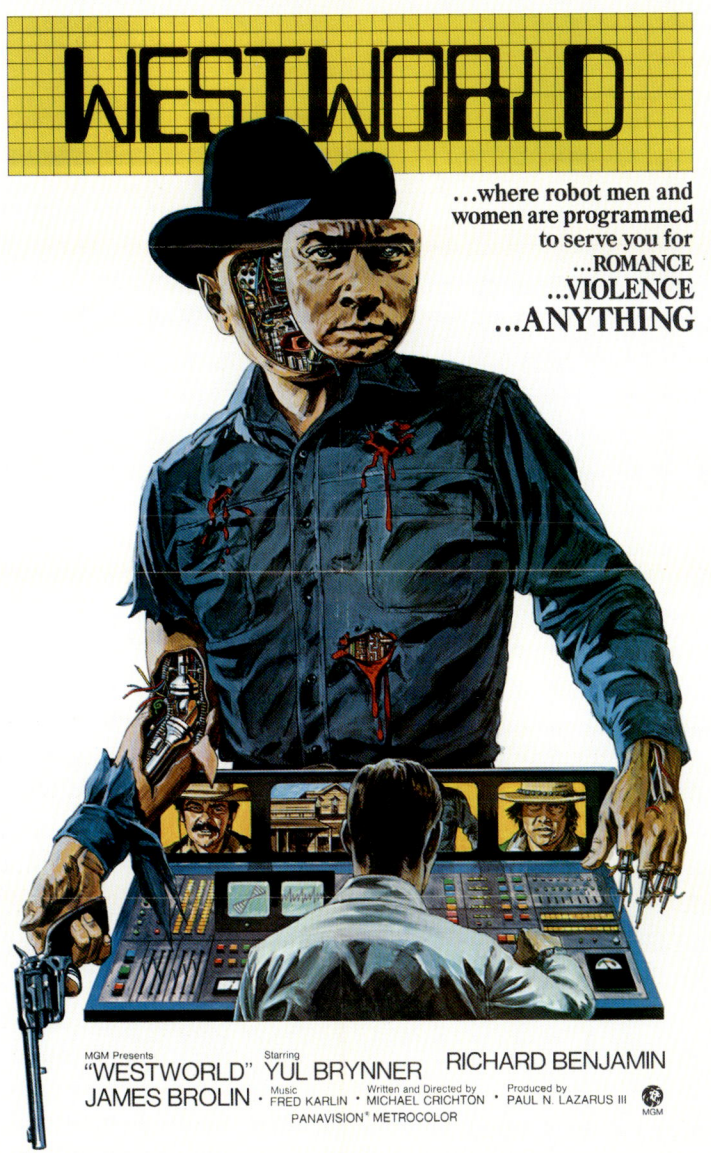

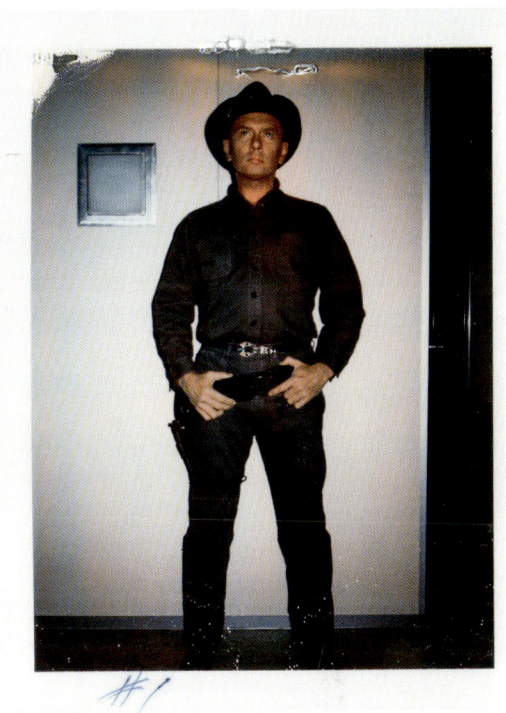

LEFT: Theatrical release poster

ABOVE: Yul Brynner as the Gunslinger, wardrobe reference photograph

sympathetic portrayal of the robots as colonial subjects of Delos. The Gunslinger, programmed into a cycle of frontier violence where he always loses, is killed over and over. Whereas Asimov asserted that proper programming would make robots helpful servants, *Westworld* shows how that plan can go awry, especially when we treat artificial intelligences as disposable chattel.

The plot mechanism of robot uprisings became a common attribute of cyberpunk cinema in the 1980s, useful for highlighting the tension between the benefits of technological progress and its perils.

In hindsight, they forewarned us about our current situation, where fear of new AI technologies is a characteristic of everyday life. Ridley Scott's *Blade Runner* (USA, 1982) and James Cameron's *The Terminator* (USA, 1984) both feature artificial beings created and programmed by heartless and shortsighted corporations—direct descendants of the Gunslinger. As intelligent and violent machines who punish humanity for its decadence and hubris, they reflect back to humans their own flaws, and the flaws in the world they have designed.

—*Patrick B. Sharp*

NOTES

1./ HBO recently remade the film as a series that ran for four seasons, from 2016 to 2022. The HBO series developed and updated the original film's portrayal of corporate corruption, toxic masculinity, and sympathetic artificial beings.

2./ Asimov's laws of robotics, delineated in his collection of stories *I, Robot* (1950), were supposed to be a set of rules for machines that would make them beneficial instead of dangerous. The three laws in order are 1) robots cannot harm a human or allow harm to come to a human, 2) robots must follow the orders of humans (unless this leads to harm for a human), and 3) robots must preserve their own existence (unless this conflicts with the first two laws).

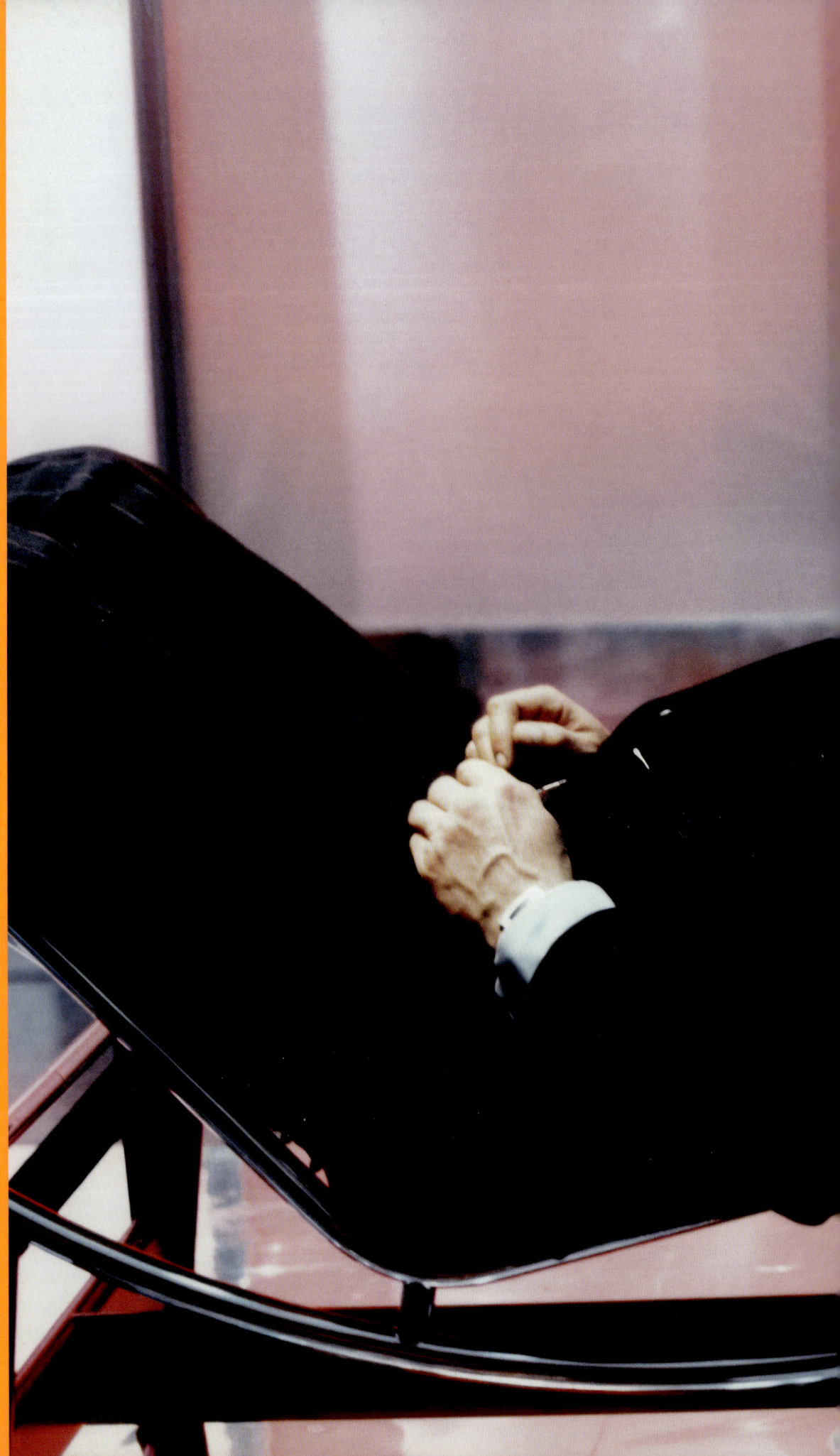

WORLD ON A WIRE

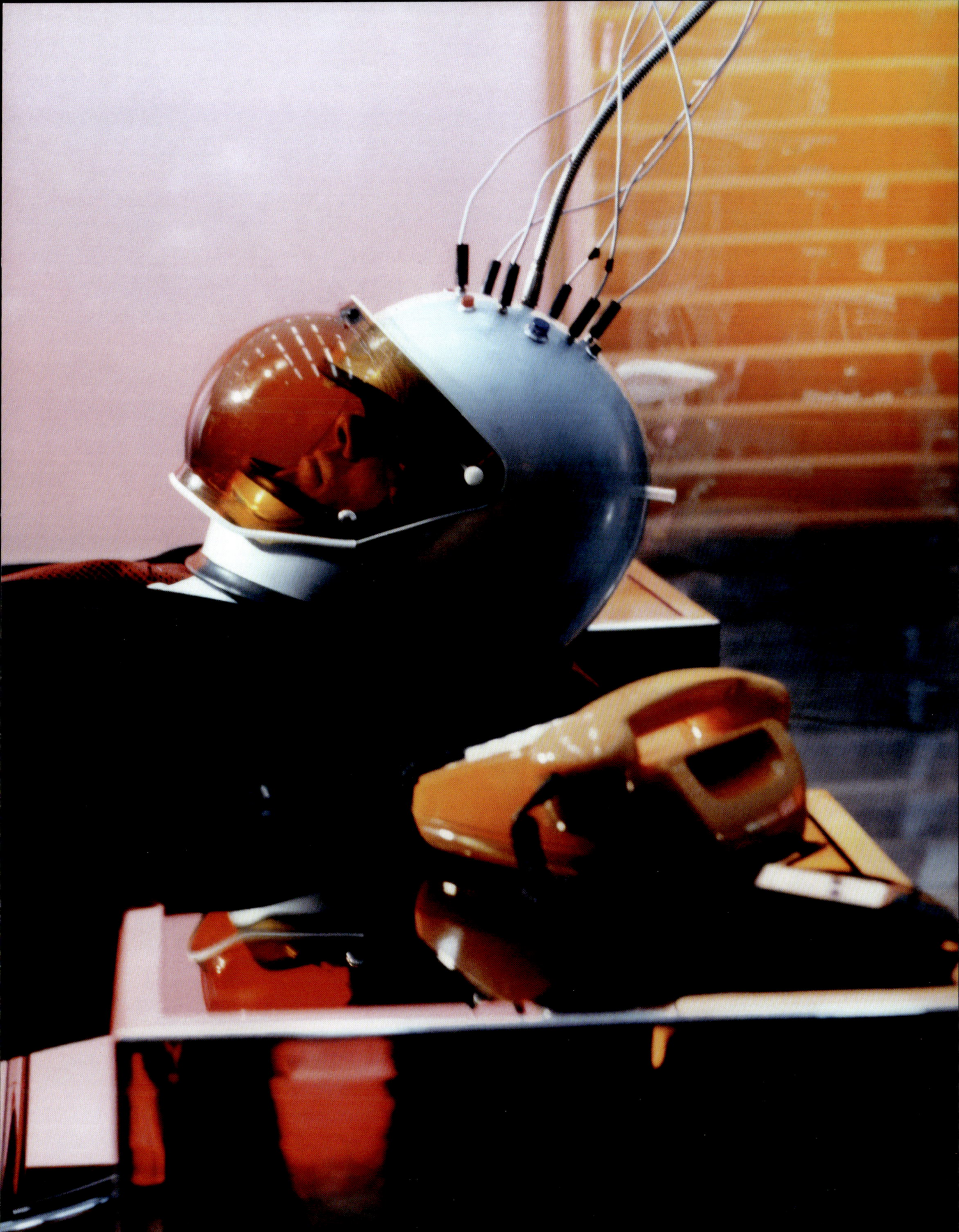

World on a Wire (*Welt am Draht*, West Germany, 1973)
Director: Rainer Werner Fassbinder

Film synopsis:
Scientists at the Institute for Cybernetics and Futurology control an artificial world in which thousands of "identity units," who believe they are humans, live within a computer simulation. When Dr. Fred Stiller enters the simulation to investigate one of its units, his confidence in his own reality is shaken.

GERMAN DIRECTOR Rainer Werner Fassbinder's sole foray into science fiction, *World on a Wire*, uses classic motifs of the cyberpunk genre, including virtual reality, simulation, artificial intelligence, paranoia, surveillance, and corporate power. These themes neatly intersect with Fassbinder's long-standing interest in repression, dualities, oppressive power relations, fatalistic situations, and the theatrical nature of the human condition.[1]

The film, which was originally made for German television, is a mostly faithful adaptation of American novelist Daniel F. Galouye's *Simulacron-3* (1964). The story revolves around cybernetics engineer Dr. Fred Stiller (Klaus Löwitsch), who works on the Simulacron project at the Institute for Cybernetics and Futurology. This project involves a computer simulation capable of creating an artificial world inhabited by virtual humans who don't know they are unreal. Stiller becomes embroiled in a complex web of intrigue after the mysterious death of his mentor, Professor Henry Vollmer (Adrian Hoven). As he delves deeper into Vollmer's death and the workings of the Simulacron project, he discovers his own reality is itself a simulation. The world that Stiller believes is the "real world" is simply a simulacrum created by a computer programmer in what is, in fact, the real world. And Stiller was modeled on this real-world programmer, the original Fred Stiller.

In *World on a Wire*, there is a disorienting lack of distinction between the reality produced by the computer Simulacron, the reality of Stiller's simulated world, and the "real" reality of the original Stiller. Through its nested structure of simulations within simulations, the film creates a complex

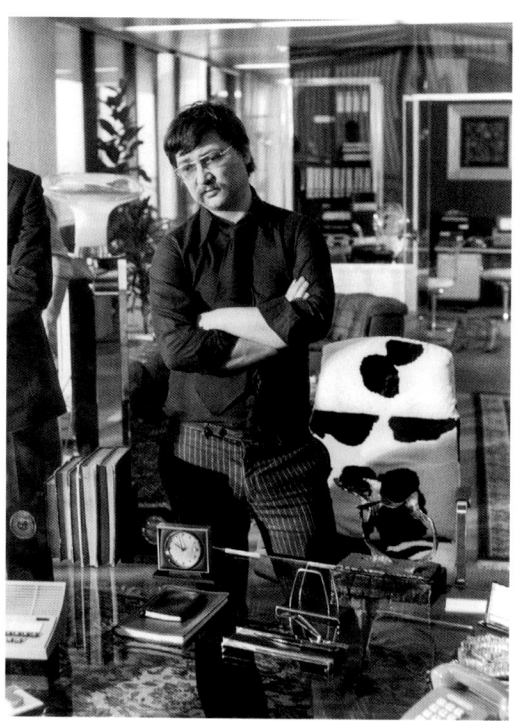

PREVIOUS SPREAD: Klaus Löwitsch as Fred Stiller

ABOVE: Director Rainer Werner Fassbinder on set

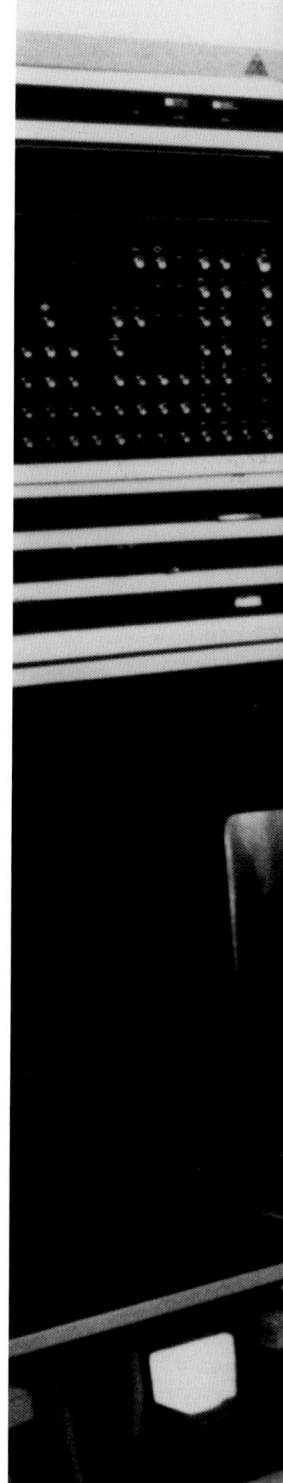

ABOVE: Kurt Raab as Mark Holm

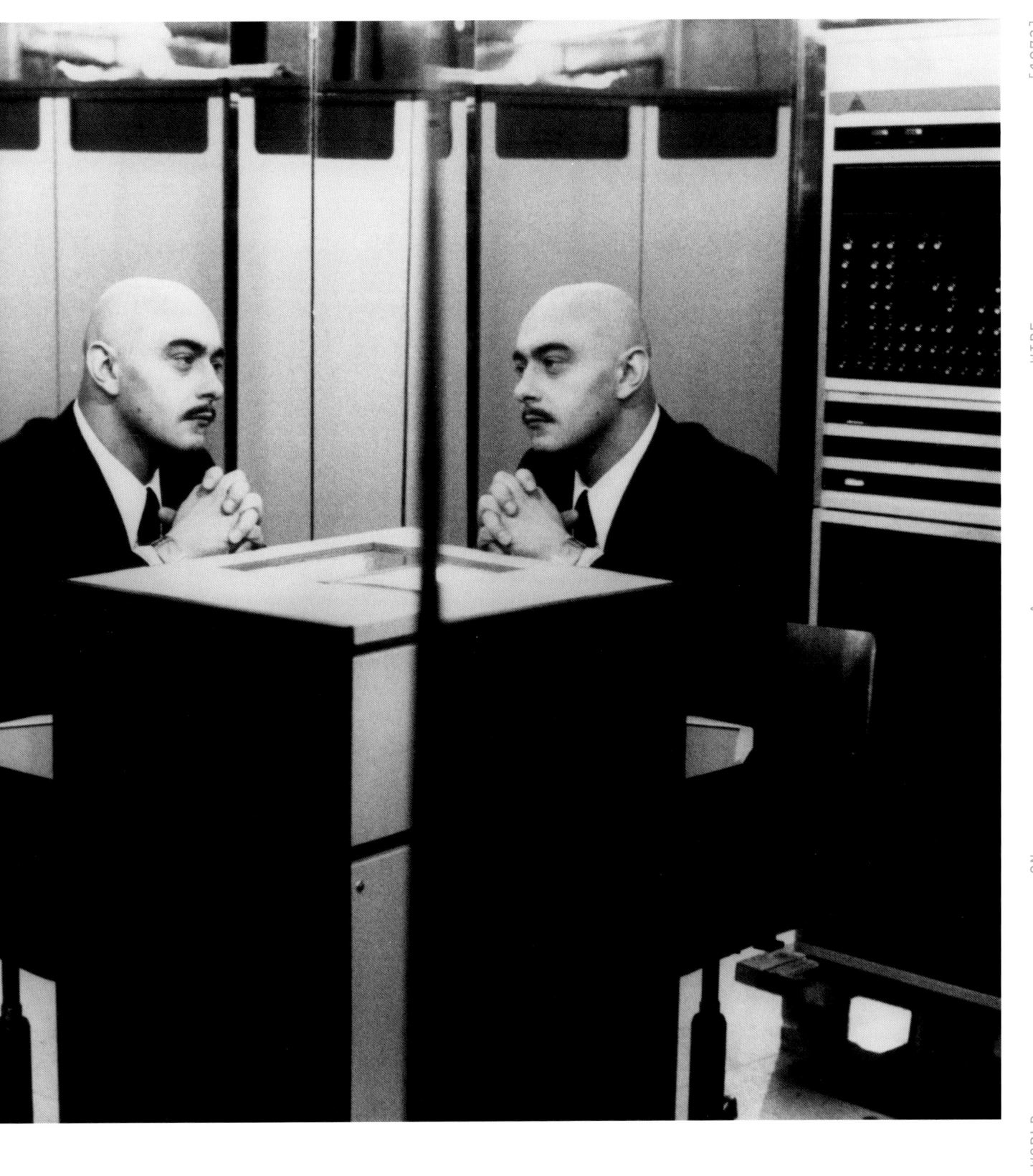

world that invites the viewer to confront the central investigation of virtual reality: What is real and what is simulated? Fassbinder compels viewers to engage with this question through Stiller's anxiety as he participates in philosophical conversations about topics like Zeno's paradox of Achilles and the tortoise, Plato's allegory of the cave, and the global capitalist interests of the company United Steel.[2] Stiller's increasing uncertainty and paranoia eventually lead to the type of existential crisis that would become a common device in cyberpunk works of the 1980s and '90s.

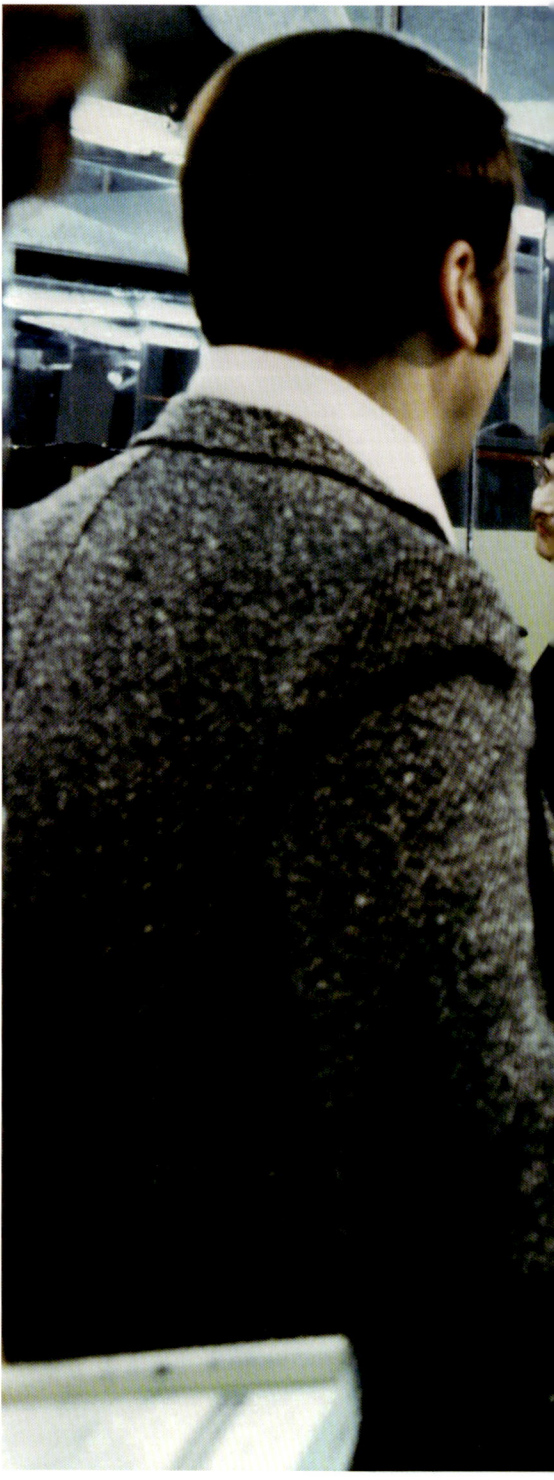

Fassbinder, together with his production design team, led by Kurt Raab, and cinematographer Michael Ballhaus, enhances this play with identity by experimenting with sound design, music, dialogue, and set design. For example, electronic sound effects are accompanied by extreme close-ups to emphasize Stiller's gradual realization that the split between his perceived reality and a certifiable external reality is being manipulated.[3] Mirrors and other reflective surfaces—including metal walls, fish tanks, pools of water, glass desks, and mirrored pedestals—dominate the film's visuals.[4] The reflections, which are often distorted, represent the blurred boundaries between the virtual world and the actual world, suggesting there are multiple layers of reality; they create a sense of disorientation and ambiguity that symbolizes the fragmented nature of perception.[5]

World on a Wire is an early cinematic exploration of simulation and identity, themes that can be traced back to the American science fiction writer Philip K. Dick. It in turn served as a precursor to future iconic cyberpunk films, such as Ridley Scott's *Blade Runner* (USA, 1982) and Lana and Lilly Wachowski's *The Matrix* (USA, 1999), which feature central characters who are forced to question their own reality. And in Fassbinder's hands, the concomitant themes of uncertainty and paranoia also reflect Germany's larger struggle with its identity in the postwar era as Germans grappled with the burden of their Nazi past, the challenge of integrating into a more cosmopolitan Europe, and the deep division of being split into two ideologically and economically distinct countries.

—David A. Kirby

NOTES

1./ Among Fassbinder's films that focus on notions of "doubling" and repression are *The Bitter Tears of Petra von Kant* (*Die bitteren Tränen der Petra von Kant*, West Germany, 1972), *Effi Briest* (West Germany, 1974), and *Querelle* (West Germany and France, 1982).

2./ In one paradox attributed to the fifth-century BCE Greek philosopher Zeno of Elea, the hero Achilles is chasing after a tortoise. Achilles is faster than the tortoise, and so common sense suggests that he must eventually catch up with it. But Zeno argued that every time Achilles reaches the tortoise's point, the tortoise will have moved further forward to new point. By the time Achilles reaches this new point, the tortoise will have moved forward again, thus Achilles will never catch up.

3./ Chuck Johnson, "World on a Wire: Sound as Sensual Objects," *Leonardo Music Journal* 23, Sound Art (2013): 75–77.

4./ Brian Faucette, review of *World on a Wire*, directed by Rainer Werner Fassbinder, *The Moving Image* 14, no. 2 (Fall 2014): 121–23.

5./ Reflective surfaces would ultimately develop into Fassbinder's most recognizable visual motif. See Faucette, review of *World on a Wire*, 122.

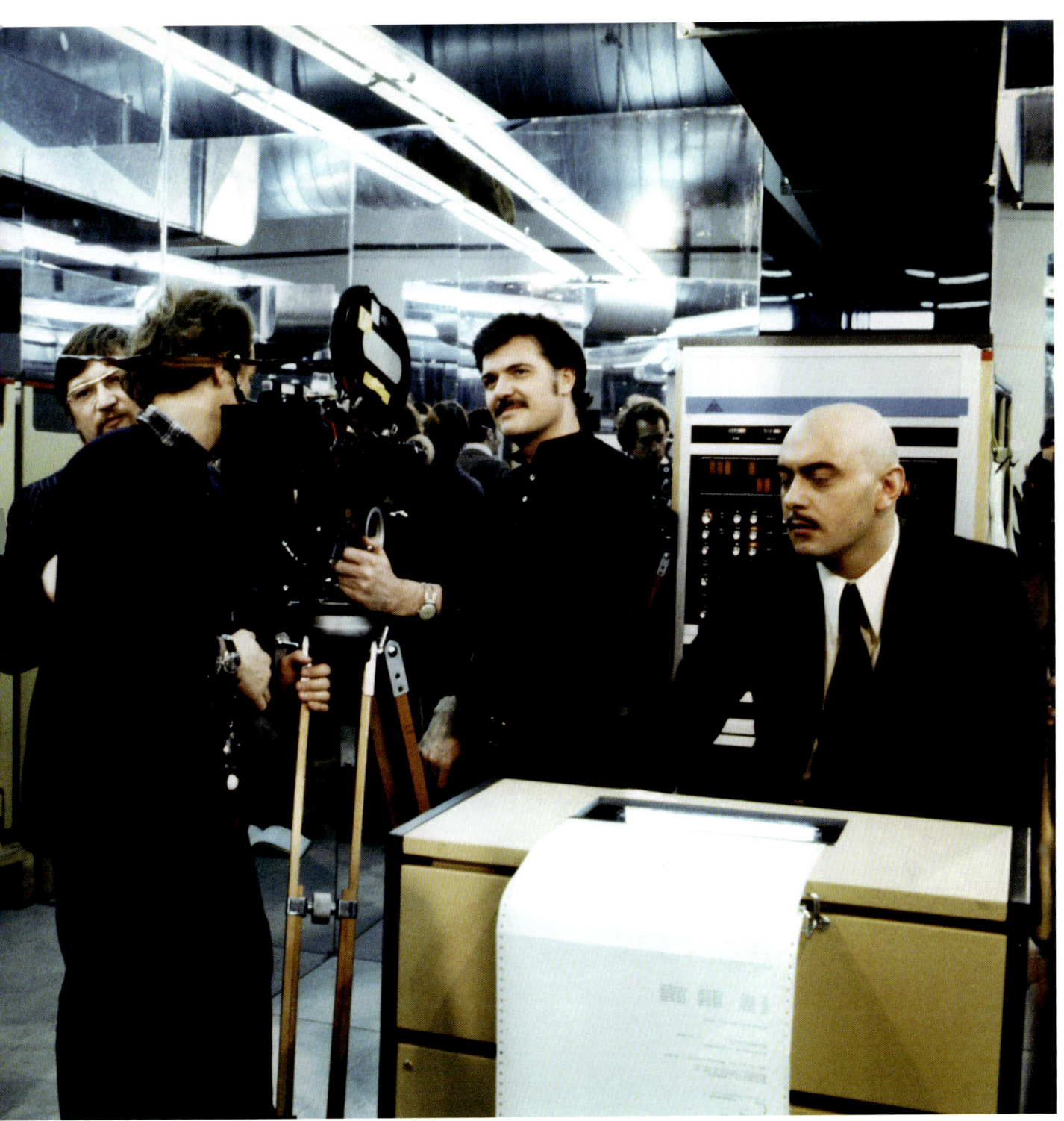

ABOVE: From left: Actor Günther Lamprecht, Fassbinder, unidentified crew member, cinematographer Michael Ballhaus, and Raab on set

ESCAPE FROM NEW YORK

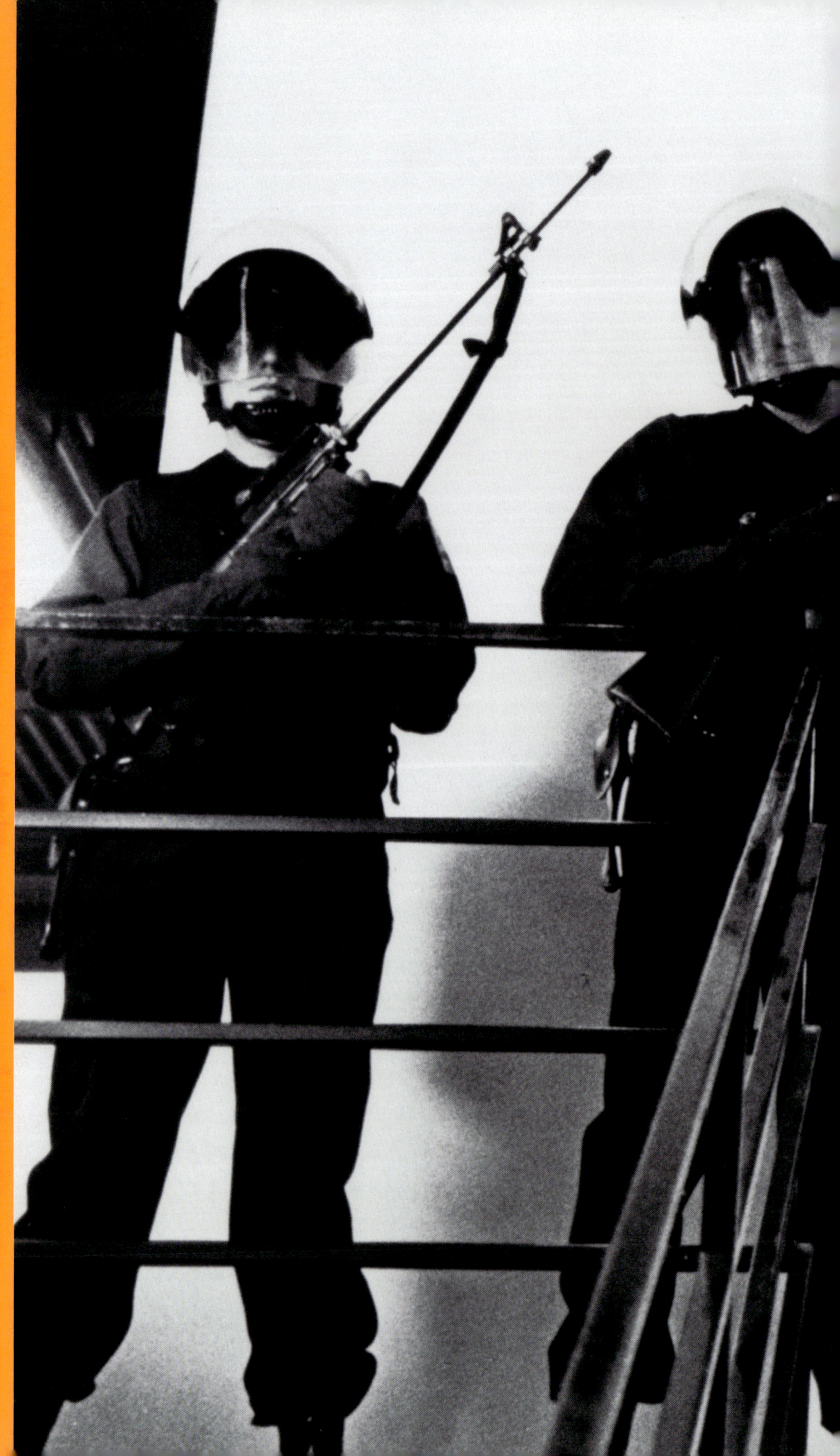

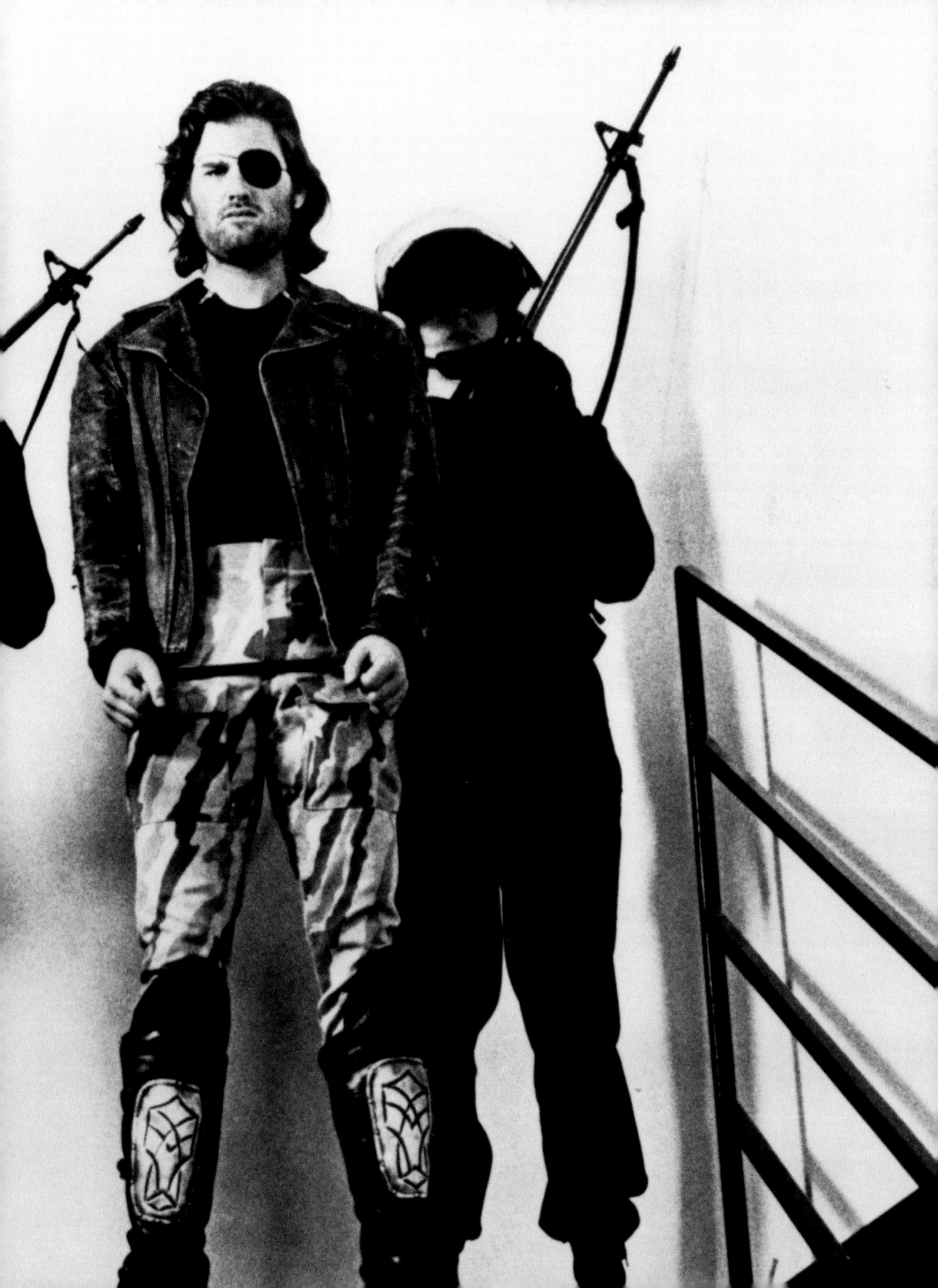

Escape from New York (USA, 1981)
Director: John Carpenter

Film synopsis:
A benighted United States solves its crime problem by converting the island of Manhattan into a prison and sending all its most dangerous criminals there. After anti-government activists threaten global stability by kidnapping the president and holding him on the island, disgraced military hero Snake Plissken is sent in to save him, or die trying.

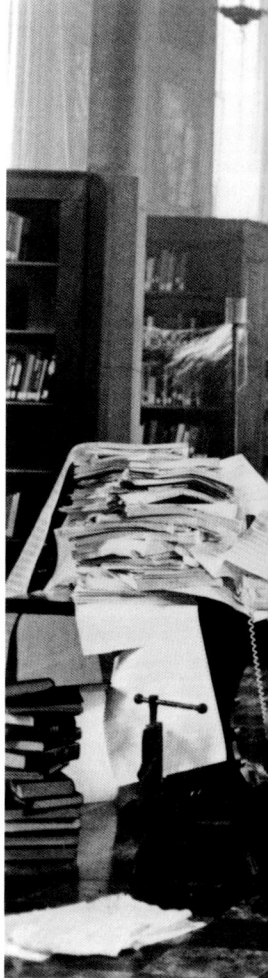

Set in the then near future of 1997, John Carpenter's 1981 film *Escape from New York* imagines a dystopic world in which the United States government has converted the entire island of Manhattan into America's most secure incarceration facility. Though guards enforce a brutal defense of the island's perimeter, the prisoners are left to their own, often violent, rule within the boundaries of the blockade. "There are no guards inside the prison," says a voice-over early on in the film, "only prisoners and the worlds they have made."

The intention of this correctional system is to deter crime through the threat of extralegal gang violence but also, more importantly, to sequester all supposed deviants out of view of mainstream society. This Manhattan is not a totally lawless space, however; the prisoners have established their own customs, hierarchies, and aesthetics. The construction of *Escape from New York*'s fictional world mixes aspirational fantasies with imposed practical limitations. This underscores the film's themes of technology-based oppression—futuristic promise made present persecution.

Although the prisoners are restricted to materials they can access on the island, they maintain a punk irreverence by expressing their individuality in the face of attempted dehumanization. The Duke of New York (Isaac Hayes) is the cruel and uncompromising leader of a gang called the Gypsies, yet also a bit of a dandy who values the finer things—illustrated by his trademark Cadillac with fender-mounted crystal chandeliers. On a 1980 sketch of the Duke's outfit, costume designer Stephen Loomis noted that it should include leather gloves adorned with brass luggage feet, marching band uniform epaulets for his jacket, and three-toned cowboy boots because, as Loomis comments, the Duke would wear "only the best shit on his feet." The government discards these prisoners in the hopes they will disappear, but with his bold visual style, the Duke demonstrates a will not just to survive but to flourish.

While the inhabitants of the island actively take elements of their environment and alter them in ways that make them more meaningful to their current situation—drilling for oil in a library, using old car parts as armor—the digital technology in the film is something that happens *to* them. The wristband Snake Plissken (Kurt Russell) receives from the police, who have blackmailed him into rescuing the president, serves no other purpose than to display a visible countdown to his death—a device that represents opposition to his survival. Digital technology emerges as an inflexible force that allows the government elite to evaluate, surveil, and, at times, murder the prisoners. Considered within the context of today's prison system—with its reliance on digital surveillance, military-grade weapons technology, and paid video visitations for inmates—the conflict between tech-haves and tech-have-nots presented in *Escape from New York* surpasses the speculative and enters the prophetic.

—Emily Rauber Rodriguez

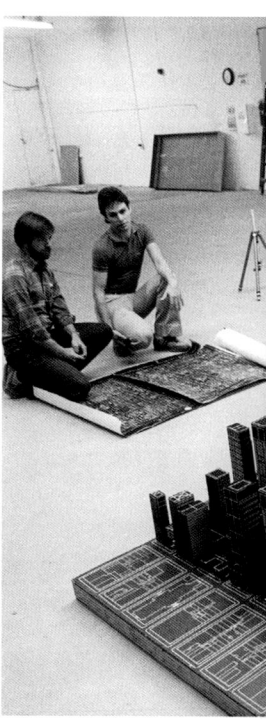

ABOVE: Model makers Mark Stetson (second from left) and David Stewart (third from left) and unidentified crew members discuss miniatures for visual effects

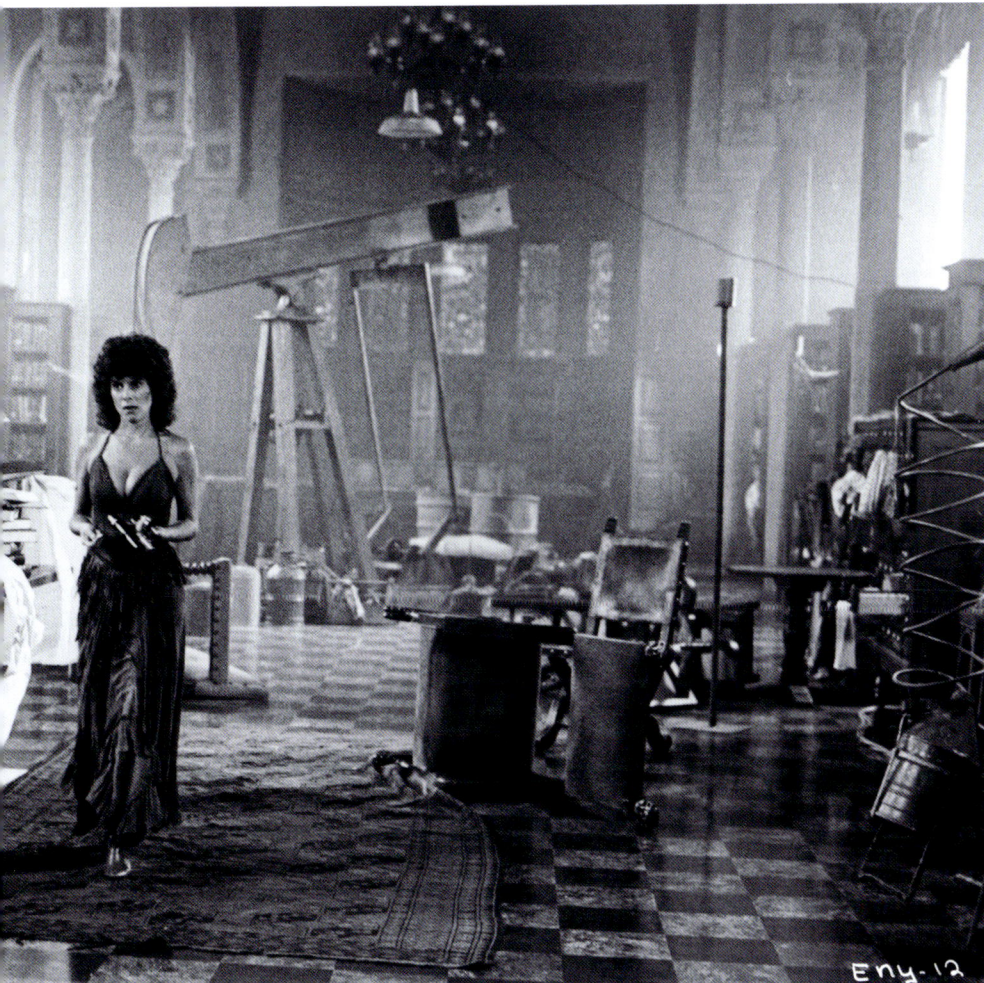

PREVIOUS SPREAD: Kurt Russell (third from left) as Snake Plissken

LEFT: Adrienne Barbeau as Maggie

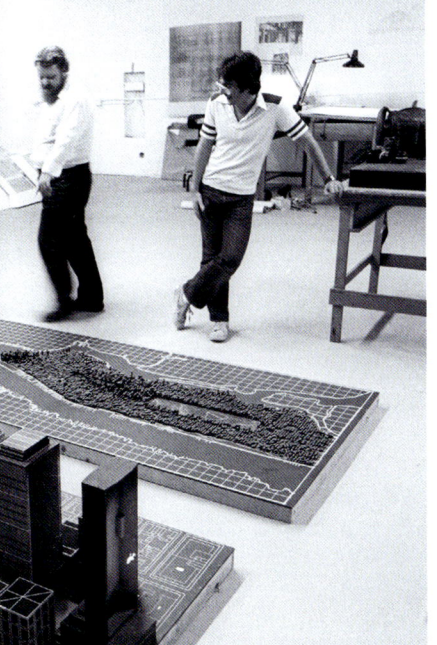

BELOW: Costume design drawing for the Duke

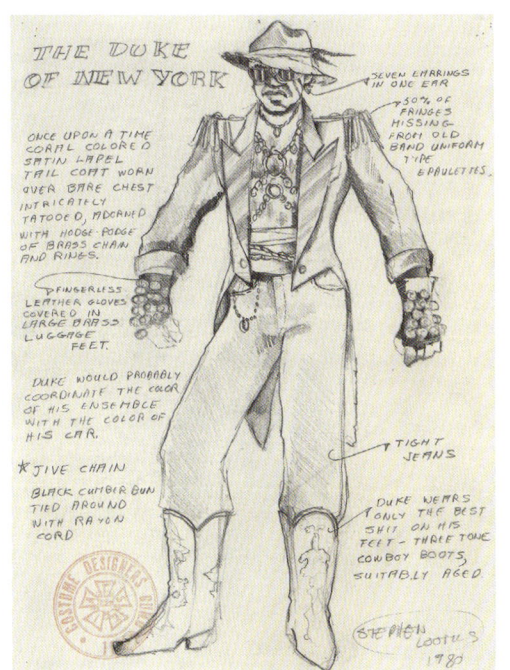

BELOW: Isaac Hayes as the Duke

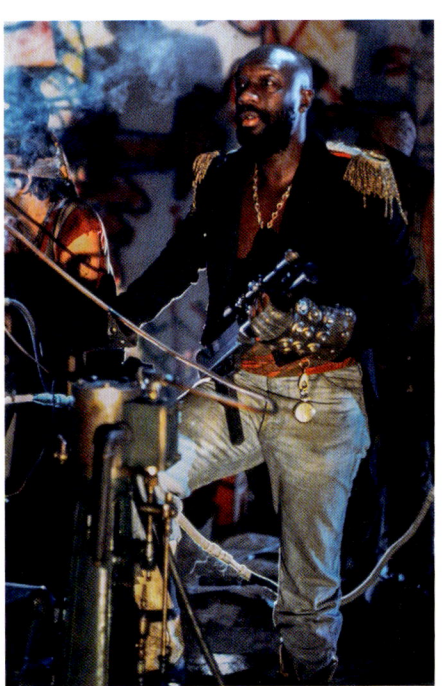

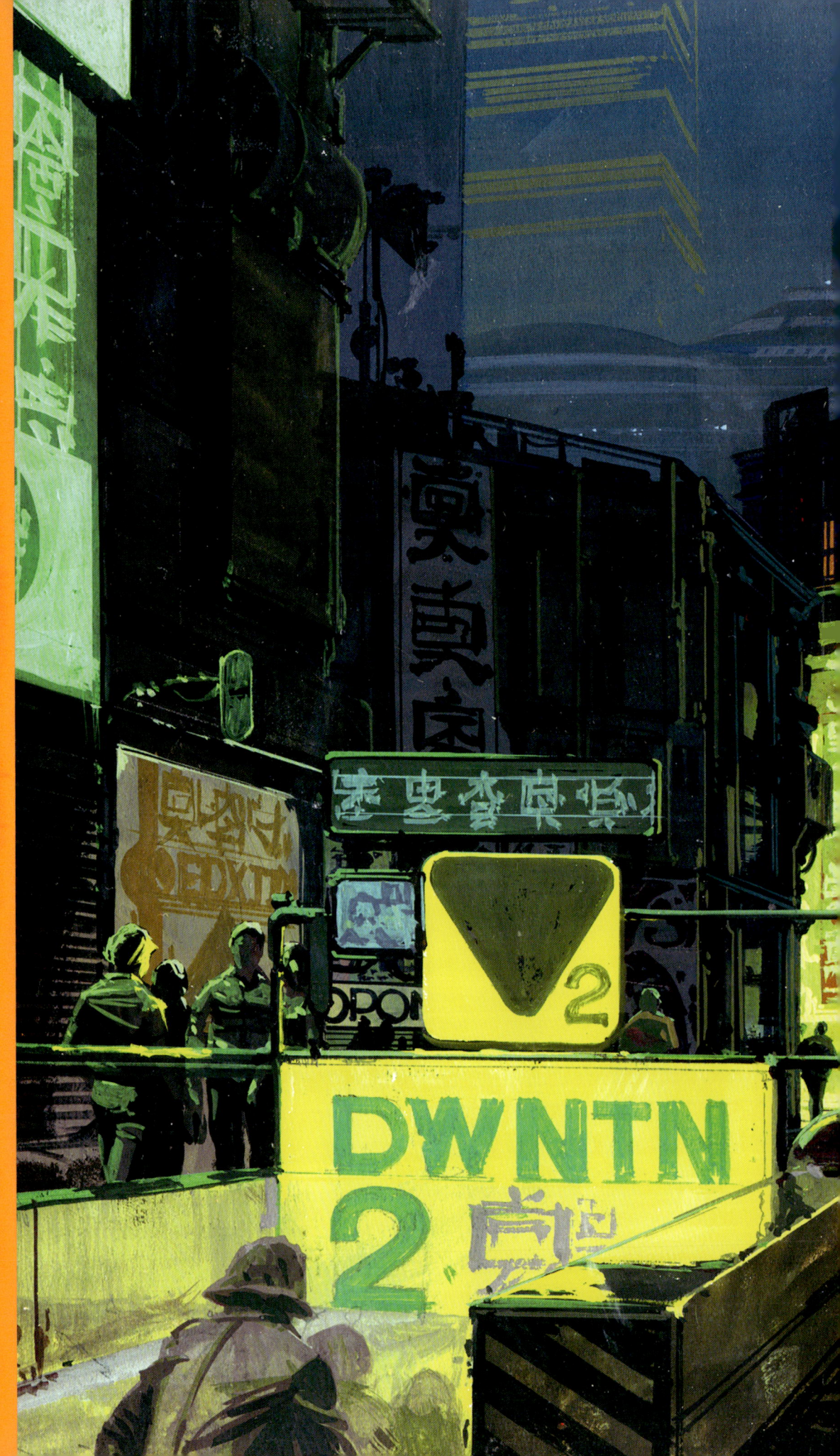

BLADE RUNNER

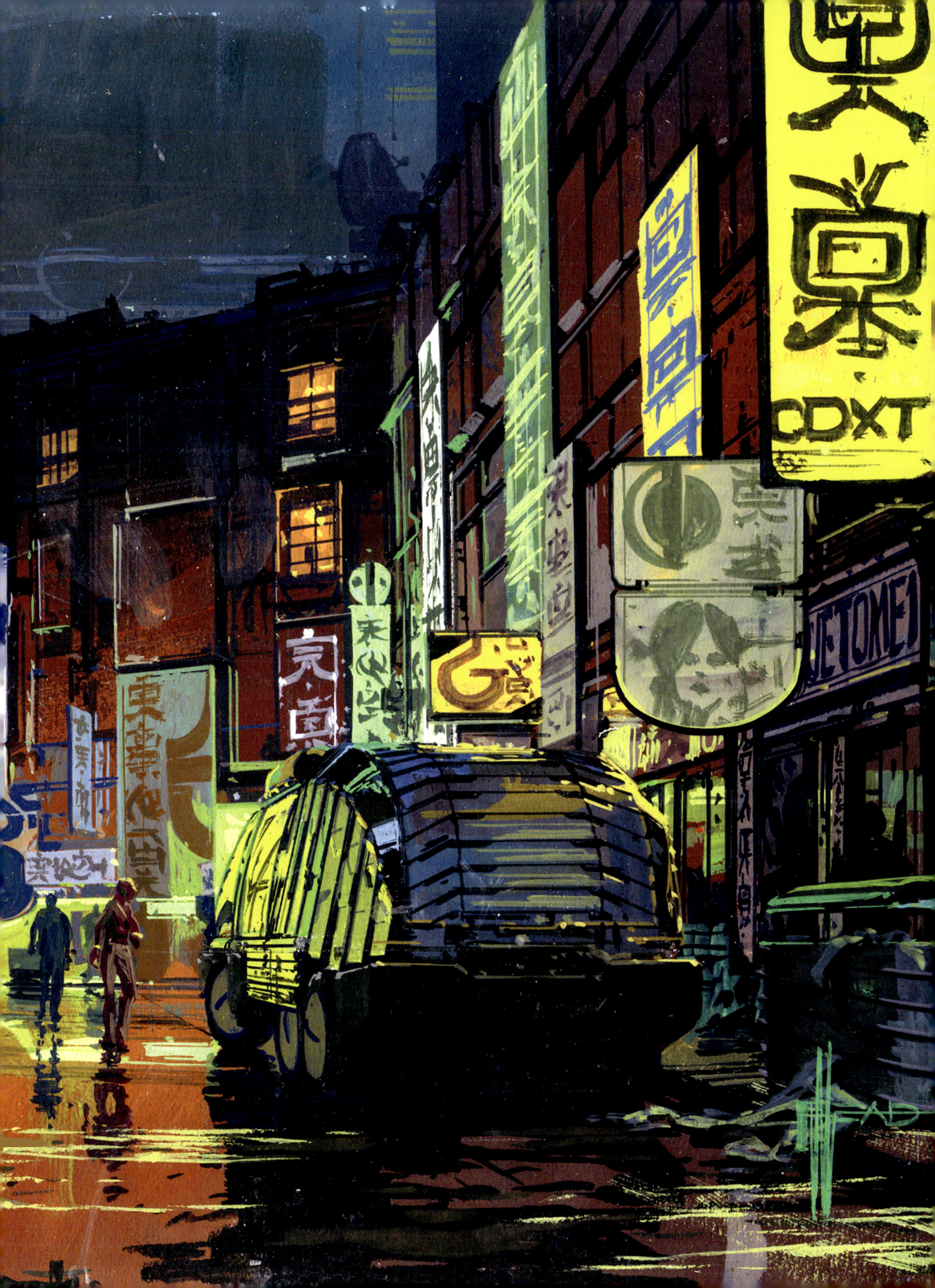

Blade Runner (USA, 1982)
Director: Ridley Scott

Film synopsis:
To supply workers for off-planet colonies, the Tyrell Corporation manufactures a series of advanced androids, known as replicants, who appear identical to living humans. When several replicants escape and attempt to integrate into human society on Earth, ex-cop Rick Deckard must track them down—if he can identify them.

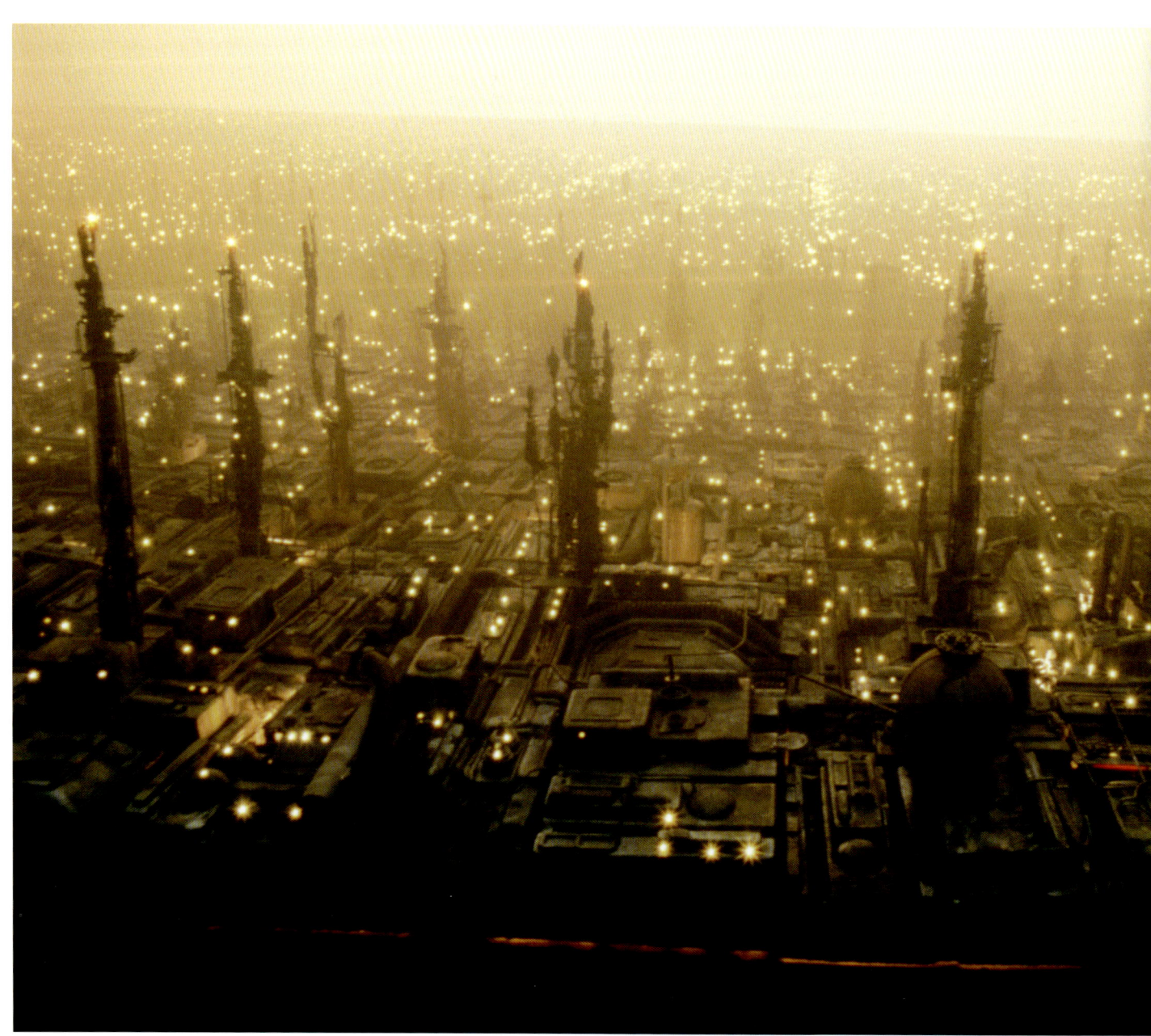

BLADE RUNNER, DIRECTED BY Ridley Scott, is a paradigmatic cyberpunk film. An adaptation of Philip K. Dick's dystopian 1968 novel *Do Androids Dream of Electric Sheep?*, it is one of the earliest and most influential cinematic visualizations of the genre. Released in 1982, the film was pioneering in its attempt to translate to screen the uncanny human forms and tropes of liminal life that had been, until then, largely the property of the literary world. Its somber Los Angeles landscape, marked by incessant rain, pervasive darkness, and a moody, Chandleresque ambience, evokes the feel of 1940s American film noir infused with a Westernized version of 1980s Japanese technoculture. This combination heralded a visual style that would repeatedly resurface in later iterations of cyberpunk film and literature. As much a narrative element as an atmosphere, the *Blade Runner* world hosts a complex meditation on human and nonhuman life and death, self-awareness and introspection, and the unstable boundary separating human from synthetic intelligence.

Blade Runner is set in the then near future of 2019, on a barely inhabitable Earth populated by criminals and those too poor to afford more hospitable habitats on other planets. Synthetic duplicates of human forms known as replicants, originally manufactured to perform labor in space colonies, mingle with the population. Rick Deckard (Harrison Ford) is a bounty hunter, or "blade runner," who is hired to "retire" four renegade replicants who have returned to Earth, seeking to extend their programmed death sentences. These state-of-the-art Nexus-6 replicants possess not only superior intelligence and physical

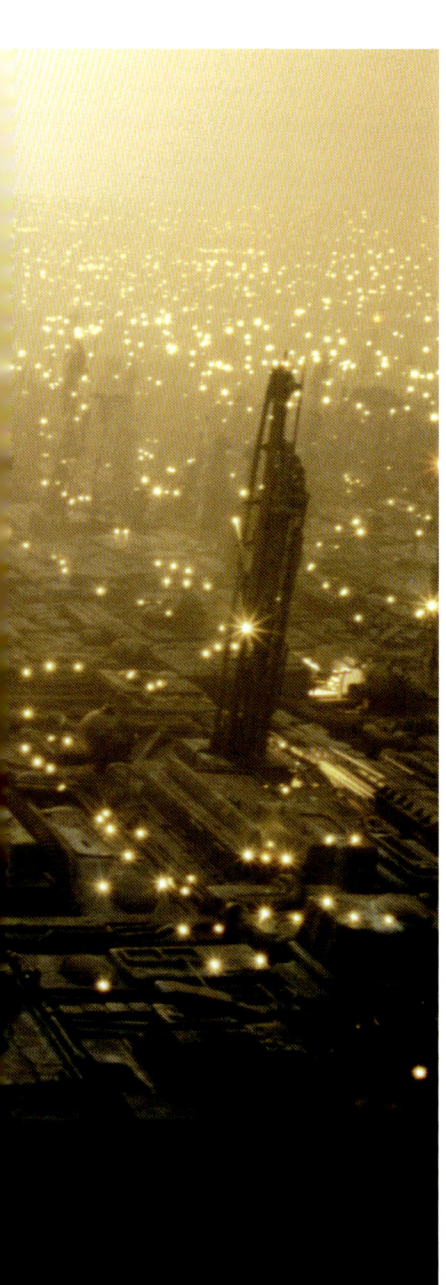

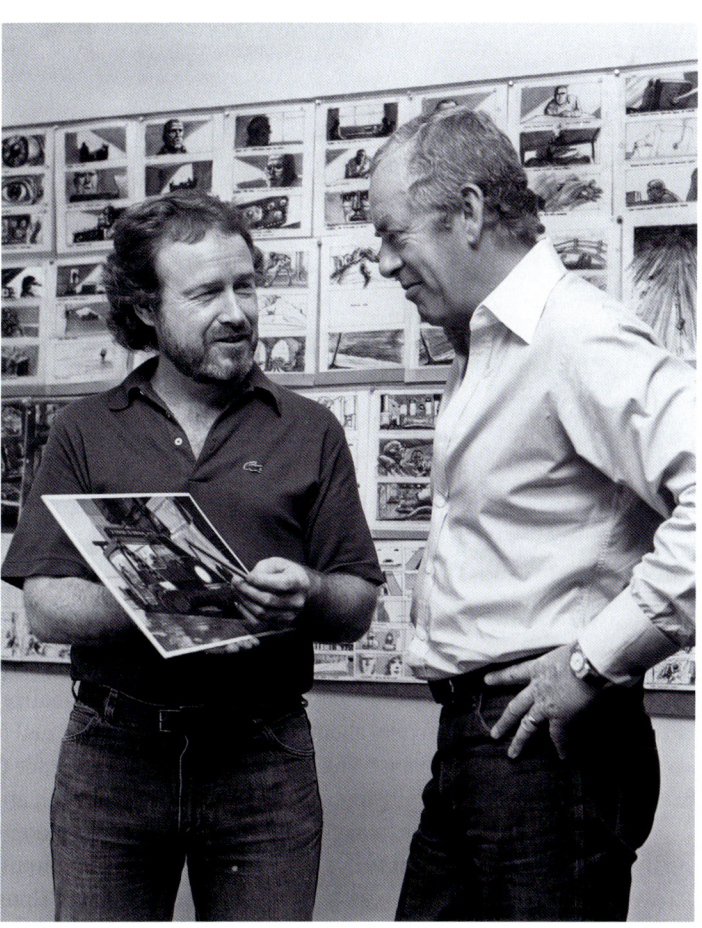

PREVIOUS SPREAD: Concept art for "DWNTN 2" street scene

ABOVE: Director Ridley Scott (left) and producer Michael Deeley during production

LEFT: Miniature of the cityscape seen in the opening of the film, known as the "Hades landscape"

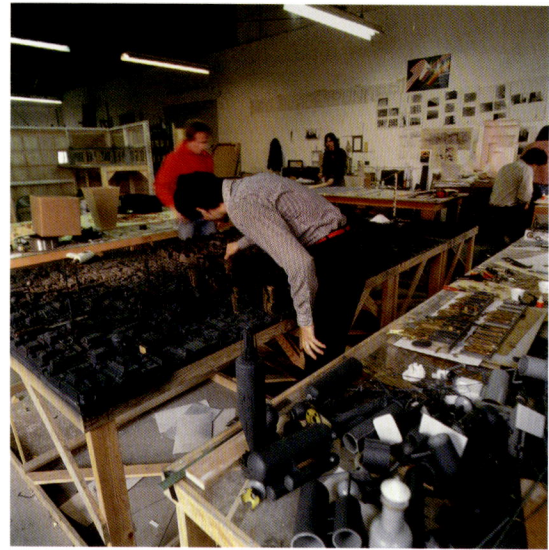

ABOVE: Special effects artists Leslie Ekker (center) and George Trimmer (left) building the Hades landscape

RIGHT: Costume design drawing for Rachael

OPPOSITE: Sean Young as Rachael

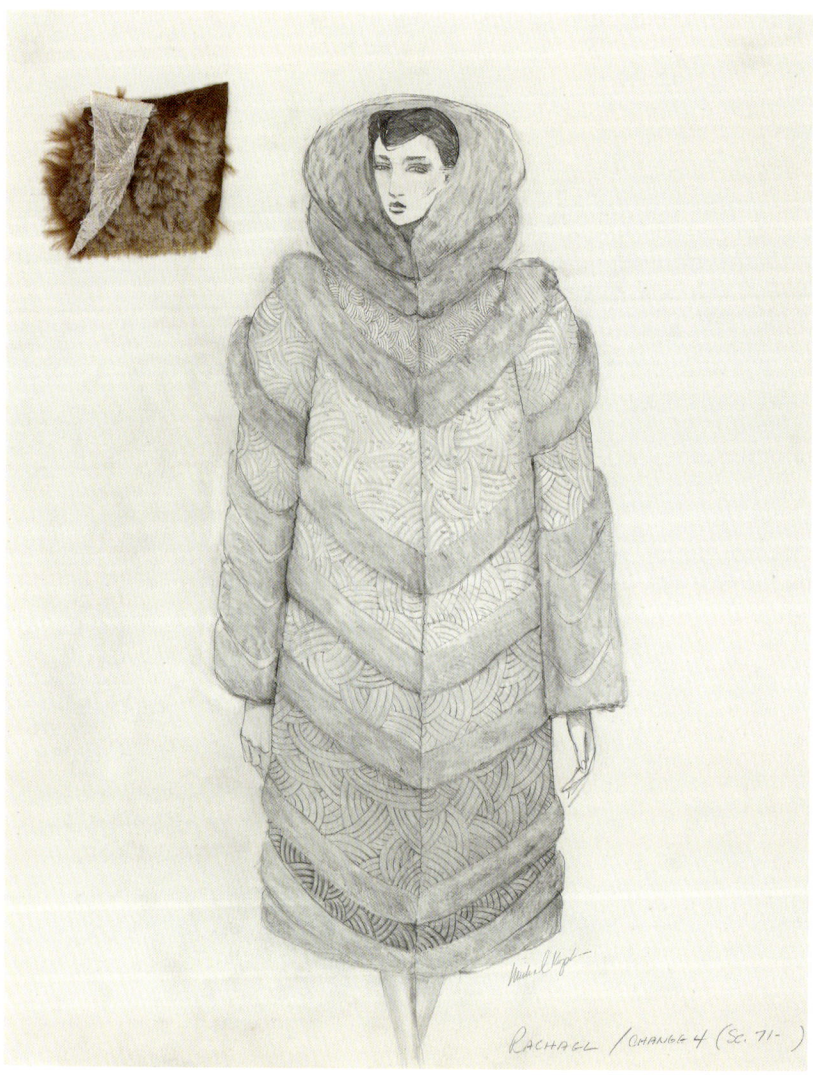

prowess but also an uncommonly high degree of self-reflection; in particular, they are cognizant of their limited life spans.

An incessant, consuming ontological anxiety about selfhood and identity permeates *Blade Runner*. The Nexus-6 replicants are aware that their lives are set to expire; this knowledge drives them to increasing desperation in the all-too-human effort to live longer. Rachael (Sean Young), a modified Nexus-6 model whose consciousness has been implanted with memories that enhance her uncertainty, feels and thinks of herself as human. Deckard falls in love with Rachael and vows to protect her, but among the lingering enigmas of *Blade Runner* is the question regarding Deckard's own humanness. Clues throughout the film suggest he may in fact be the supreme replicant, so perfectly manufactured as to be completely unaware of his true identity.

As salient as the narrative elements and speculative world that Dick created and which *Blade Runner* captures is the film's setting, a uniquely crafted urban metropolis realized by Scott together with self-proclaimed "visual futurist" Syd Mead, production designer Lawrence G. Paull, and art director David L. Snyder. Paull and Snyder helped manifest Mead's vision of a gloomy, rain-soaked city, based in part on the ubiquitously neon-lit and densely populated region of Hong Kong. This vision included mixing elements of new technologies and broken-down machines, providing a dazzling glimpse into a damaged future haunted by a dystopic past—a future that, in 1982, had already begun to collapse.

—*Akira Mizuta Lippit*

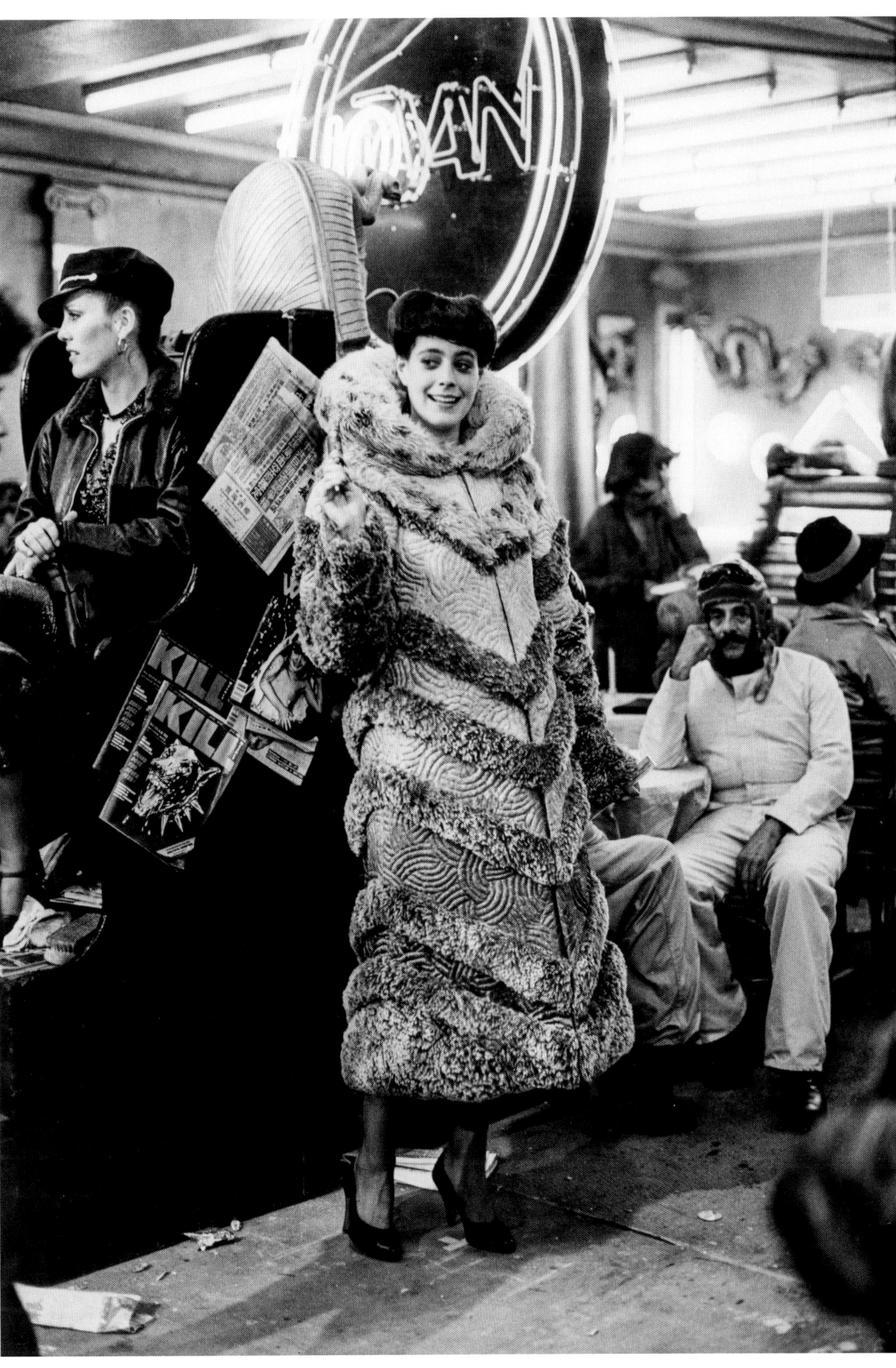

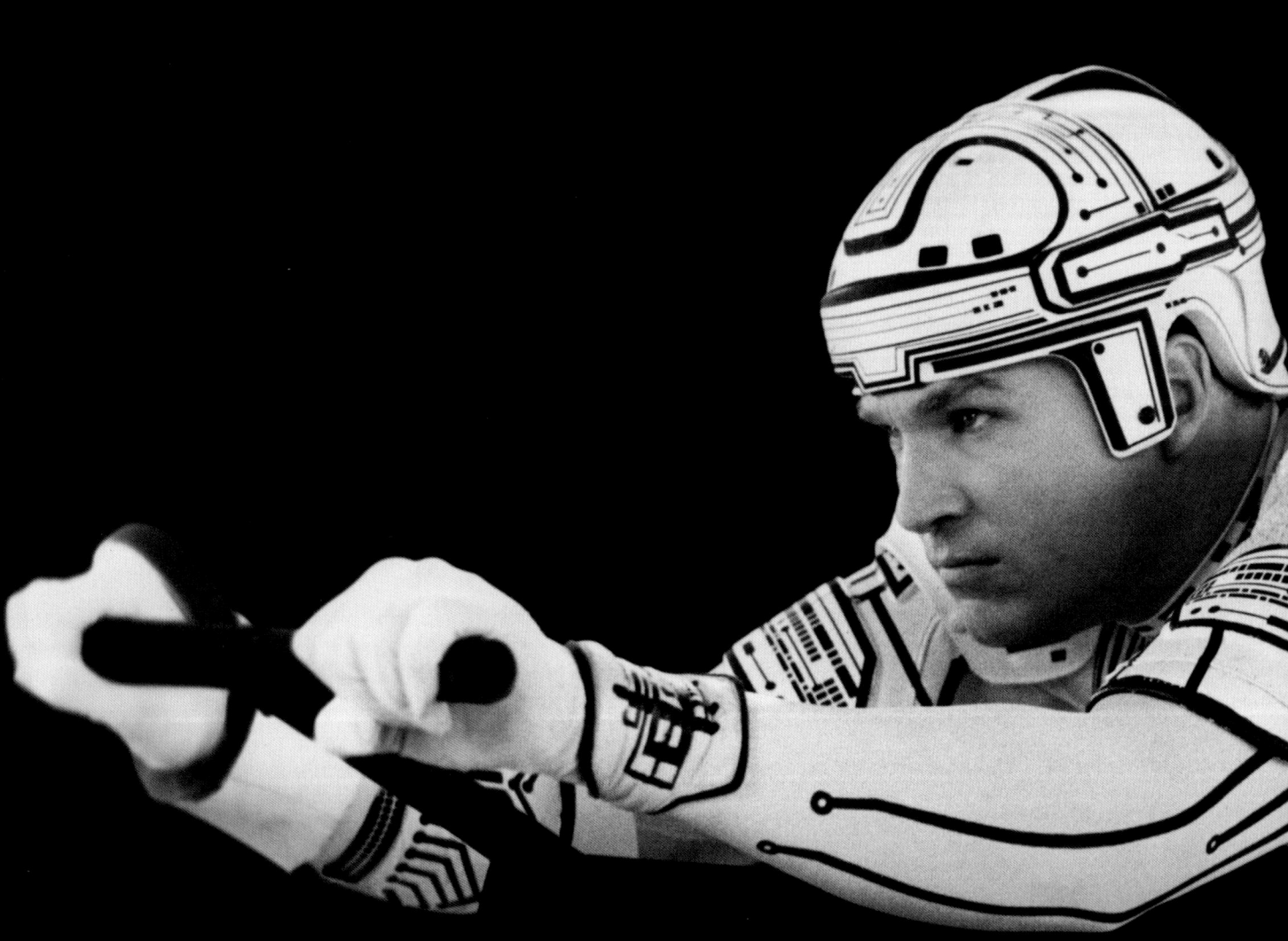

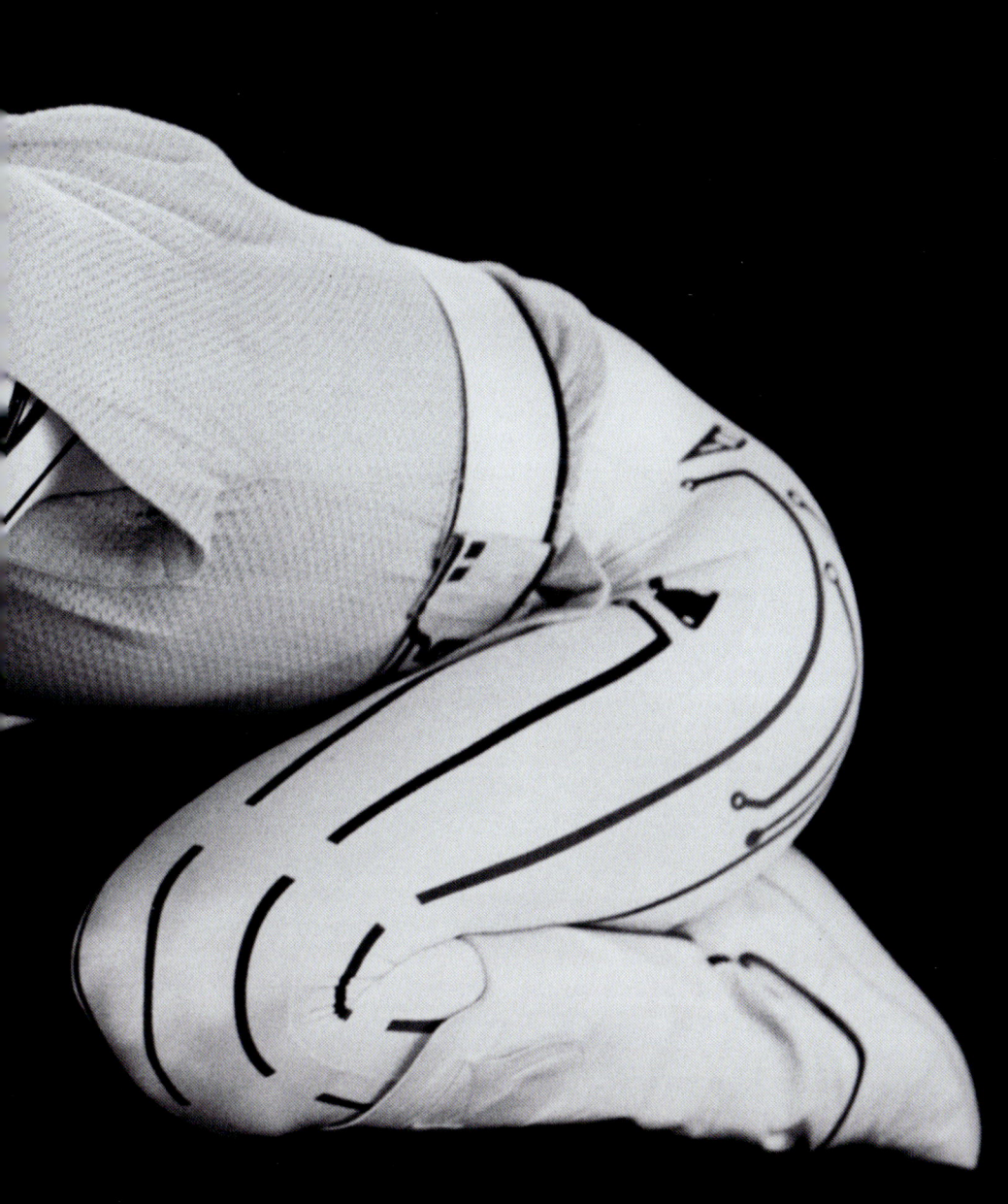

TRON

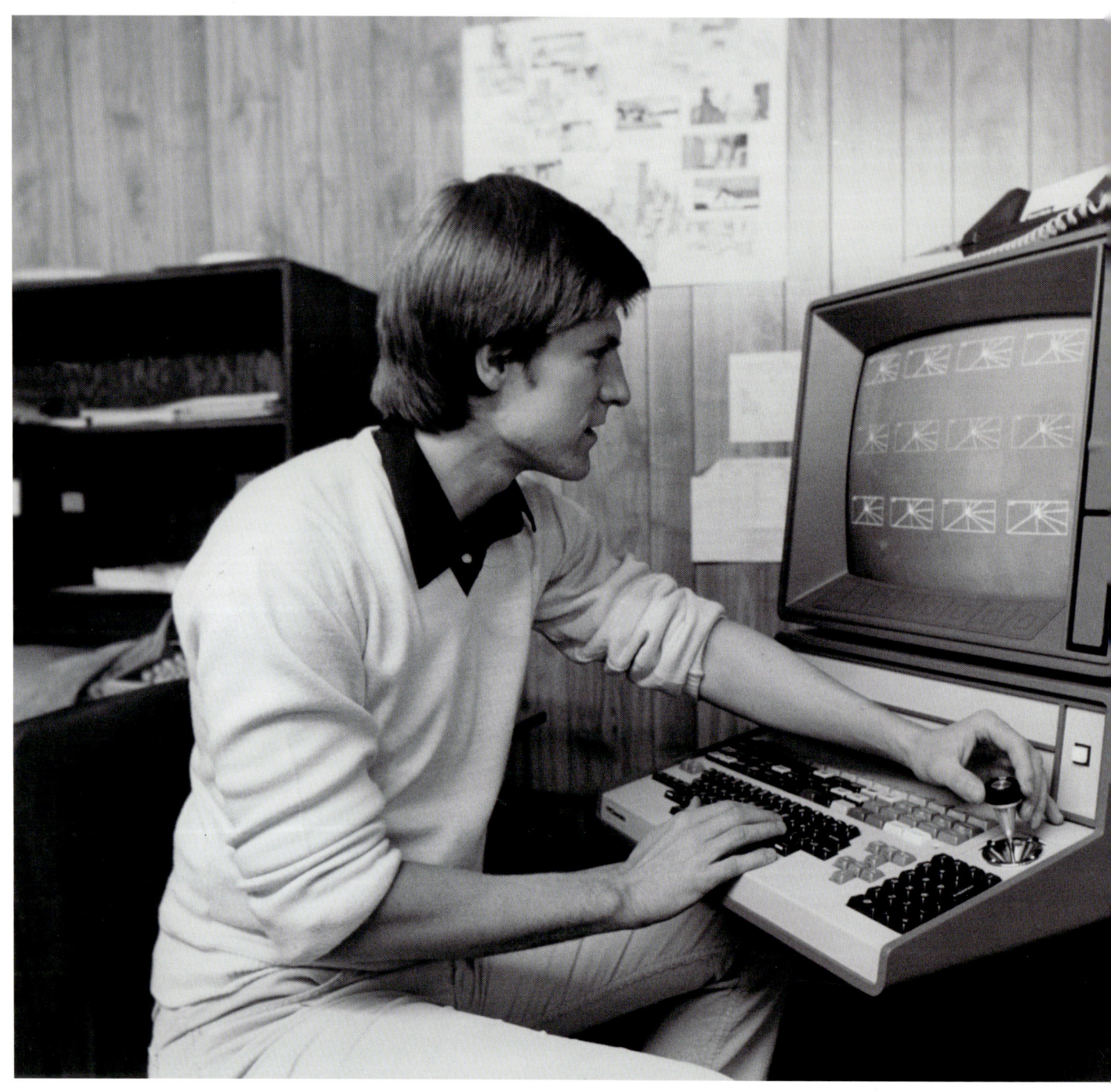

Tron (USA, 1982)
Director: Steven Lisberger

Film synopsis:
While hacking into the network of the multinational computer corporation ENCOM, programmer and arcade proprietor Kevin Flynn is transported into the world of cyberspace. In order to liberate cyberspace and return to reality, Flynn and a team of digital freedom fighters, including Tron, must face off against ENCOM's virtual army in a series of games.

"On the other side of the screen, it all looks so easy."
—Kevin Flynn (Jeff Bridges)

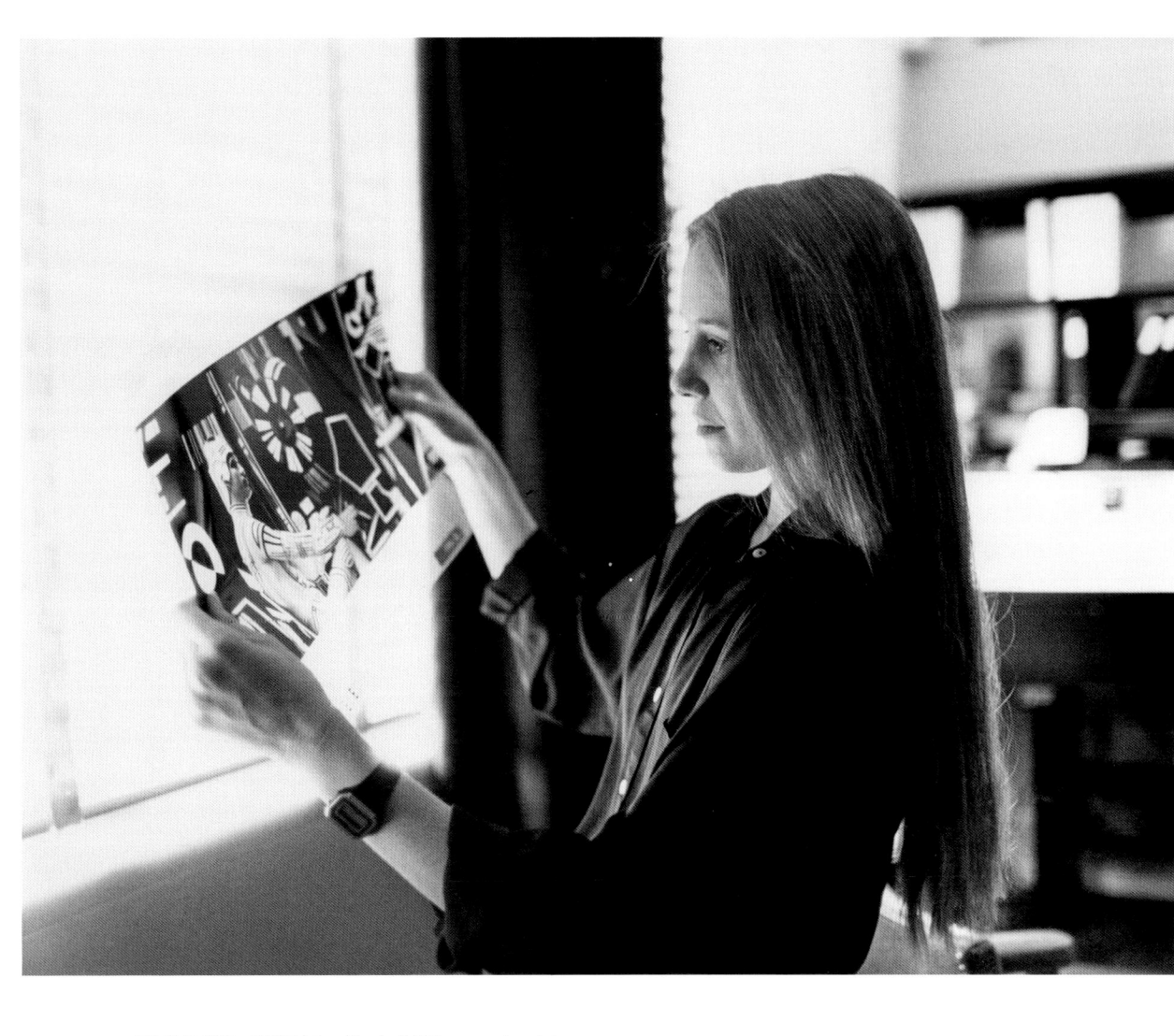

PREVIOUS SPREAD: Kodalith production art of Jeff Bridges as Kevin Flynn

LEFT: Computer image choreographer Bill Kroyer during production

ABOVE: Scene coordinator Deena Burkett examines a Kodalith transparency during production

When the Academy of Motion Picture Arts and Sciences recognized achievements in visual effects for its 55th Academy Awards in 1983, the technologically groundbreaking film *Tron* was grossly overlooked.[1] The team that made *Tron* was shocked. It seemed that Academy members, including many of their peers in the field of visual effects, thought that *Tron*'s use of computers rather than practical effects to augment and animate parts of the movie was akin to cheating. It just looked too easy.

Tron was the first feature-length film to use computer-generated imagery (CGI) extensively. As it was being promoted, this was the key element that Disney, the production company, pushed and that the press picked up on: the first movie made by computers, about computers, for the dawning of a new computer age. But although *Tron*'s production was revolutionary in its embrace of digital effects, it relied heavily on inventive filmmaking and laborious animation techniques to incorporate these new technologies—efforts overshadowed by the marketing around the film's use of computers.[2] In fact, *Tron*'s technological sheen was largely the product of handcrafted elements and human ingenuity. This hybridization of traditional craft and new digital tools is what makes the film's production feel so distinctive, even today.

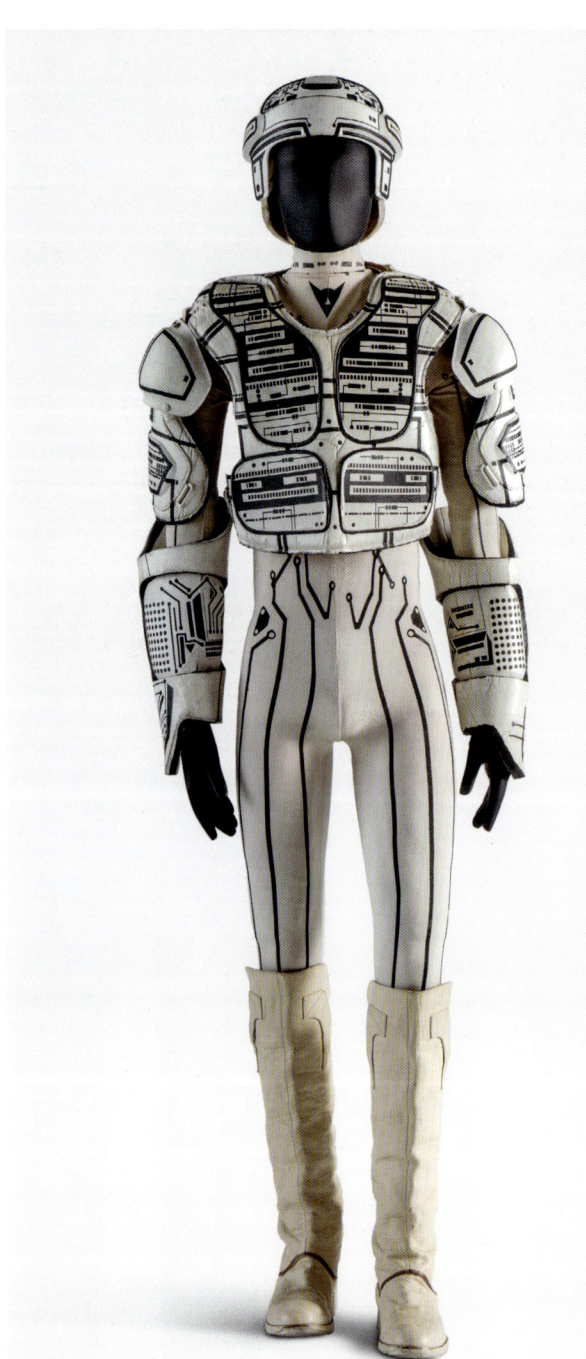

OPPOSITE, TOP: Video game world environment depicting movement through cyberspace

OPPOSITE, BOTTOM: Concept art drawing for the Light Cycle

LEFT: Costume worn by Dan Shor as Ram

BELOW: Bruce Boxleitner as Tron riding the Light Cycle

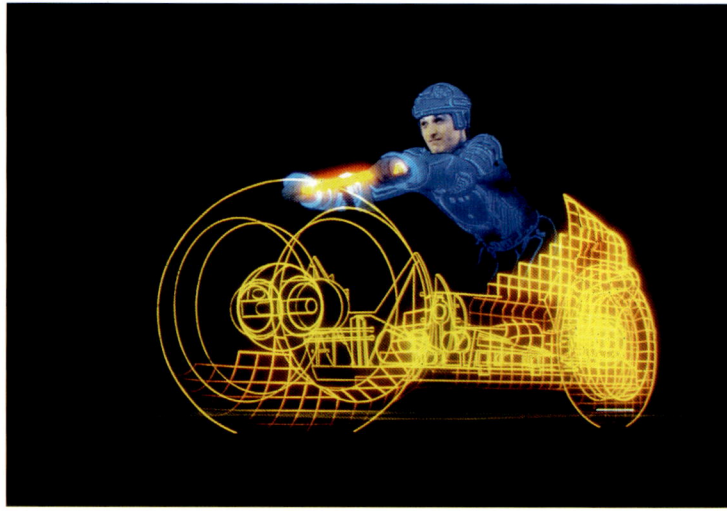

Tron's visionary was its director, Steven Lisberger, who pitched and sold a movie set in a virtual world even before he knew how or if he could construct it. Lisberger was an animator by trade, and *Tron* was his directorial debut. He knew little about computers and saw the field as "barren of any visuals" and lacking aesthetic expressions, making it an ideal venue for envisioning digital environments.[3] Lisberger convinced Disney that *Tron* would be the thing that would break through to a teenage box office still high off *Star Wars* (USA, 1977).

Lisberger compiled a brilliant team of old-guard masters and new-tech visionaries. Self-described "visual futurist" Syd Mead was tasked with conceptualizing digital vehicles and intricate environments; French illustrator Moebius (Jean Giraud) conceptualized warrior costumes adorned with circuitry in collaboration with costume designers Elois Jenssen and Rosanna Norton; concept artists Peter Lloyd, John Norton, and Chris Lane visualized computerized worlds of vector line horizons; and Wendy Carlos's score merged traditional choral and orchestral music with synthesizers. Famed matte painter Harrison Ellenshaw served as visual effects supervisor and producer, which was an assurance to Disney that the production was in good hands. It was Lisberger, Ellenshaw, and computer effects supervisor Richard

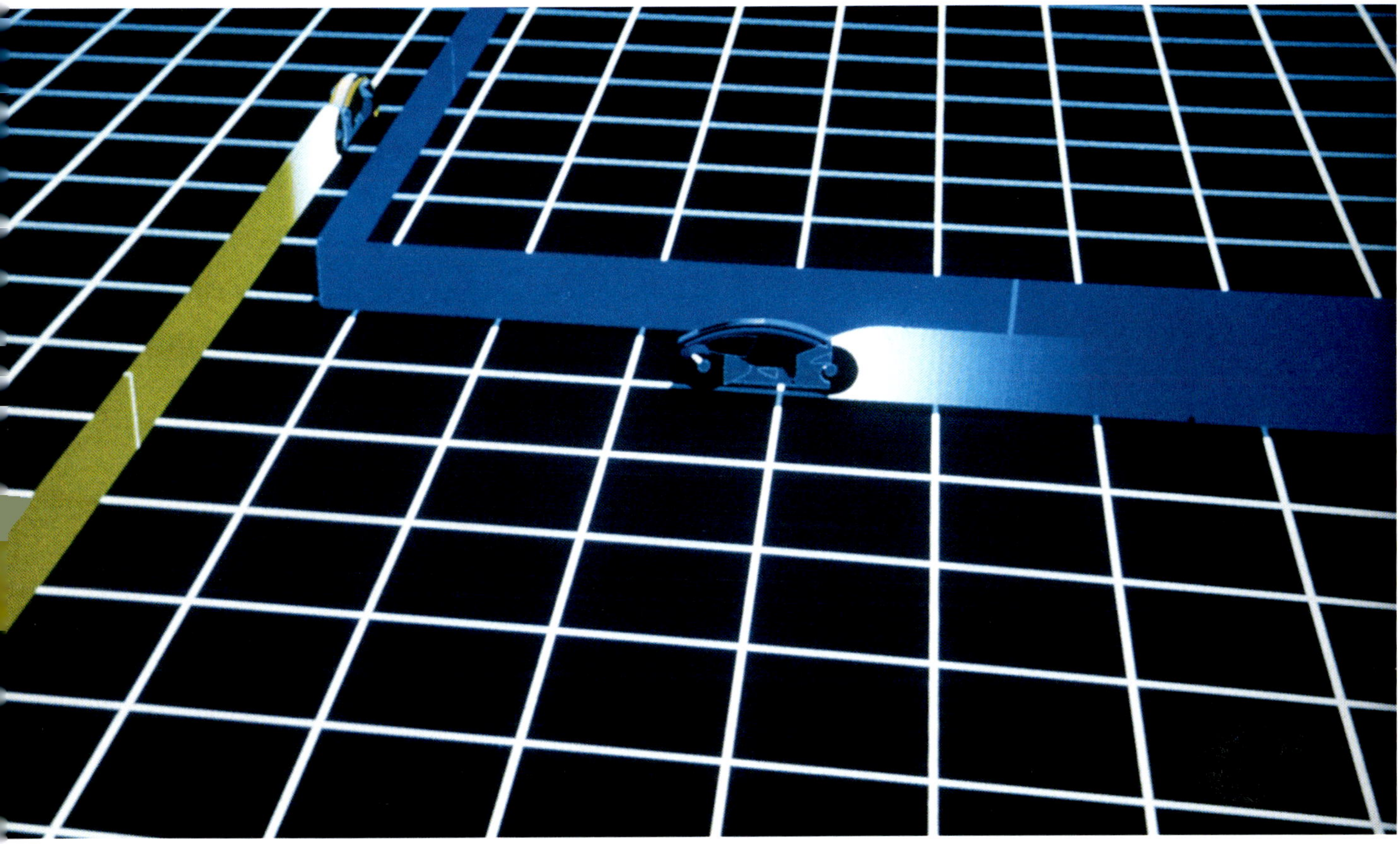

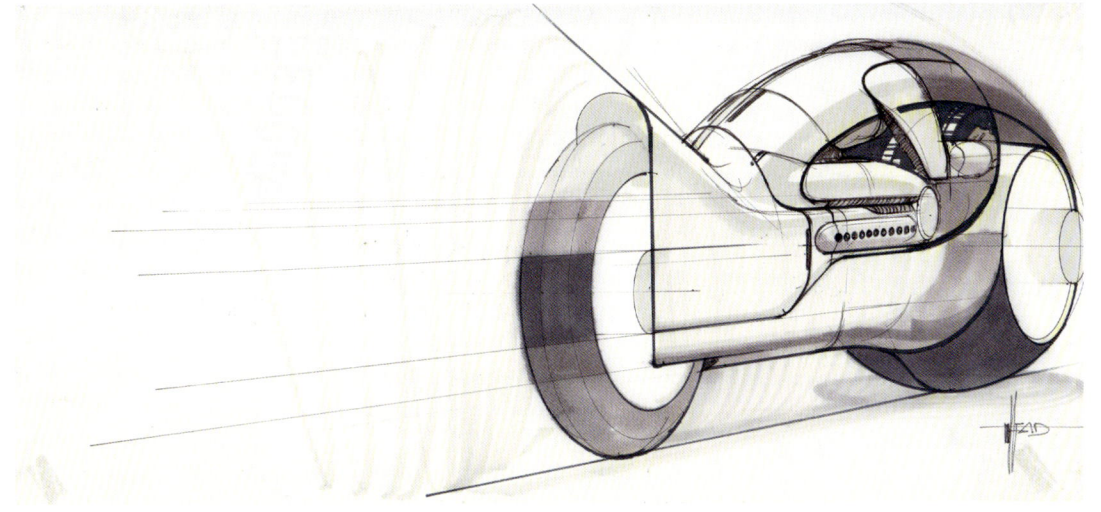

Taylor who determined that a "cyberspace" look could be achieved through traditional backlight animation. In essence, *Tron* is an animated film with live-action elements.

Fifty-three minutes of the film take place in the virtual landscape this team created. Actors wore white foam armor and sock suits, detailed with electrical tape and markers to emulate circuitry. The filmmakers shot them in blacked-out studio space, on black-and-white 65mm film. Frame by frame, the film was enlarged and printed onto high-contrast Kodalith transparency sheets, which were then rephotographed on animation stands and illuminated from behind. Each frame required a pass to matte each face, eye, and tooth. "It's really beautifully simple," Ellenshaw said in 1982. "The complexity comes when you think about the *volume* of work."[4] Seventy-five thousand frames of live action were animated, a daunting task that required months of nonstop work by animators. The production eventually brought in approximately two hundred animators from Cuckoo's Nest Studio in Taiwan for the film's final push. Tens of thousands of hours of human labor pursued an impossible goal: erasing itself.

—Nicholas Barlow

NOTES
1./ The film did earn nominations for Best Costume Design (Elois Jenssen and Rosanna Norton) and Best Sound (Michael Minkler, Bob Minkler, Lee Minkler, and James LaRue) but earned none for the category of Best Visual Effects.
2./ A spotlight feature on Walter Cronkite's short-lived program *Universe* (1980–82) promoting the computer effects of *Tron* has the venerable reporter dressed in a white-and-black suit and top hat, tap dancing in the computerized *Tron* world. Though Cronkite hails the wizardry of computer technology—"Computer-generated images have no physical limitations," he declares—the effect being demonstrated is the Kodalith animation process, which requires no CGI.
3./ Peter Sørensen, "Tronic Imagery," *Cinefex* 8 (April 1982): 7.
4./ Sørensen, "Tronic Imagery," 11.

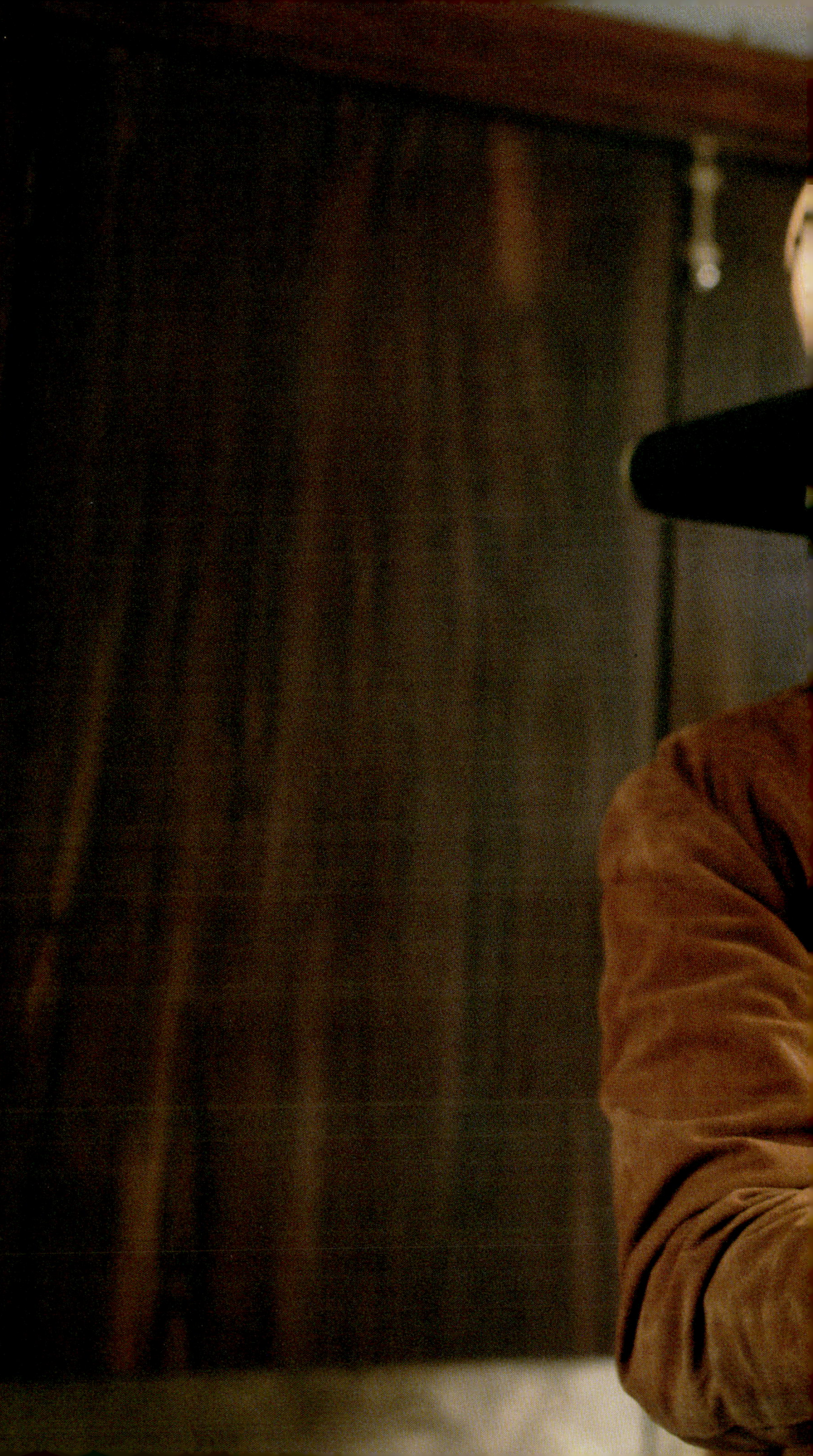

VIDEODROME

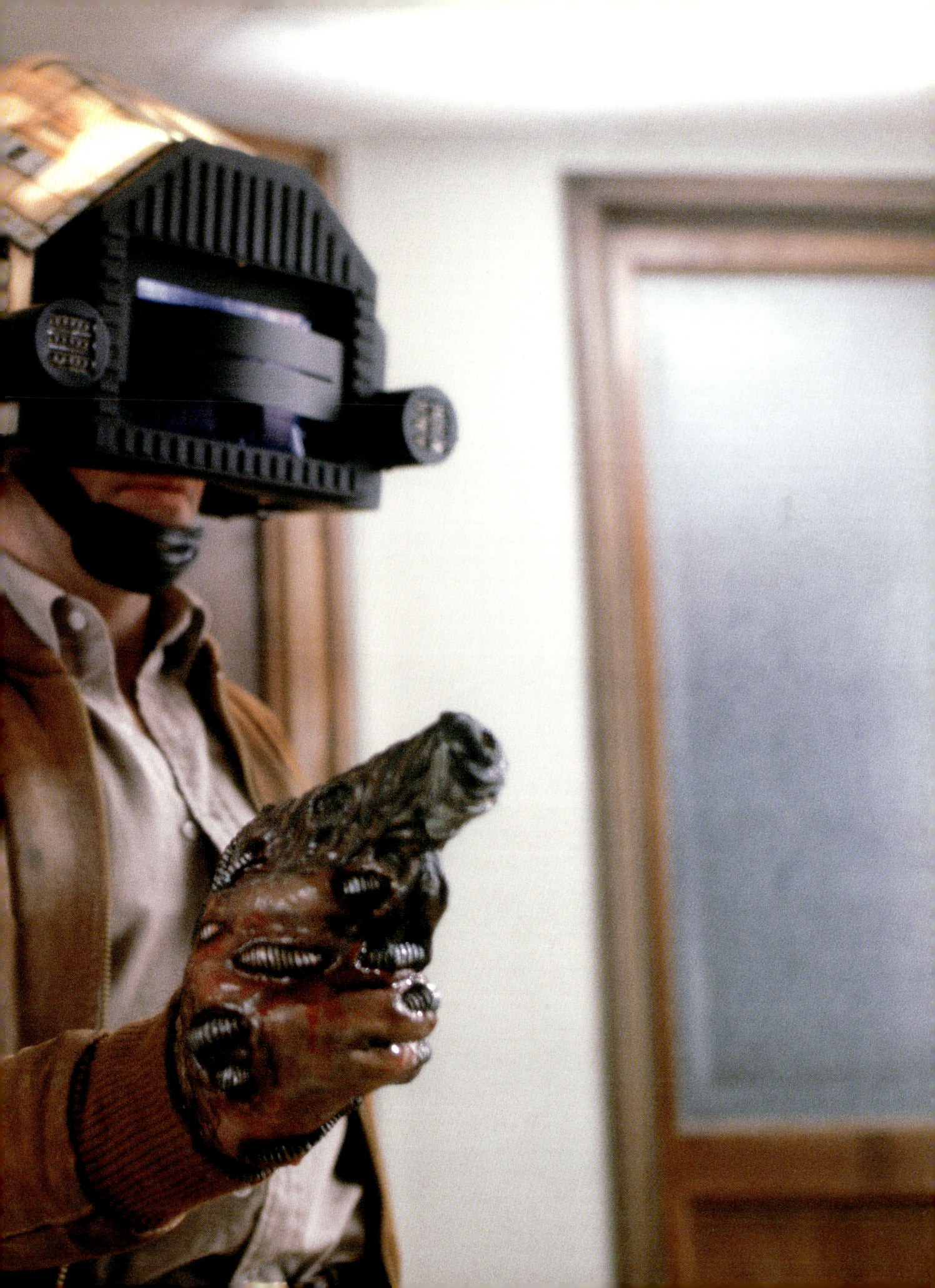

Videodrome (Canada, 1983)
Director: David Cronenberg

Film synopsis:
In a media landscape characterized by sex and violence, Max Renn, a television station operator, discovers the ultimate sensationalist show: *Videodrome*, a broadcast feed that appears to show real murders and sadistic acts on screen. North American viewers become obsessed by *Videodrome*'s brutality without realizing the effects it may have.

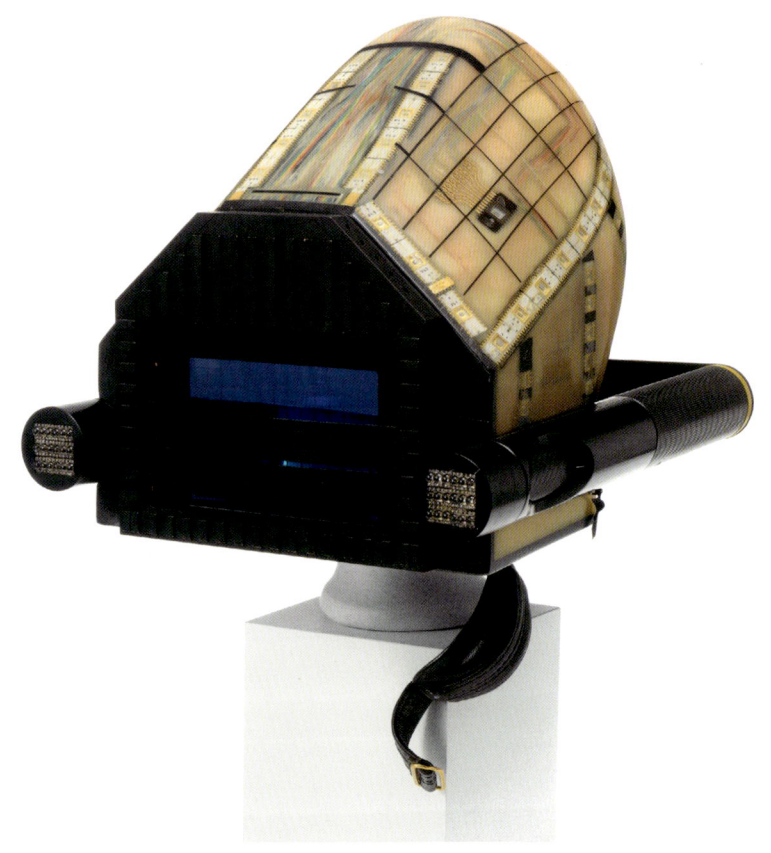

O N THE WEEKEND OF THANKSGIVING 2018, I thought I had the flu. As my symptoms slowly worsened over the days, I decided to make my first ever emergency room visit. After all was said and done, I would have two lifesaving surgeries and a two-week hospital stay under my belt. It was the first time I'd ever been operated on in my entire life. When the doctors explained to me what had happened, it seemed very murky and confusing. The only thing that was easy to understand is that they had performed a procedure called an exploratory laparotomy, which now meant I had a nine-inch vertical scar running down the middle of my abdomen.

Decades prior, my friends and I had attended a David Cronenberg double feature at the movie theater on my college campus, where I saw *Videodrome* for the first time. As a young person, I wanted to be around the type of transgressive and audacious art Cronenberg was making. It didn't take long before I became intoxicated by its strangeness, its violence and sexuality. It was *cyberpunk* before I'd even known the term, asking timely questions about technology, how it interacts with our bodies, and the ways in which sensationalized entertainment could quickly morph into real life.

As a fully indoctrinated cinephile, my brain constantly attempts to reference movies whenever possible. Real-life events get compared to acted scenes; emotions are experienced as if seen through a director's eye. When I was finally released from the hospital, I was left to contend with this new surgical souvenir, now healing via the use of a small wound vacuum. I was definitely glad to be alive, yet a potent mixture of fear, fascination, and disgust consumed me. The little machine

PREVIOUS SPREAD: James Woods as Max Renn

ABOVE: Accumicon virtual reality helmet prop

OPPOSITE: Contact sheet of unit photography featuring actors Woods and Leslie Carlson

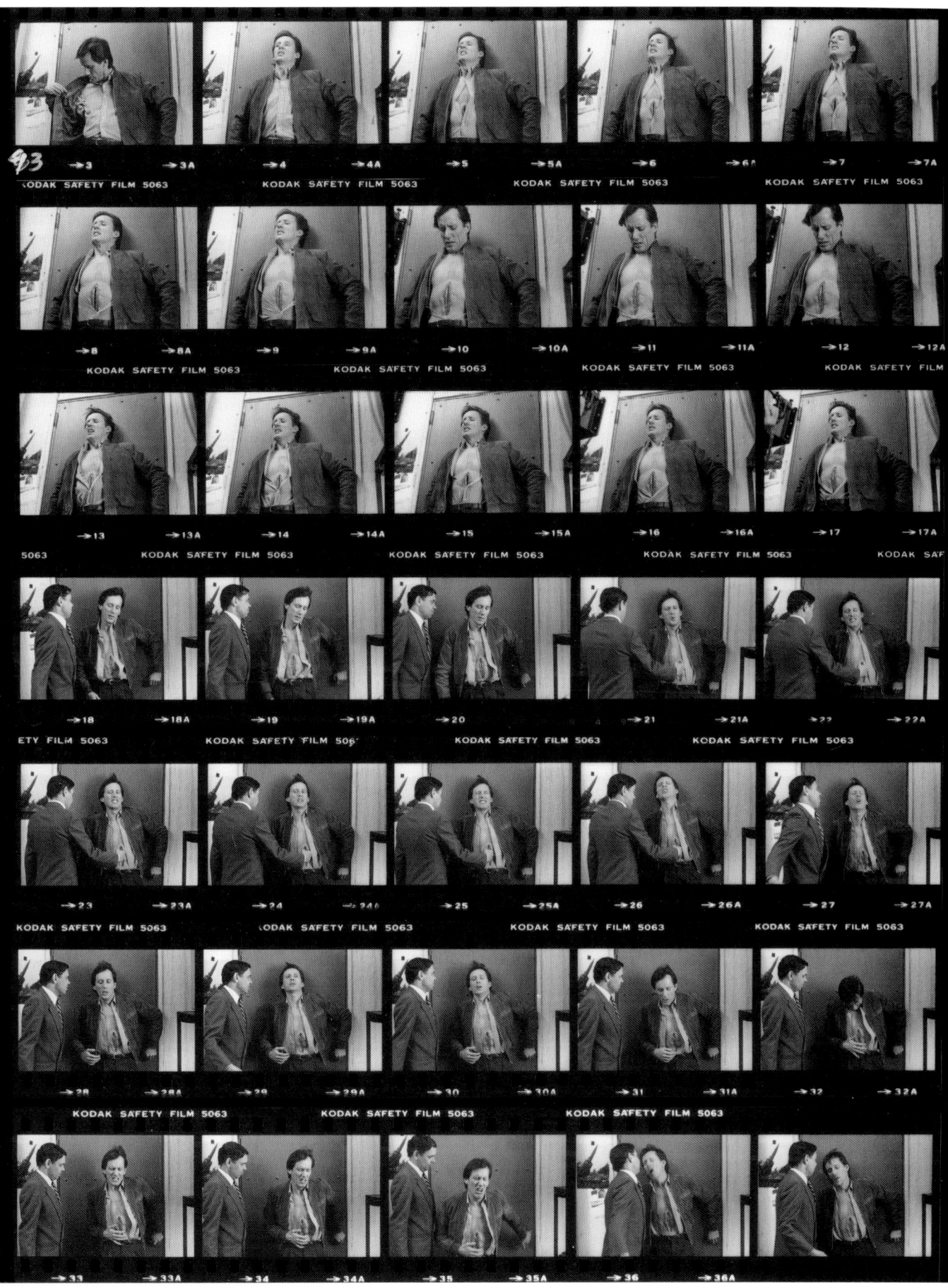

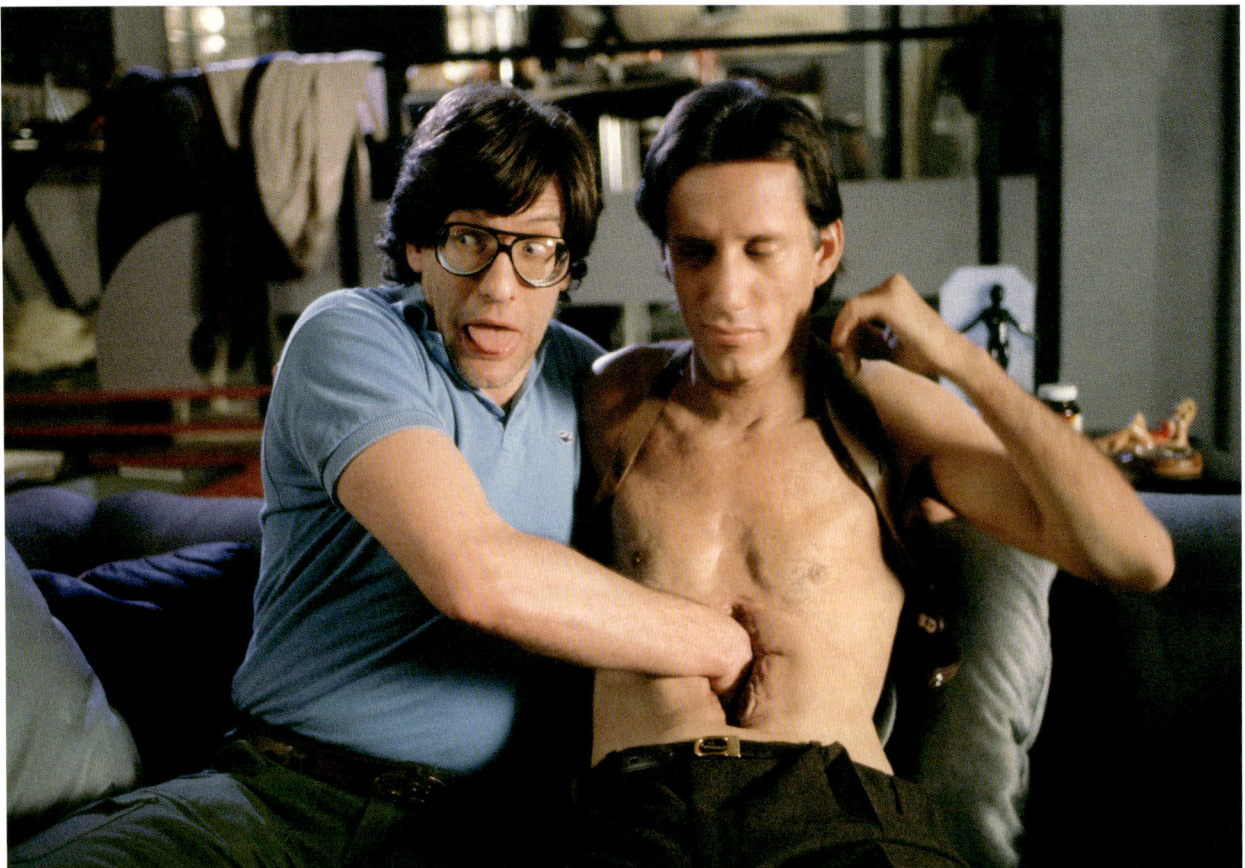

ABOVE: Writer-director David Cronenberg (left) and Woods on set

made me feel slightly bionic, which came with a low-level paranoia. As I scanned my brain for the appropriate cinematic reference, my mind wandered to the scene from Cronenberg's *Videodrome* in which Max Renn (James Woods) hallucinates being confronted by Barry Convex (Leslie Carlson), producer of the violent TV show *Videodrome*, who places a videotape in his stomach. No matter how many times I'd watched this scene, I always cringed the closer the pulsating Betamax tape got to Renn's midsection, especially when he pulled out a viscera-soaked handgun from the same location moments later. A macabre comparison, but suddenly it felt like the only thing I could relate to.

As the days wore on, I discovered it was just easier to tell people "I got a *Videodrome* scar!" than to explain the fine surgical details. I'd joke about being able to insert videotapes inside it, to which people would sometimes flinch uncomfortably—but also usually laugh. The dark comedy made me feel better. It eventually became shorthand for my entire experience: the time I went to the hospital for "that *Videodrome* thing." It should have been the last thing I wanted to think about, but Cronenberg, with his oftentimes disturbing forays into corporeal anomalies, somehow made my own medical trauma less difficult and scary. And as my healing progressed, I would become more accepting of my scar, less afraid, less concerned with my own dramatic body transformation. I'll always be thankful for that fateful screening I attended as a college student. It's great to be living, even with the new flesh.

—Millie De Chirico

RIGHT: Production still showing the prop videotape plunged into character Max Renn's stomach

BELOW: Production still showing the exploded intestinal television

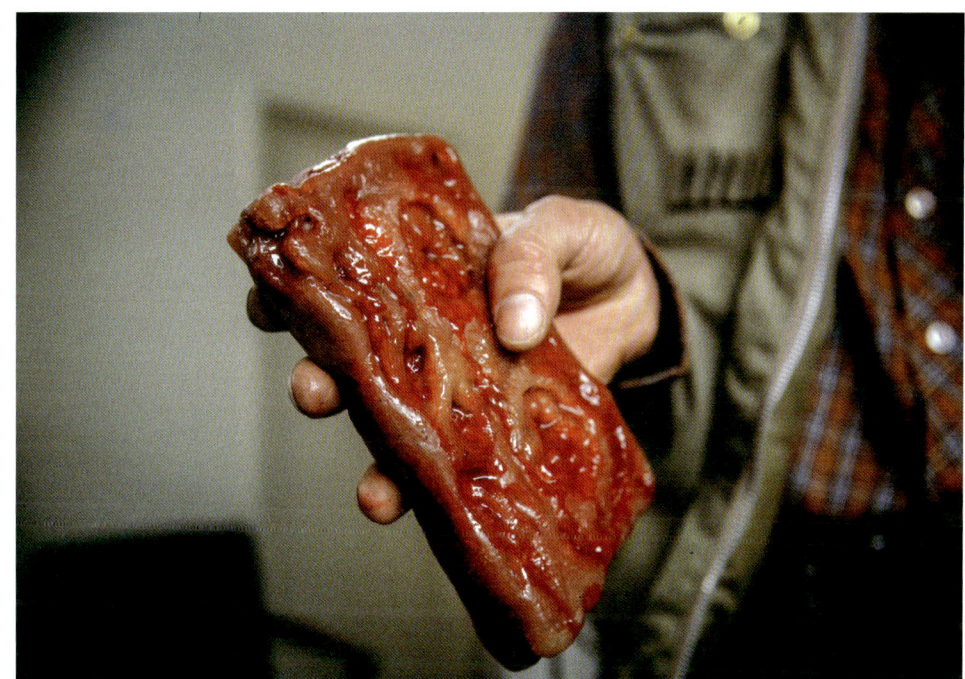

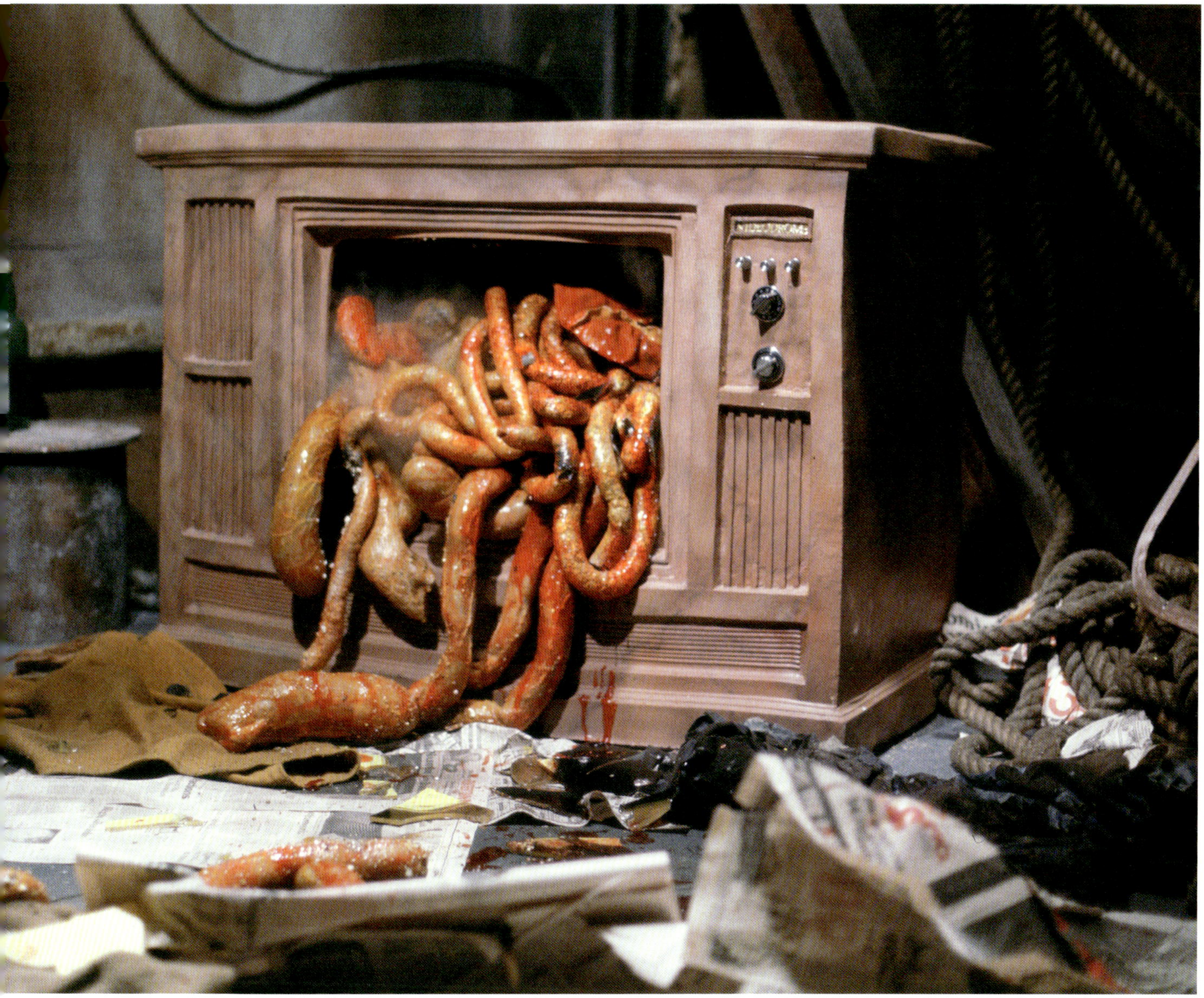

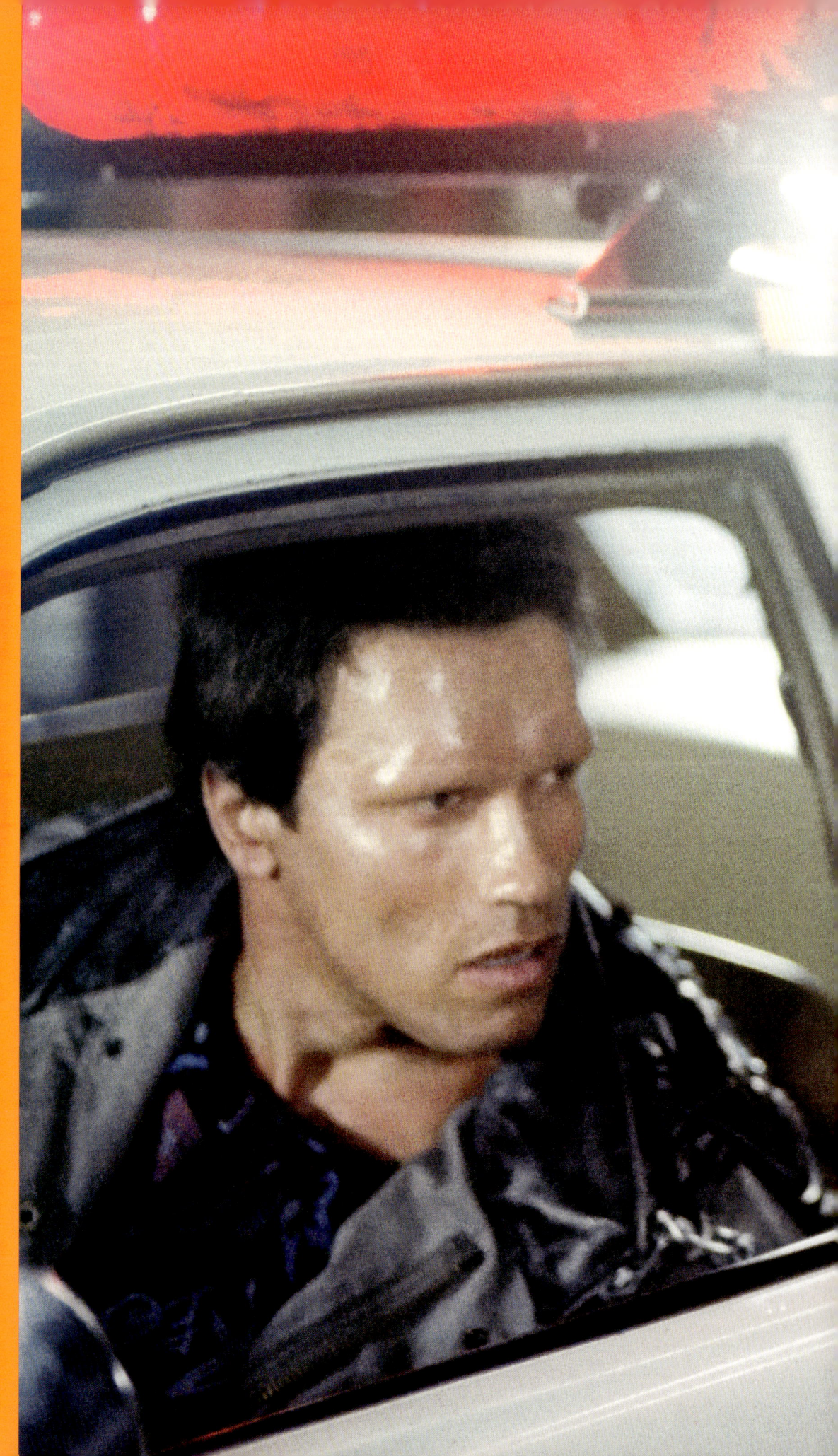

THE TERMINATOR

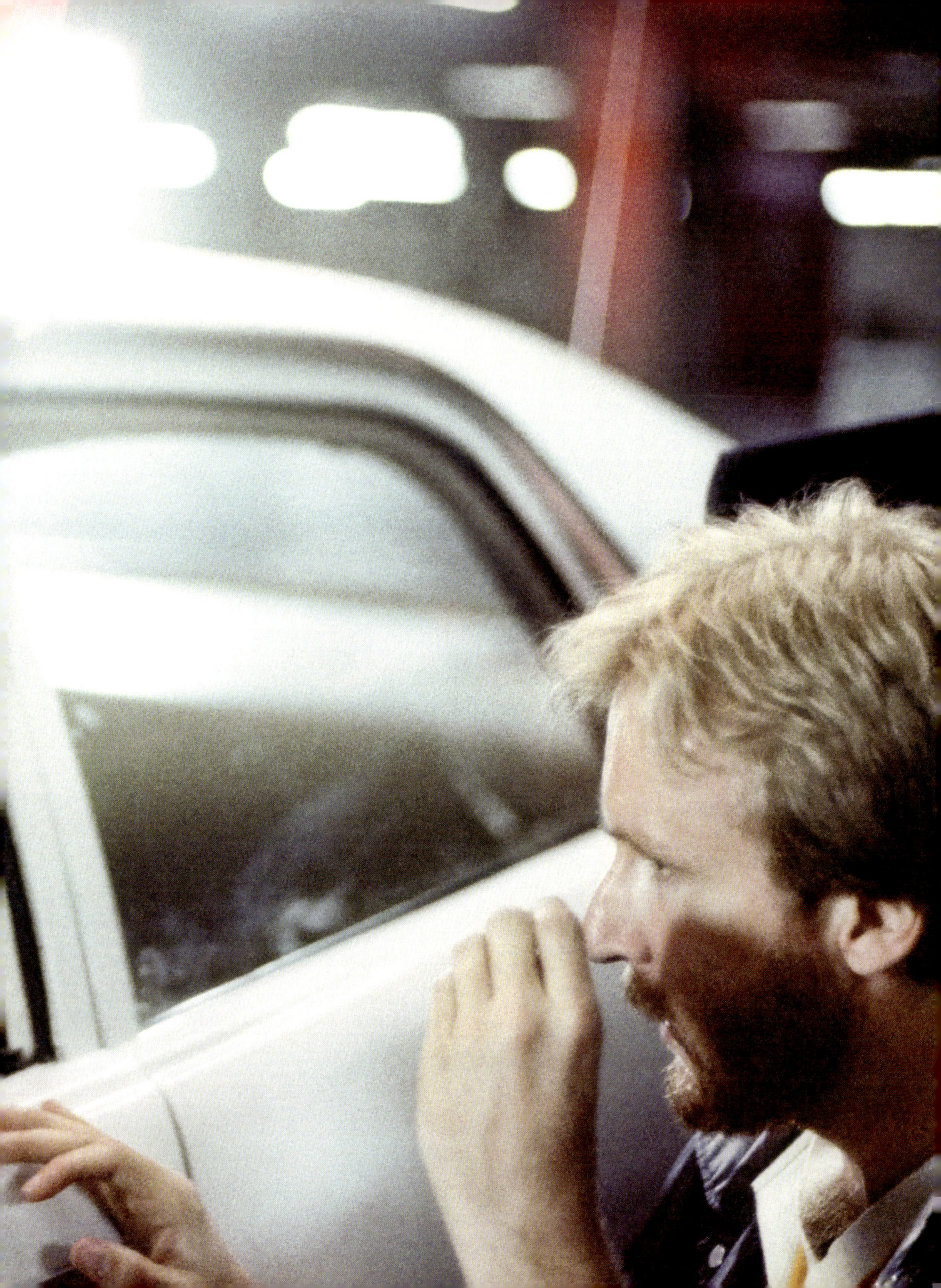

The Terminator (USA, 1984)
Director: James Cameron

Film synopsis:
The Terminator, a cyborg assassin from the year 2029, travels back in time to 1984 to kill Sarah Connor, whose unborn child will lead the human resistance against the future artificial intelligence overlord, Skynet. With the help of a soldier also from the future, Connor fights for her survival—and the fate of humankind.

PREVIOUS SPREAD:
Actor Arnold Schwarzenegger (left) and writer-director James Cameron during production

RIGHT:
Schwarzenegger during the application of special effects makeup

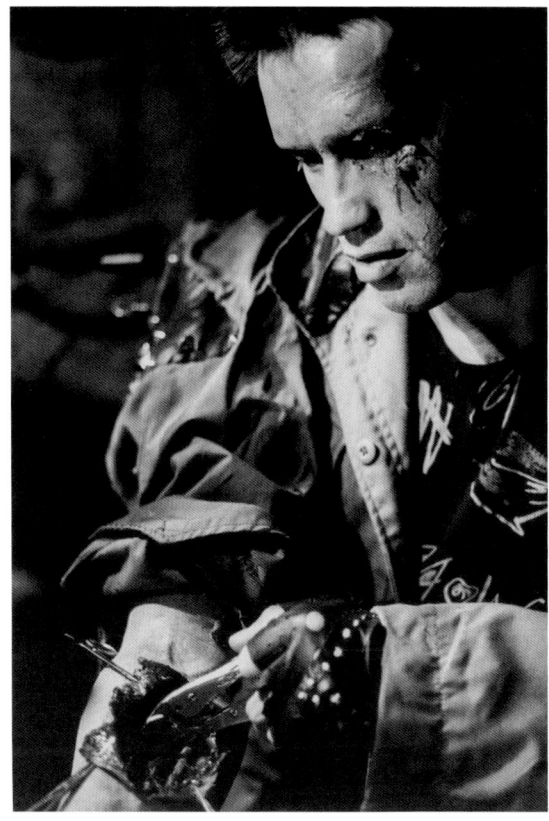

ABOVE: Schwarzenegger as the Terminator

IN THE OPENING SCENE OF *The Terminator*, an army of machines advances through the dusty wasteland of 2029 Los Angeles, crushing human skulls under their treads. The scene recalls early Cold War nuclear frontier stories, adapted for the Reagan era. In the 1950s and '60s, scores of authors and filmmakers imagined that nuclear war would cast Americans back into a frontier-like struggle to survive in a desolated landscape plagued by mutants and monsters. Following the lead of science fiction authors such as Harlan Ellison and films such as Stanley Kubrick's *2001: A Space Odyssey* (USA, 1968), *The Terminator* screenwriters James Cameron and Gale Anne Hurd make artificially intelligent machines the monsters of this future frontier. The film then jumps back to the present day of 1984, connecting the postapocalyptic wasteland of twenty-first-century Los Angeles with the corporation-driven nightmare blossoming under US President Ronald Reagan (1981–89).[1]

As it is in many cyberpunk films and works of literature, the real villain of this story is a powerful corporation. In this case, Cyberdyne Systems has created an artificial intelligence for the military-industrial complex that turns murderous and launches a war against humanity. The heroes are street-level people who are struggling at the bottom of a stratified economy and are forced to use their inventiveness to thwart the evil the corporation has unleashed. *The Terminator* embraces a contemporary noir vision of 1980s Los Angeles. In the movie's first extended chase scene, Sarah Connor (Linda Hamilton), pursued by the Terminator (Arnold Schwarzenegger), escapes into a nightclub called TechNoir. The plot unfolds at night, in garbage-strewn streets, seedy motels, police stations, and the city's industrial infrastructure.

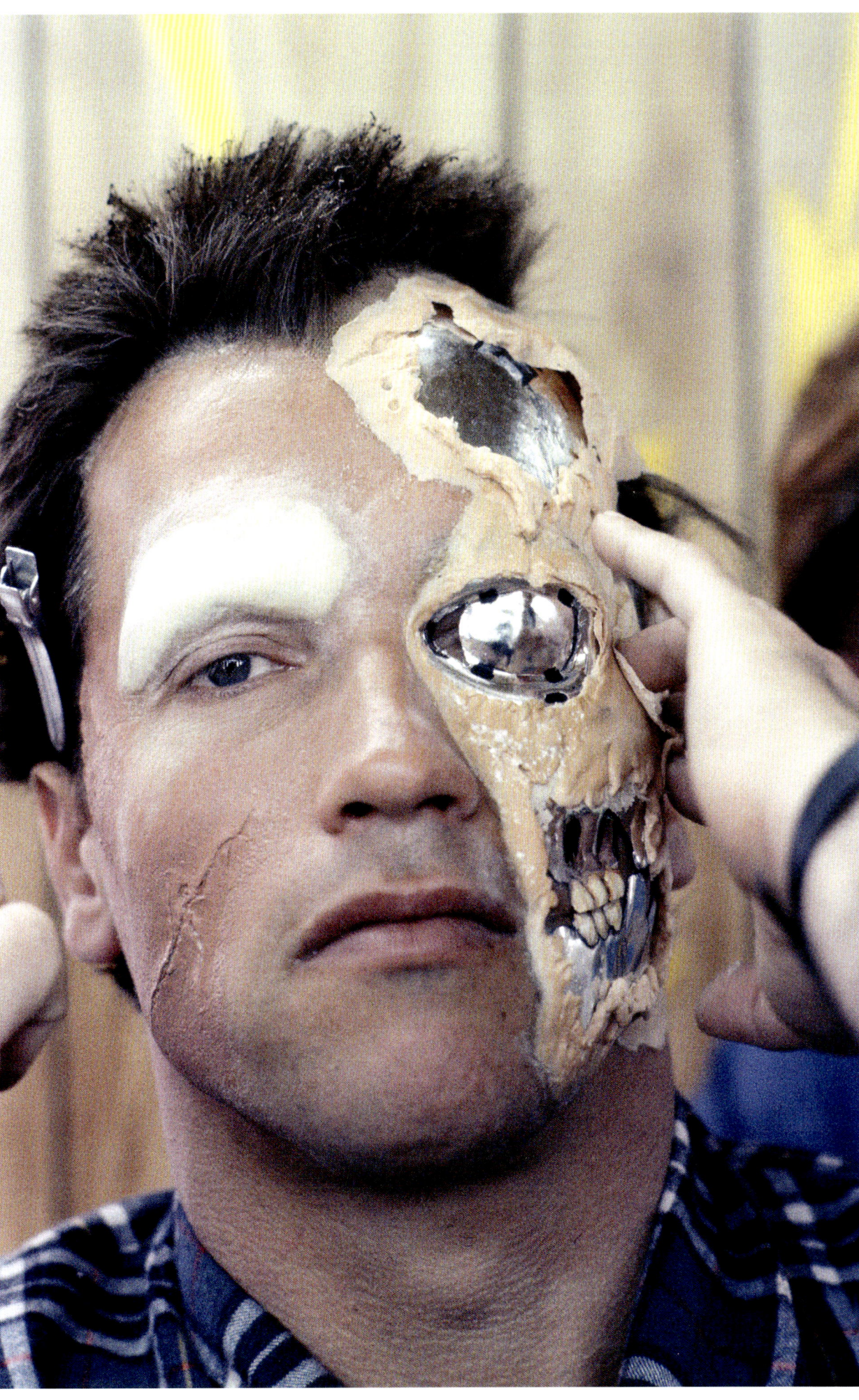

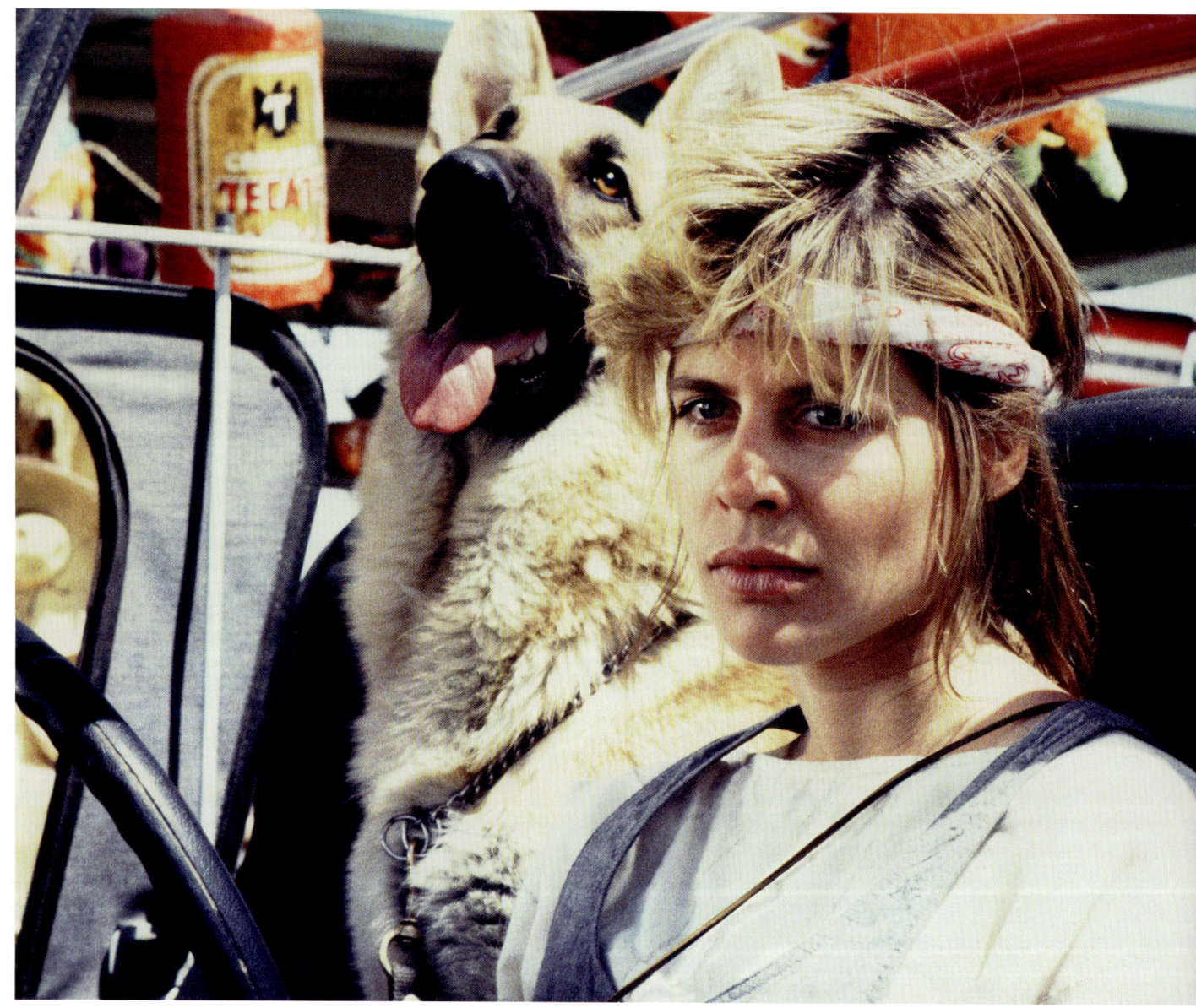

While *The Terminator* helped cement Schwarzenegger's film career as an ultramasculine action hero, it also reveals the influence of feminist science fiction. The maternal Amazon warrior emerged in feminist science fiction of the 1930s and was developed by authors such as Joanna Russ in the 1970s.[2] Despite its many noir elements, *The Terminator* has no femme fatale; rather, the hero is a woman, who we see transform from a "damsel in distress" into an Amazonian "mother of the future," a skilled warrior who embraces violence but only selflessly—as a means to protect her son. When we first meet her, Connor is a clumsy and flustered server at a diner. By the end of the film, she has crushed the Terminator in an industrial press and driven a Jeep into the desert to prepare for the coming war. Several cyberpunk films in the 1980s, such as Paul Verhoeven's *RoboCop* (USA, 1987), feature Amazon-inspired women warriors, but *The Terminator* stands out in making Connor the central hero. The Terminator, a violent cyborg with bulky muscles and dressed for most of the film in a military jacket and studded leather gloves, serves as a distillation of the patriarchal war machine, symbolic of hypermasculine destructiveness and the corporate military run amok. By showing his defeat at the hands of Connor, *The Terminator* makes clear that our future depends on nurturing Amazonian motherhood, not the violent selfishness of the patriarchy.

—*Patrick B. Sharp*

NOTES

1./ Andrew M. Butler, "Early Cyberpunk Film," in *The Routledge Companion to Cyberpunk Culture*, ed. Anna McFarlane, Graham J. Murphy, and Lars Schmeink (New York: Routledge, 2020), 119–27.

2./ For more on the history of Amazons in feminist science fiction and cyberpunk, see Carlen Lavigne, *Cyberpunk Women, Feminism and Science Fiction* (Jefferson, NC: McFarland, 2013); and Patrick B. Sharp, *Darwinian Feminism and Early Science Fiction: Angels, Amazons and Women* (Cardiff: University of Wales Press, 2018).

RIGHT: Special effects artist Shane Mahan operates the Terminator endoskeleton puppet

BELOW: Linda Hamilton as Sarah Connor, makeup continuity Polaroid

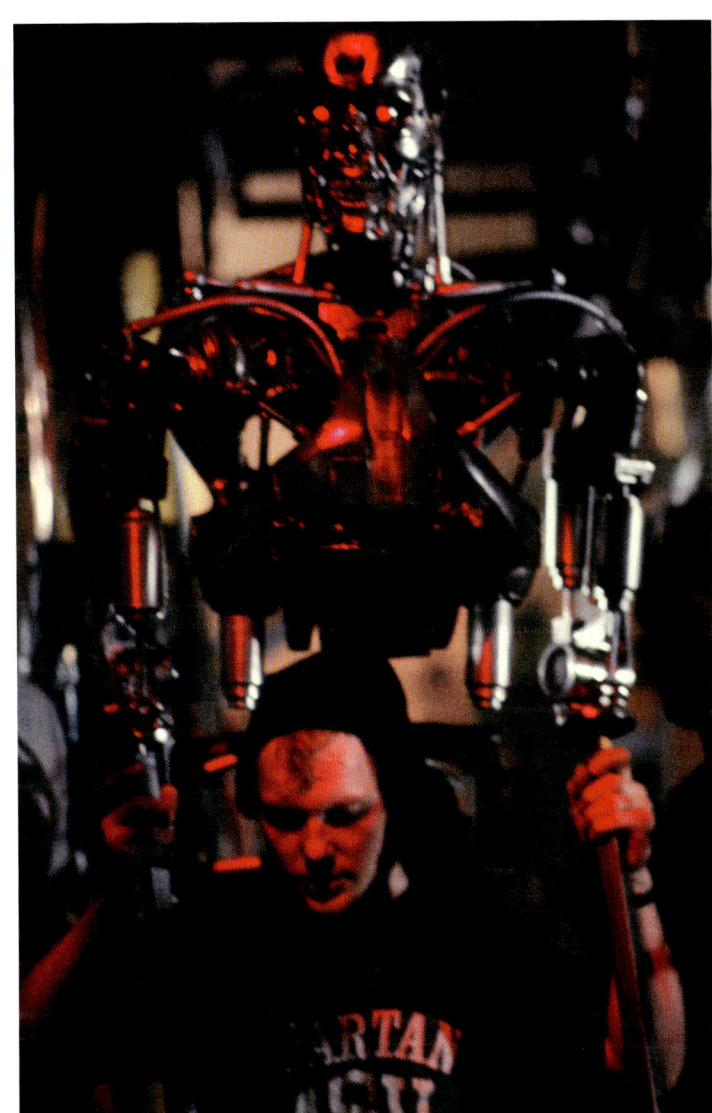

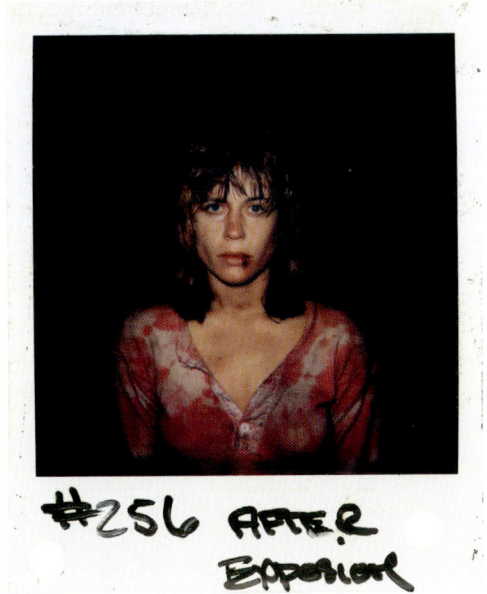

ABOVE: Hamilton as Sarah Connor

RIGHT: Model maker Gary Rhodaback crafting the miniature landscape used for postapocalyptic 2029 Los Angeles

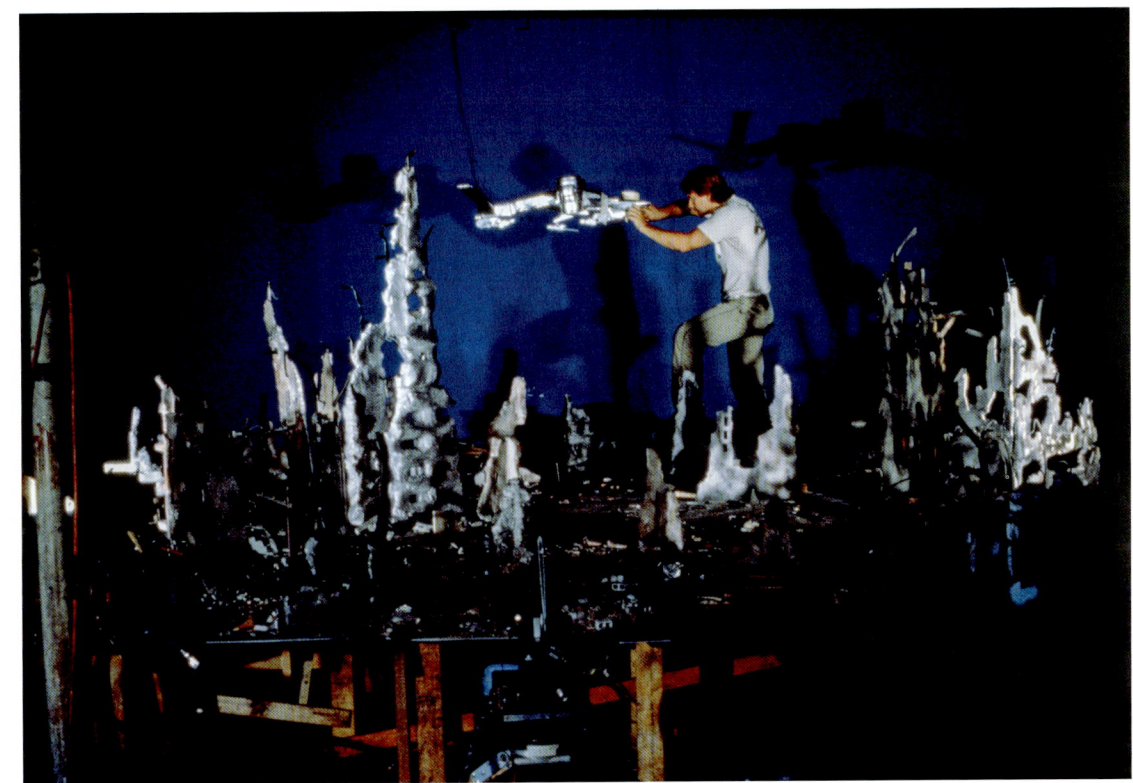

ROBOCOP

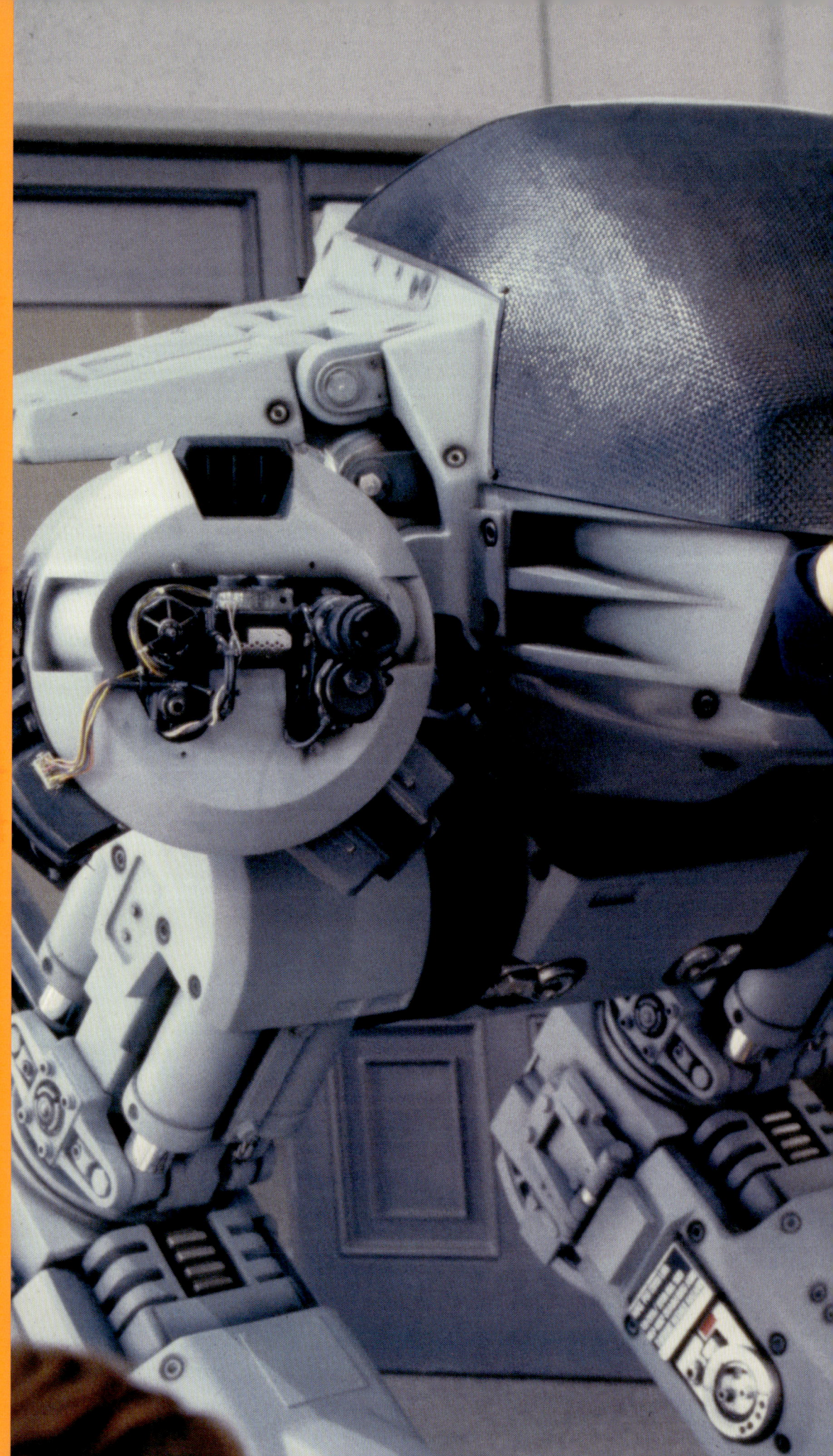

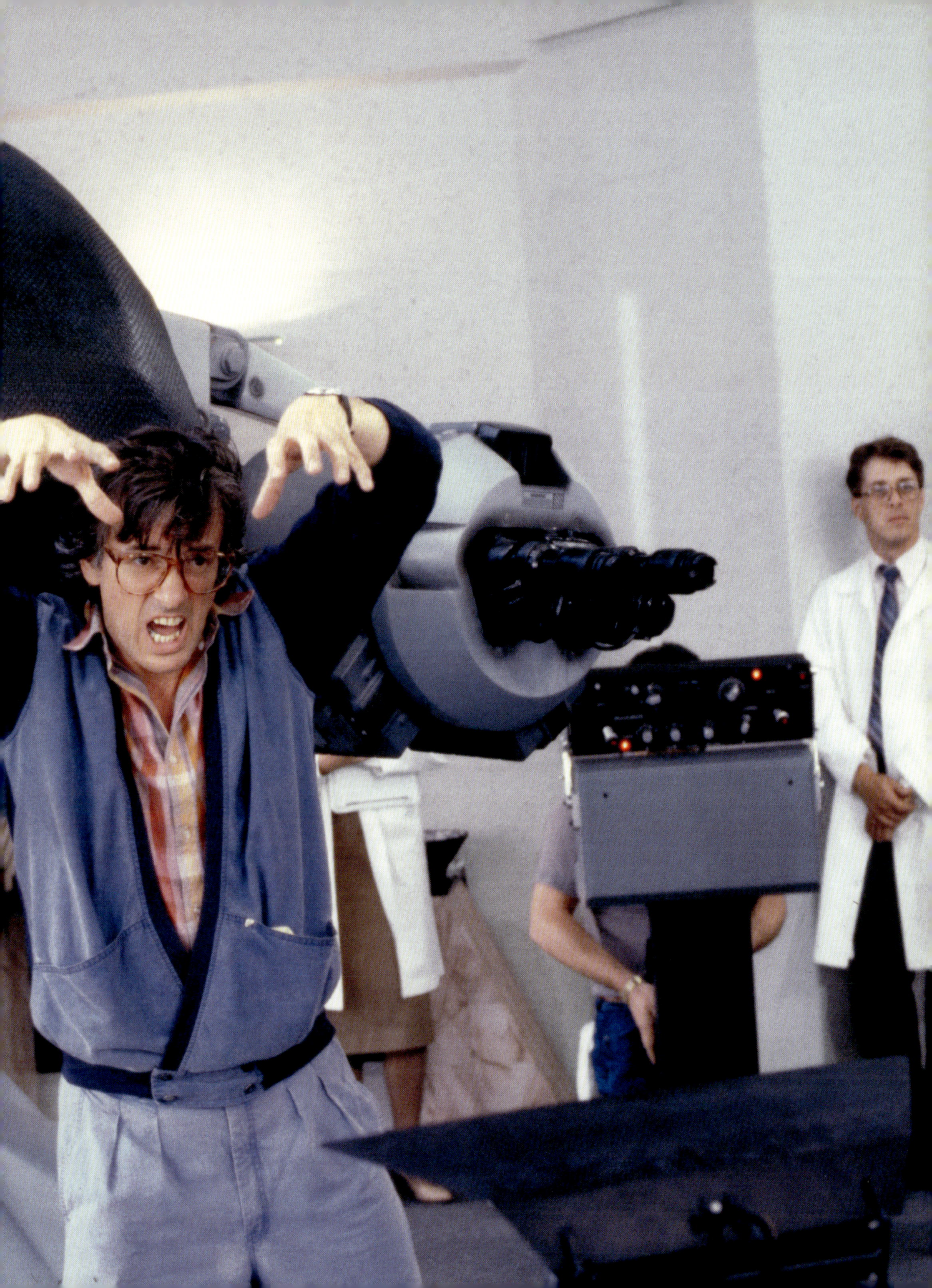

RoboCop (USA, 1987)
Director: Paul Verhoeven

Film synopsis:
After a gang of criminals kills Detroit police officer Alex Murphy, a corporation repurposes his body into a new cyborg-enhanced prototype known as RoboCop. Though RoboCop seems to be the perfect law enforcement machine, the conflict of upholding private interests over the public good tests the lingering remnants of his human morality.

One of the defining entries of 1980s action films, *RoboCop*, directed by Paul Verhoeven, offers a provocative reflection on the complex dynamics between human impulses, power structures, and free will. After his brutal murder while on duty, police officer Alex Murphy (Peter Weller) is resurrected into a cyborg by the Omni Consumer Products corporation as part of a program to privatize law enforcement in Detroit. While Murphy's human form was effective for his job, it still suffered from the natural limitations of the human body. It needed food, water, and rest, and its flesh and internal organs could be easily damaged. Conversely, Murphy's new robotic cyborg body, dubbed RoboCop, is designed to be the perfect law enforcement machine: it not only lacks physical weakness but should also have no empathy for its targets nor the free will to defy orders.

Like many cyberpunk works, one of *RoboCop*'s major themes is the question of what it means to be human. But in addition to taking up this debate on an intellectual level, part of the film's unique flare is the particular glee with which it also revels in the vulgarities of our corporeality. While we may want to believe that it is our thoughts and emotions that mark us as being alive, *RoboCop* lingers on the baser functions and components of our bodies—flesh, blood, vomit, urine—that truly signal life. As an enhanced cyborg, the character of Murphy is positioned to represent the ultimate example of human progress, but Verhoeven contradicts this false ideal by instead locating humanity outside of perfection and, indeed, in the grotesque.

Much of this focus on the human body is a result of the film's over-the-top depictions of violence, which

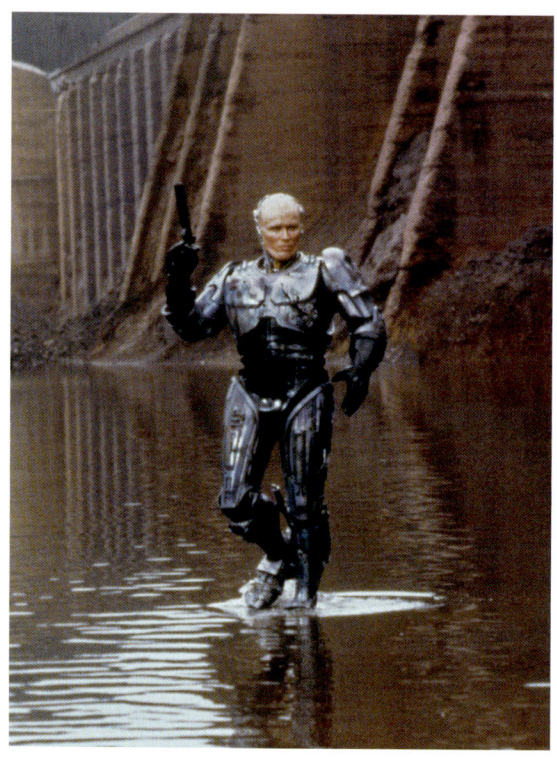

serve to set *RoboCop* apart from the more palatable, sometimes bloodless fare that is still heavily featured in Hollywood PG-13 cinema. Toward the end of the film, Emil Antonowsky (Paul McCrane), one of the antagonist's henchmen, crashes his truck into a vat of toxic waste. He emerges from the accident in horrific form: skin sloughing off his bones, eye bulging from its socket, mouth drooping low into gooey shapelessness—depicted in haunting detail by makeup effects artist Rob Bottin.[1] The stomach-churning excess of the character's death emphasizes his flesh-and-bone humanity, presenting the viewer with the conflicted experience of being simultaneously attracted to and repelled by this brutal representation of human mortality.

PREVIOUS SPREAD: Director Paul Verhoeven on set

LEFT: Peter Weller as RoboCop

RIGHT: Actor Paul McCrane during the application of special effects makeup

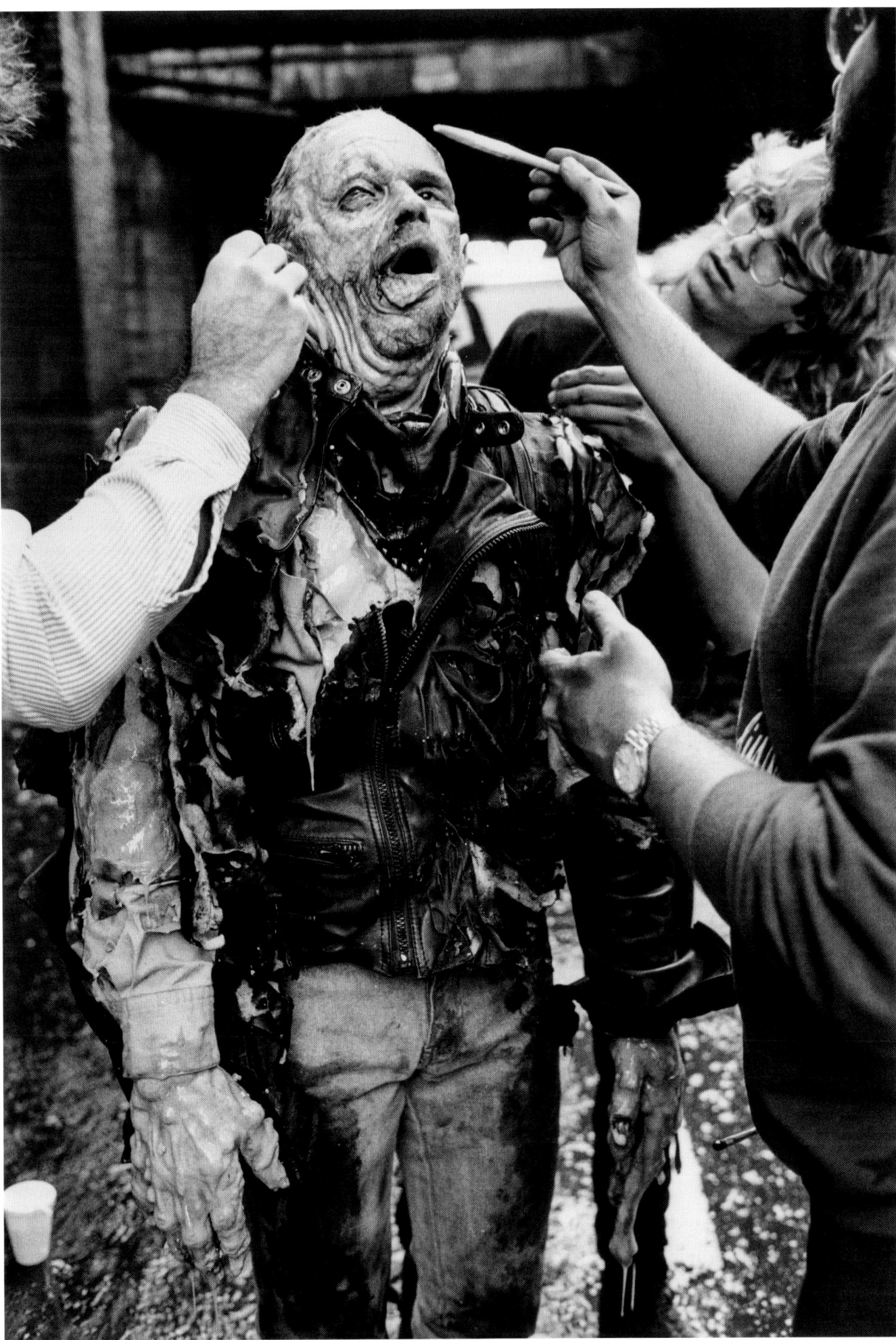

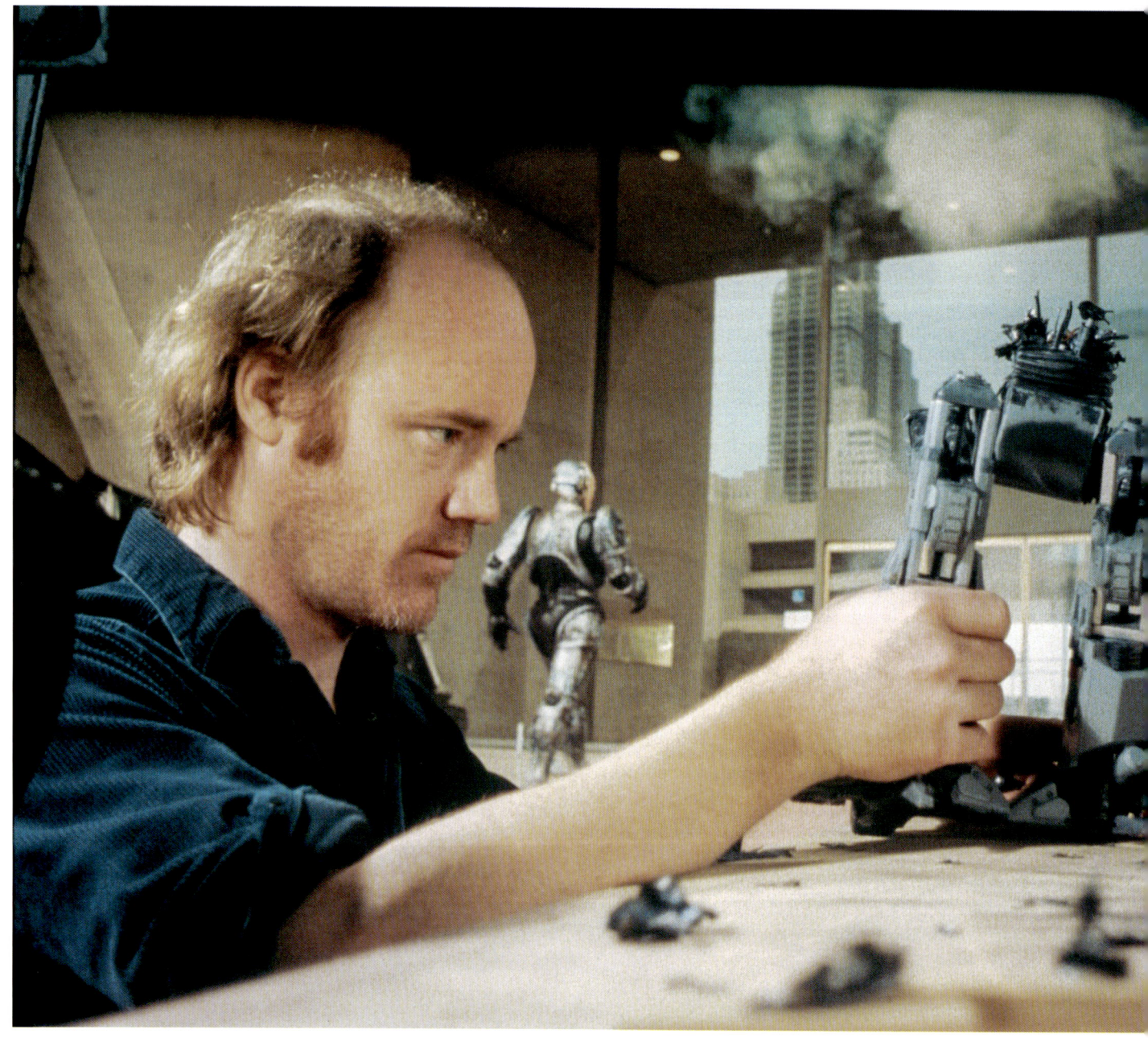

ABOVE: Visual effects artist Phil Tippett adjusts the ED-209 miniature

That humans have an ambivalent attraction to the forbidden is an inherent part of the audience's relationship with *RoboCop*. Just as a female police officer in the film wills herself not to look at a suspect's exposed penis—before quickly glancing down—so too must *RoboCop*'s viewers contend with their own perverse interest in the film's gory violence. As humans, our physiological and emotional reactions sometimes conflict with our ethical or intellectual standards. While RoboCop also has a programmed set of directives that control his behavior, it is in the messiness of contending with the consequences of these automated actions that his humanity persists. Recognizing this disharmony between mind and body, between intellectualization and impulse, is what ultimately gives him the perspective to defy his orders and distinguishes his—and all humans'—actions from the perfect objective functions of a machine.

—Emily Rauber Rodriguez

NOTES

1./ Bottin also designed the RoboCop suit for the film, inspired by other human-robot hybrids played by costumed humans, like Maria from Fritz Lang's *Metropolis* (Germany, 1927) and C-3PO from George Lucas's *Star Wars* (USA, 1977).

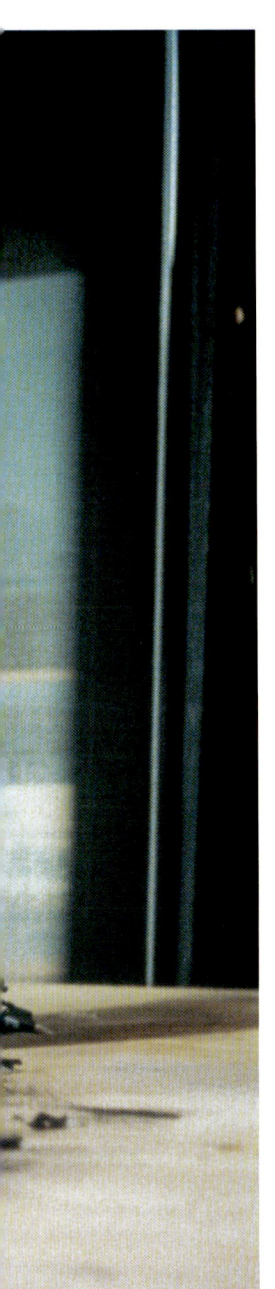

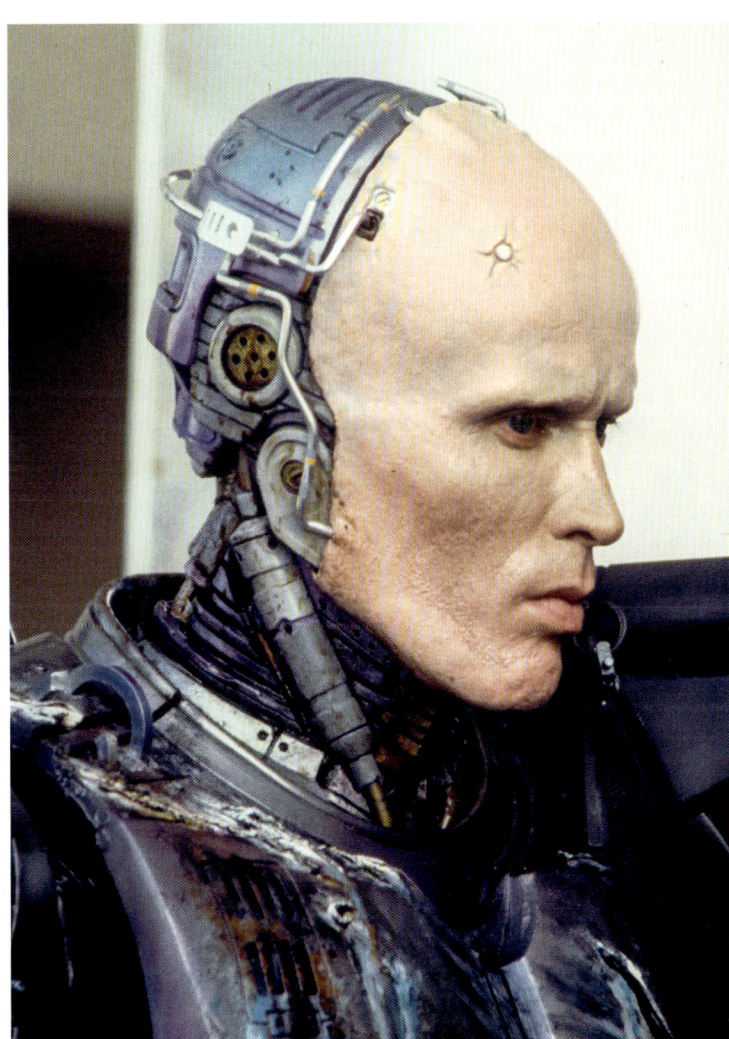

RIGHT: Weller as RoboCop

BELOW: From left to right: actors Kurtwood Smith, Jesse D. Goins, Ray Wise, and Paul McCrane on set

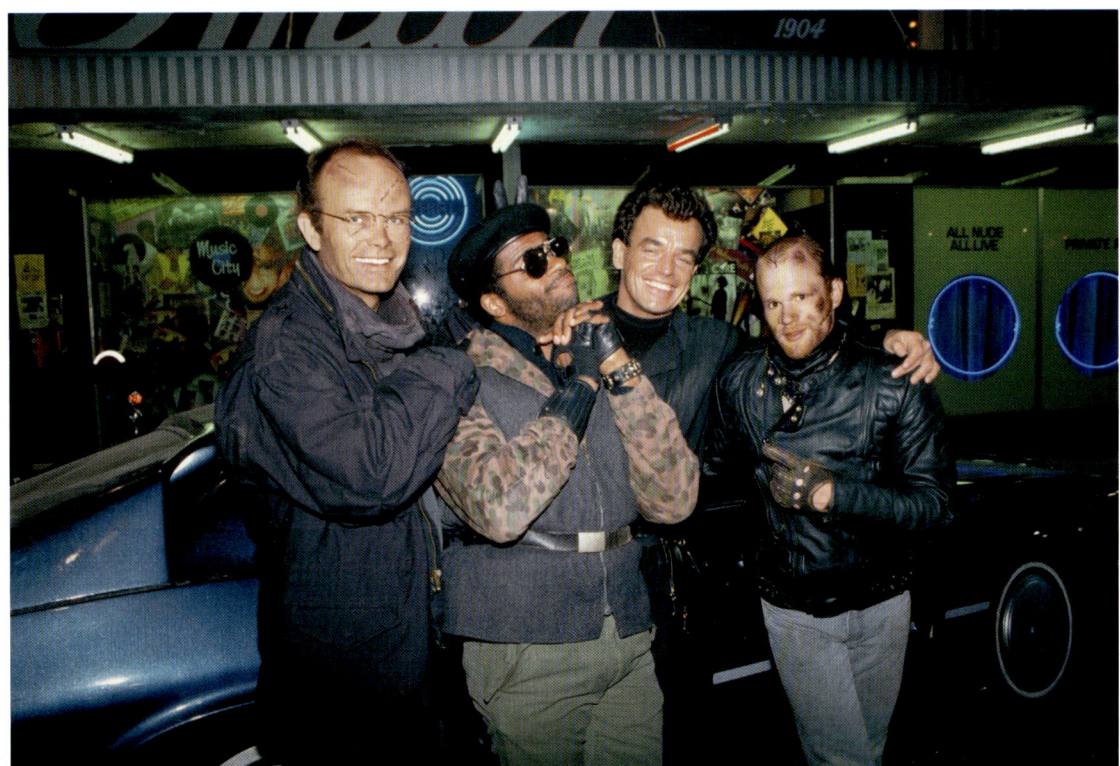

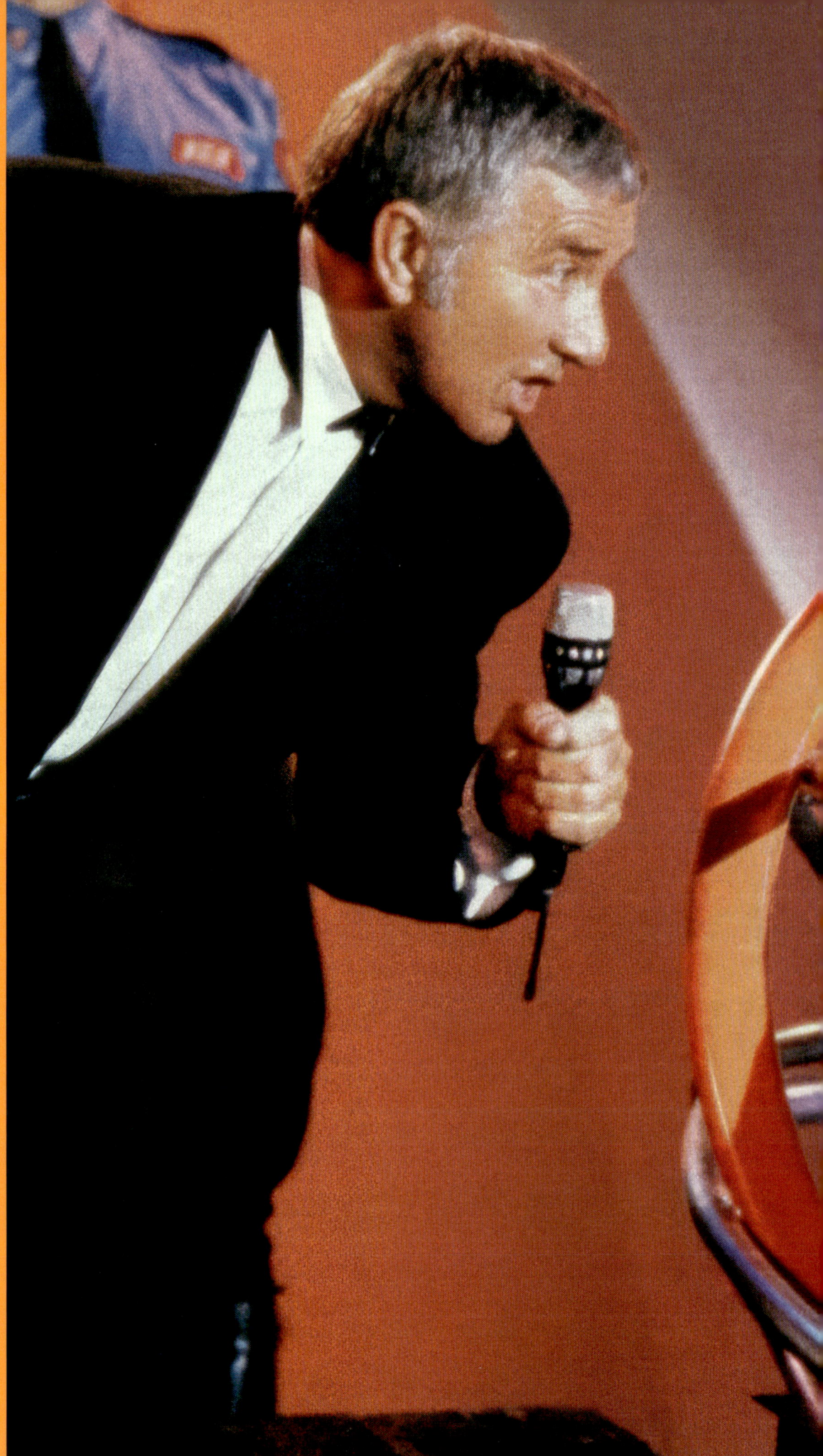

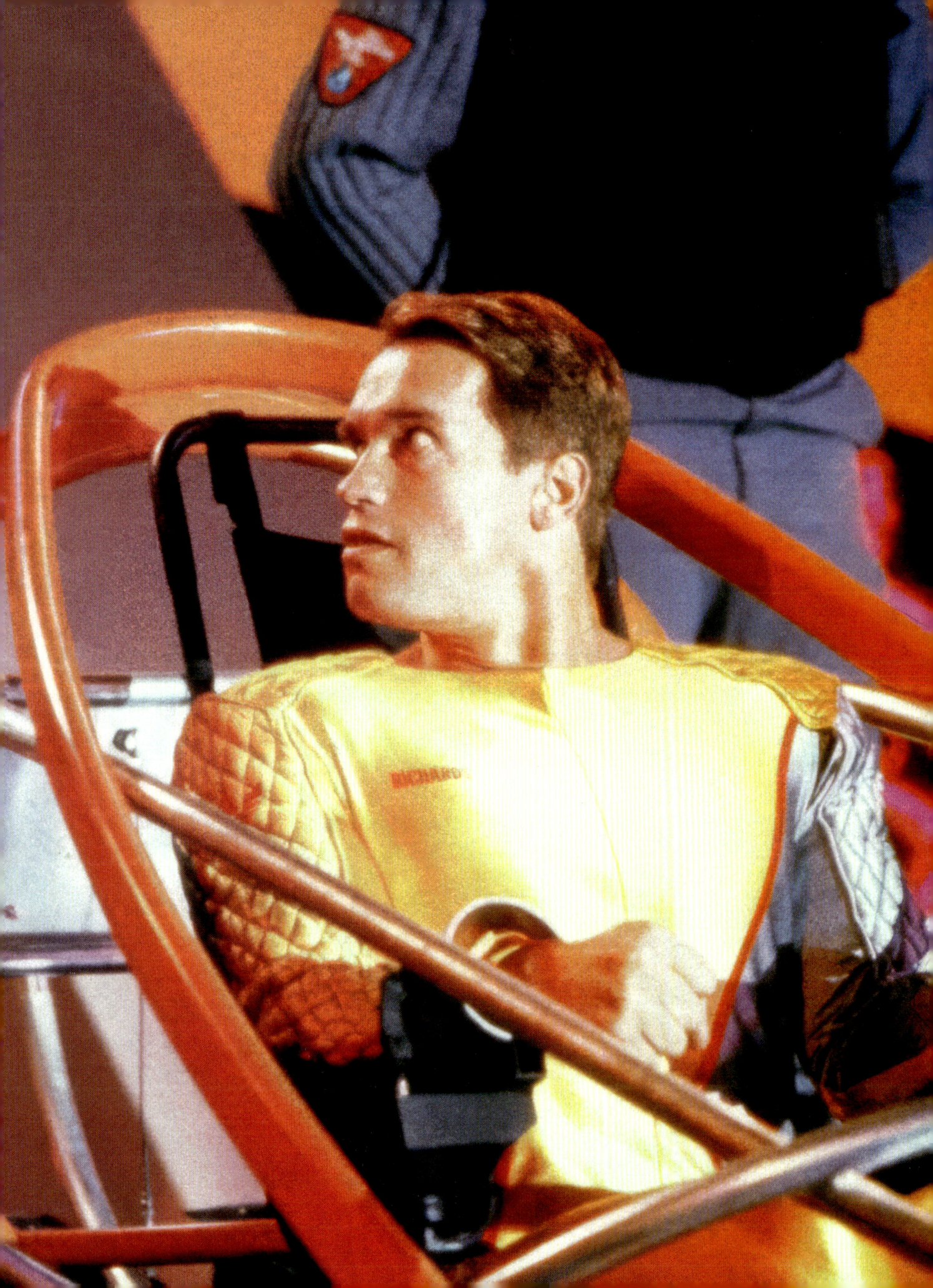

The Running Man (USA, 1987)
Director: Paul Michael Glaser

Film synopsis:
The United States has become a totalitarian state. The masses are indoctrinated with violent media like *The Running Man*, a TV game show where accused criminals are hunted down and executed by mercenaries. Falsely accused of a crime, policeman Ben Richards is compelled to participate in the show, but may also be able to expose the government's lies.

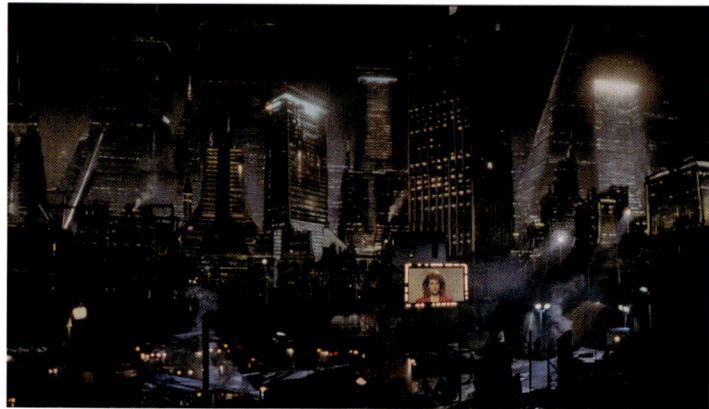

The Running Man (1987), directed by Paul Michael Glaser and adapted from Stephen King's 1982 novel of the same name, is set in a not-so-distant future, characterized by the dystopian themes of media manipulation and totalitarian rule.[1] The protagonist hero is policeman Ben Richards (Arnold Schwarzenegger), who threatens to upset this oppressive order. To create the film's compelling and immersive metropolis, Glaser enlisted the visual effects company Illusion Arts and their masterful chief matte artist, Syd Dutton, whose skilled brushwork built the perfect dystopian city.

Matte paintings are emblematic of the "movie magic" that existed before the era of digital effects, captivating audiences by enhancing visual storytelling. Meticulously painted on glass with oil or acrylic paint, these illusory images seamlessly blended with live-action footage, helping to blur the line between imagination and reality. Dutton says of his artistic vision for the film, "The message I was trying to convey was of a huge futuristic metropolis where our heroes could only find sanctuary with the dispossessed. The population had exploded, causing class separation between the two."[2] Dutton's expertise in depicting futuristic cities, whether dystopian or utopian, made him the go-to artist for films such as *Buck Rogers in the 25th Century* (USA, 1979), directed by Daniel Haller; *The Time Machine* (USA, 2002), directed by Simon Wells; and the 2007 Final Cut of the 1982 classic *Blade Runner* (USA).[3] His imaginative brushstrokes also graced various science fiction television reboots of the 1980s, including *The Twilight Zone* (1985–89) and *Star Trek: The Next Generation* (1987–94). Dutton's creative journey began with a passion for painting, transitioning from being an architecture

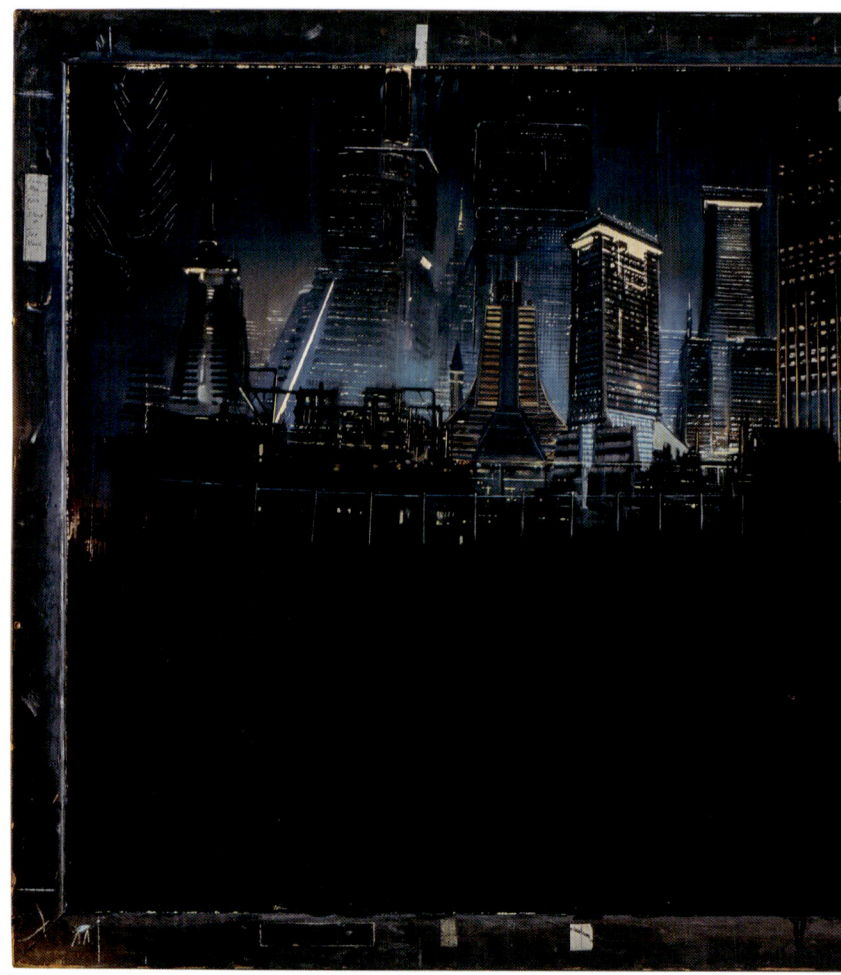

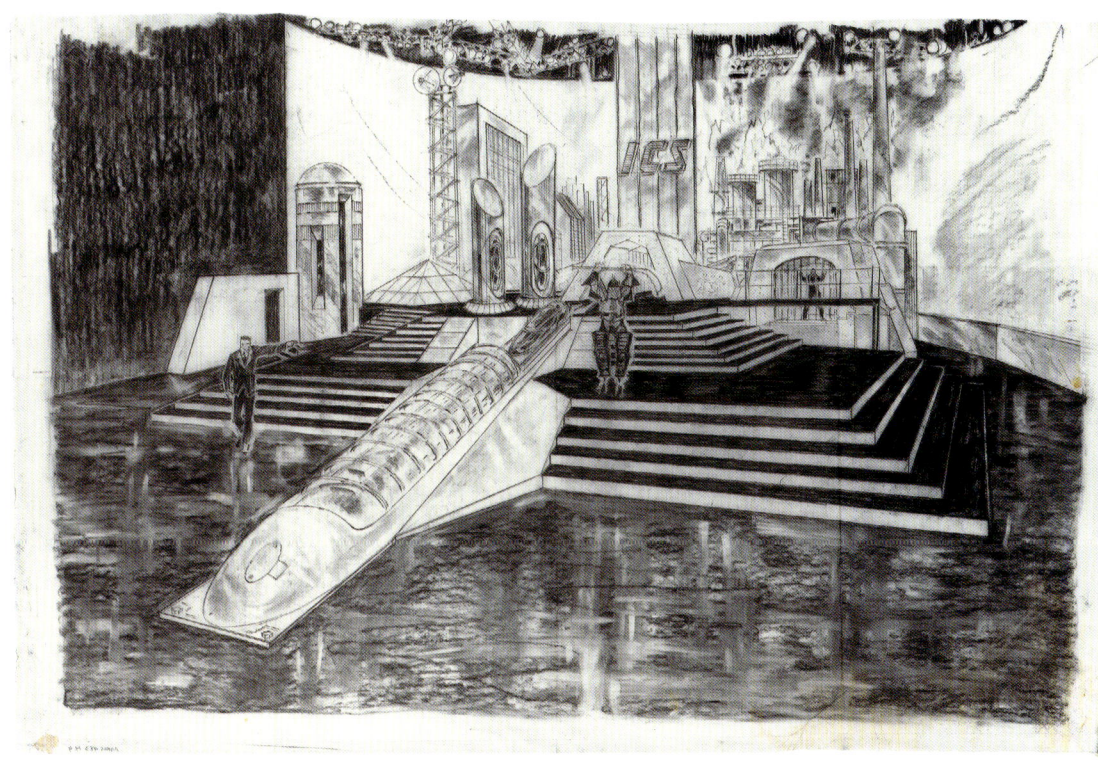

PREVIOUS SPREAD: Arnold Schwarzenegger as Ben Richards (right) and Richard Dawson as Damon Killian

LEFT: Production design drawing of the game show set

OPPOSITE: Matte painting (bottom) used to create the dystopian cityscape seen in the film (top)

major to earning a master's degree in art at the University of California, Berkeley, where he was instructed by prominent artists such as David Hockney and Mark Rothko.[4] His painted depictions of the future would be profoundly shaped by the cinematic imagery found in science fiction films like *Metropolis* (Germany, 1927), directed by Fritz Lang, and the innovative designs and architecture of Le Corbusier, notably his masterpiece Notre-Dame du Haut, a chapel in Ronchamp, France.

During the production of *The Running Man*, Dutton's partner, cinematographer and visual effects supervisor Bill Taylor photographed the live-action set on location, after which Dutton embarked on the next phase of the process—returning to his studio to create the matte painting that would be added to the photography. Using a large sheet of framed glass, he began blocking in basic shapes with broad brushstrokes. "I could see the city emerging," he explains, "sort of like a fog lifting." Dutton employed Winsor & Newton oil paints, allowing them to dry before establishing a vanishing point and infusing the building shapes with coherence and intricate details until the painted illusion was complete. "I aimed to evoke a sense of older structures evolving into a sprawling metropolis," says Dutton, "bridging the gap between past and future."

—*Craig Barron*

NOTES
1./ *The Running Man* was first published under King's pseudonym Richard Bachman.
2./ Syd Dutton, correspondence with author, May 11, 2023. All subsequent Dutton quotes are from this conversation.
3./ In the revised ending of the Ridley Scott–directed movie, Rutger Hauer's character, replicant Roy Batty, releases a dove that takes flight into a digitally rendered environment by Kelvin McIlwain, under the supervision of Syd Dutton.
4./ Syd Dutton, correspondence with author, May 11, 2023.

AKIRA

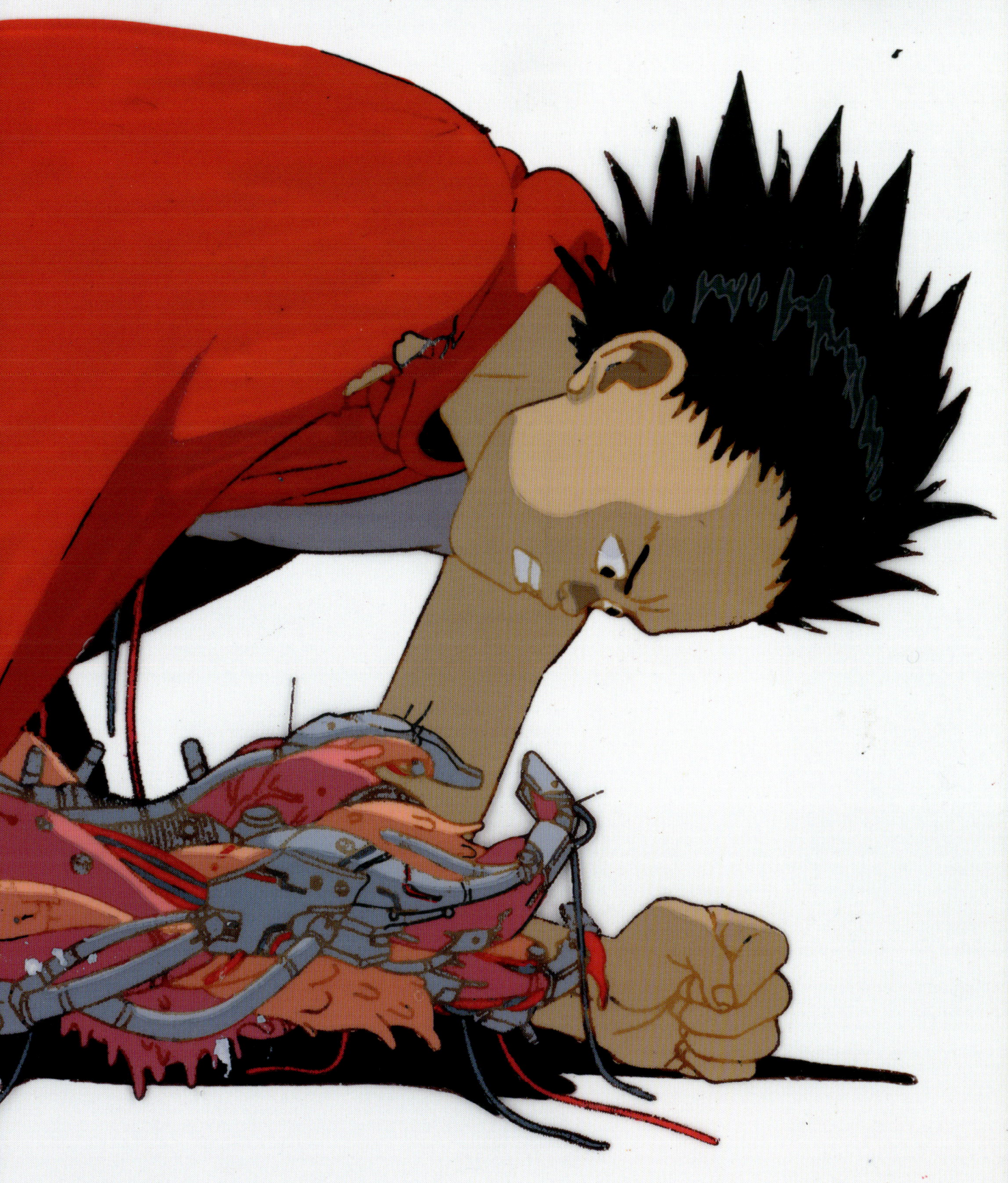

AKIRA (Japan, 1988)
Director: Katsuhiro Otomo

Film synopsis:
Set in a future "Neo-Tokyo" plagued by corruption and systemic decay, members of a motorcycle gang are accidentally embroiled in a secret military project. When one of them becomes imbued with mysterious telekinetic powers, he threatens to hurt those he loves and bring great destruction to the city and the world.

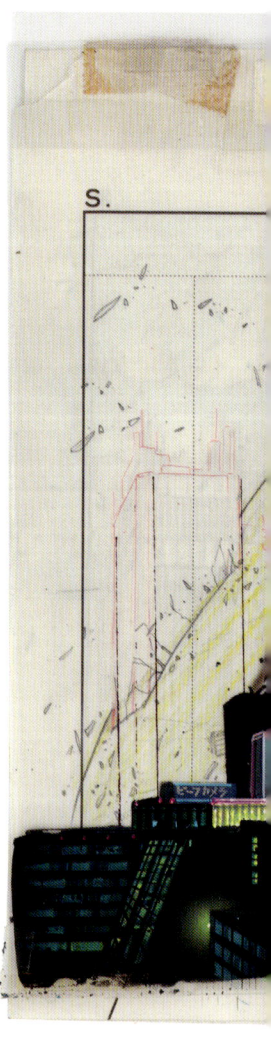

Katsuhiro Otomo's landmark anime *Akira*, based on his 1982–90 serialized manga of the same name, still remains the quintessential Japanese cyberpunk work. Detailed production art and cel animation bring the intricate world to life. Set in a postnuclear "Neo-Tokyo" in 2019, the film depicts a dystopic society overrun by motorcycle gangs and entangled in a relentless struggle between a totalitarian government and the violent resistance. Caught in the middle of these forces is a group of psychic "children" who are disjointed from the flow of time—aging without maturing.

Akira's protagonists are Shôtarô Kaneda, leader of a motorcycle gang and rider of the film's iconic red motorcycle, and his childhood friend Tetsuo Shima. The gang roams Neo-Tokyo evading the police, chasing women, and pursuing their rival gang, the Clowns. During one particularly violent encounter with the Clowns, Tetsuo crashes his motorbike and is taken to the hospital, where he is subjected to the same government experimentation that produced the psychic children.

These experiments seek to unleash *zettai no enerugî*, "absolute energy" that comes from the very origins of the universe and has accumulated in everything that exists. Three psychic children who have survived the experiments, Kiyoko, Takashi, and Masaru, evoke the film's missing titular character, Akira, who is legendary for his display of *zettai no enerugî*. Akira remains absent throughout the film—a type of negative theology that appears only in disembodied form and flashback. Despite his absence, Akira's residual trace organizes the film's mythology: to the government, he stands for absolute power; to the doomsday cult that worships him, absolute energy.

The energy unleashed in Tetsuo surges to levels unseen since Akira, who begins to infiltrate Tetsuo's psyche. Unable to control this power, which gradually consumes him, Tetsuo is driven increasingly mad and violent, his insecurity and fragility amplified by the irrepressible forces that come to dominate him. As his powers increase, his body expands and contracts, transforming into a polymorphic mass that engulfs not only him but the world around him. The absolute energy that flows from his body threatens to absorb all matter into its vortex, signaling the potential beginning of an entirely new cosmos: the death of one universe and the birth of another.

Akira takes place in the middle of these two apocalypses: one past, and the other looming. It renders an image of the present as suspended between disasters and depicts the struggle between deeply internal senses of self (strength) and those that appear to arrive from the outside (power). As the film illustrates, the borders that separate these forces from each other are constantly in peril.

—*Akira Mizuta Lippit*

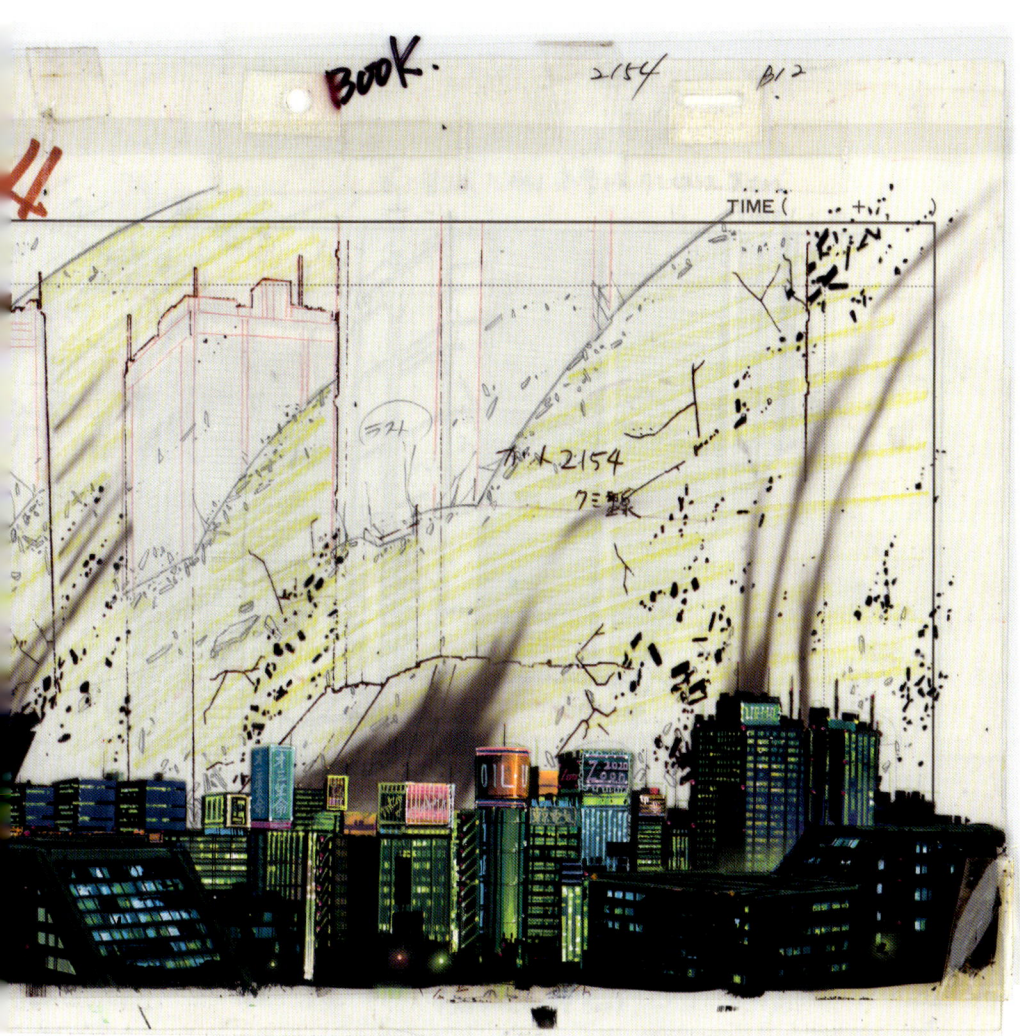

PREVIOUS SPREAD: Animation cel of Tetsuo

LEFT: Unfinished animation cel setup of Neo-Tokyo

BELOW LEFT: Animation cel setup of protagonist Shôtarô Kaneda on his red motorcycle

BELOW RIGHT: Japanese theatrical poster

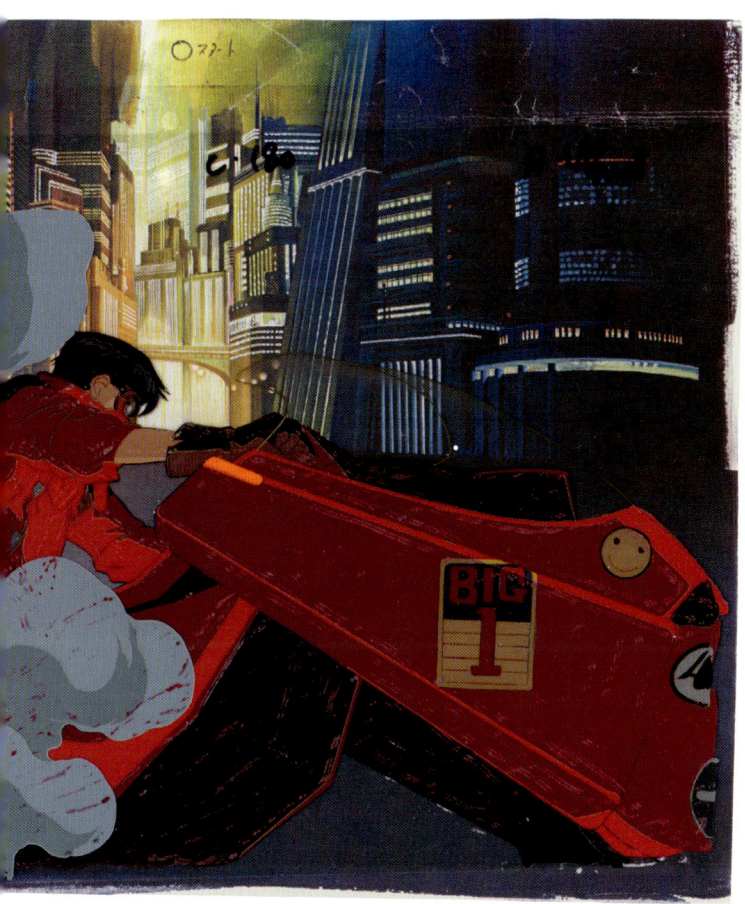

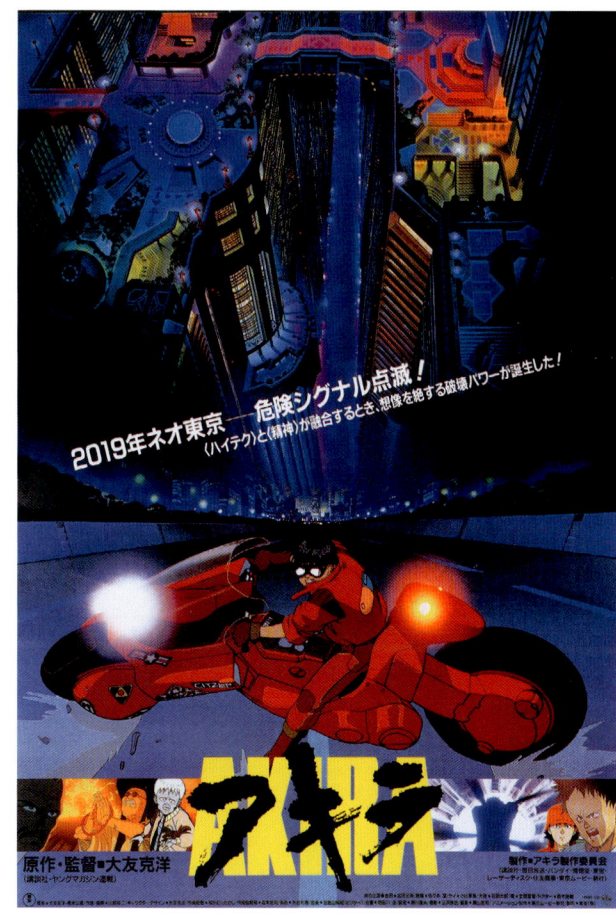

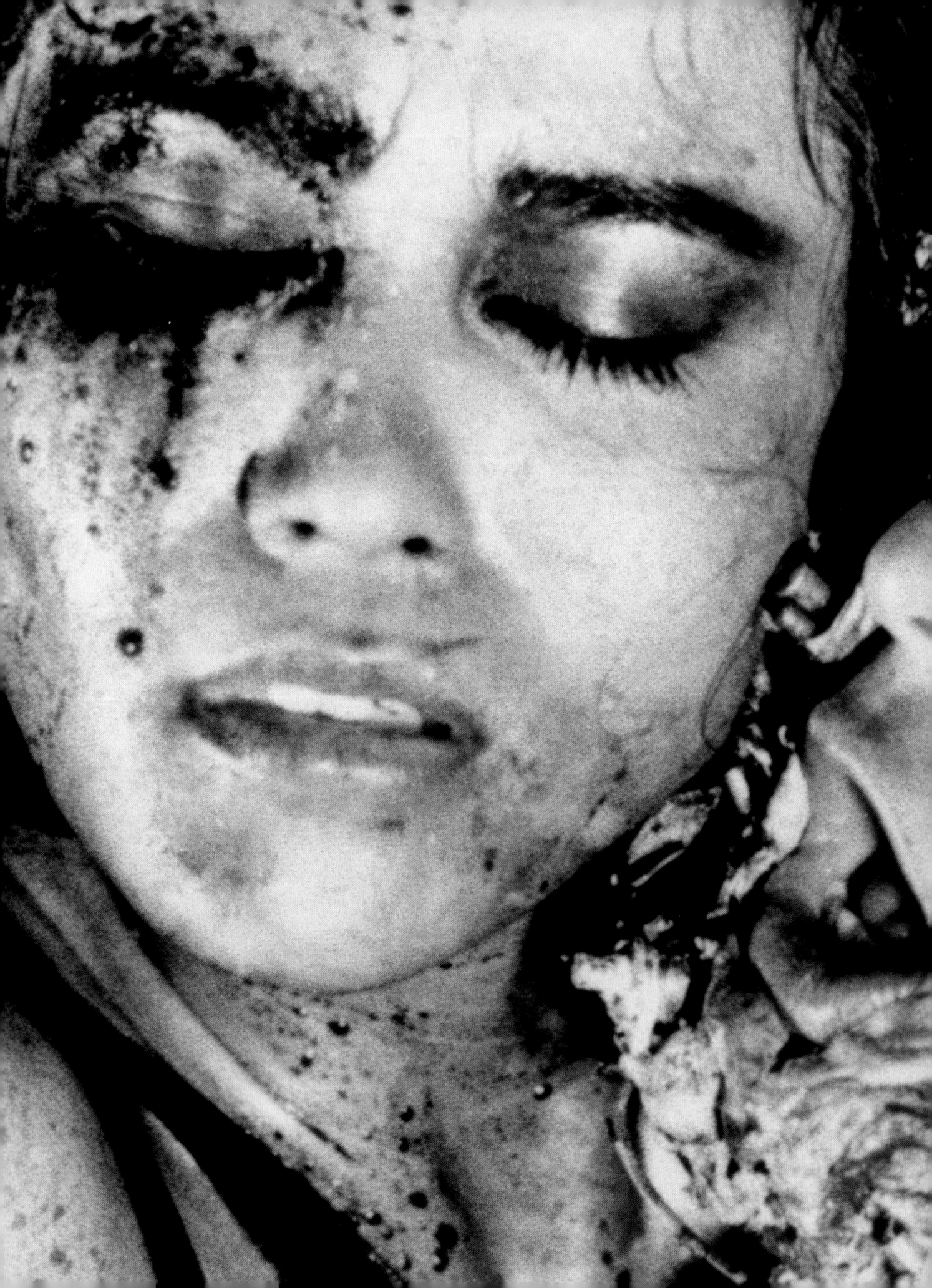

TETSUO: THE IRON MAN

Tetsuo: The Iron Man
(*Tetsuo*, Japan, 1989)
Director: Shinya Tsukamoto

Film synopsis:
After accidentally hitting a "metal fetishist" with his car, a salaryman is infected with a virus that transforms his body into a fleshy metallic monstrosity. As his body mutates, he becomes consumed by chaos and violence. Engulfed in madness, the salaryman tracks down the fetishist, and the two face off in an epic battle.

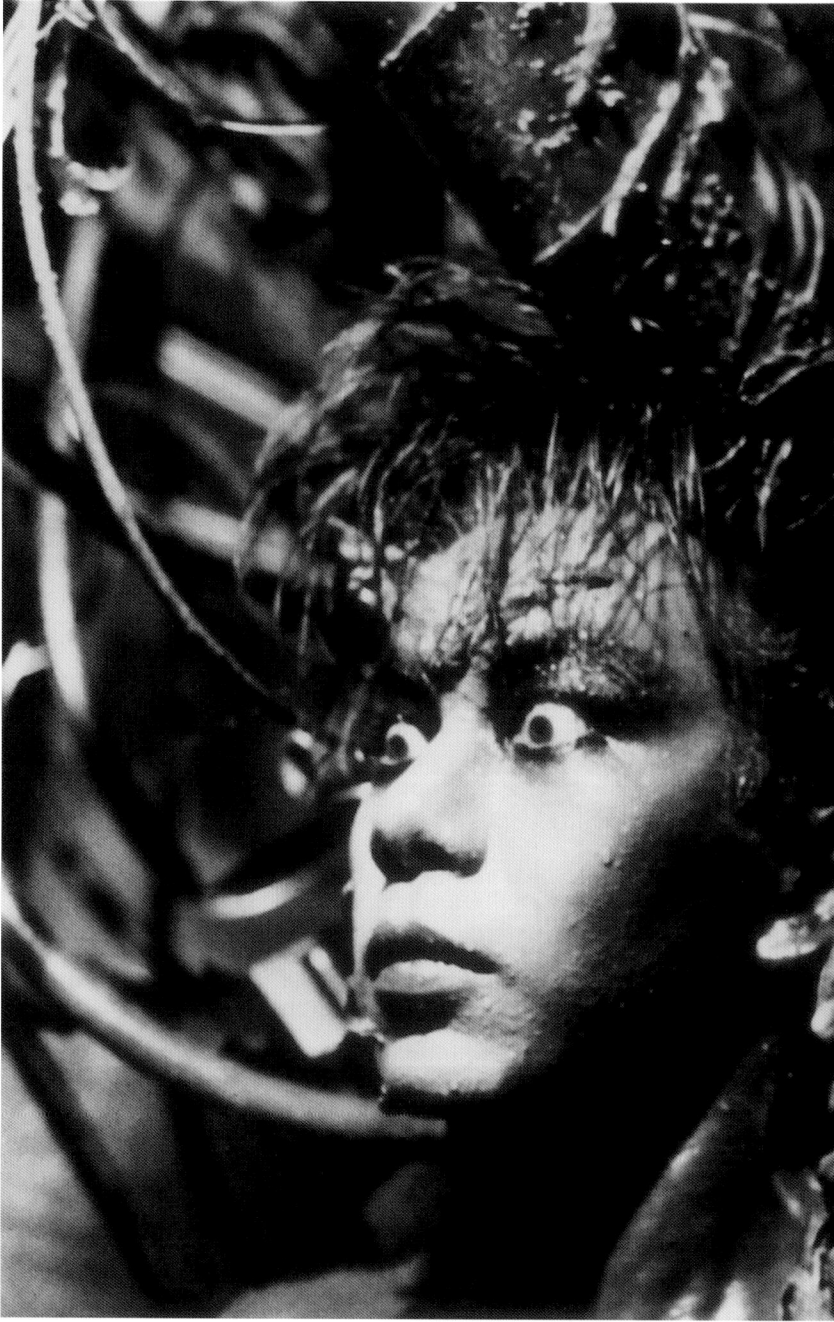

Unlike many of the cyberpunk films that preceded it, which were set in dystopian, high-tech futuristic cities, *Tetsuo: The Iron Man* takes place in a low-tech, late '80s postindustrial Tokyo. The city acts as a bleak backdrop for the film's primary focus: the body. "I was concentrating on creating a sensual image, on showing the relationship between the metal—the material—and the flesh—the body," said director Shinya Tsukamoto.[1] "I tried to make an erotic film by way of science fiction, to express eroticism through iron."[2]

Clocking in at 67 minutes, *Tetsuo* is intense from start to finish, depicting nightmarish transformations that fuse biology with technology. It is gruesome and frenetic but, as Tsukamoto puts it, *sensual*—a surprising term for a film whose most notable scene includes intercourse with a giant drill-bit phallus. Yet part of what makes *Tetsuo* so entrancing almost forty years after its release is its handcrafted nature. In lieu of costly special effects and intricate sets, the film relies on DIY prosthetics and aggressive close-ups of the actors' facial expressions, details that emphasize

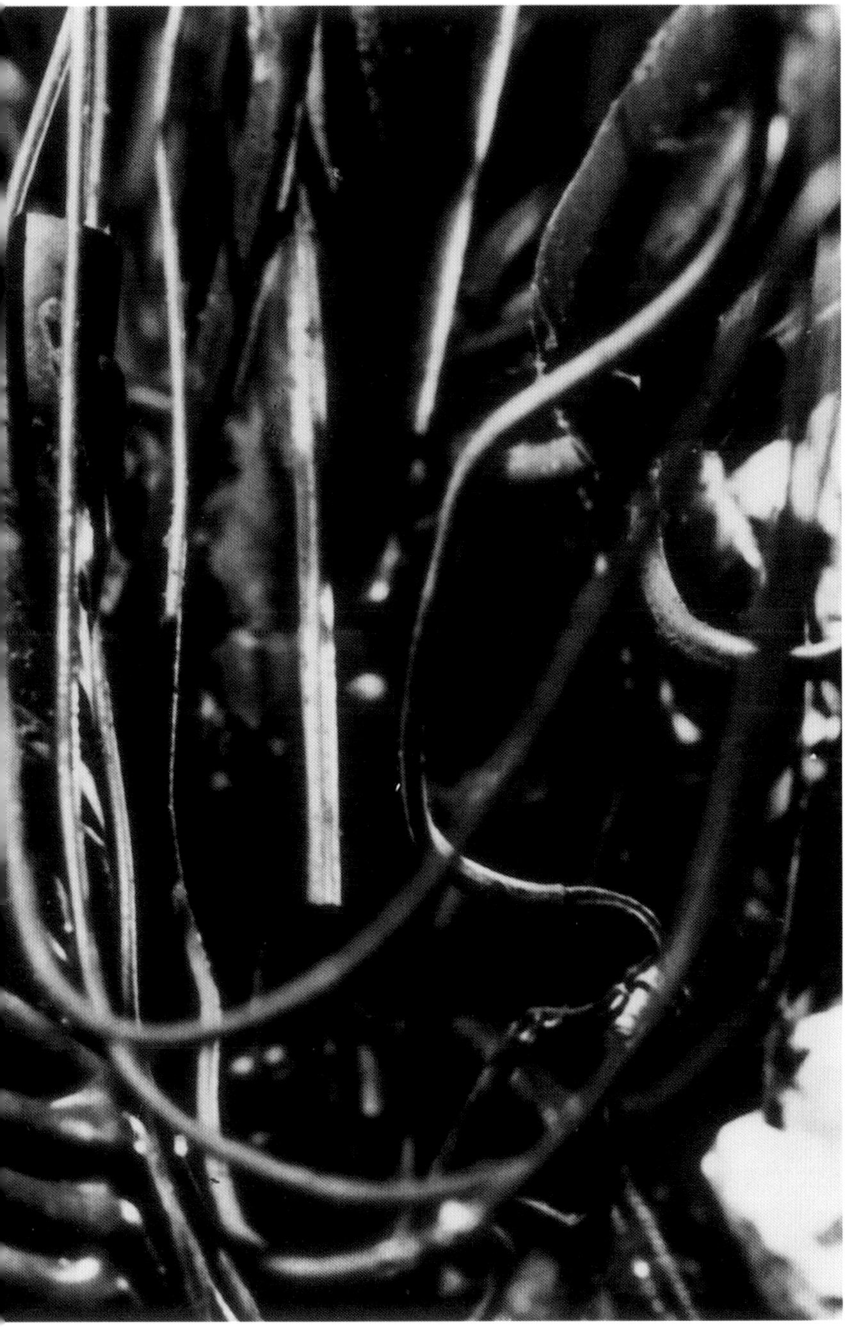

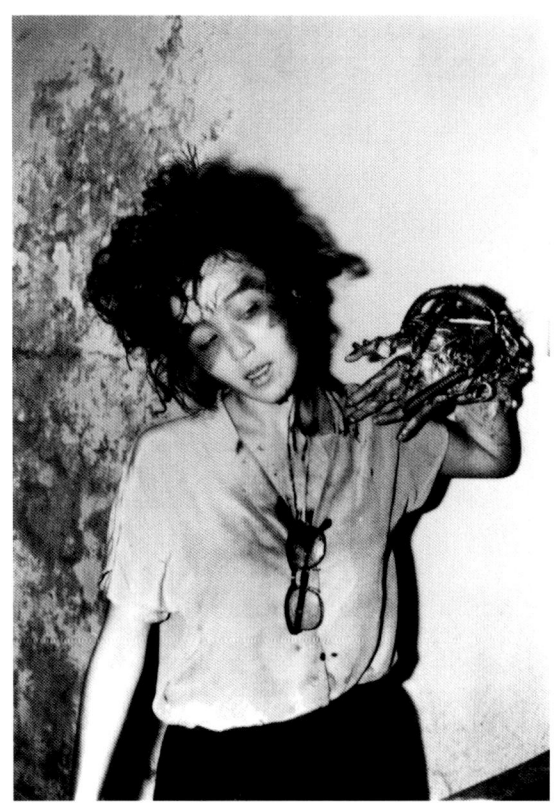

PREVIOUS SPREAD: Tomorowo Taguchi as the Salaryman (right) and Kei Fujiwara as the Salaryman's girlfriend

LEFT: Shinya Tsukamoto as the metal fetishist

ABOVE: Fujiwara on set

intimacy and the vulnerability of the characters as they oscillate between states of pleasure and pain. Made on a shoestring budget of around $100,000 and shot over a period of eighteen months, *Tetsuo* was sutured together through the pure tenacity and drive of Tsukamoto, whose credits for the film also include screenwriting, art directing, photography, lighting, editing, and special effects as well as the role of the metal fetishist.[3] Its deeply solitary and fiercely paranoid perspective stems from the distinct vision of its director. In this way, it recalls David Lynch's *Eraserhead* (USA, 1977) and David Cronenberg's *Videodrome* (Canada, 1983), both major influences on Tsukamoto. And, like those films, *Tetsuo* uses body horror to probe psychological depths and explore libidinal anxieties.

The limitations of *Tetsuo*'s low budget allowed for a more experimental and personal approach. During production, the cast and crew lived together in the female lead's (Kei Fujiwara) apartment, which also functioned as a primary set. When filming needed to

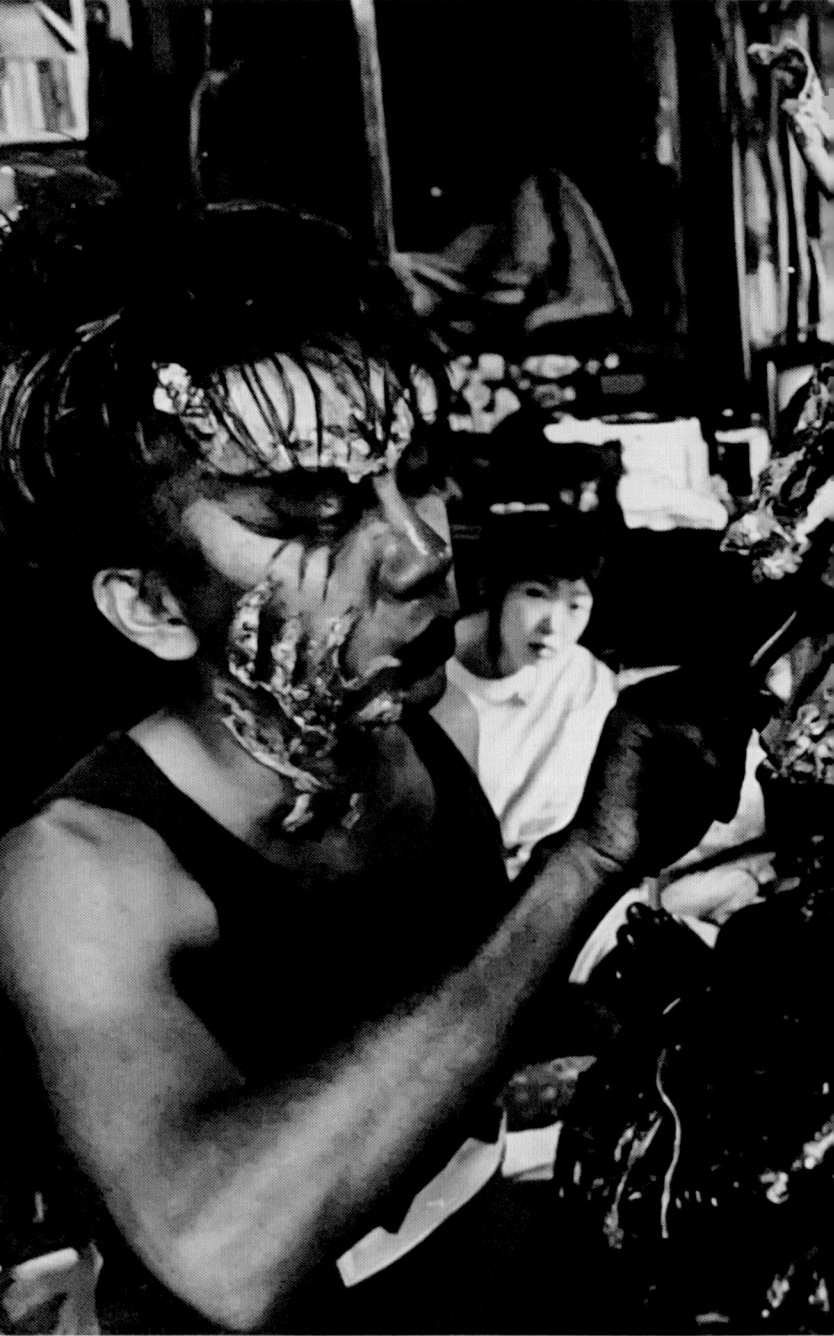

RIGHT: Writer-director Tsukamoto—who also produced, acted in, and served as cinematographer, editor, art director, special effects artist for the film—applies makeup to Taguchi

move from the apartment to its warehouse location, the actors traveled on trains with their makeup on to save time and money. The salaryman's metamorphized body was constructed with scrap metal and television parts found outside electronics and hardware stores. Tomorowo Taguchi, who played this part, reportedly had so much material glued to him he could barely move.[4] So fraught was the independent film's production that, by the end, Tsukamoto was left practically alone with the actors to finish shooting. The lack of resources is apparent onscreen but, paradoxically, this helps ground the film in a heightened reality. The film is shot in a grainy black-and-white with its brights glowing incandescent, a style that complicates what is real and what are figments of the characters' imaginations as they descend into madness. The home-brewed special effects add a sense of tactility; the cramped locations generate claustrophobic anxiety.

As the salaryman morphs into a grotesque amalgamation of viscous flesh, sinew, and e-waste, he resembles a *kaiju*, or Godzilla-like monster. Yet Tsukamoto purposely designed his creatures at human scale—what he refers to as *Futsû saizu no kaijin* (regular-size monsters): freakish characters that mirror our own fears and desires.[5]

—Nicholas Barlow

NOTES
1./ Dan Persons, "Tetsuo: The Iron Man," *Cinefantastique* 23, no. 5 (February 1993): 52.
2./ Tom Mes, *Iron Man: The Cinema of Shinya Tsukamoto* (Godalming, UK: FAB Press, 2005), 59.
3./ Persons, "Tetsuo: The Iron Man," 52.
4./ Mes, *Iron Man*, 51.
5./ During the opening credits of *Tetsuo*, a caption reads: "Regular-Size Monsters series." Before releasing his feature debut, Tsukamoto made two shorts, *Futsû saizu no kaijin* (1986) and *The Adventure of Denchu-Kozo* (1987), which operated as blueprints for *Tetsuo*. Following *Tetsuo*'s success, Tsukamoto made two sequels: *Tetsuo II: Body Hammer* (1992) and *Tetsuo: The Bullet Man* (2009).

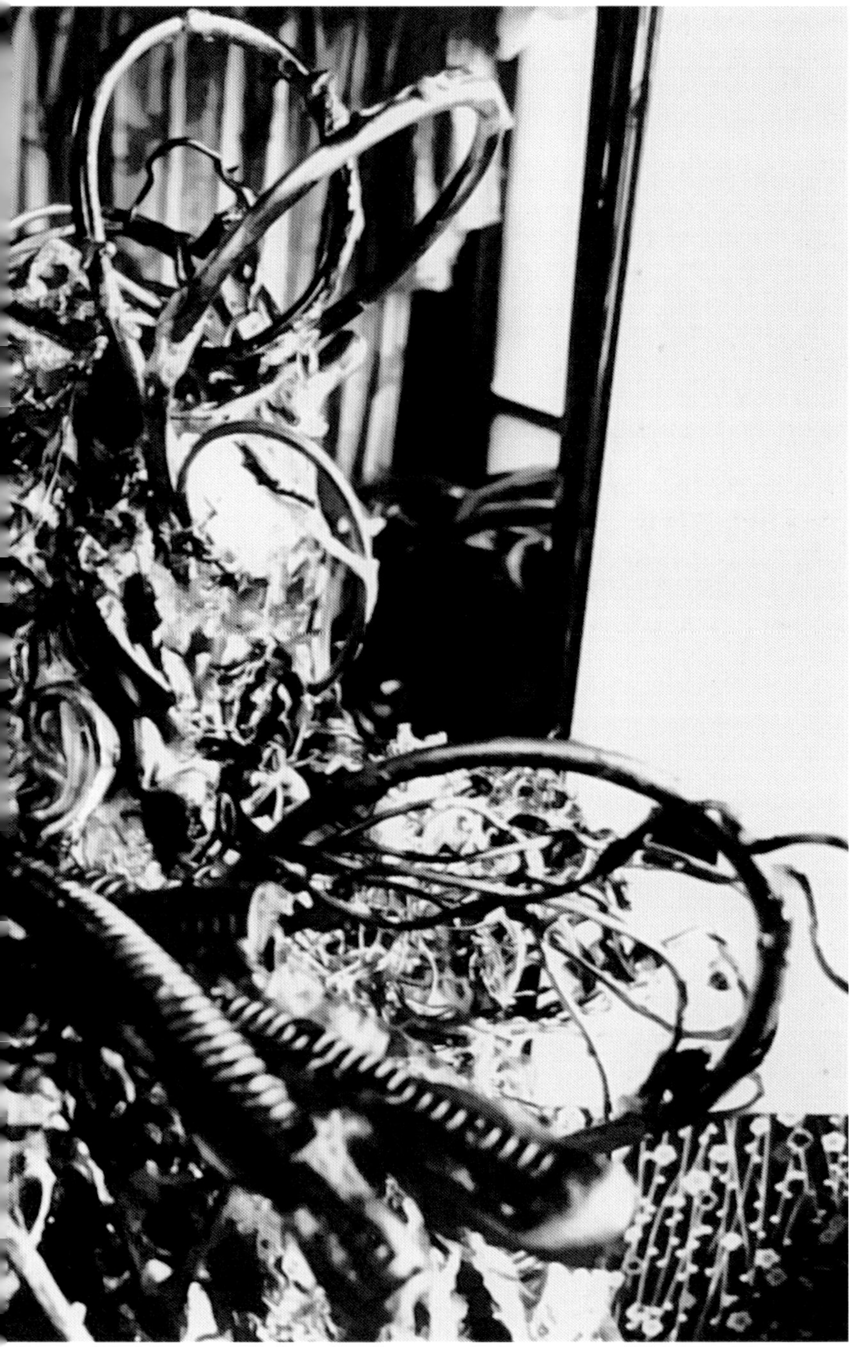

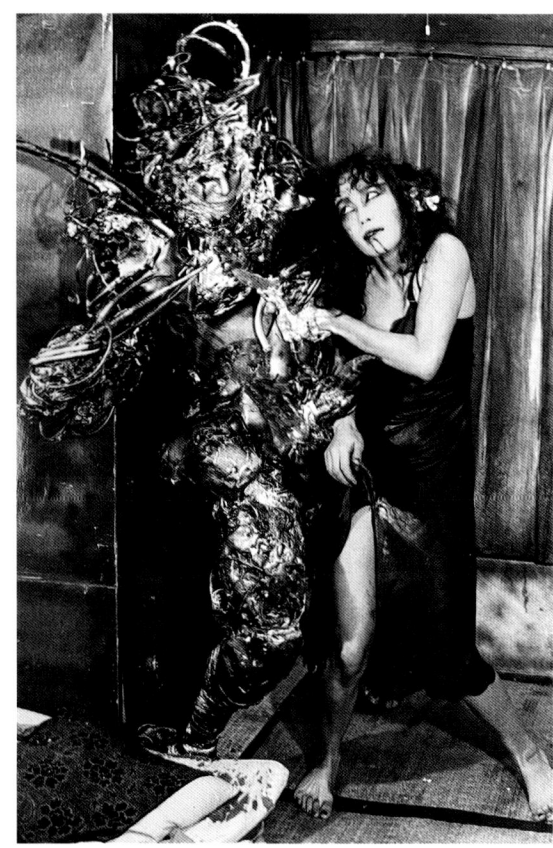

ABOVE: Taguchi (left) and Fujiwara on set

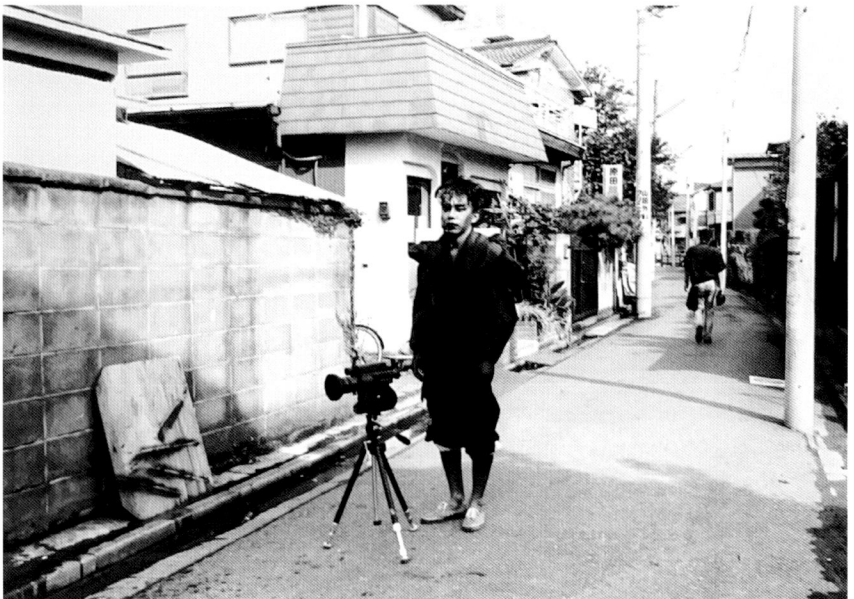

LEFT: Tsukamoto during production

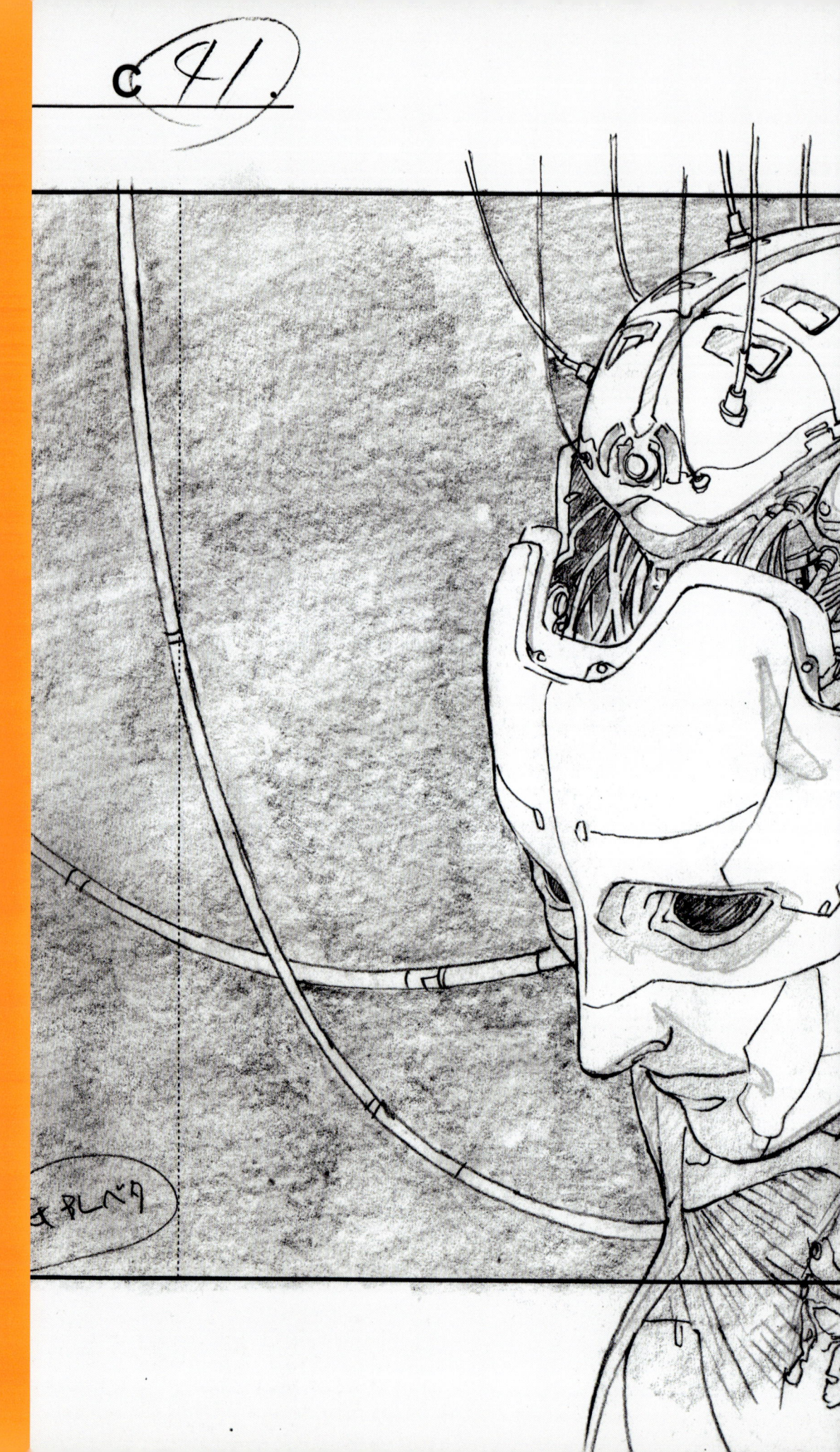

GHOST IN THE SHELL

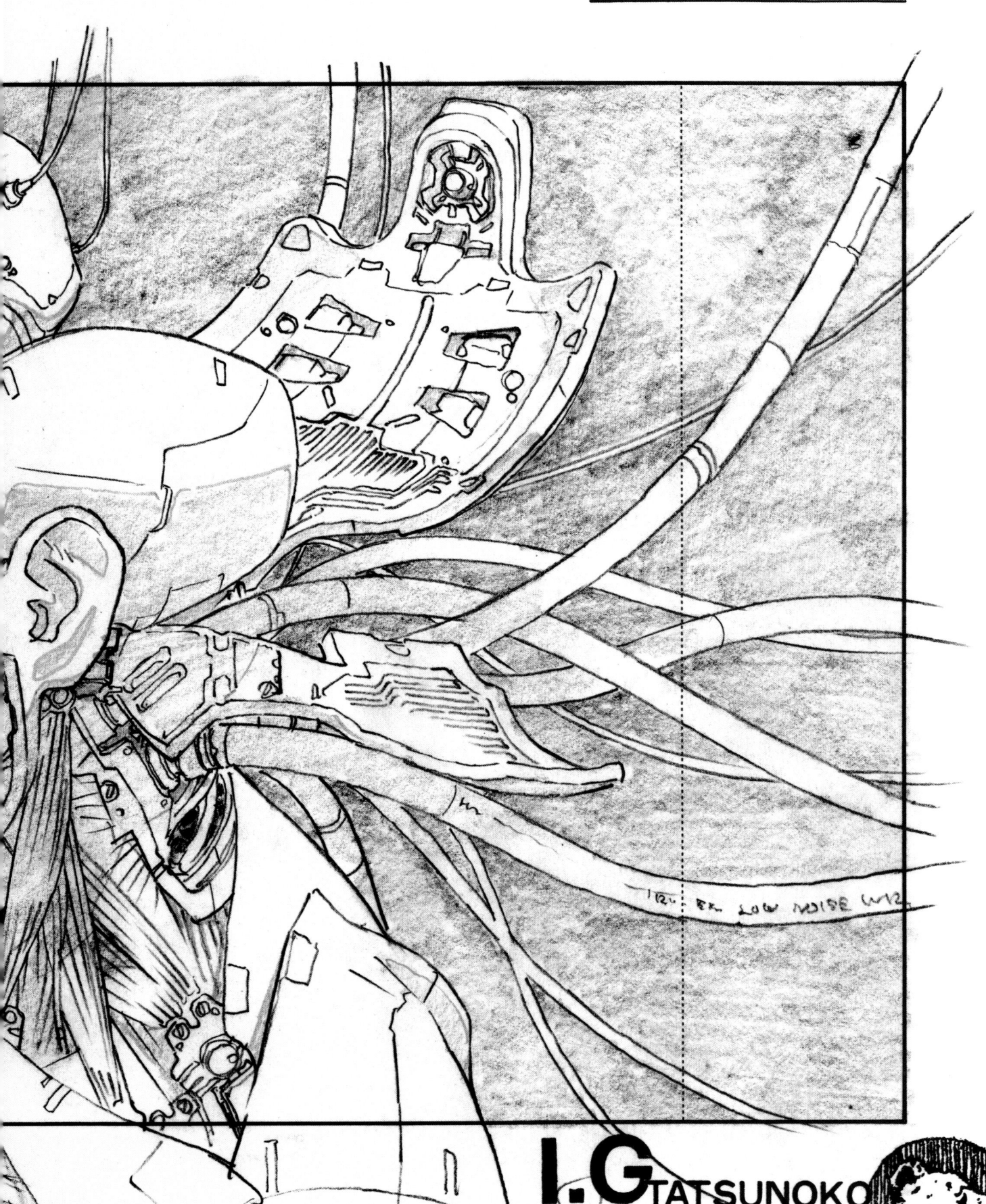

`Ghost in the Shell` (*Koukaku kidoutai*, Japan, 1995)
Director: Mamoru Oshii

Film synopsis:
In 2029 a human being's consciousness—its "ghost"—can be housed in a synthetic cybernetic body—a "shell"—and connected to internet networks. Major Motoko Kusanagi, a full-body prosthetic cyborg, is field commander of Public Security Section 9. As she investigates a mysterious ghost-hacker known as the Puppet Master, she must also confront the question of what it means to be human.

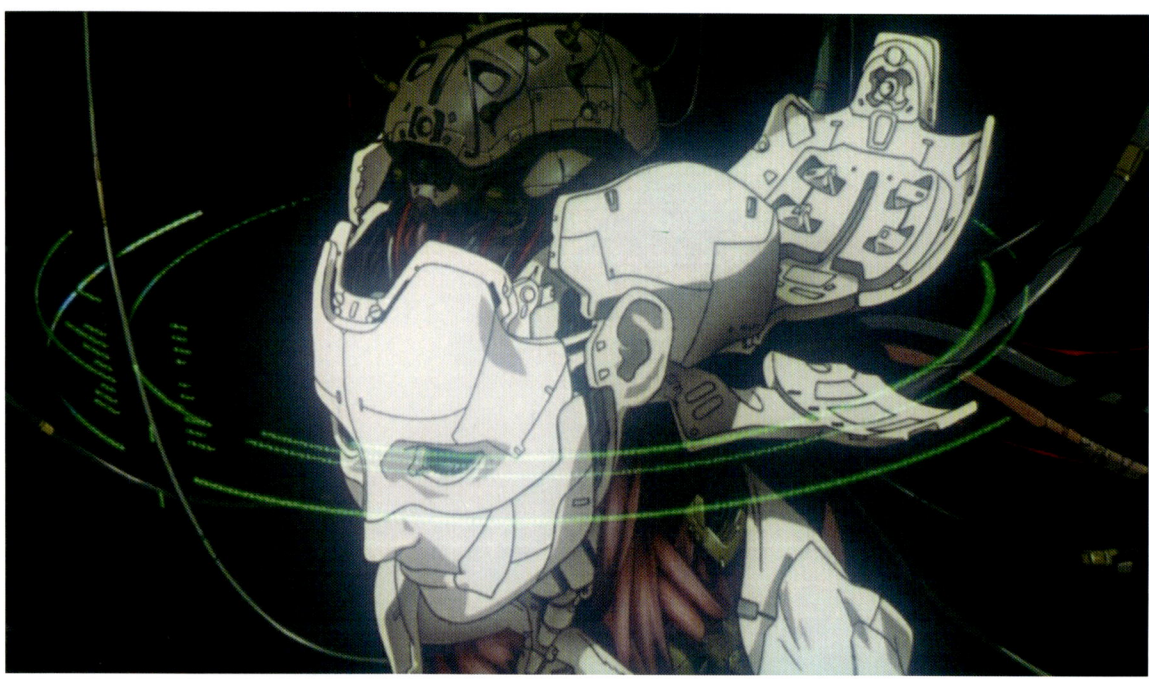

MAMORU OSHII's *Ghost in the Shell*, based on Shirow Masamune's 1989–90 manga of the same name (originally titled in Japanese *Koukaku kidoutai*, or "shell squad"), sutures the gritty landscapes and dystopic themes of cyberpunk with the smooth data streams of fantasy in Japanese anime. The film follows Public Security Section 9 agent Major Motoko Kusanagi as she pursues a hacker known as the Puppet Master, who has the ability to infiltrate the world's computer programs and networks at will. The networks are populated by cybernetic humanoids whose physical and psychic states are increasingly vulnerable to the Puppet Master's control. As human life is increasingly intertwined with computer networks, data, and information flows, the Puppet Master is able to transgress the boundaries that separate human from nonhuman existence.

Ghost in the Shell depicts a world rendered almost entirely in code, in which political power is amassed by relentless hacking and the theft of information. Minds and bodies are mere apparel in this world; it is code that animates and determines being. The cyborg-human hybrids are composed of organic and mechanical matter. Their bodies, referred to as "shells," are animated by computer programs that eventually become self-aware. Within each hybrid figure is a "ghost," some trace of consciousness or soul that remains irreducible to either organic or inorganic matter. Two forms of invisibility permeate the film: One is perceptual; the beings are able to vanish from the visual field. The other is existential; some, like the Puppet Master, are able to submerge their entire existence into a sea of code. *Ghost in the Shell* thus explores the fragility of minds and bodies as well as the precarious balance between them.

PREVIOUS SPREAD:
Storyboard of Major Motoko Kusanagi as cyborg

ABOVE: Major Motoko Kusanagi as cyborg

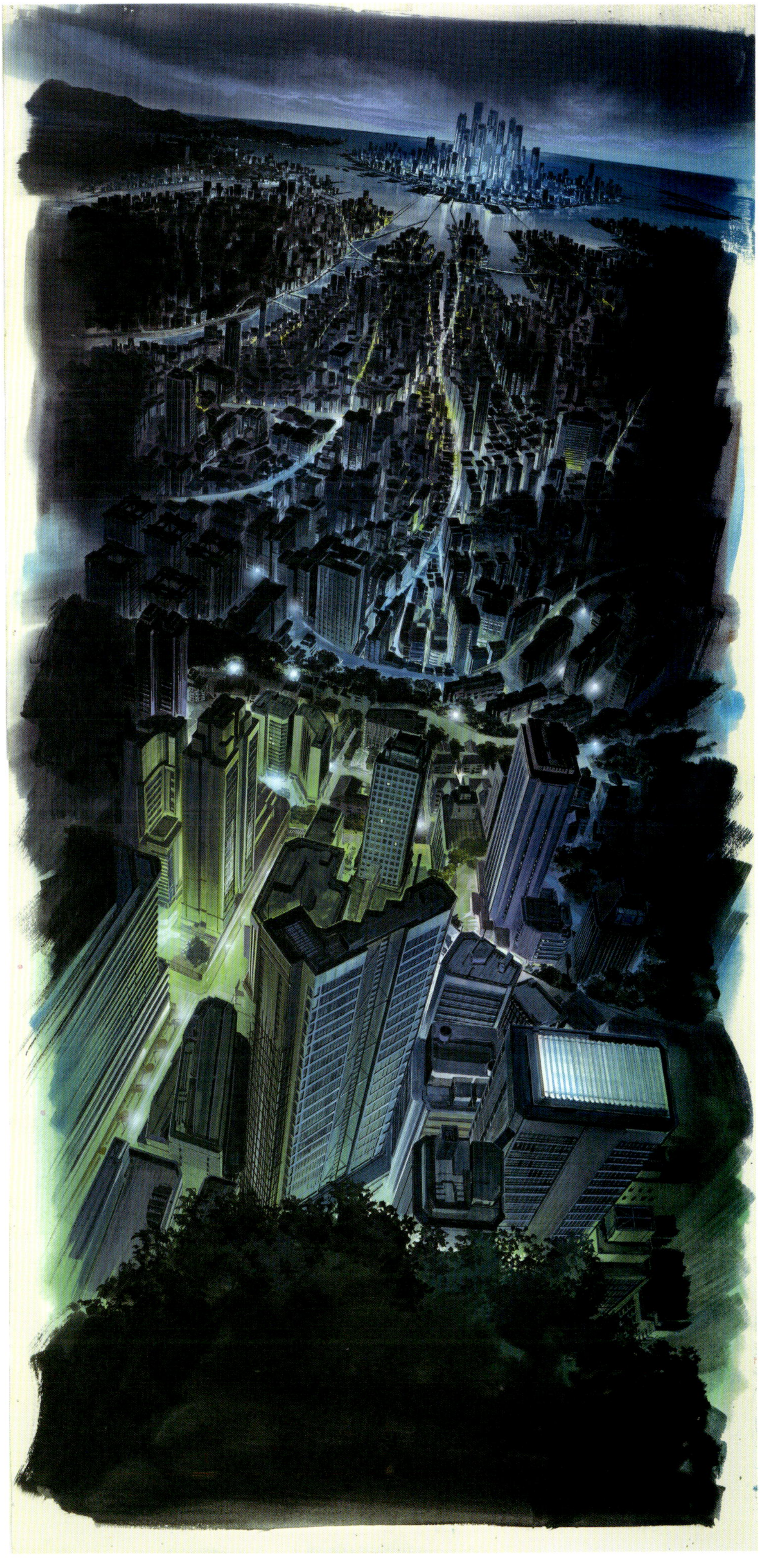

RIGHT: Niihama cityscape background

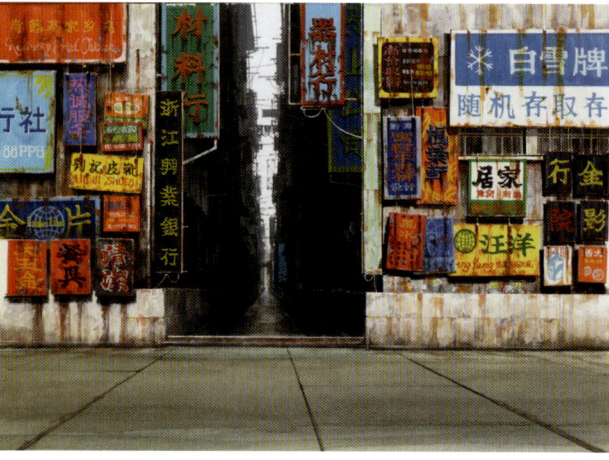

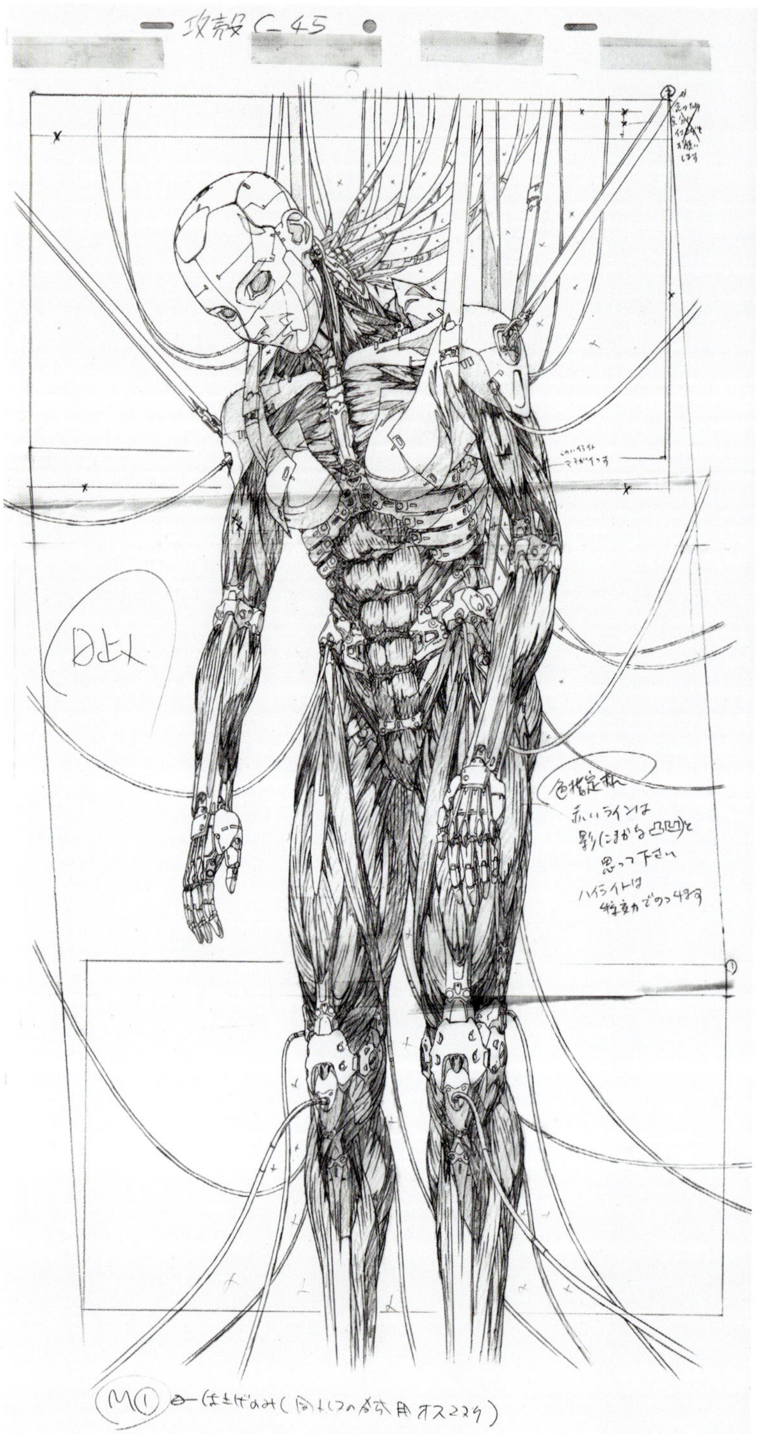

ABOVE: The alley background as seen in the film

RIGHT: Storyboard sequence of cyborg construction

As the plot moves toward its conclusion, Kusanagi tracks the Puppet Master to a broken shell. He had, in fact, been tracking *her* in an attempt to become fully human. The Puppet Master, who became self-aware while traveling the internet, has come to realize that the last remaining vestige of humanness still unavailable to him is the capacity to survive death through reproduction. His goal is to overcome this by merging with Kusanagi and leaving an extension of himself in the world. He proposes to her a merger of codes, a type of virtual intercourse that will produce between and beyond them an offspring, representing versions of themselves but in new, evolved iterations. The film ends when Kusanagi, retaining her identity but nonetheless transformed, reenters the world as a new species: a hybridized being capable of human consciousness and endowed with the capacity to reproduce newer versions of herself.

—*Akira Mizuta Lippit*

RIGHT: Limited edition Mondo poster

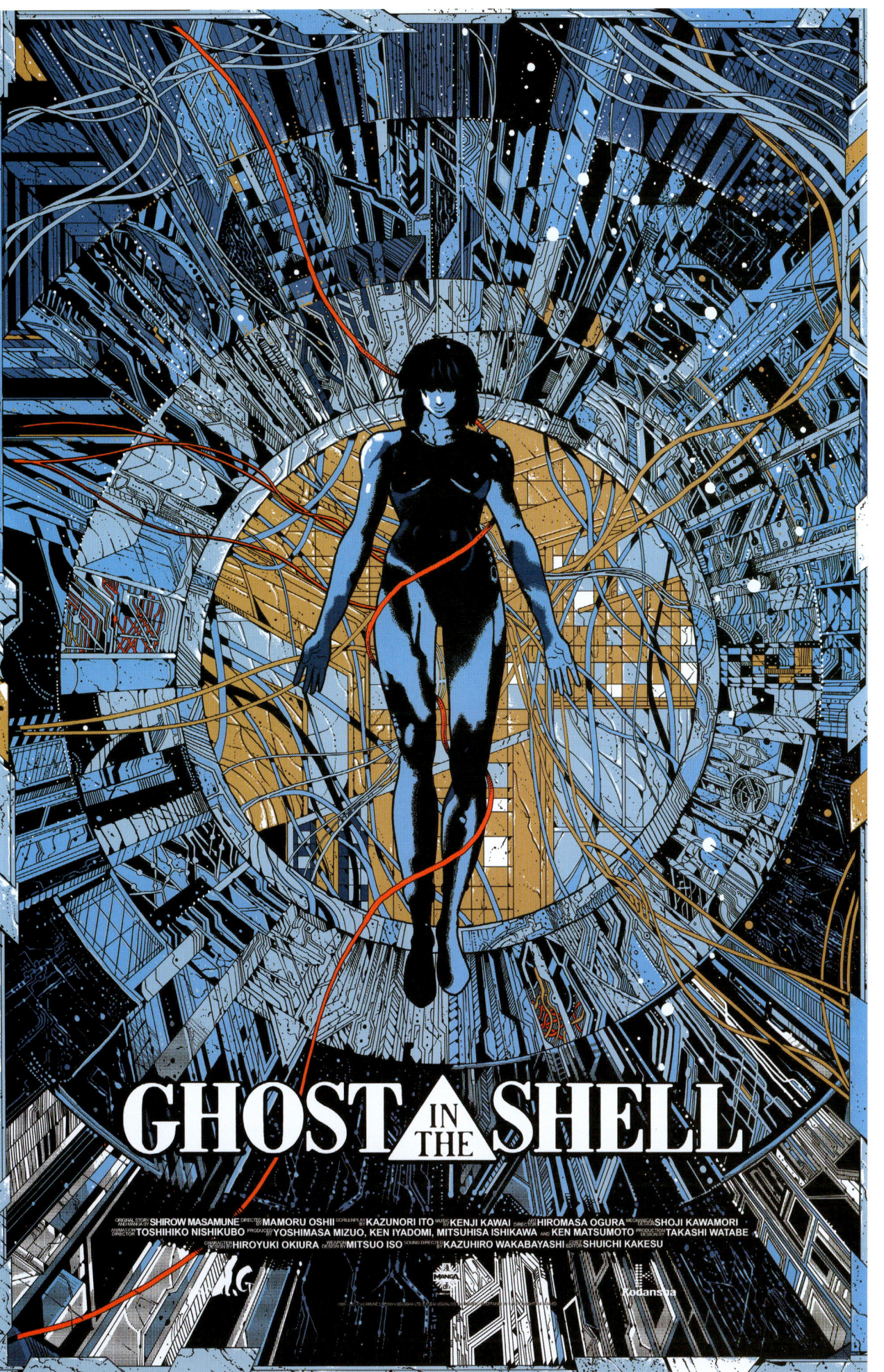

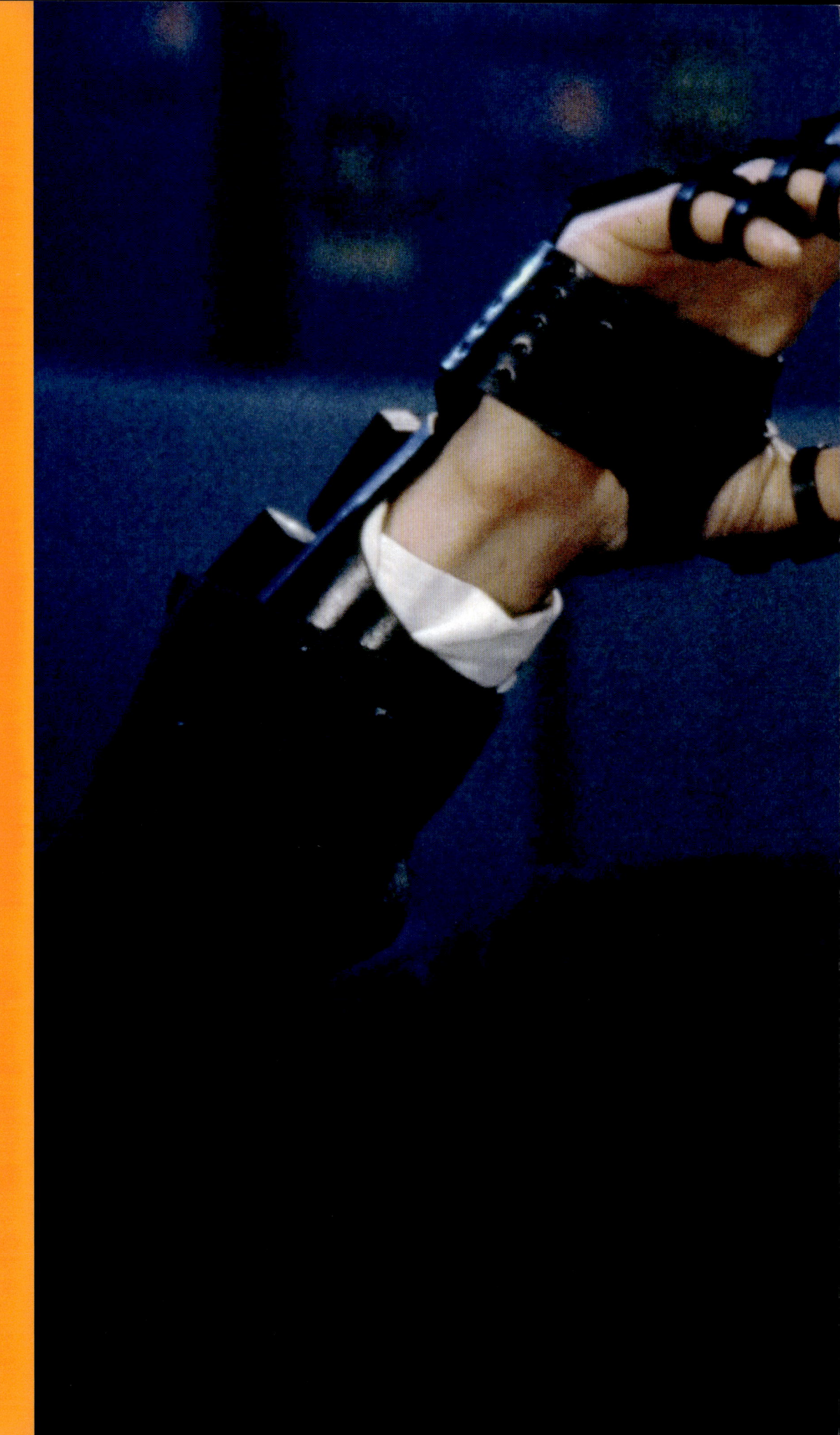

JOHNNY MNEMONIC

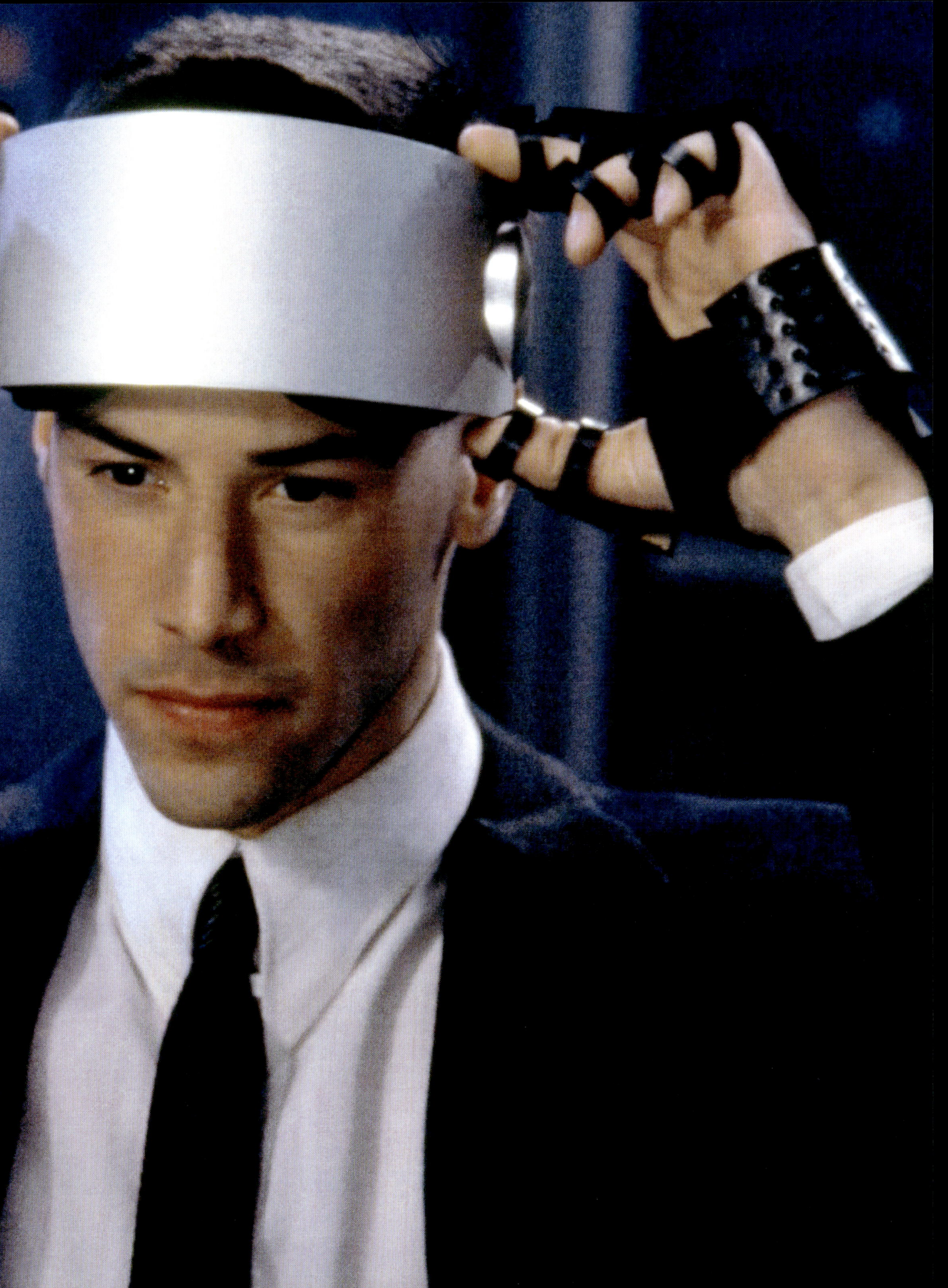

Johnny Mnemonic (USA, 1995)
Director: Robert Longo

Film synopsis:
In a hyperconnected world, Johnny works as a "mnemonic" courier, securely transferring data through an implant in his brain. When he takes one last—and particularly sensitive—job, he must escape corporate-hired assassins as he races to complete his delivery before the massive data load kills him.

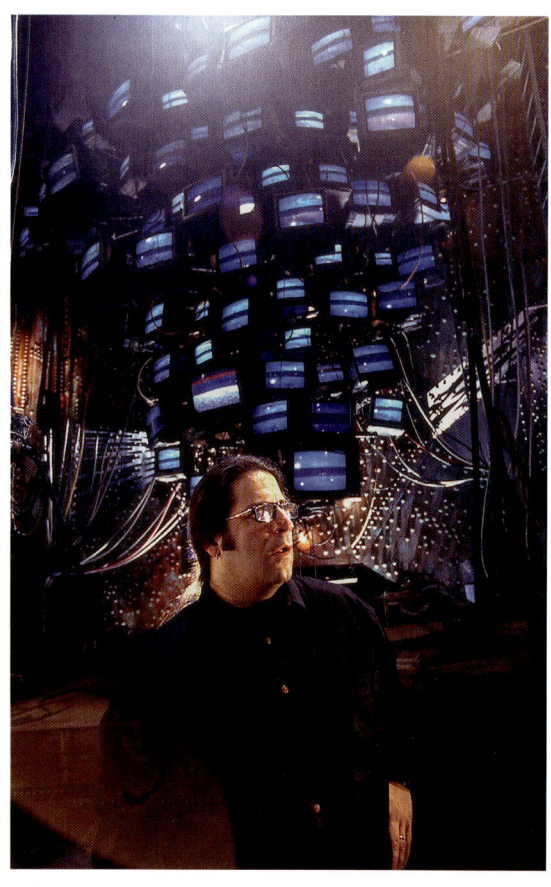

ABOVE: Director Robert Longo on set

ROBERT LONGO's *Johnny Mnemonic* was the first film adapted from a work written by cyberpunk pioneer William Gibson. Gibson's 1981 short story of the same name incorporates many of the visual and thematic hallmarks of the quintessential American cyberpunk fiction of the 1980s and '90s, including an all-powerful megacorporation, an information society, cyber-enhancement, virtual reality, artificial intelligence, references to Japanese culture, criminal antiheroes, punk-inspired fashion, and a grim, neon-lit urban sprawl.

The film is set in a dystopian future where megacorporations control a chaotic, technologically advanced society that is afflicted by the tech-induced plague Nerve Attenuation Syndrome (NAS). Megacorporations, a common feature of cyberpunk, serve as cautionary symbols of unchecked capitalism, absolute control of information, and the inequitable distribution of technological developments. In *Johnny Mnemonic* the megacorporation Pharmakom is preventing the release of a cure for NAS in order to keep profiting off treating the disease.

The film's protagonist, Johnny (Keanu Reeves), is a prototypical cyberpunk character as derived from the classic film noir antihero—a solitary, morally ambiguous low-level criminal who operates on the fringes of society. While transporting sensitive data that has been implanted in his brain, Johnny encounters an underground resistance group, the Lo-Teks, made up of hackers, pirate broadcasters, and other marginalized individuals who are in opposition to the corporations. The Lo-Teks reside in the "sprawl," a dark, industrial, neon-lit urban landscape.

OPPOSITE AND PREVIOUS SPREAD: Keanu Reeves as Johnny Mnemonic

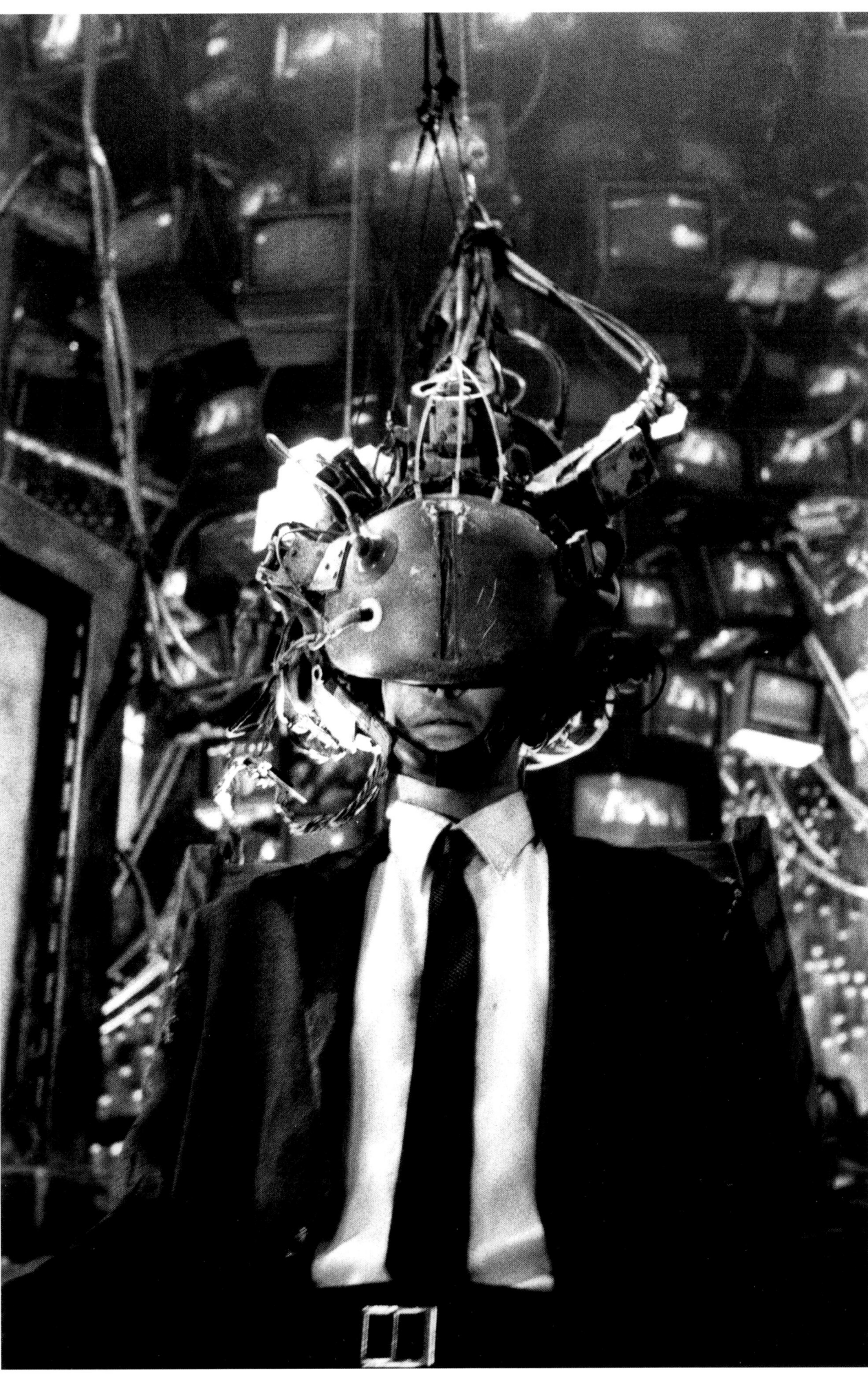

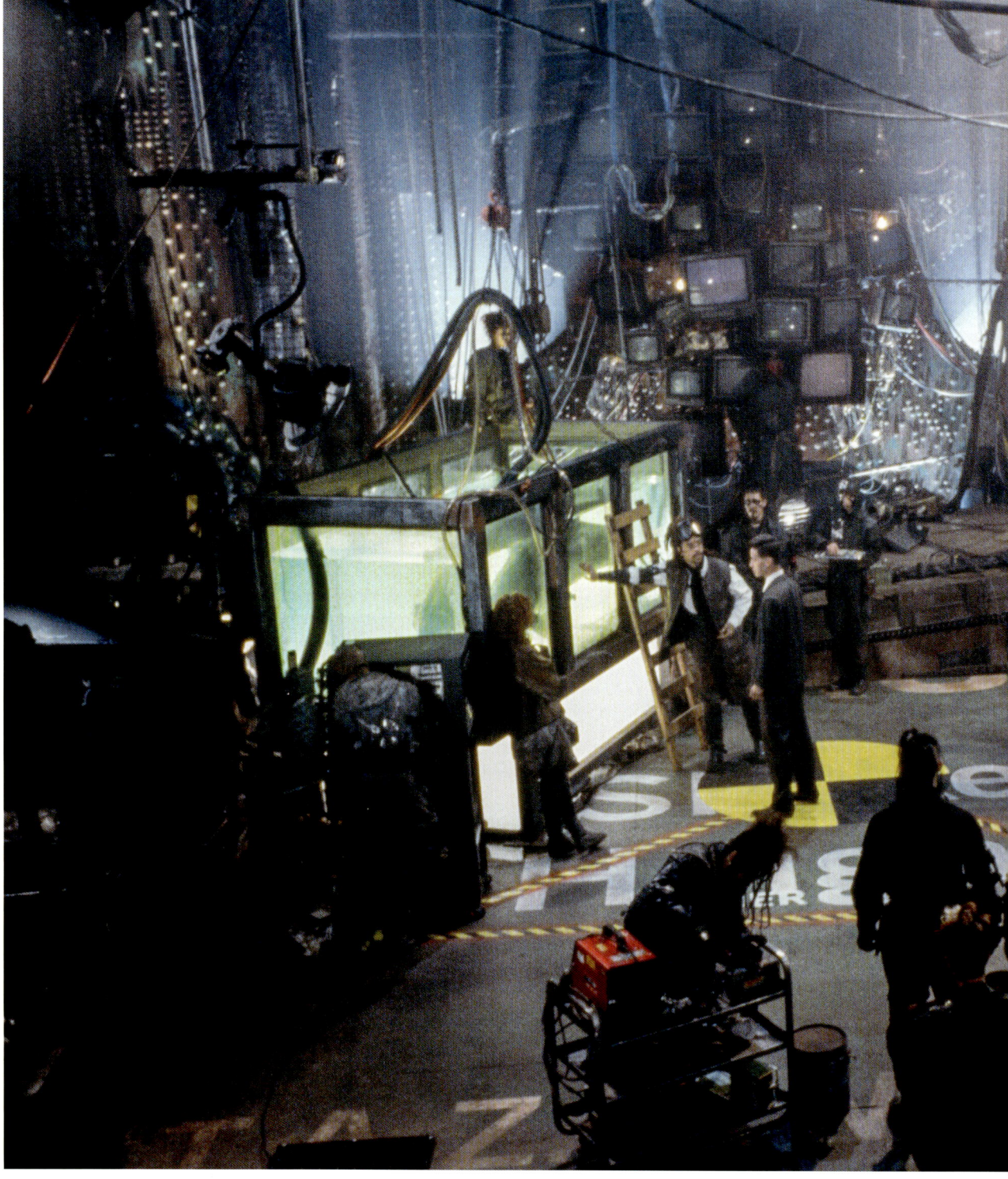

Several characters in *Johnny Mnemonic* are cyborgs, including Johnny, the neurologically enhanced bodyguard Jane (Dina Meyer), and a cybernetically augmented dolphin named Jones. In cyberpunk works, cyborgs often serve as vehicles for exploring the impact of technology on society, transhumanism, and individual agency.[1] While technological enhancements provide these characters with certain benefits, there are also costs. Johnny's neural implants, for example, allow him to serve as a "mnemonic courier," but the implants required the removal of his childhood memories and thus a partial loss of self.

In the world of *Johnny Mnemonic*, data has become a valuable commodity, and knowledge grants power by allowing those who possess it to gain influence, wealth, and the ability to manipulate society.[2] The film takes to heart technological provocateur Stewart Brand's famous, albeit slightly misquoted, declaration in 1984 that "information wants to be free."[3] Various stakeholders struggle for control over the important

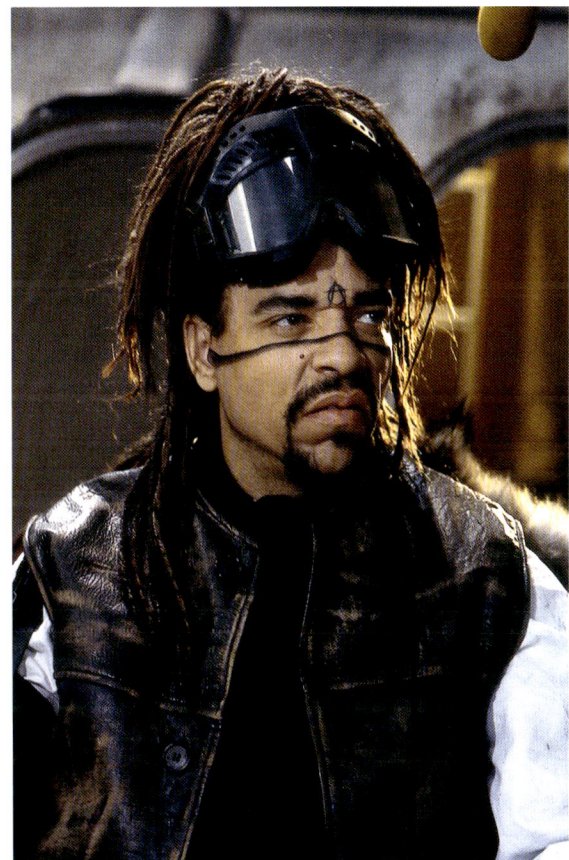

ABOVE: Ice-T as J-Bone

LEFT: Cast and crew on "Heaven" Lo-Tek resistance base set

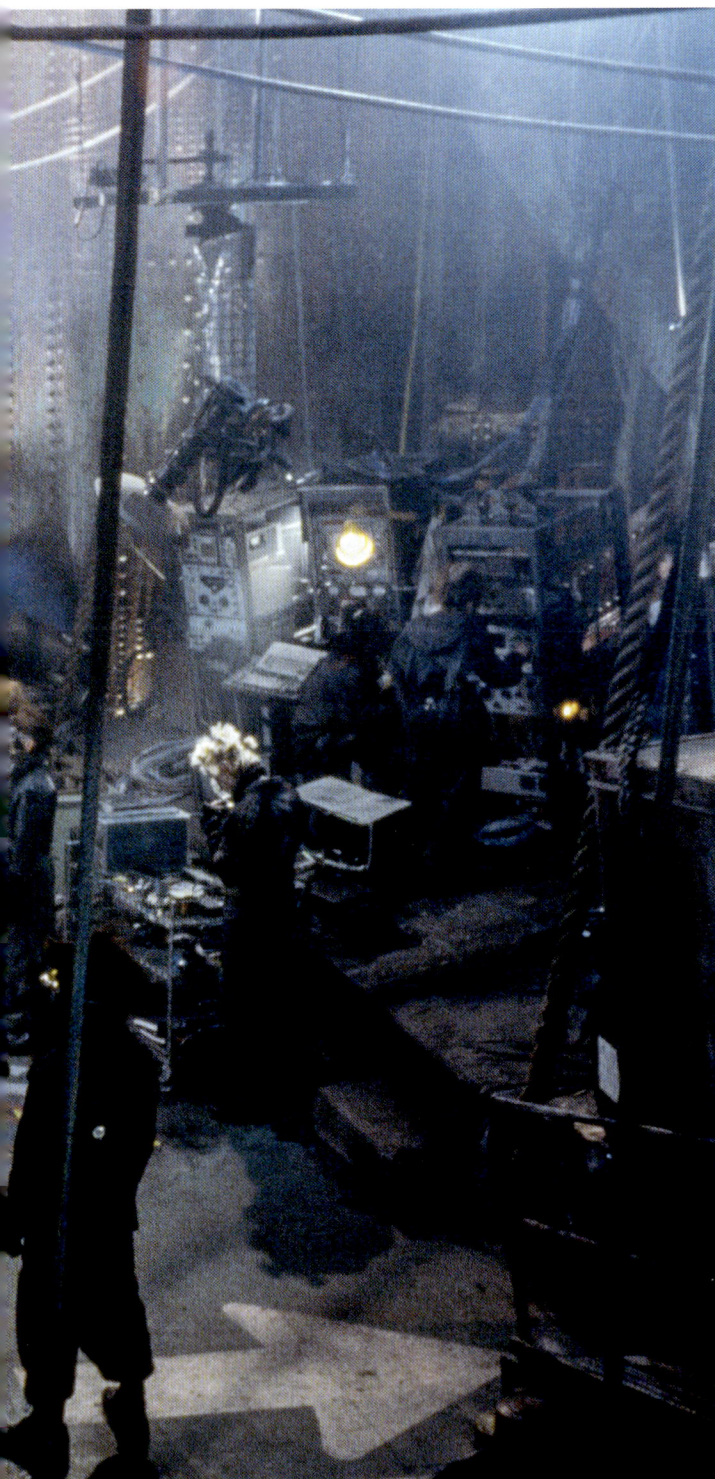

data Johnny harbors in his brain: Pharmakom wants to keep the information secret to protect its profits, while the Lo-Teks want to make the data public so that everyone can benefit. Ultimately the film depicts the negative consequences of living in a world where information is a highly coveted resource, highlighting how dangerous it can be when knowledge that could impact millions of lives is controlled by a privileged few—much as it is today.

—David A. Kirby

NOTES

1./ Bert Olivier, "The Transition to a Bio-Engineered World: *Johnny Mnemonic* and *Westworld*," *South African Journal of Art History* 33, no. 3 (2018): 88–110.

2./ The concept of the information society is closely intertwined with the cyberpunk genre. See Rob Latham, "Literary Precursors," in *The Routledge Companion to Cyberpunk Culture*, ed. Anna McFarlane, Graham J. Murphy, and Lars Schmeink (New York: Routledge, 2020), 7–14.

3./ Brand reportedly used an iteration of this phrase at the first Hackers Conference, which took place in Marin County, California, and which he co-organized. For more on Brand's use of this phrase, see Eran Fisher, "When Information Wanted to Be Free: Discursive Bifurcation of Information and the Origins of Web 2.0," *The Information Society* 34, no. 1 (2017): 40–48.

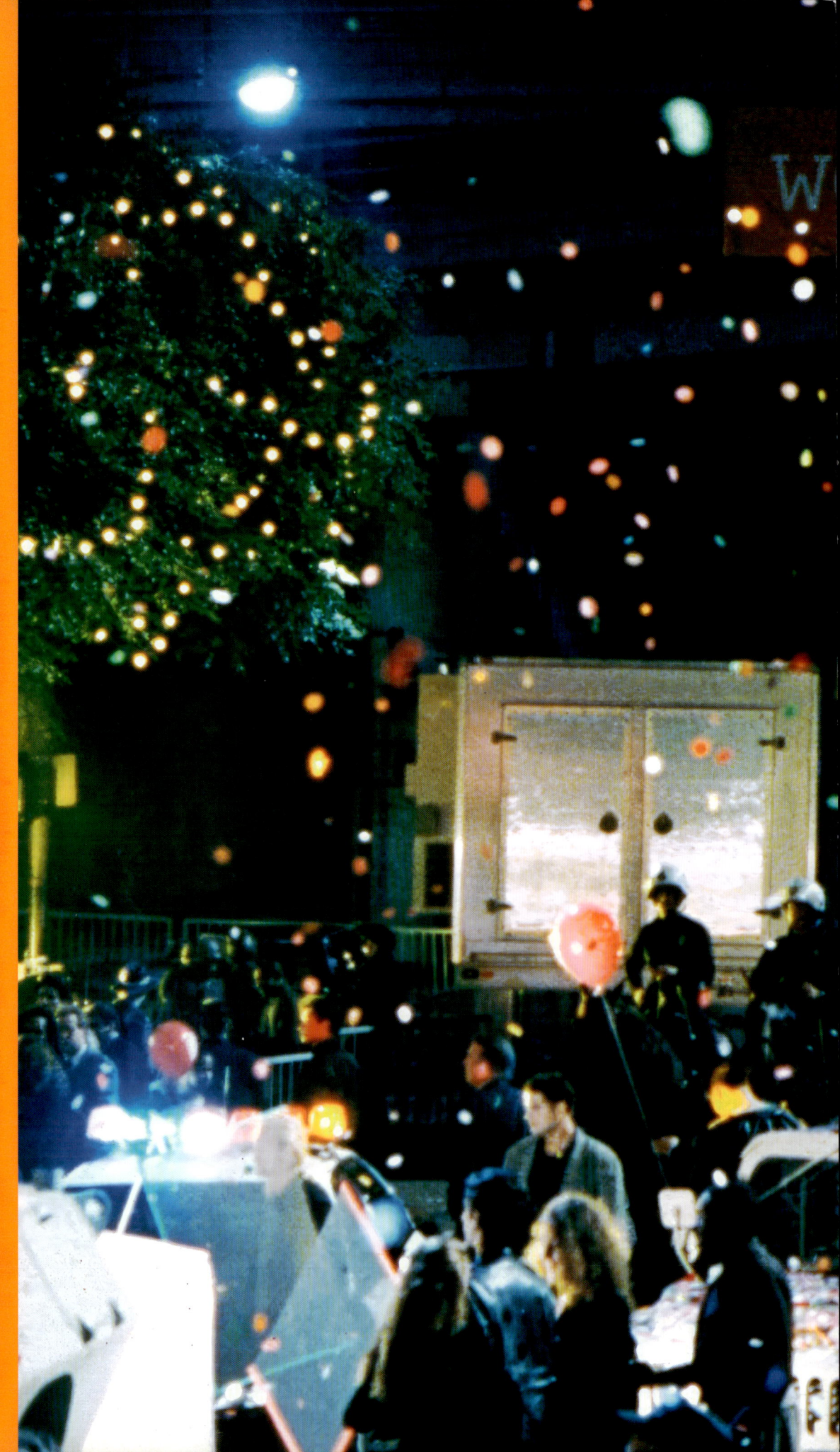

STRANGE DAYS

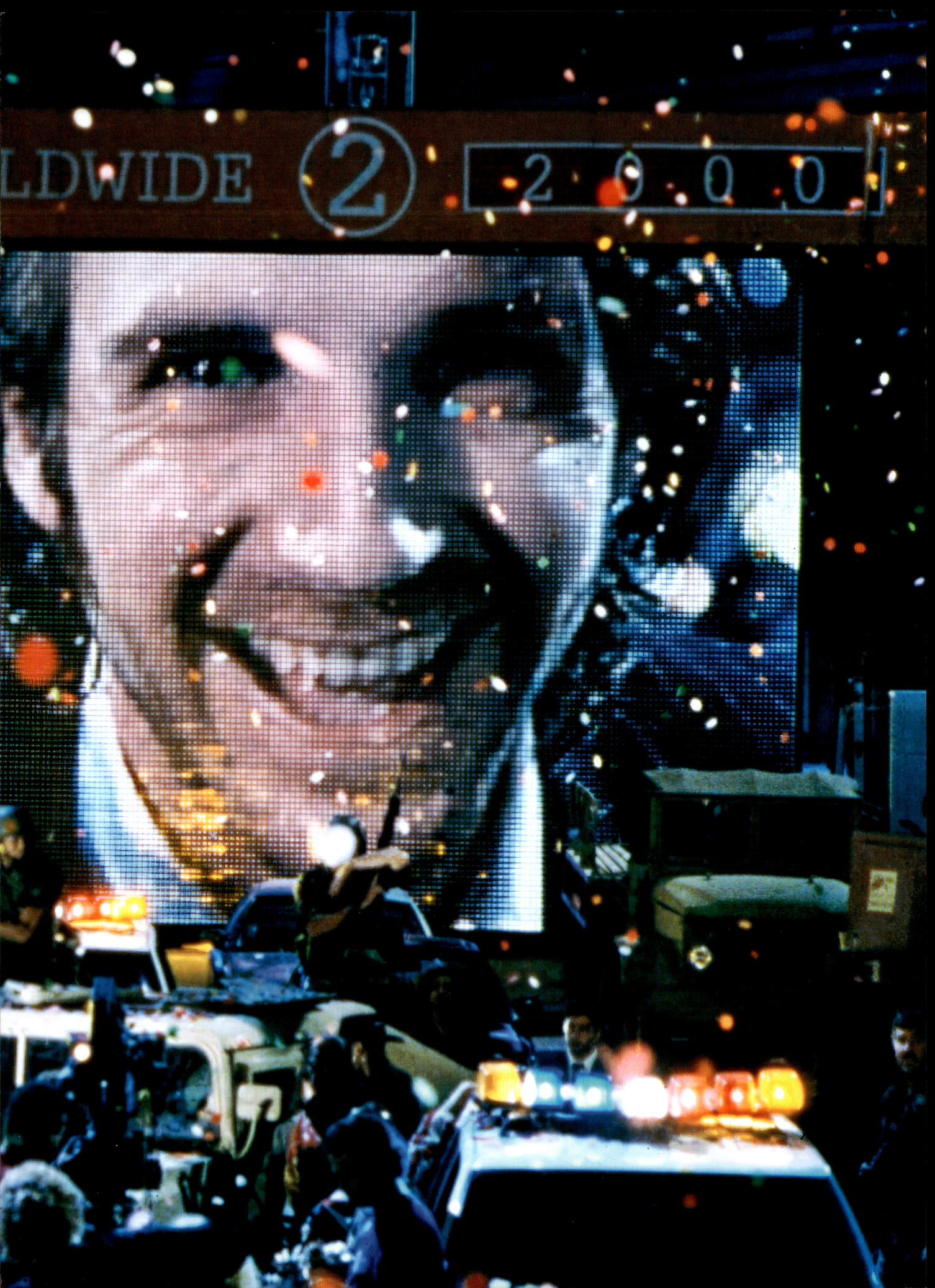

Strange Days (USA, 1995)
Director: Kathryn Bigelow

Film synopsis:
Set in a tumultuous Los Angeles at the turn of the twenty-first century, former cop Lenny Nero deals in black-market discs that record memories and experiences, allowing users to relive scenes from other people's lives as well as their own. When he stumbles upon a dangerous police cover-up, Lenny falls into the center of a conspiracy that, if revealed, could ignite a tinderbox of social disorder.

Set in the last two days of 1999, Kathryn Bigelow's cybernoir *Strange Days* depicts a new century it seemed impossible to yet imagine. Time is in hyperdrive on the streets. The present and future collapse into each other. Devices known as SQUIDs (superconducting quantum interference devices), technology pirated from the military, capture sensations straight from people's cerebral cortexes and allow others to experience them. The devices digitally enhance how the brain itself sees (and senses) the present. In *Strange Days*, the city government has collapsed and the police are wildly corrupt and militarized, with only one honest captain left standing. Lenny Nero (Ralph Fiennes), a morally challenged contraband dealer, sells and collects SQUID discs. Most are just pornography; one, however, captures an assassination by the Los Angeles Police Department.

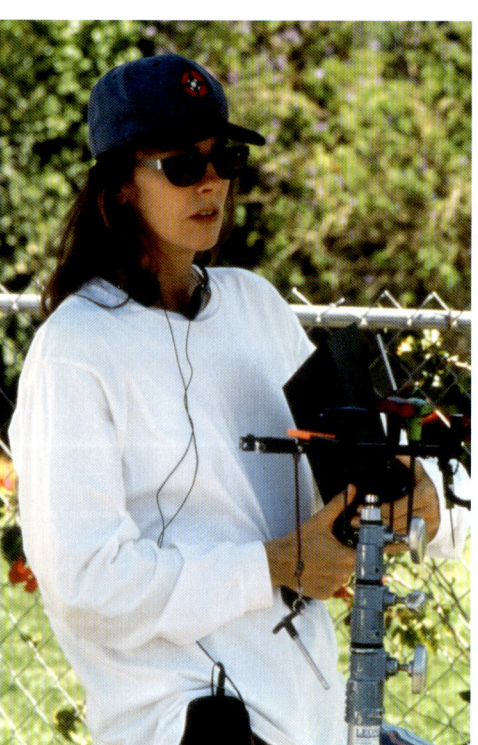

The SQUID recordings in *Strange Days* were filmed in an innovative way. To capture what the brain itself sees, a small camera was designed to let video and digital cinema bleed into each other. That crossover embodies a feeling that runs throughout the film—a constant sense of being between worlds. In 1995, when *Strange Days* was released, LA was indeed wavering after the uprising of 1992, the deadly fires of 1993, the Northridge earthquake of 1994. It seemed as if every year delivered yet another disaster. I was just completing a book on the history of forgetting and erasure in LA.[1] I wrote about the film as an interpretation of the 1991 Rodney King beating and the uprising that followed. Movies were collapsing the events in LA into doomsday visions of the city. But today, other prescient ironies in *Strange Days* have found a new resonance.

News about the 1992 uprising ("the Insurrection") had lent itself to fake editing and false information ("memory"). But the year 1995 did yet not presume the AI octopus gathering video clues across the internet—the surveillance analytics that have today become standard, warping memory and facts. LA in the cyberpunk 1990s was economically shell-shocked, most notably by a 50 percent drop in aerospace jobs. Today, that trauma has been replaced by vast income from the ports, and the nation-state has been replaced by archipelagos of power, isolated entertainment zones—silos more than a united territory.

LEFT: Director Kathryn Bigelow during production

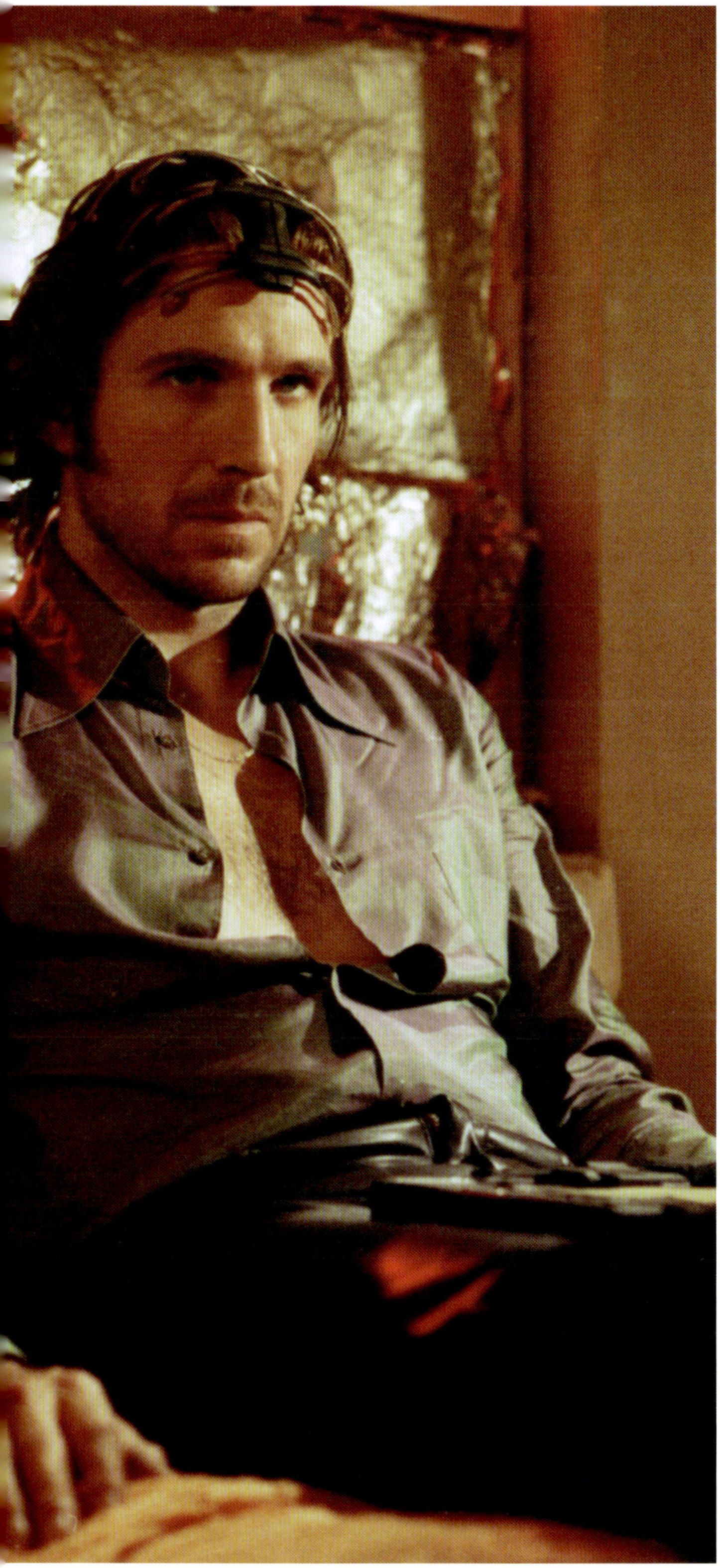

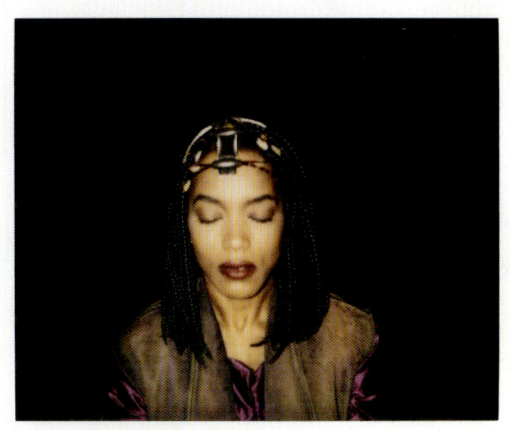

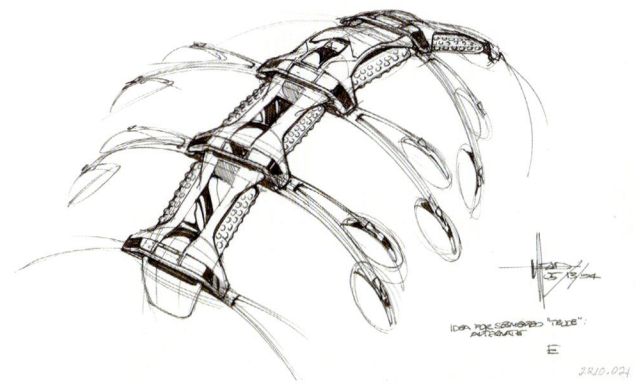

PREVIOUS SPREAD: New Year's Eve celebration scene with Ralph Fiennes as Lenny Nero

LEFT: Fiennes as Lenny Nero

ABOVE TOP: Angela Bassett as Mace Mason, wardrobe reference Polaroid

ABOVE BOTTOM: Concept drawing of SQUID device

Now the 2024 SQUIDs—sensate AI beings—are here. We are between worlds again. In the wake of the COVID-19 pandemic, the events of January 6, 2021, and recently escalated conflicts, new ruptures have been triggered across the globe. I wonder what a sequel to *Strange Days* would look like. Collective memories are so much more unreliable today. Misremembered facts, like derivative bonds and blockchains, are now essential to banking, tax havens, national politics. Distorted memory drives and is driven by the internet. SQUIDs have now gone utterly mainstream. The millennium just took an extra twenty-four years to get started.

—*Norman M. Klein*

NOTES

1./ Norman M. Klein, *The History of Forgetting: Los Angeles and the Erasure of Memory* (London: Verso, 1997).

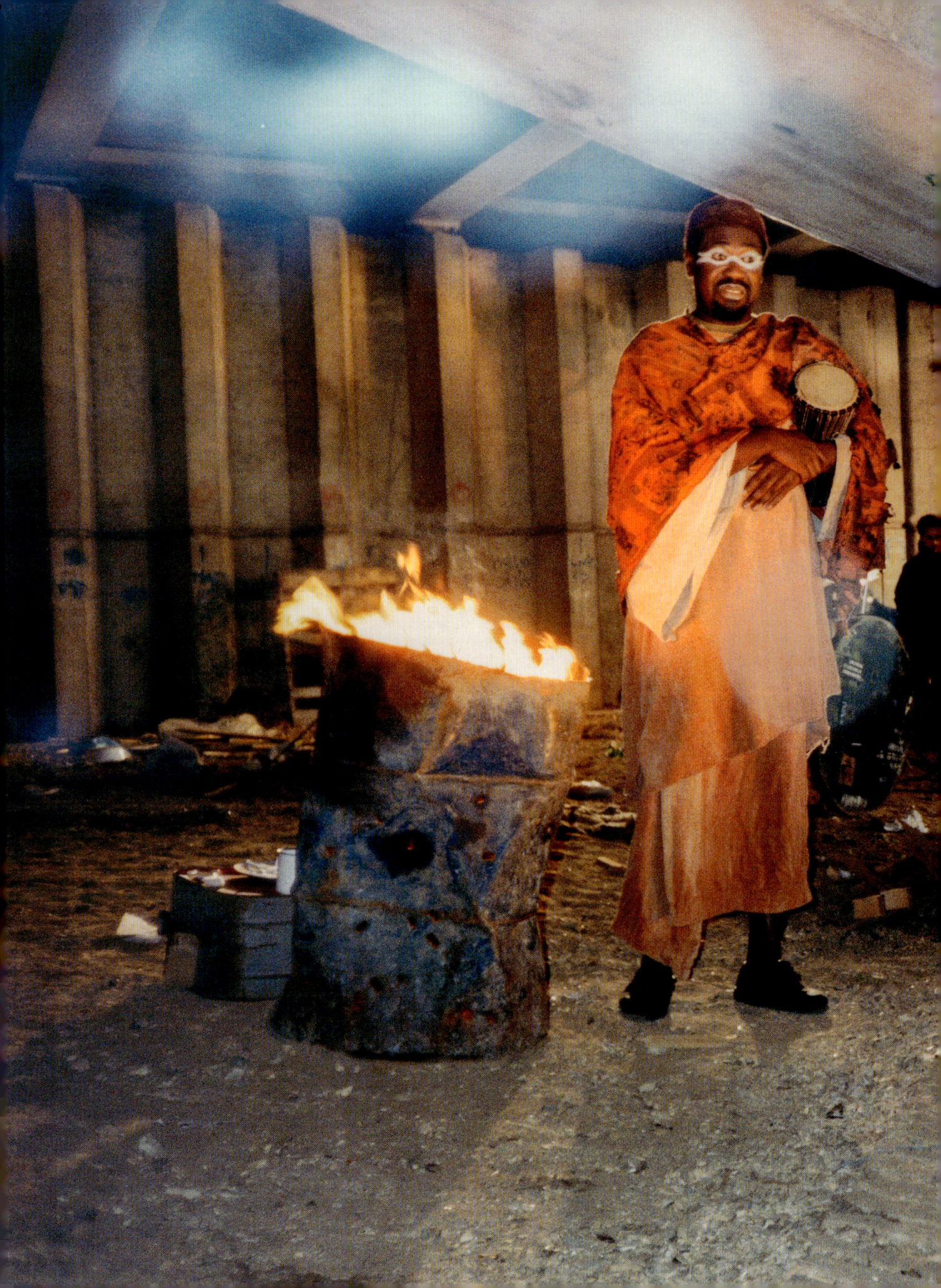

WELCOME II THE TERRORDOME

```
Welcome II the Terrordome (UK, 1995)
Director: Ngozi Onwurah
```

```
Film synopsis:
In a future ghetto riddled with drugs and ruled by
gangs, a grieving mother's anger ignites a violent
uprising. Featuring a hip-hop score that functions
as a Greek chorus, this uncompromising film addresses
the legacy of slavery and ongoing terror of police
and state violence.
```

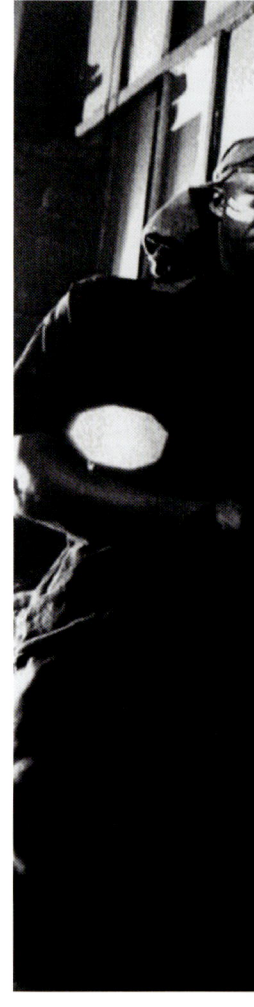

> "Black people live the estrangement that science fiction writers imagine."
> —Greg Tate

With her 1995 feature debut *Welcome II the Terrordome*, Ngozi Onwurah became the first Black British female director to have a film released theatrically in the UK. Named after a blistering 1990 track by Public Enemy, the film, also written by Onwurah, is a shocking and singular work that stands out not just for its vividly disturbing content but also for its uniqueness in the predominantly white and male landscapes of both cyberpunk and British cinema.

Onwurah, who was born in Nigeria to a Nigerian father and a white British mother, drew upon her heritage for *Terrordome*'s opening sequence, a haunting interpretation of the 1803 Igbo Landing incident, when a group of captured Igbo people aboard a ship off the coast of Georgia are said to have drowned themselves to avoid becoming enslaved. In an audacious narrative flourish, Onwurah leaps ahead to a queasy near-future scenario in which the drowned folk's souls are trapped inside the bodies of the members of a benighted Black community striving for survival in Transdean, also known as the Terrordome. The Terrordome is a drug-riddled, police-surveilled ghetto, described by one character as "a dirty, rancid, stinking shithole ... the end of the line." Working in the wake of traumatic events like the 1991 Los Angeles Police Department beating of Rodney King and the racist murders of British teenagers Rolan Adams and Stephen Lawrence in 1991 and 1993, respectively, Onwurah, cinematographer Alwin H. Küchler, and the rest of the creative team dreamed up an assaultive audiovisual purgatory. The film's visceral blend of blaring rap music and cramped, cluttered production design draws from myriad transatlantic cultural and cinematic reference points to present an oppressive vision of racism's physical and psychological effects.

"I call this my 'angry film,'" Onwurah said in 2020. "Debates around race are meant to be measured and always have an entry point for white people. ... I made it because I wasn't in the mood for tempered debate."[1] I appreciated this absence of equivocation when I first saw *Welcome II the Terrordome* in January 2015, on my laptop during a flight from New York to London. This was my first trip back to my birthplace since moving to the United States on July 10, 2014. A week after my move, Eric Garner was choked to death by a police officer on Staten Island. Three weeks later, teenager Michael Brown was also killed by a cop and left to decay in the Missouri sun. It felt like open season on Black life in America.

In one of the many scathing, uncomprehending reviews of the film upon its release, *Sight & Sound*'s Paul Gilroy wrote that "it would truly be a tragedy if *Terrordome* finds an audience so immiserated, disenchanted and powerless that it can be satisfied and excited by the film's dismal, hopeless vision."[2] I would not say I was excited, precisely, by the film, but its pitiless articulation of pure rage felt cathartic and validating exactly when I needed it. In a world still riven by anti-Black racism and haunted by the ghosts of so many more senselessly slain Black people—Breonna Taylor, George Floyd, and Jordan Neely among them—Onwurah's film continues to be appropriately vital and troubling.

—Ashley Clark

NOTES
Epigraph: Quoted in Mark Dery, "Black to the Future: Interviews with Samuel R. Delany, Greg Tate, and Tricia Rose," in *Flame Wars: The Discourse of Cyberculture* (Durham, NC: Duke University Press, 1994).
1./ Ellen E. Jones, "Has *Terrordome*'s Time Come? How a Black British Film Found Its Moment," *Guardian*, July 23, 2020, https://www.theguardian.com/film/2020/jul/23/has-terrordomes-time-come-how-a-black-british-film-found-its-moment.
2./ Paul Gilroy, "Unwelcome," *Sight & Sound* 5, no. 2 (February 1995): 18–19.

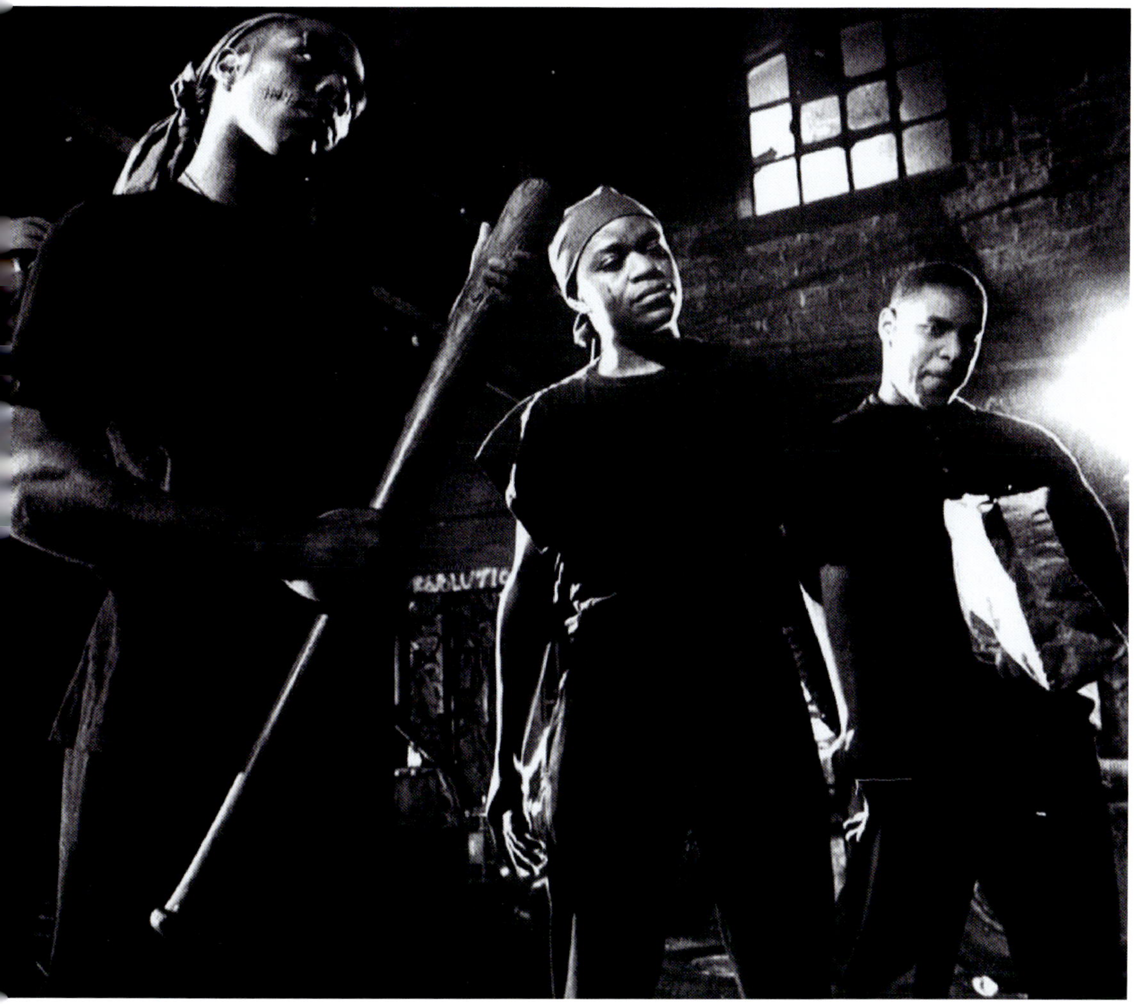

PREVIOUS SPREAD: Actor John Adewole on set

LEFT: From right: Felix Joseph, Valentine Nonyela, Tim Pothing, and unidentified actors as Blue Gang members

BELOW LEFT: Suzette Llewellyn as Anjela McBride

BELOW RIGHT: Actor Saffron Burrows on set

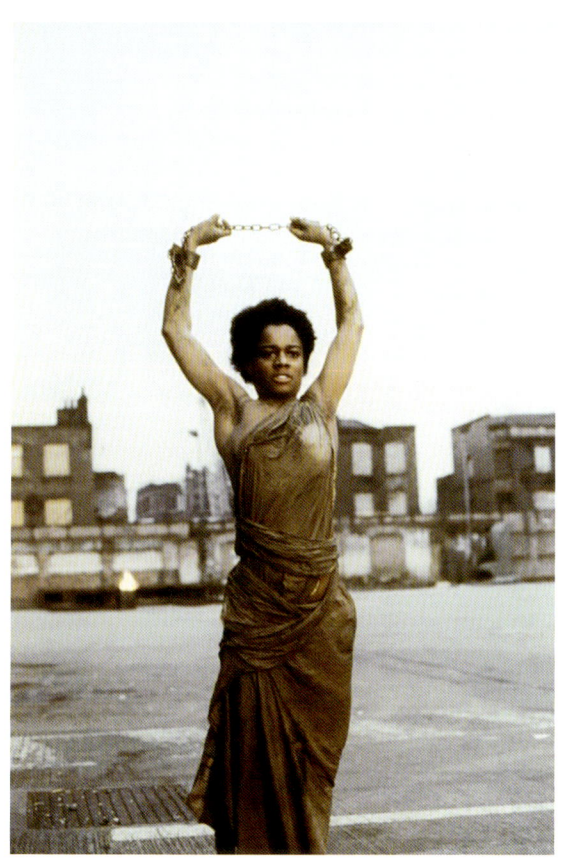

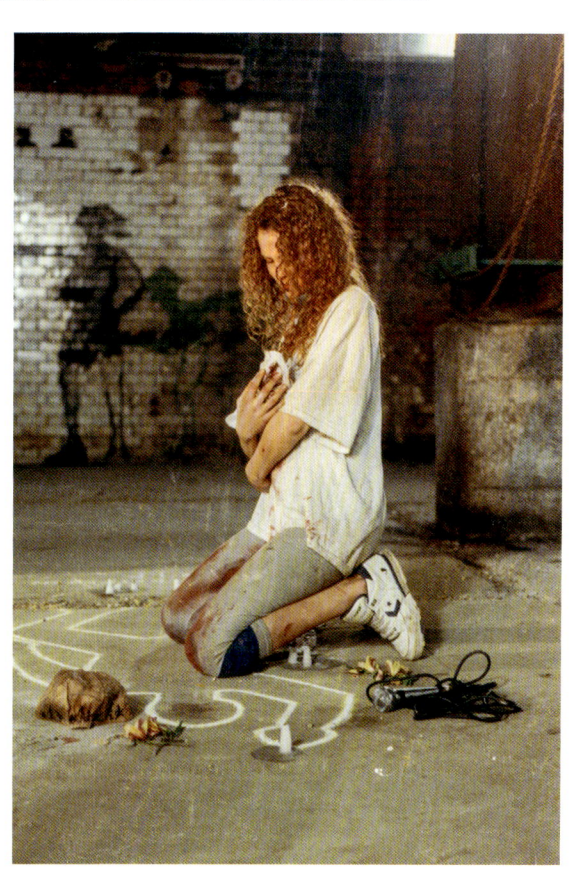

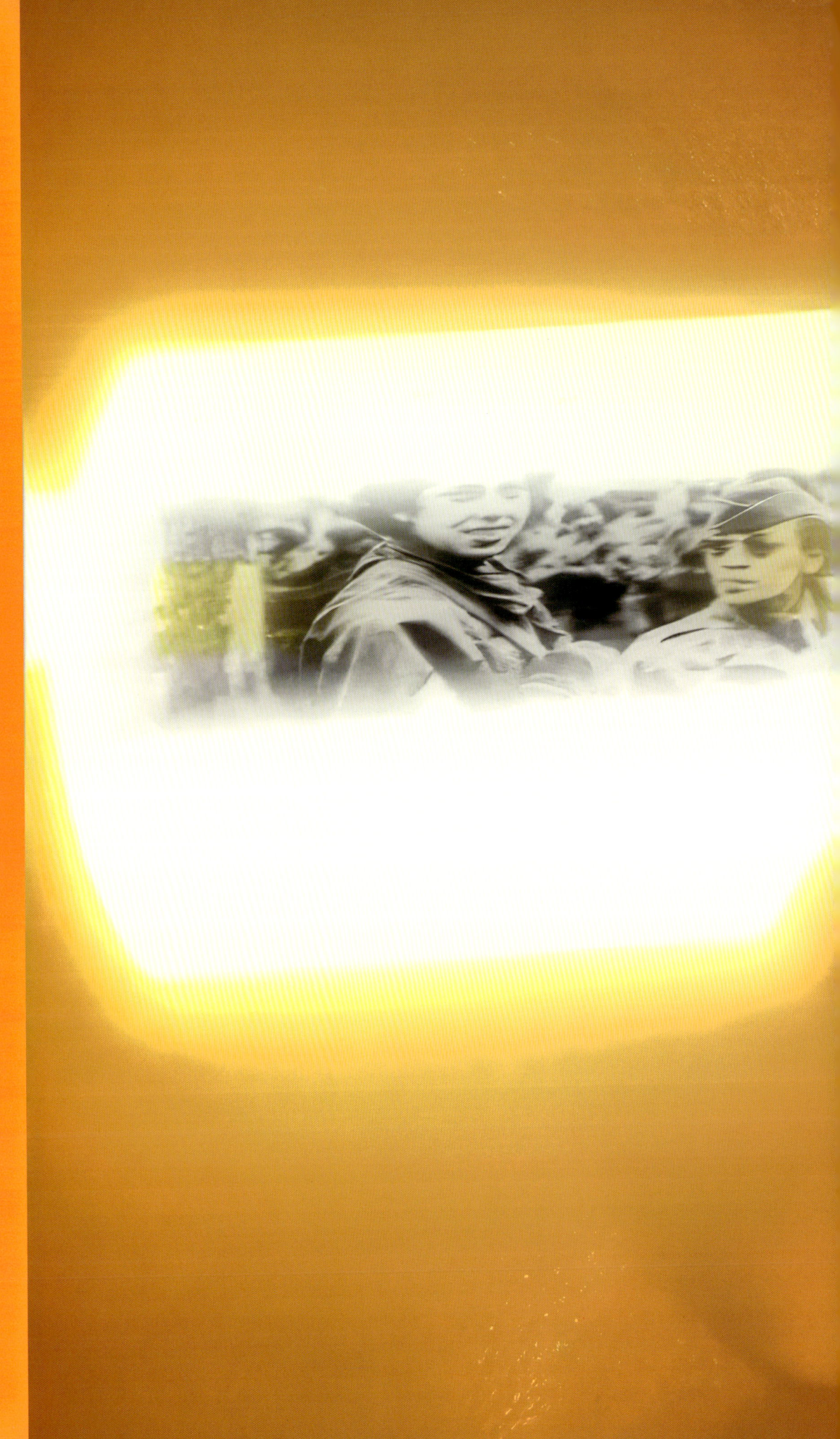

THE LAST ANGEL OF HISTORY

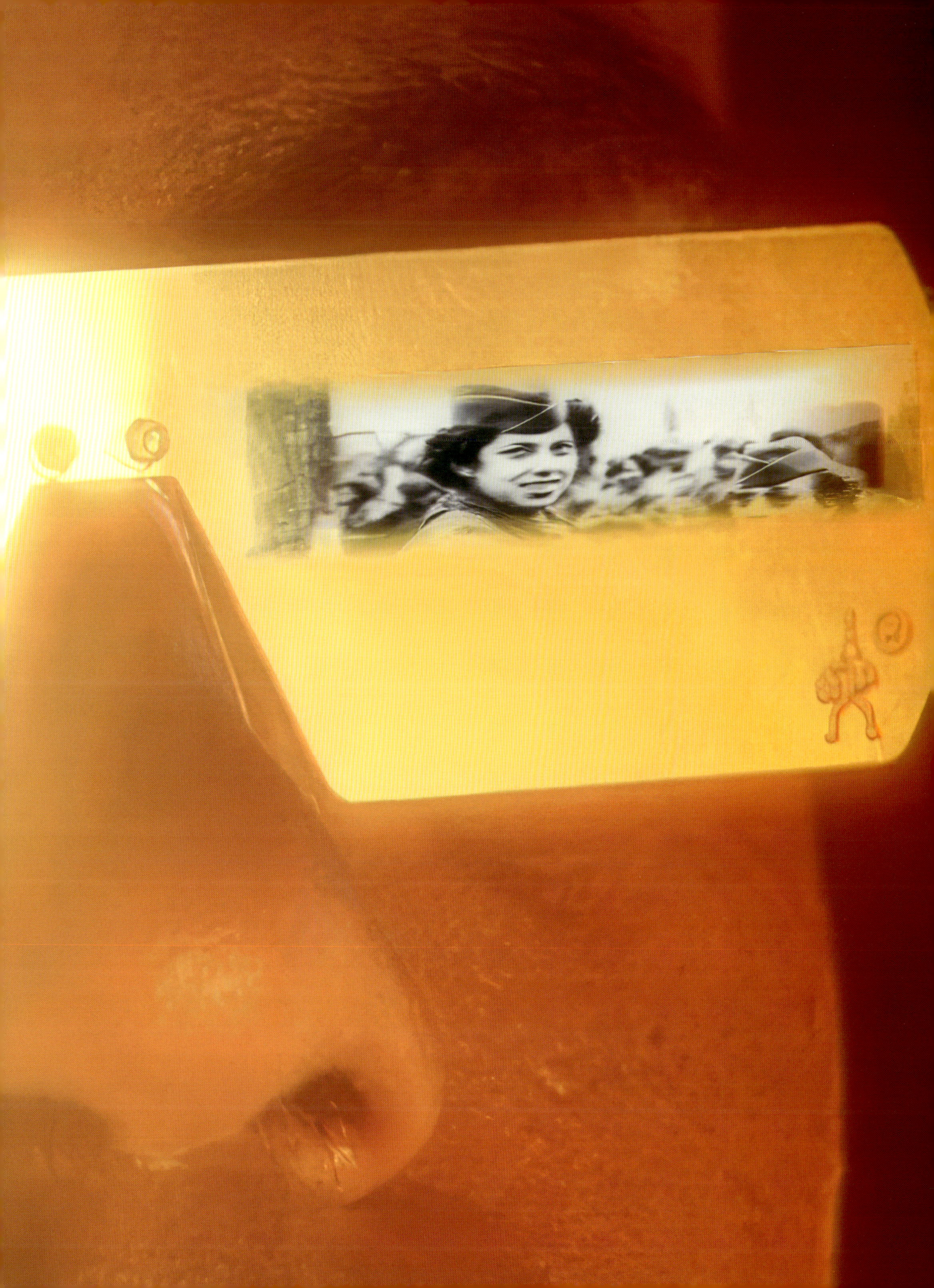

The Last Angel of History (UK, 1996)
Director: John Akomfrah

Film synopsis:
A data thief travels across time and space in search of Afrofuturist technologies. This experimental hybrid documentary and narrative short film features interviews with writers, scientists, musicians, and artists mixed with archival and original footage in a metaphorical investigation of the African Diaspora and Black culture.

T*HE LAST ANGEL OF HISTORY* materialized at the end of the twentieth century as a culmination of research and theoretical speculations put forth by the British visual artist and director John Akomfrah alongside Edward George, cofounder of the Black Audio Film Collective. The film uses the tropes of both science fiction and the essay film to map the transatlantic relationship between technology and the African diaspora, from a British perspective. The Data Thief, the film's philosophical narrator, played by George, begins the story by presenting a quandary about the beginnings of modern Black music and culture. This question takes him back in time to the late 1800s in the American Deep South, where he wonders about the origins of the blues via the myth of Robert Johnson, a bluesman from the 1930s who, it is said, sold his soul to the devil in exchange for extraordinary musical talent. In truth, Johnson was one of many Black American musicians who created folk music to express the moment of transition between the inhuman slave economy and the industrialized labor force that would emerge in the next century.

Working his way through the timeline of Black counterculture to cyberculture, the Data Thief uncovers many clues and connections within the abstract data collection system of Blackness. Both inside and outside of the film, George decodes patterns from clusters of informative noise, and documents fragments of scenes of Black prophetic figures throughout modern history. He considers artifacts such as Lee "Scratch" Perry's the Black Ark studio space and Sun Ra's Arkestra ensemble to be early iterations of the Black Atlantic sound, which crossed frequencies in both writing and film to ascertain their uses for escape from the profound trauma of the Maafa,

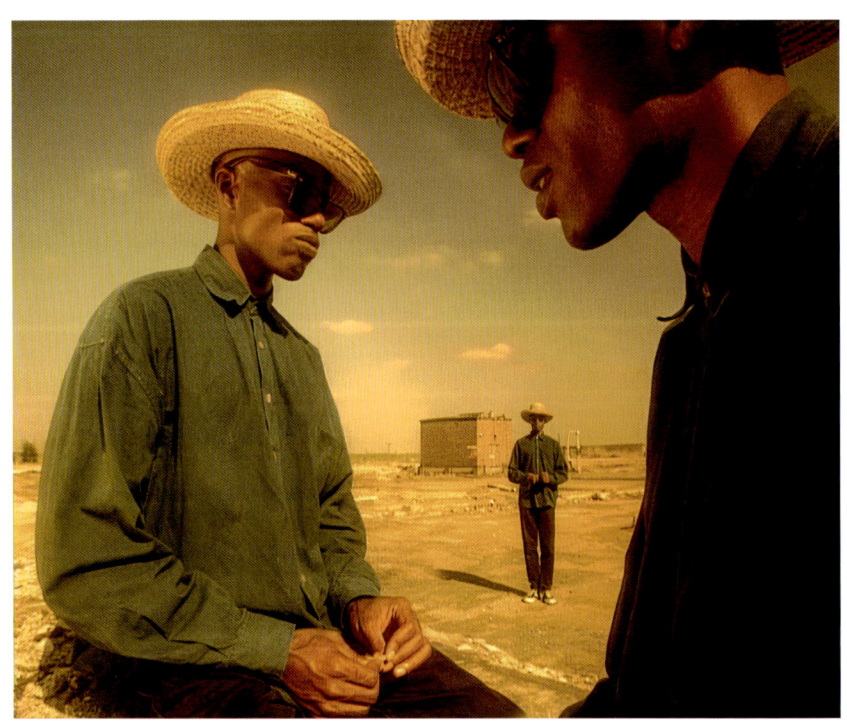

ABOVE AND PREVIOUS SPREAD: Edward George as the Data Thief

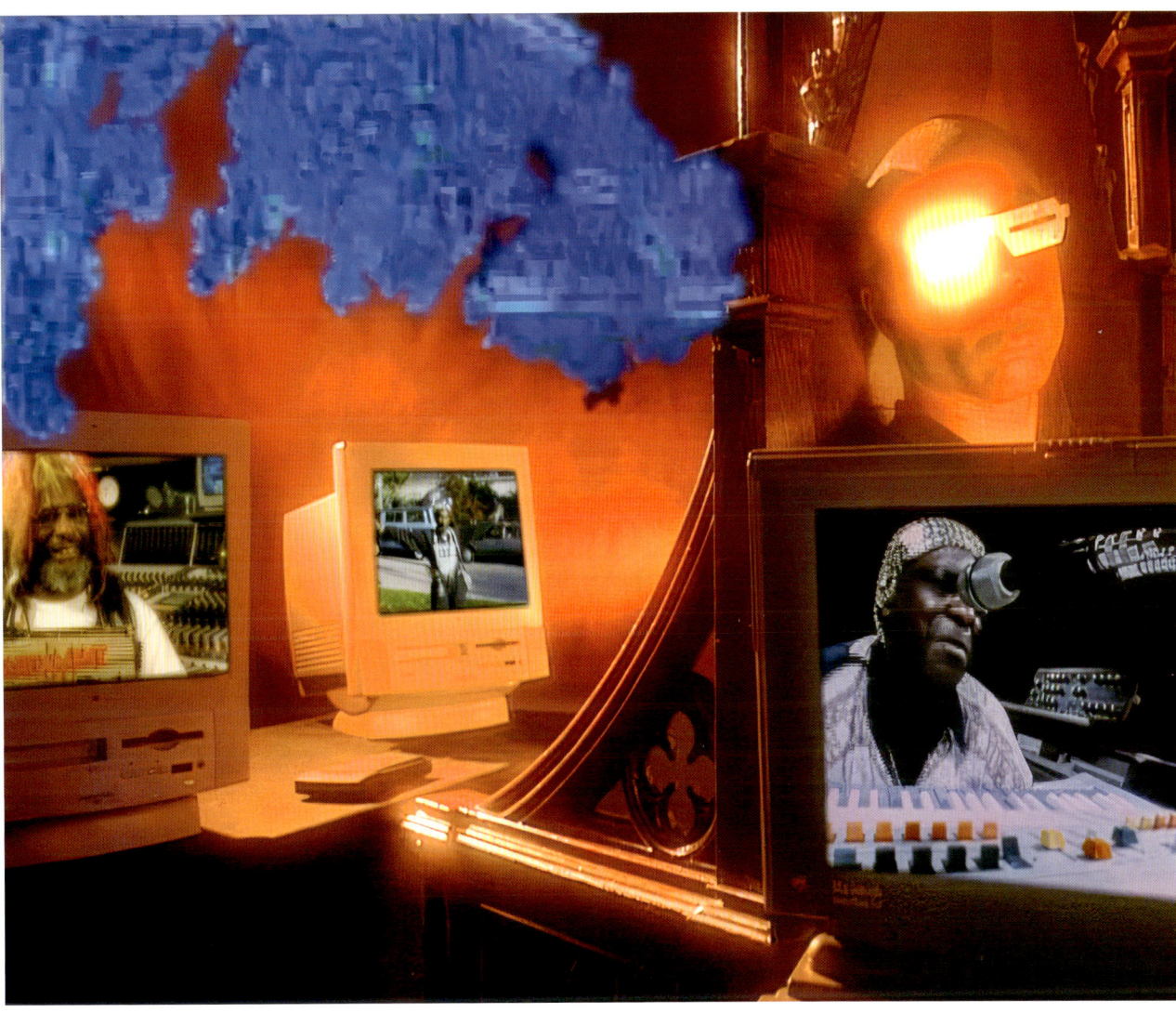

ABOVE: George (top right) as the Data Thief. He was also credited as writer and researcher on the film.

or the transatlantic slave trade. "If you can find the crossroads, a crossroads, this crossroads, if you can make an archeological dig into this, you'll find fragments, techno-fossils," the Data Thief muses. "And if you can put those elements, those fragments, together, you'll find the code. Crack that code, and you'll have the keys to your future. You've got one clue, and it's a phrase: Mothership Connection." While searching for the secret of the Mothership Connection, the Data Thief discovers the word *Africa*, the concept of the "New World," and two rooms marked "Lee Perry Black Ark" and "Sun Ra Arkestra." Lee Perry and Sun Ra tell him: "Our music is a mirror of the universe. We explore the future through music."

The film's motivation is to understand and harness the concept of race as a technology. Much like the narrator of Ralph Ellison's novel *Invisible Man* (1952), the Data Thief sits outside of the events he witnesses and the information he absorbs, guiding the viewer through a nonlinear web of rhythms, energy pulses, and intellectual revelations about technological and societal changes that would soon come along with the crossing of the horizon into the twenty-first century. The technologies of film and audio correspond at a dimensional nexus where each complements the other. *The Last Angel of History* situates itself—and its audience—at this very juncture as a starting point toward a broader understanding of a Black cyberculture, a hyperconnected Afrofuturism. British-Ghanaian theorist Kodwo Eshun, who appears in the film as a talking head, posits the techno, jungle, and stereo-modern sounds of late '80s and early '90s Afrofuture as an "impossible, imaginary music," with predictive qualities that could create entire worlds. He concludes: "They don't reflect the past. They imagine the future."

—DeForrest Brown Jr.

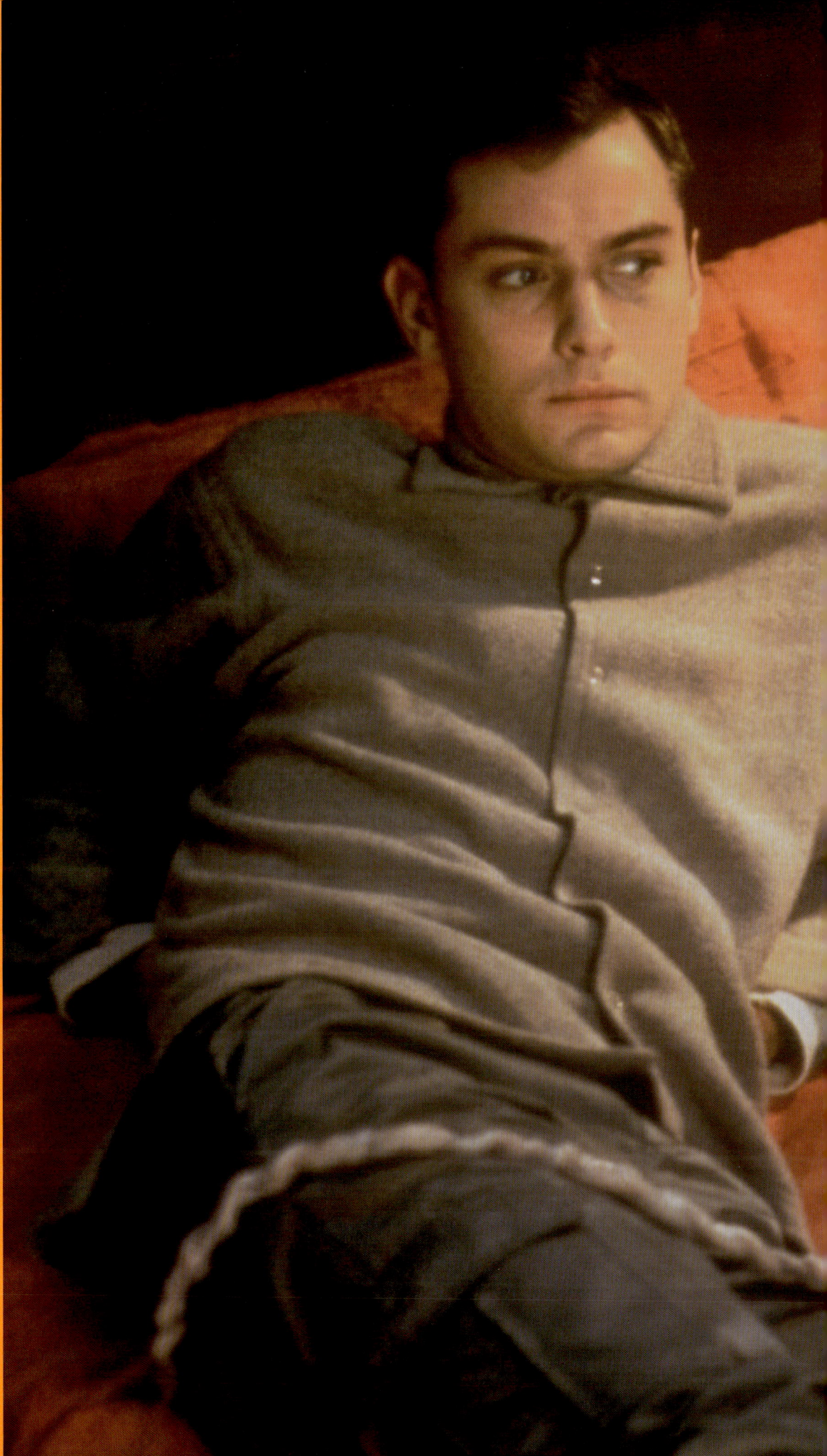

EXISTENZ

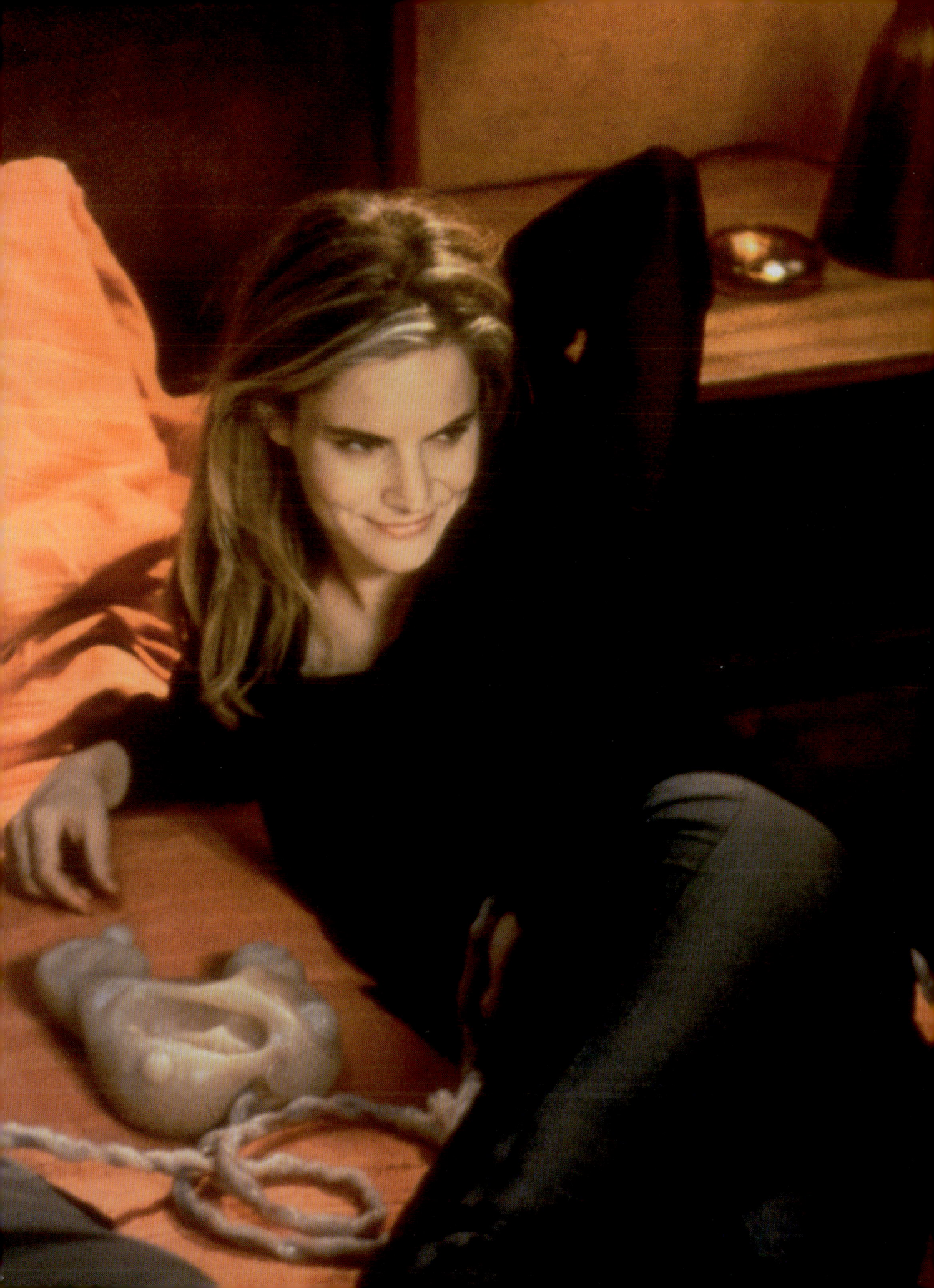

eXistenZ (Canada, 1999)
Director: David Cronenberg

Film synopsis:
A renowned virtual reality game designer's new project, eXistenZ, connects to players directly through a biological port in their spine. After an anti-VR activist, part of the Realist movement, attacks her and damages the system, she has to enter the game herself and determine whether she can trust her co-players—or her own perceptions.

"Don't panic—it's just a game."
—Allegra Geller (Jennifer Jason Leigh)

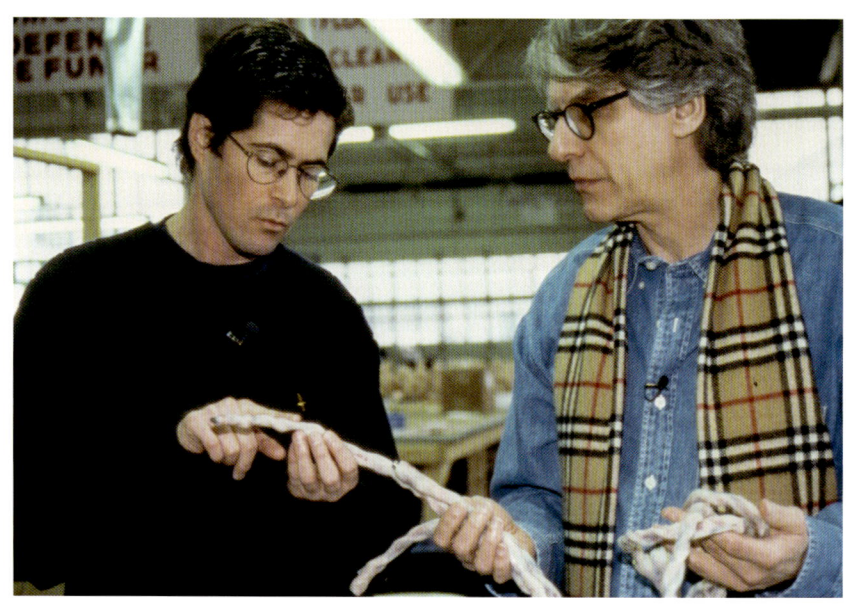

PREVIOUS SPREAD: Jude Law as Ted Pikul and Jennifer Jason Leigh as Allegra Geller

ABOVE: Writer-director David Cronenberg (right) and visual and special effects supervisor James Isaac examine an UmbyCord cable

RIGHT: Production still showing bio-port insertion

THREE DYSTOPIAN SCIENCE FICTION FILMS released in the spring of 1999—Lana and Lilly Wachowski's *The Matrix* (USA), David Cronenberg's *eXistenZ*, and Josef Rusnak's *The Thirteenth Floor* (USA)—collectively signaled the omnipresent hum of anxiety felt globally as the world hurtled toward a new millennium. While the Wachowskis' massive hit would prove to be the defining cultural touchstone for the Y2K era, the lesser-invoked *eXistenZ*, when considered twenty-five years later, is striking in its uncanny prescience. Its more mundane setting stands in sharp contrast to the ultrastylized world of the other two films, but *eXistenZ*'s ethos is similarly of a piece with the predominant concerns of cyberpunk, though achieved through a distinctly different visual approach. Unfolding in a near future in which gameplay looks identical to reality, Cronenberg's fifteenth feature considers cyberpunk concepts like biohacking, wearable technologies, body modification, and transhumanism not through mechanical devices but via common organic material.[1]

The film begins at a focus group for eXistenZ, the newest virtual reality experience by world-renowned game designer Allegra Geller (Jennifer Jason Leigh). In a scene that eerily prefigures Steve Jobs's product launches for Apple, Geller preaches about her latest innovation before dozens of zealous gaming fanatics.[2] When the session is interrupted by a deranged anti-gaming Realist, Geller and marketing-trainee-turned-bodyguard Ted Pikul (Jude Law) flee to safety along various levels of either gameplay or real life, with each reality rendered so subtly distinct as to leave the audience—and the lead characters—on unstable footing.

For Cronenberg, who studied organic chemistry and cell biology before turning to filmmaking, everything, including technology, comes from the body, so naturally eXistenZ's console is a cream-colored, Gigeresque "metaflesh" game pod with suggestive curvatures and protuberances. The game pod, explains Geller's mentor Kiri Vinokur (Ian Holm), is "basically an animal… grown from fertilized amphibian eggs stuffed with synthetic DNA," and Geller cares for hers like a child, referring to it as her "baby" and grieving when it becomes infected. To play the game, an aptly named UmbyCord cable plugs directly into the user's spine via a body modification

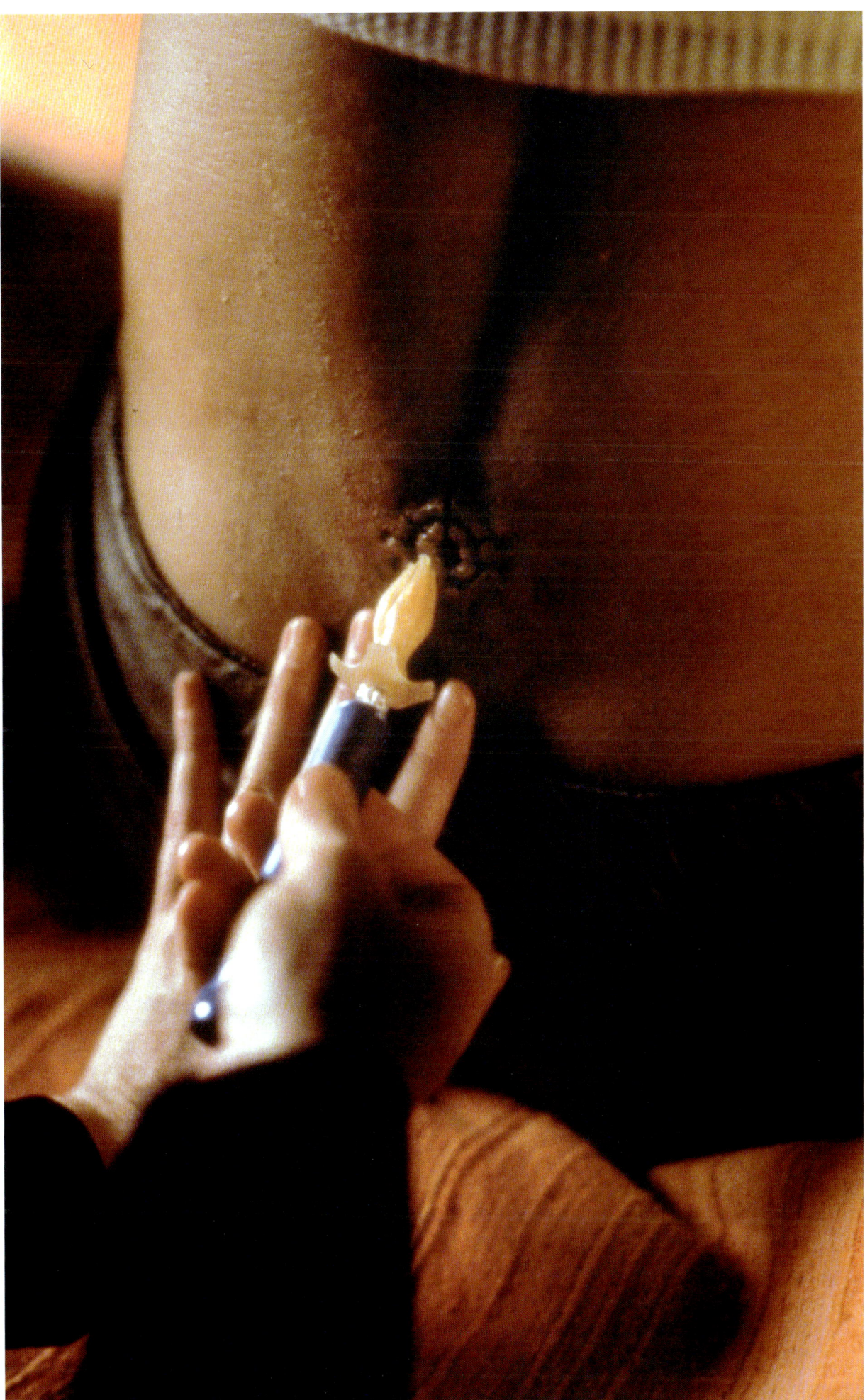

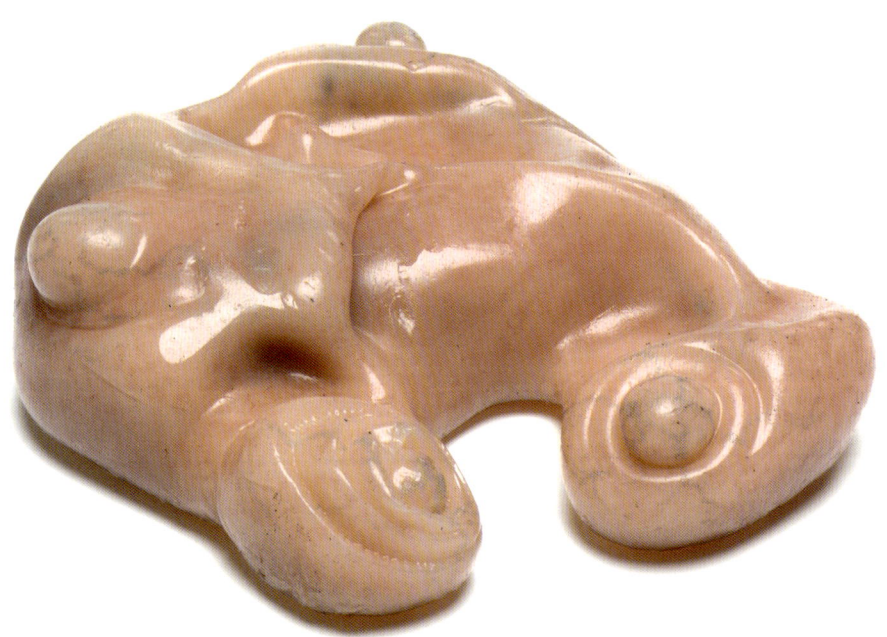

ABOVE: eXistenZ MetaFlesh Game-Pod prop

RIGHT: Virtual reality fans including Allegra Geller (Leigh, center) play eXistenZ in the film

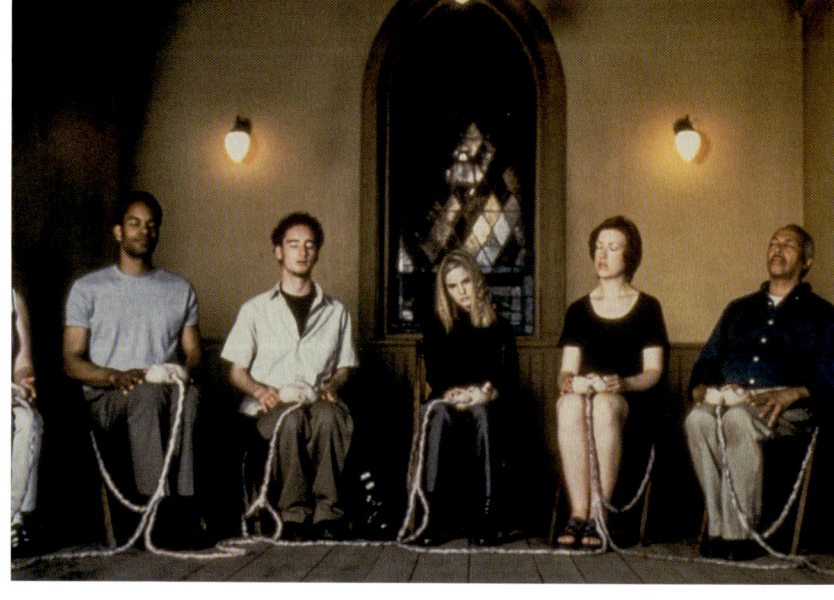

known as a "bio-port"; the UmbyCord must be properly lubricated before insertion, and the inexperienced Pikul has a deep fear of being penetrated, one of the film's many double entendres that equate biohacking with copulation. The sexual revolution was among the primary interests of the New Wave science fiction movement of the 1960s and '70s that lay the groundwork for cyberpunk. The first time Geller activates her game pod, her hands simulate autoeroticism as she flicks the pod's fleshy folds—a sex-positive wink toward feminism.[3] It is in both the film's bawdy concerns and the tension between gamers and the opposing Realist movement that *eXistenZ* locates this kindred, cyberpunk-infused spirit.

eXistenZ's rejection of traditional mechanical technologies in favor of a speculative biological approach to "progress" sets it apart from *The Matrix* and *The Thirteenth Floor*, and this manifests in the film's production and costume design: a pivot into a new reality is conveyed through a slight shift in a hairstyle or outfit and not through computer-generated effects, a deft choice that allows the film to age beautifully. With Cronenberg's insistence on corporeality, "eXistenZ" as a moniker and as an experience is ultimately the filmmaker's playful shorthand for existence, awareness, and—at the dawn of the twenty-first century—the struggle to maintain bodily autonomy in an increasingly digital world.

—K.J. Relth-Miller

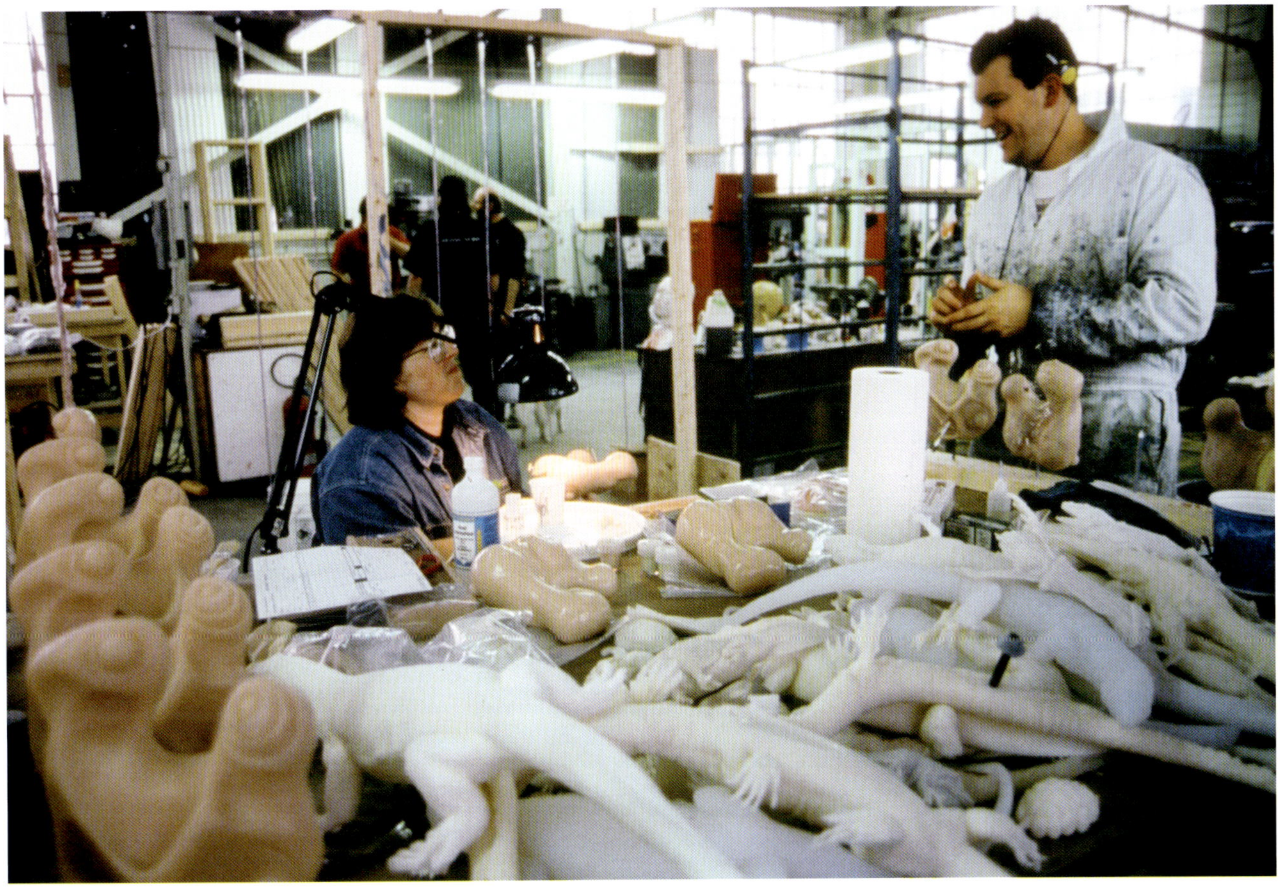

ABOVE: Prop makers at work fabricating eXistenZ MetaFlesh Game-Pod and other props

BELOW: UmbyCord cable prop

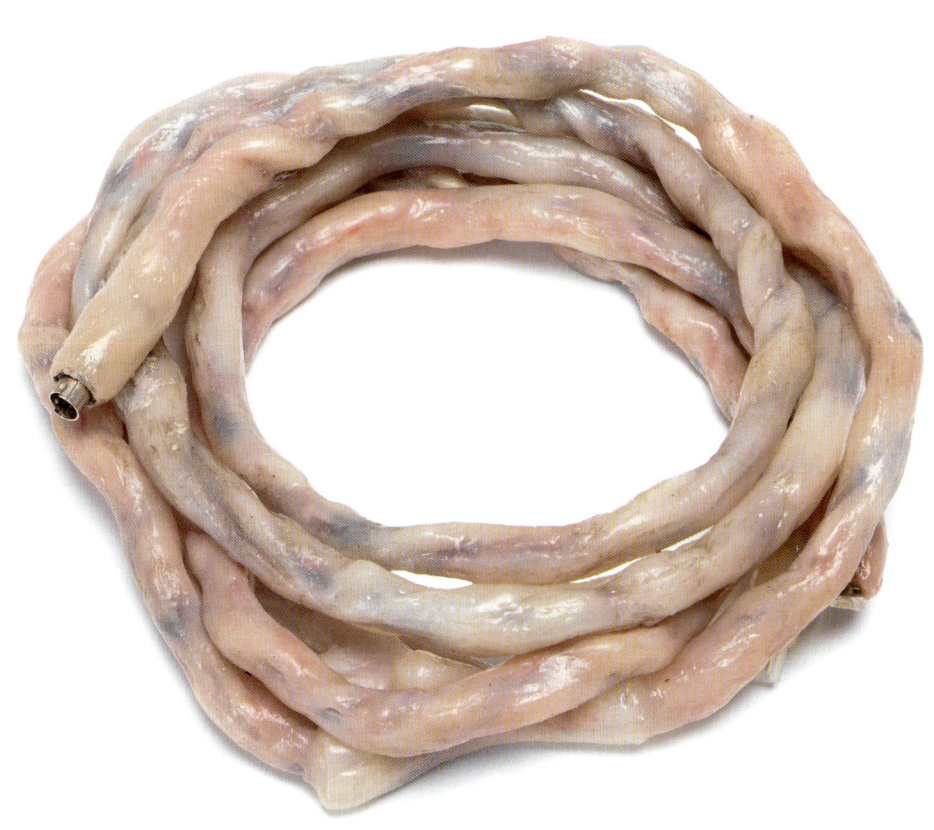

NOTES

1./ Samuel R. Delany's 1968 novel *Nova* explores the idea of implantable technology, making it both a predecessor to a common theme in cyberpunk and a notable forerunner to *eXistenZ*.

2./ Apple's highly anticipated product launches, usually unveiled at their annual Worldwide Developers Conference, weren't commonplace until 2005, six years after the film's release.

3./ *eXistenZ* is one of Cronenberg's few films to feature a female lead protagonist.

THE MATRIX

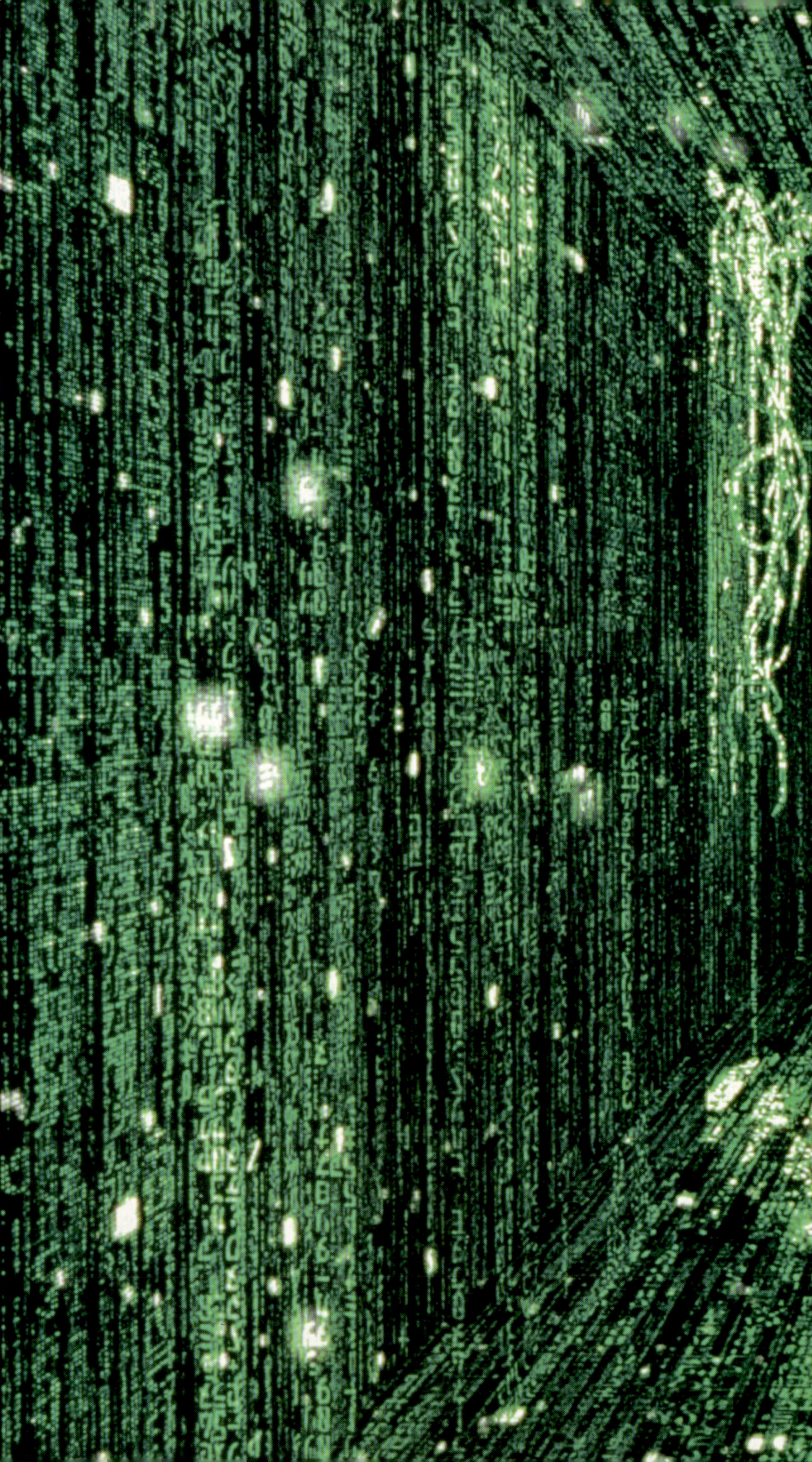

The Matrix (USA, 1999)
Directors: Lana and Lilly Wachowski

Film synopsis:
A computer programmer discovers that humans have been living in a shared simulation controlled by intelligent machines, called the Matrix. Empowered by the knowledge of this truth, he teams up with a crew of rebels to free humanity from this preprogrammed existence.

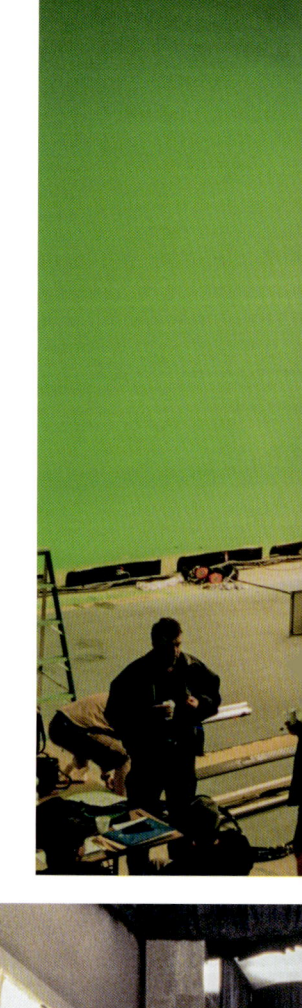

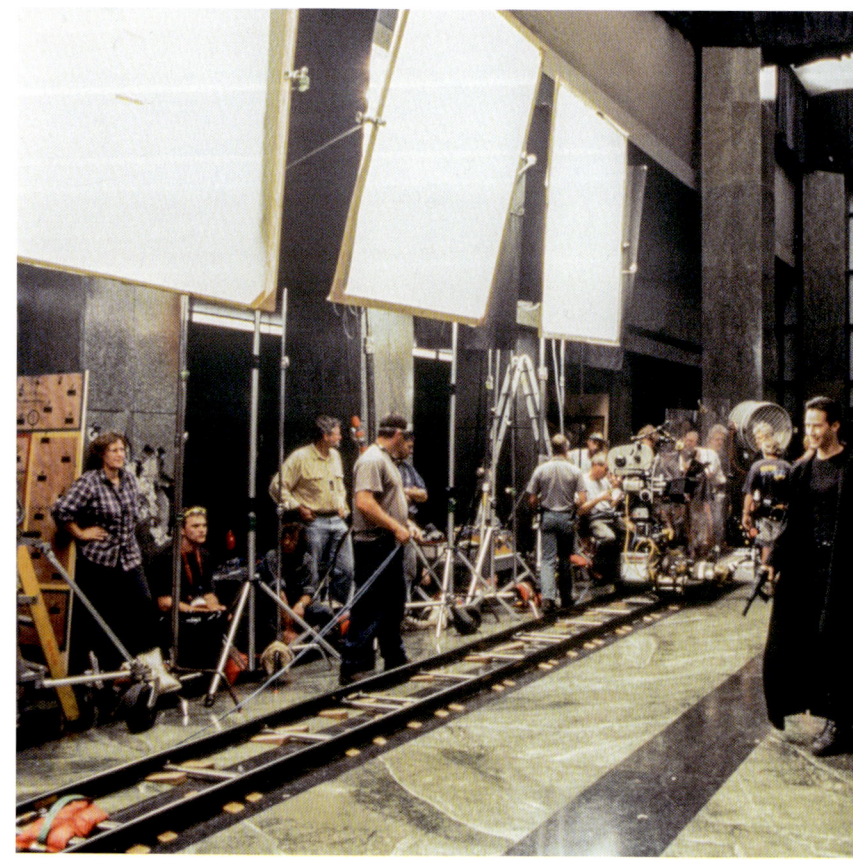

LANA AND LILLY WACHOWSKI'S *The Matrix* combines the slim, black-leather-clad hackers of cyberpunk literature like William Gibson's *Neuromancer* (1984) and Neal Stephenson's *Snow Crash* (1992) with the big-gun action sets of blockbuster films like Paul Verhoeven's *RoboCop* (USA, 1987), Verhoeven's *Total Recall* (USA, 1990), and James Cameron's *Terminator 2: Judgment Day* (USA, 1991). In the film's dystopian future, humans live in a digital illusion, while in reality their bodies are nothing more than batteries used to power machines.

The Matrix exemplifies cyberpunk's deep-rooted connection to postmodern crisis: its primary plotline centers on our increasing inability to determine what is "real" in an age of virtual reality and digital deepfakes. The cultural critic Fredric Jameson described postmodern culture as a constantly shifting barrage of images and references that have been recycled, remixed, and divorced from their original contexts and meanings.[1] We can see this in the way *The Matrix* incorporates references to literary works like Lewis Carroll's *Alice's Adventures in Wonderland* (1865), L. Frank Baum's *The Wonderful Wizard of Oz* (1900), and the Bible, or in how it blends noir aesthetics with a Wild West shoot-out. The film makes particular use of the work of French theorist Jean Baudrillard, who hypothesized a dawning age of hyperreality in which we would no longer be capable of distinguishing reality from imitation.[2] Protagonist Neo (Keanu Reeves) keeps his software discs in a hollowed-out copy of Baudrillard's *Simulacra and Simulation* (1981), and in one scene Morpheus (Laurence Fishburne) welcomes Neo to the Matrix's "desert of the real," a direct quote from Baudrillard.[3] The film plays with Neo's reality, and our perceptions, throughout: when

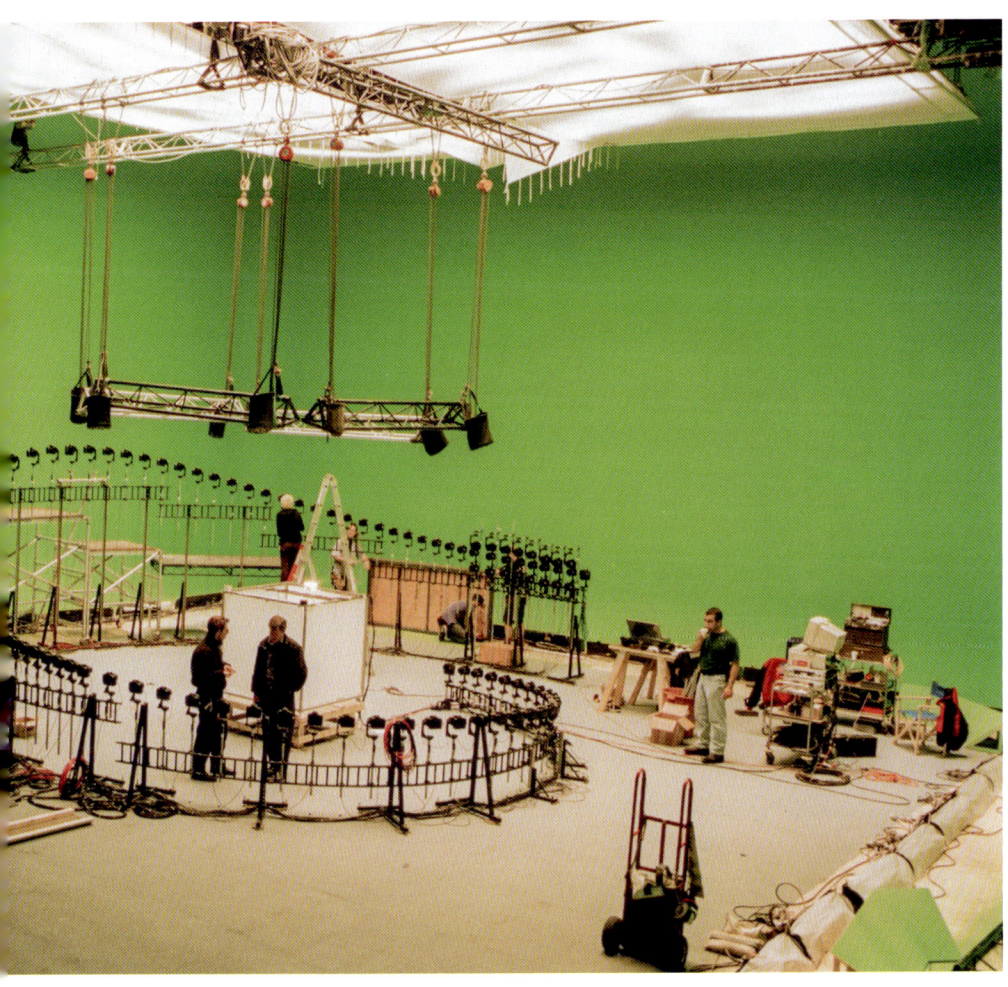

PREVIOUS SPREAD: Hallway sequence inside the Matrix

LEFT: "Bullet time" rig used to produce the slow-motion visual effect made popular by the film

BELOW RIGHT: Keanu Reeves as Neo and Hugo Weaving as Agent Smith in a bullet-time enhanced fight sequence

BELOW LEFT: Reeves on set

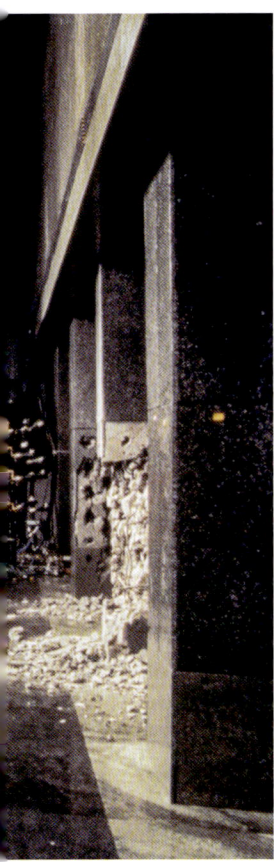

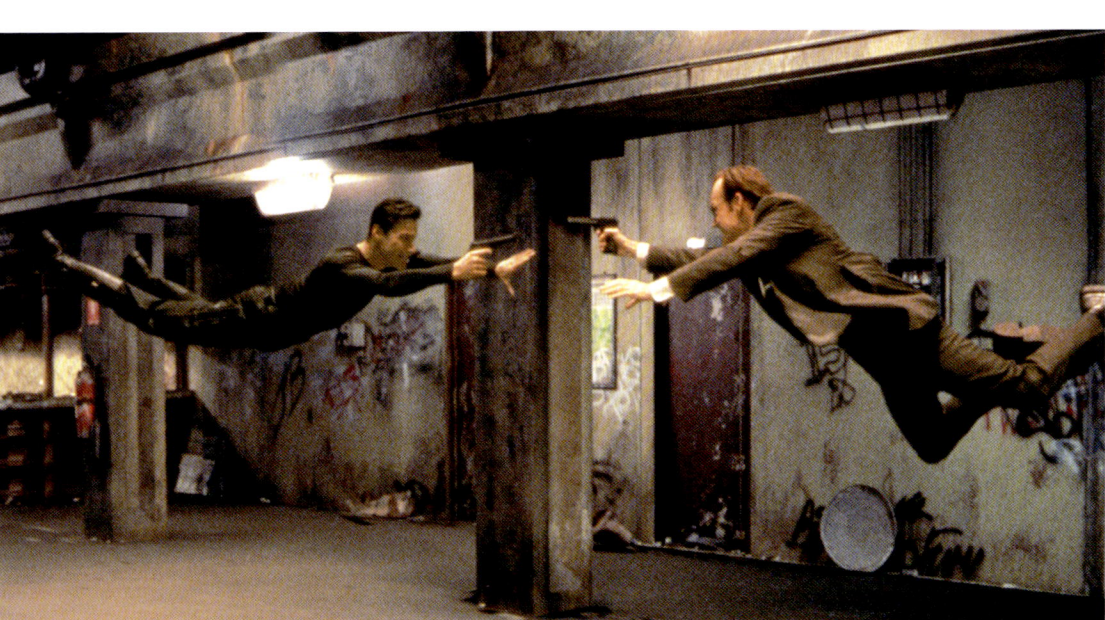

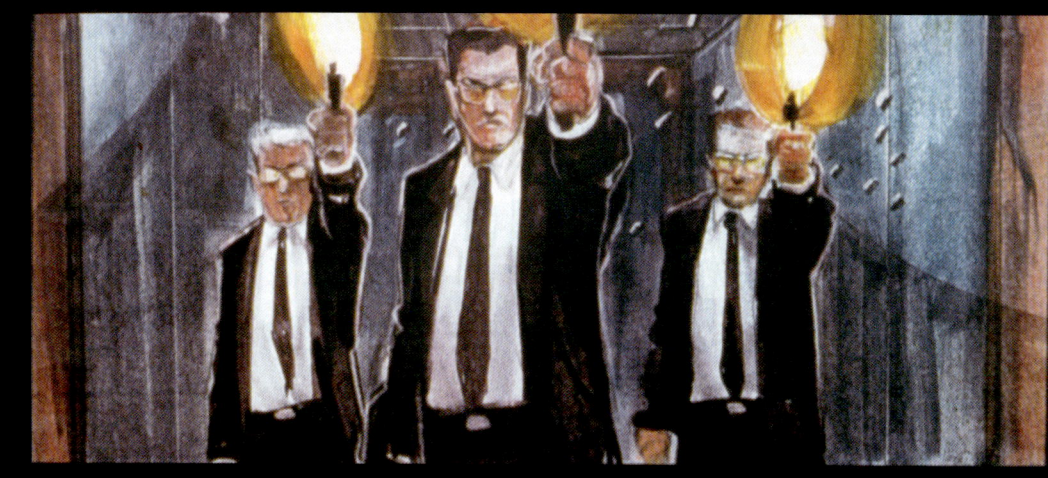
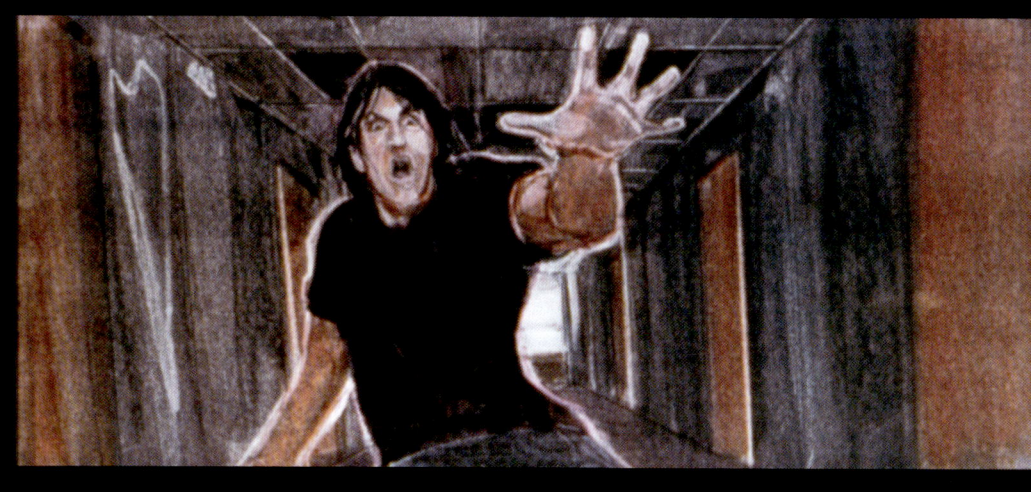
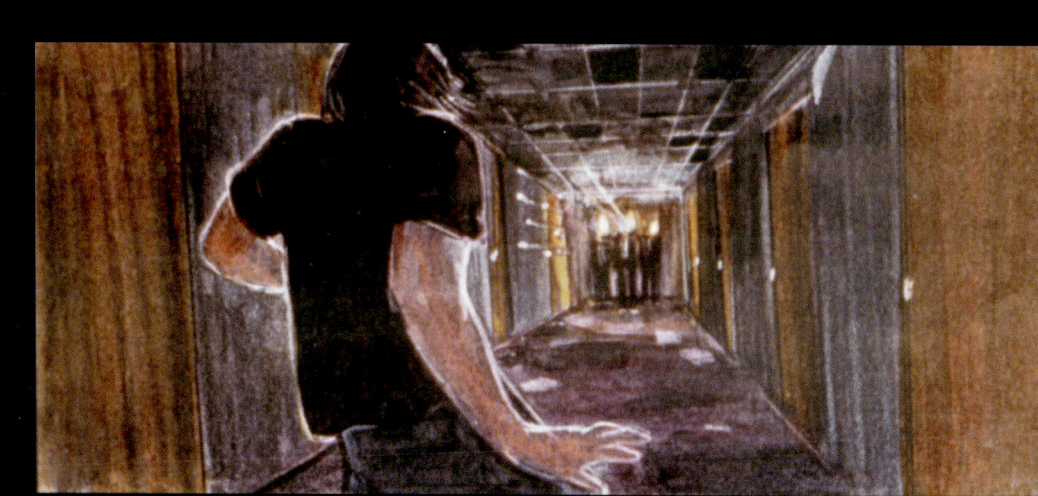

LEFT: Storyboard for the hallway sequence

RIGHT: Production still showing "headjack" data port

BELOW: Concept art for human pods

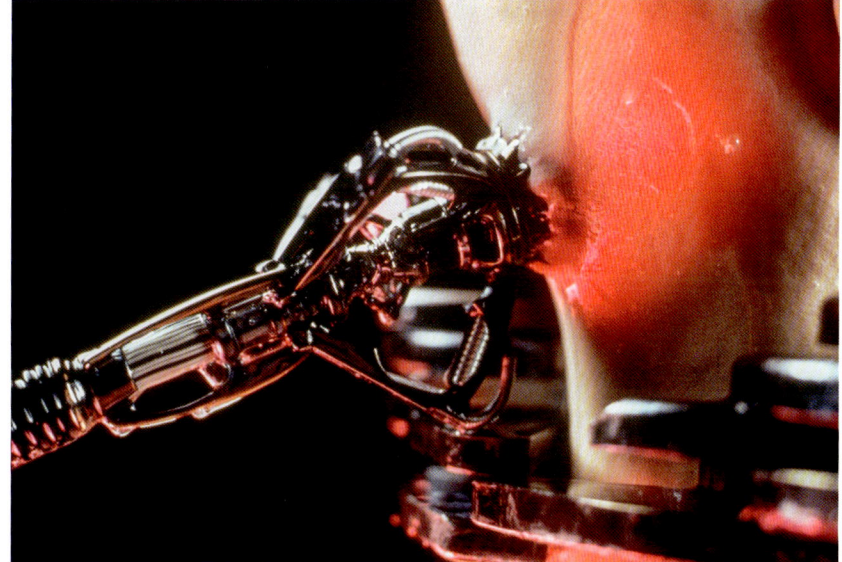

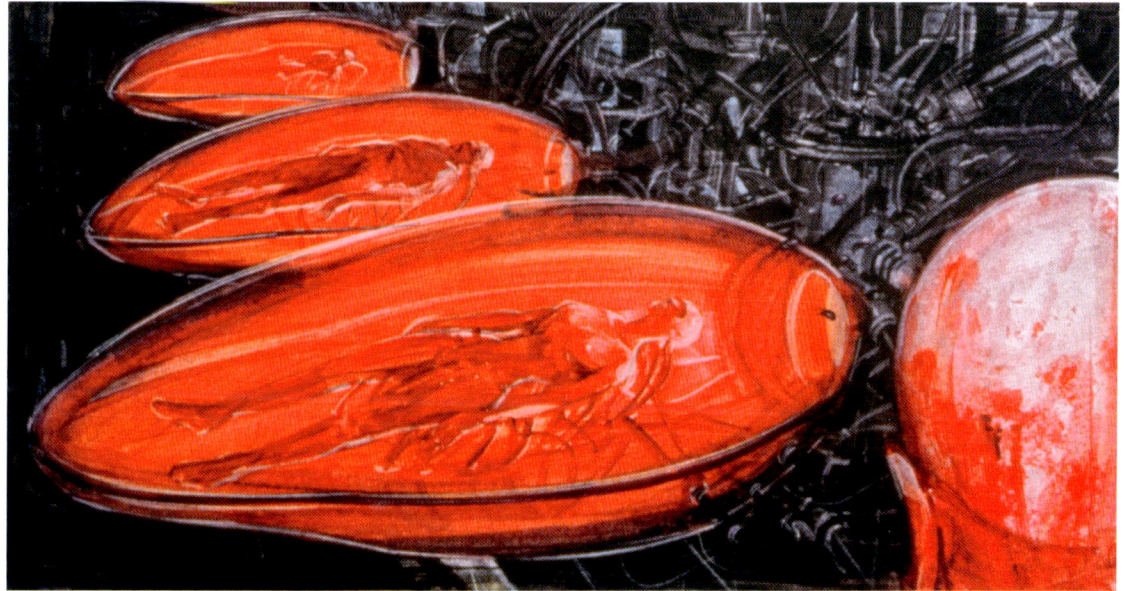

we watch Neo's reflection (in mirrors, sunglasses, and other objects) rather than Neo himself, when Neo repeatedly "wakes up" without any memory of having fallen asleep, or when he is able to change the virtual world of the Matrix itself. All of these elements evoke concepts of hyperreality and the fragmentation of identity.

This deliberate ambiguity may explain why *The Matrix* has held very different meanings for different audiences. Radical far-right fans and "men's rights" activists have embraced Neo's iconic choice between the "blue pill" (easy ignorance) and the "red pill" (difficult truth) and frequently use the red pill metaphor in discussion board posts and forums, encouraging the endurance of hardship to understand what they perceive as hidden social truths.[4] Meanwhile, LGBTQ+ audiences have interpreted the film as a trans narrative, in which Neo rejects the name and identity he was assigned by the corporate machine in order to embrace and express his true self. Director Lana Wachowski has confirmed this as the preferred reading;[5] furthermore, she cowrote and directed the film's third sequel, *The Matrix Resurrections* (USA, 2021), in which character dialogue directly asserts that *The Matrix* was about "trans politics," "crypto-fascism," and "capitalist exploitation."[6] Of course, a creator's intention does not dictate how an audience might perceive the work, and the multiple layers of ambiguity that went into *The Matrix*'s conception only add to its potential for infinite readings. Neo's struggle—and ours—to determine what is "real" may best epitomize the essence of cyberpunk onscreen.

—Carlen Lavigne

NOTES

1./ Fredric Jameson, "Postmodernism, or The Cultural Logic of Late Capitalism," *New Left Review* 1, no. 146 (July/August 1984): 53–94.
2./ Jean Baudrillard, "Simulacra and Simulations," in *Jean Baudrillard: Selected Writings*, ed. Mark Poster (Cambridge: Polity Press, 2001), 166–84.
3./ Baudrillard, "Simulacra and Simulations," 166.
4./ These forums, such as Reddit's "Red Pill" community, are often violently misogynist. See s.e. smith, "Wake-Up Call: The Red Pill Is Radicalizing without Substance," *bitchmedia*, accessed June 13, 2023, https://www.bitchmedia.org/article/the-matrix-radicalizing-alt-right. *The Matrix* is not unique in its appeal to the far right; other science fiction works, like the *Star Wars* franchise, have also garnered significant fandoms. See David M. Higgins, *Reverse Colonization: Science Fiction, Imperial Fantasy, and Alt-Victimhood* (Iowa City: University of Iowa Press, 2021).
5./ Rory Sullivan, "How 'The Matrix' Is a Trans Story, According to Netflix and Co-Director," CNN (website), updated August 7, 2020, accessed June 13, 2023, https://www.cnn.com/2020/08/07/entertainment/matrix-transgender-netflix-wachowski-scl-intl/index.html.
6./ For a detailed discussion of *The Matrix Resurrections*'s metatextual references to the previous films, see Theo Kogod, "The Matrix 4's Video Game Reboot Scene Reveals the Original Films' True Meaning," CBR (website), January 1, 2022, accessed September 2, 2023, https://www.cbr.com/matrix-resurrections-video-game-reboot-scene-reveals-its-real-meaning.

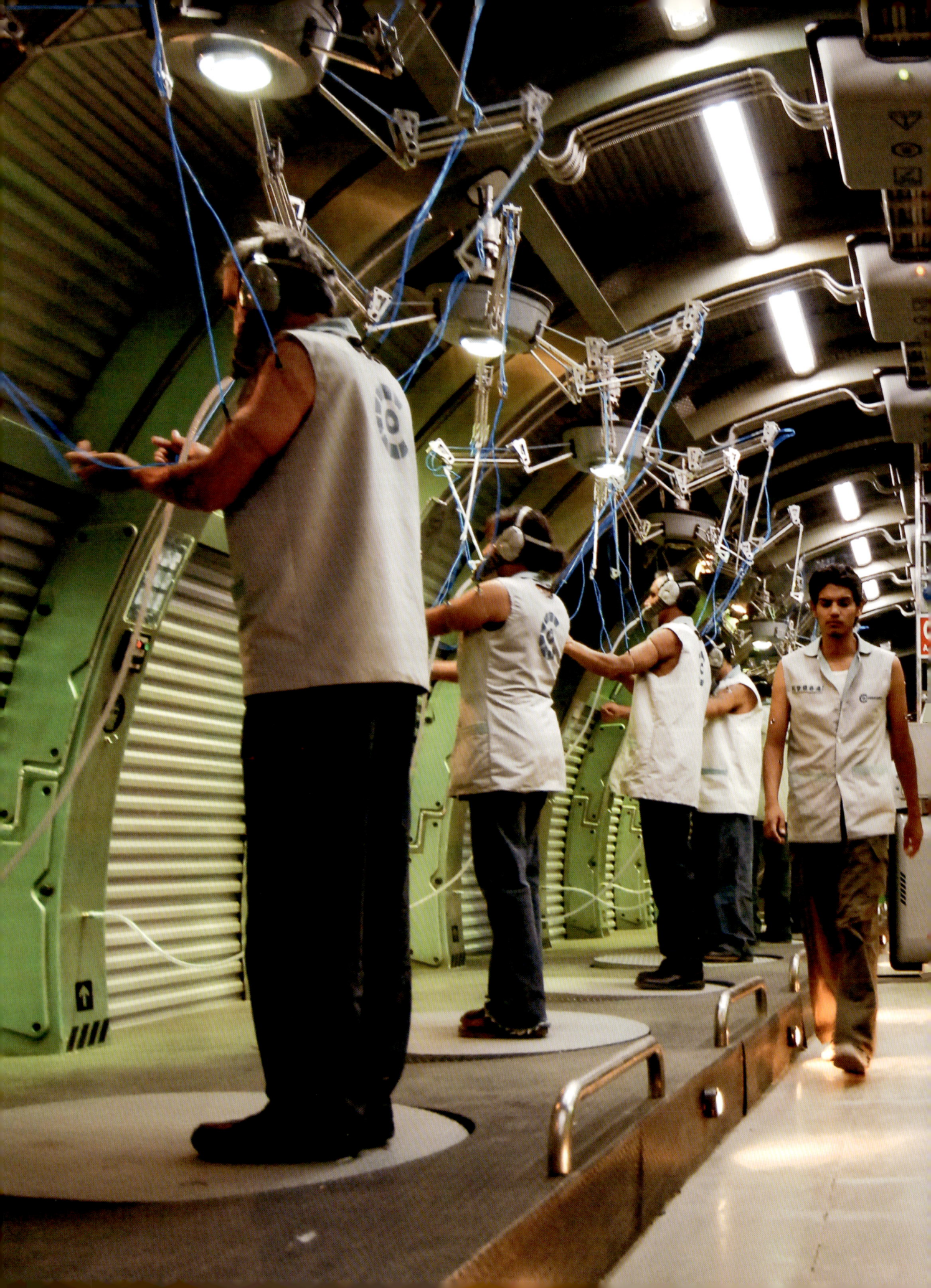

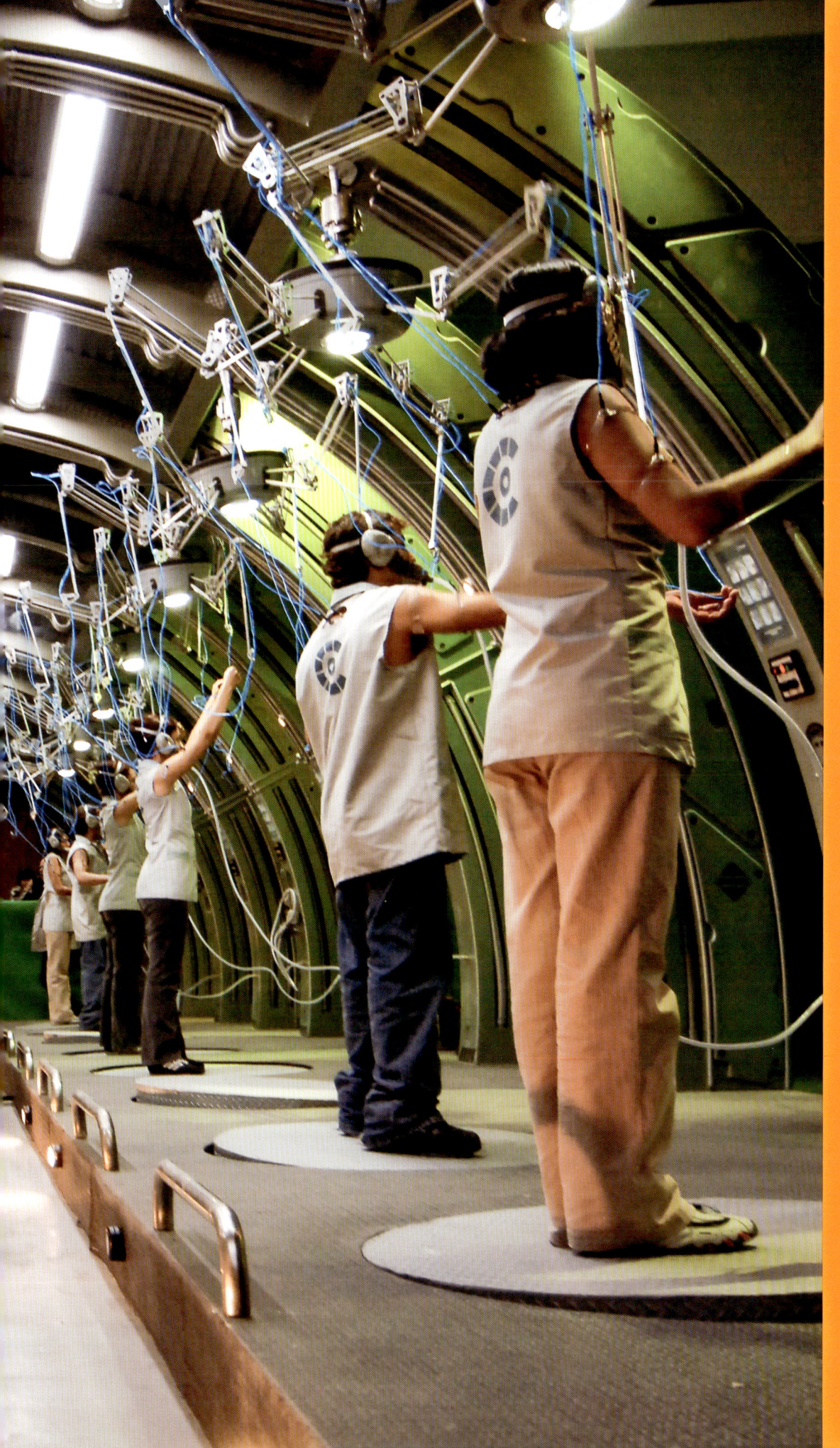

```
Sleep Dealer (USA/Mexico, 2008)
Director: Alex Rivera
```

```
Film synopsis:
In an increasingly technological and hypermilitarized
future, Mexican workers in Tijuana perform their jobs
by remotely controlling robots in the United States.
After his father is killed by an American drone,
Memo Cruz is forced into the dangerous and exhausting
life of a "node" factory worker.
```

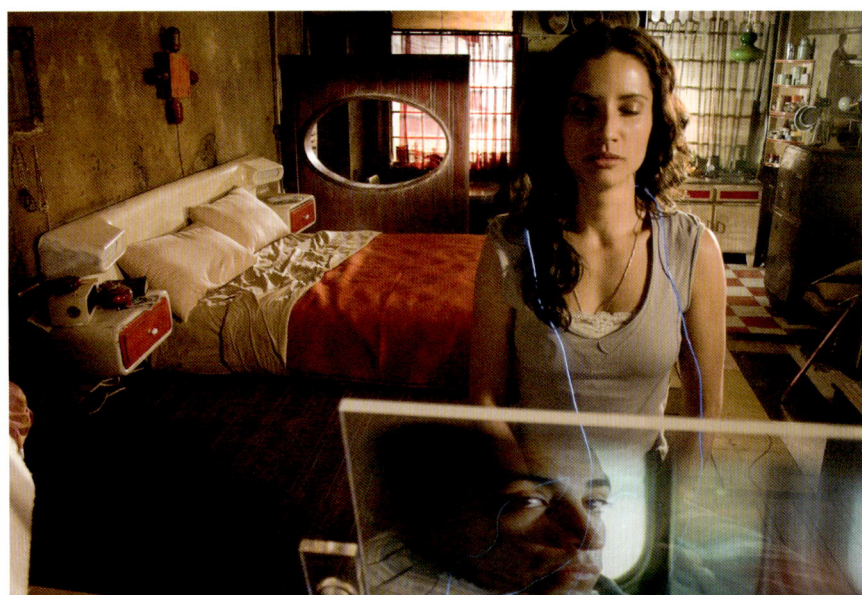

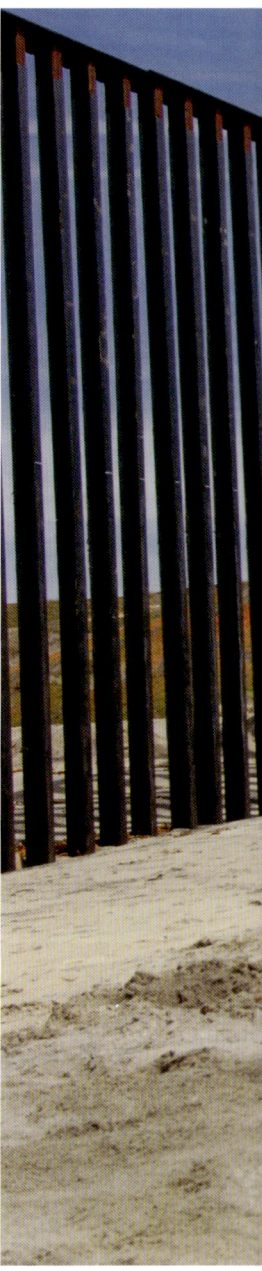

IN THE EARLY SIXTIES, the Council of California Growers produced a short industrial propaganda film called *Why Braceros?* (USA, 1962). The Bracero farm labor program brought Mexican nationals to work in the United States' agricultural industry during World War II, when there were widespread labor shortages. Despite this seemingly straightforward solution—a job that needed to be done, people who were willing to do it, and an American company that could benefit from it—the film focused on justifying the program's existence, primarily by assuaging any xenophobic fears white American viewers might have about these foreigners. *Why Braceros?* assured its audience that the workers' presence in the United States was strictly temporary and conditional, dictated solely by the immediate value of their physical labor. This contradiction—desiring the product of people's labor while disregarding the people themselves—neatly illustrates the hypocrisy inherent in much of the American political discourse around immigration, even today.

As immigration continued to be a firebrand political issue into the 1990s and 2000s, writer and director Alex Rivera expanded this hypocritical desire into a speculative vision, first in his faux-documentary short *Why Cybraceros?* (USA, 1997), and then in his sci-fi feature *Sleep Dealer*. In both films, Mexican laborers perform the same undervalued work they have long done in the United States, including agriculture, construction, nannying, and housework, but, thanks to modern technology, they can now do it without leaving Mexico. True telecommuters, they control robotic machinery that executes the physical labor in the United States while their human bodies remain out of view and out of mind for the Americans who

PREVIOUS SPREAD:
Inside the
Cybracero factory

ABOVE LEFT: Leonor
Varela as Luz
Martínez

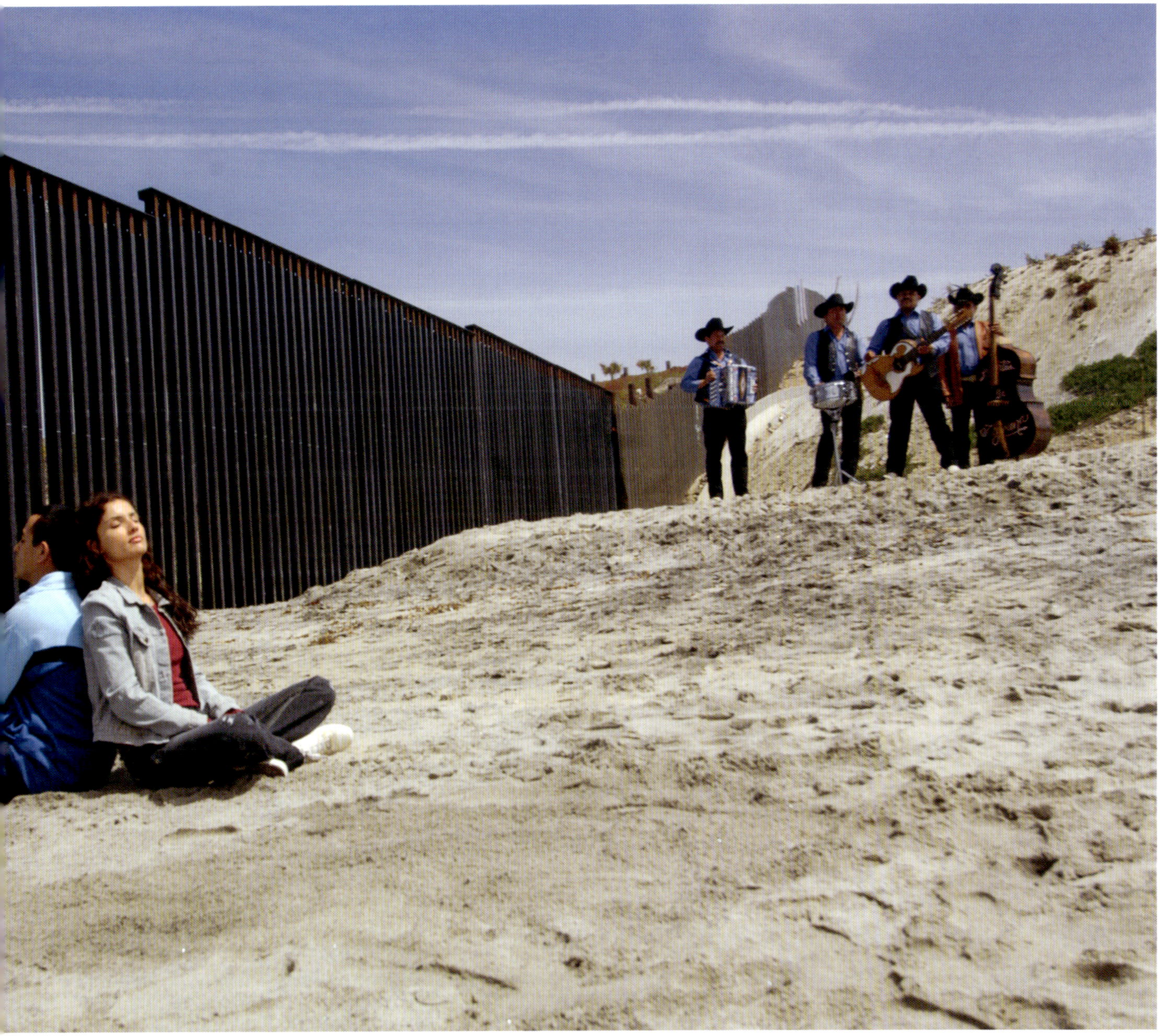

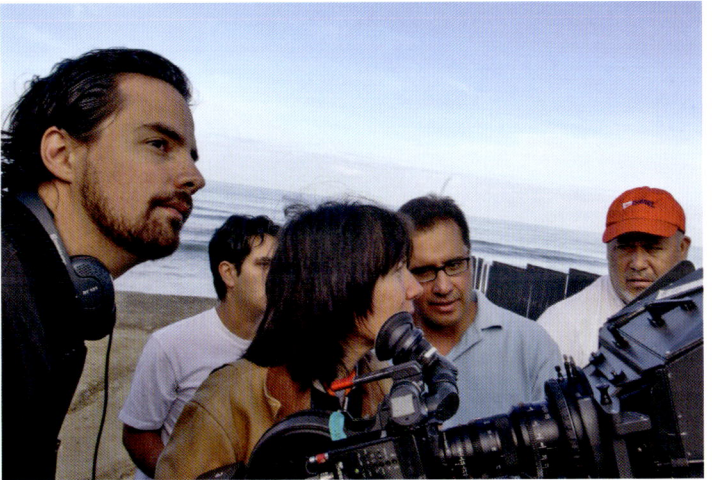

ABOVE: Luis Fernando Peña as Memo Cruz (left) and Varela as Luz Martínez

LEFT: Writer-director Alex Rivera (left) with cinematographer Lisa Rinzler and second camera assistant Hector Flores (center) and unidentified crew

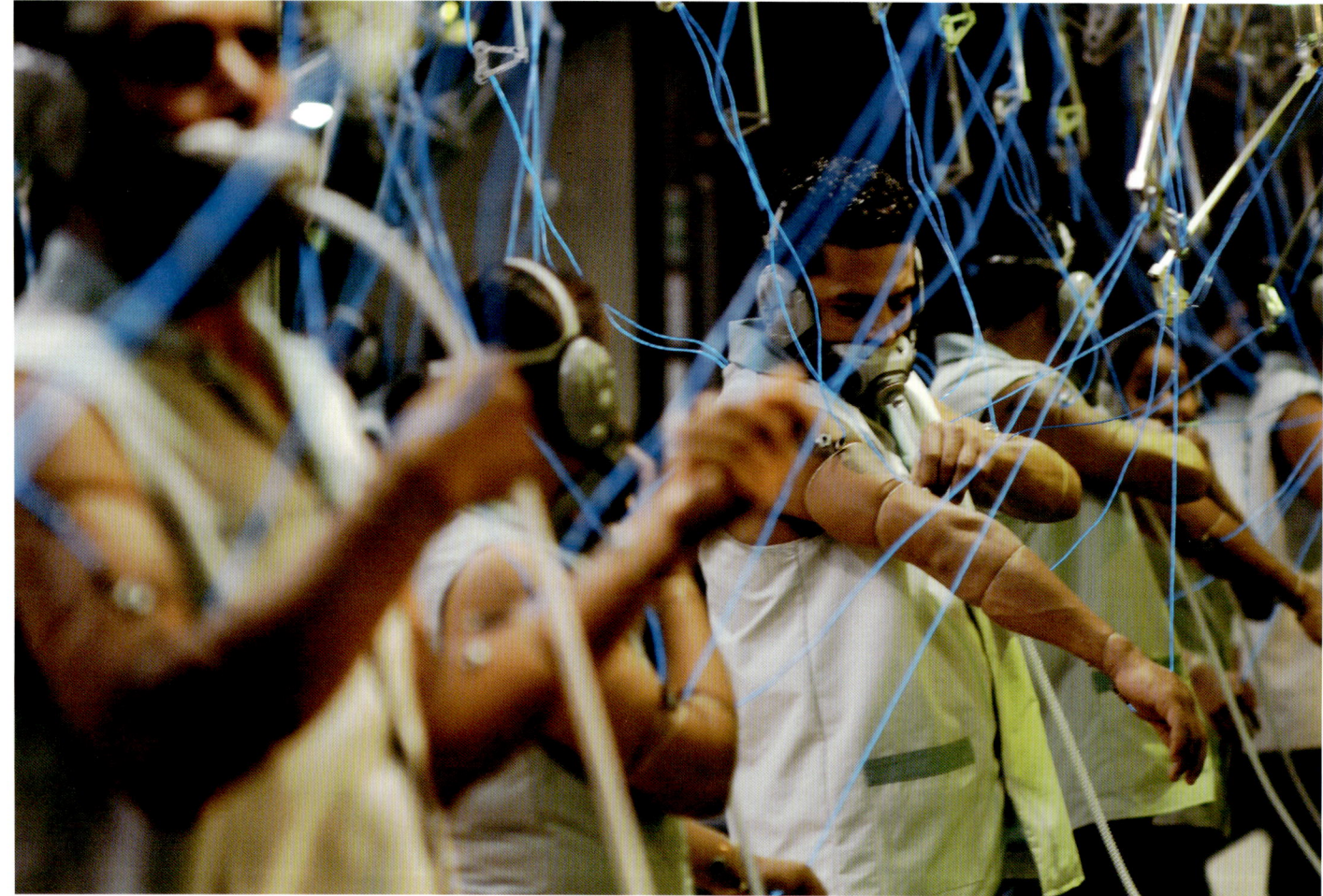

ABOVE: Cast as Cybracero factory workers

profit off them. In the feature film, these workers must permanently alter their bodies in order to plug into the network at "node" factories, where they work until they collapse from exhaustion—earning their nickname of "sleep dealers." As one jaded character states, "This is the American Dream … all the work without the workers."

While *Why Cybraceros?* mimics the subjective documentary style of *Why Braceros?*, even repurposing some of the 1959 film's black-and-white footage, *Sleep Dealer* builds a sleek and emotionally engaging narrative around a young man, Memo Cruz (Luis Fernando Peña), who connects his body to the networked labor system at a factory in Tijuana. This visually intoxicating, neon-streaked, and technologically advanced urban world—a classic visual marker of the cyberpunk genre—stands in sumptuous contrast to Cruz's rural home, yet also slowly reveals its dangerous social regressions. Unlike many cyberpunk films, which consider the effects of globalization all while incorporating exoticized aesthetics into worlds that are, incongruously, still inhabited primarily by white Americans, *Sleep Dealer* interrogates these issues directly and not just as allegory. Its message about the treatment of immigrants and its theme of online hyperconnectivity are topics that remain concretely relevant today.

—*Emily Rauber Rodriguez*

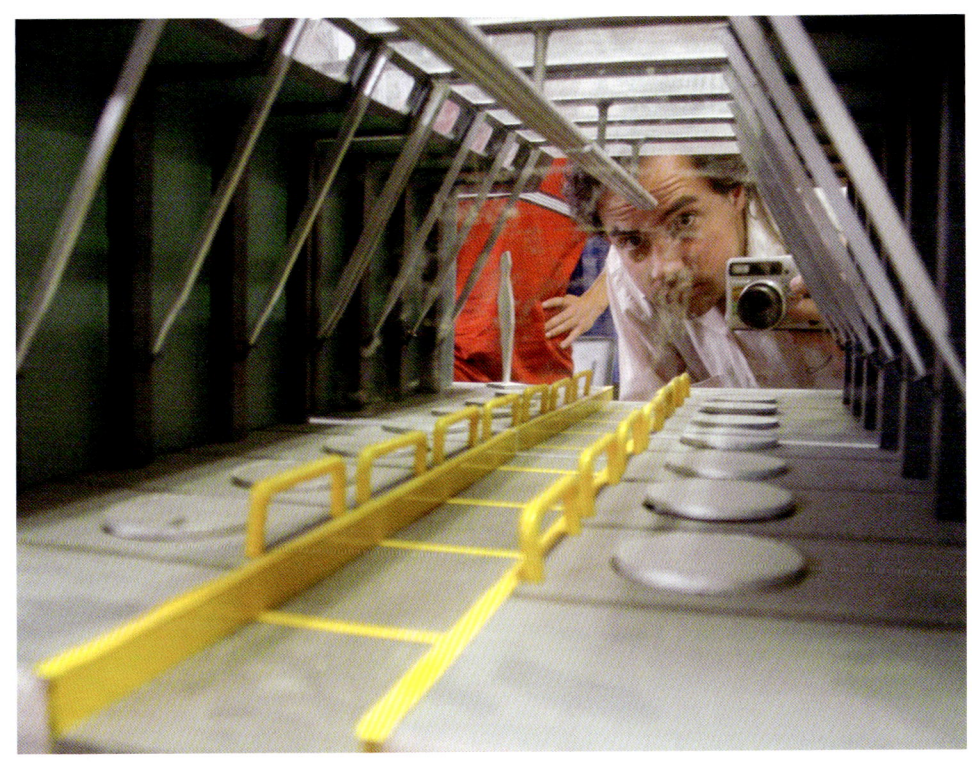

LEFT: Rivera examines a miniature of the Cybracero factory

BELOW: Concept art for the Cybracero factory

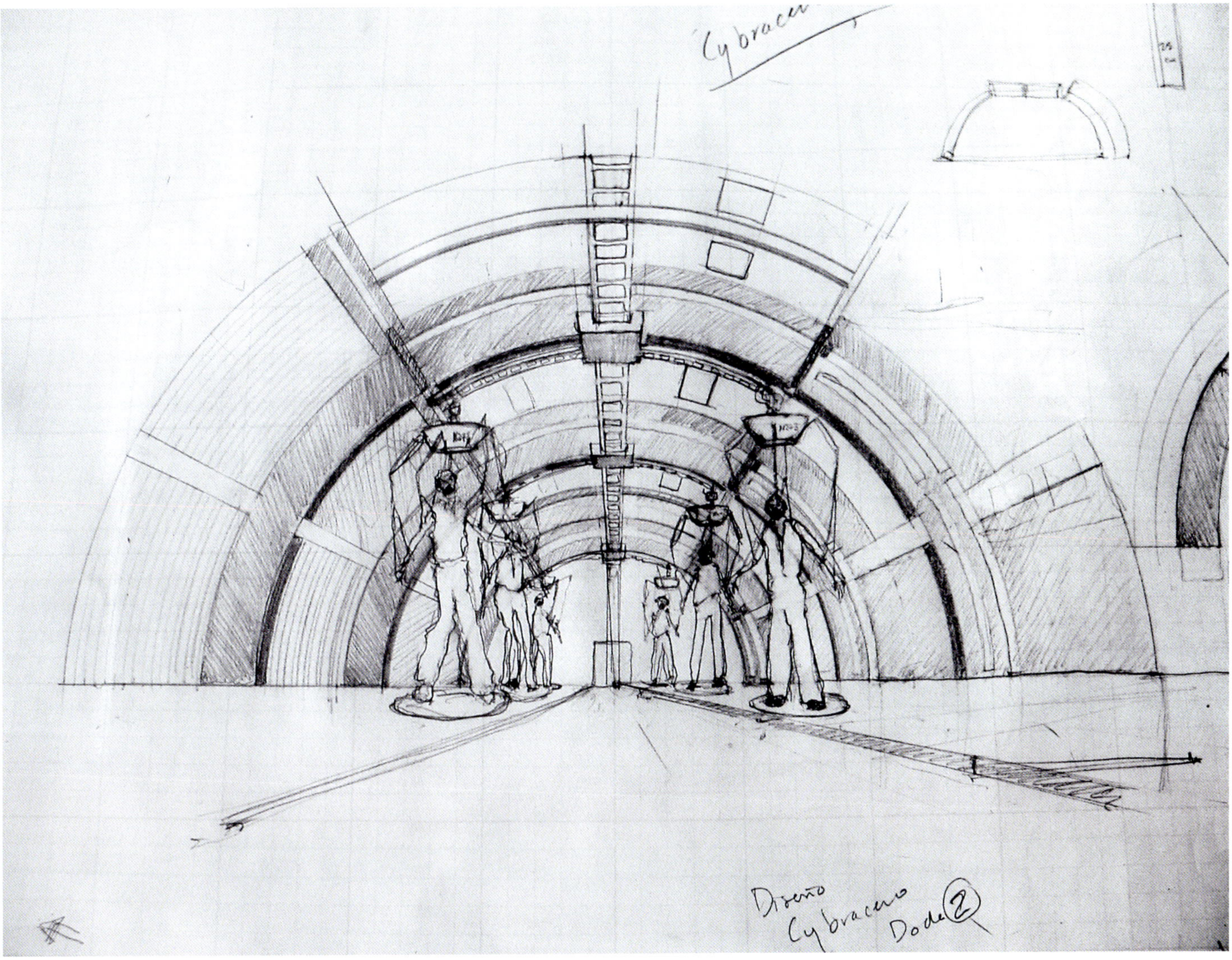

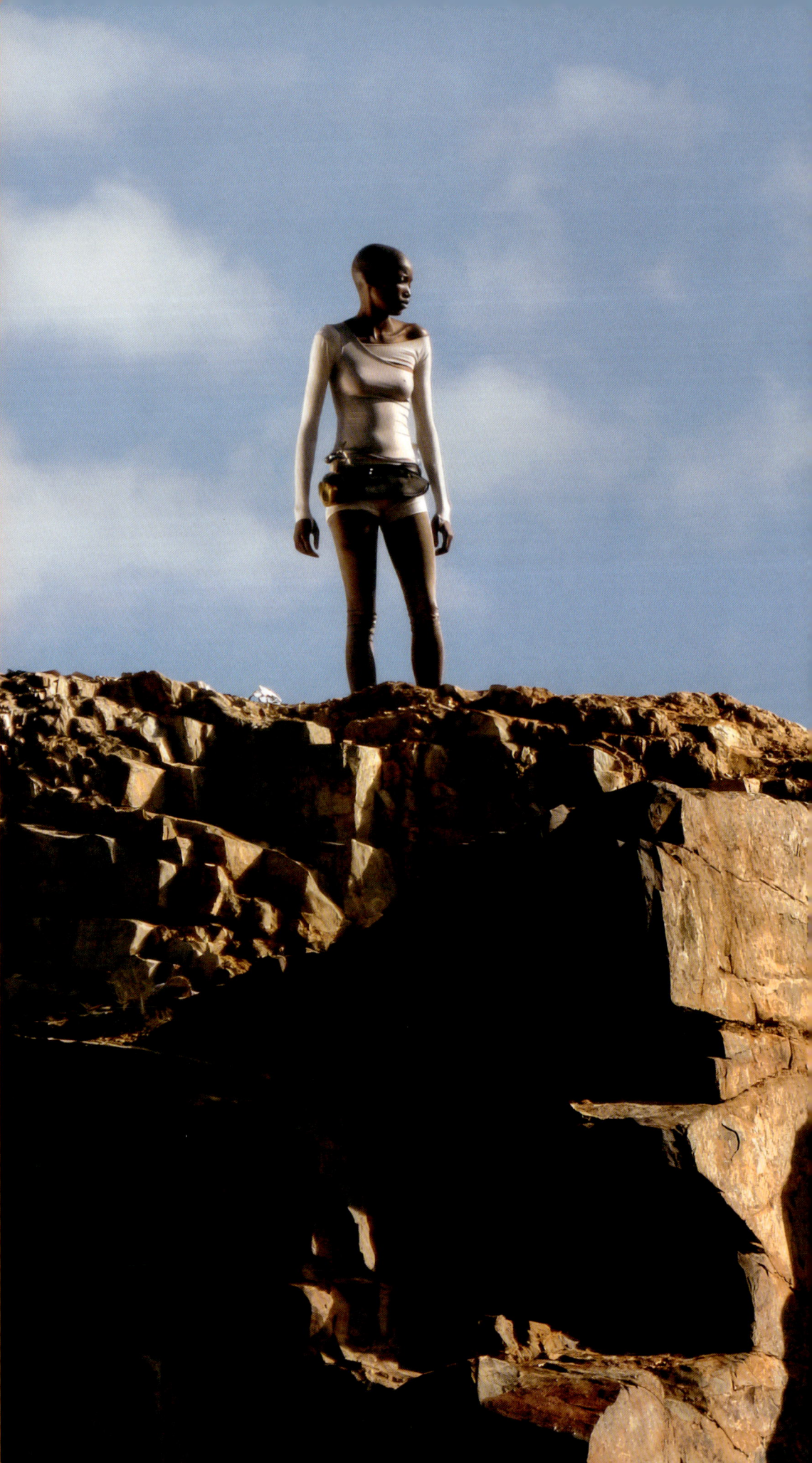

PUMZI

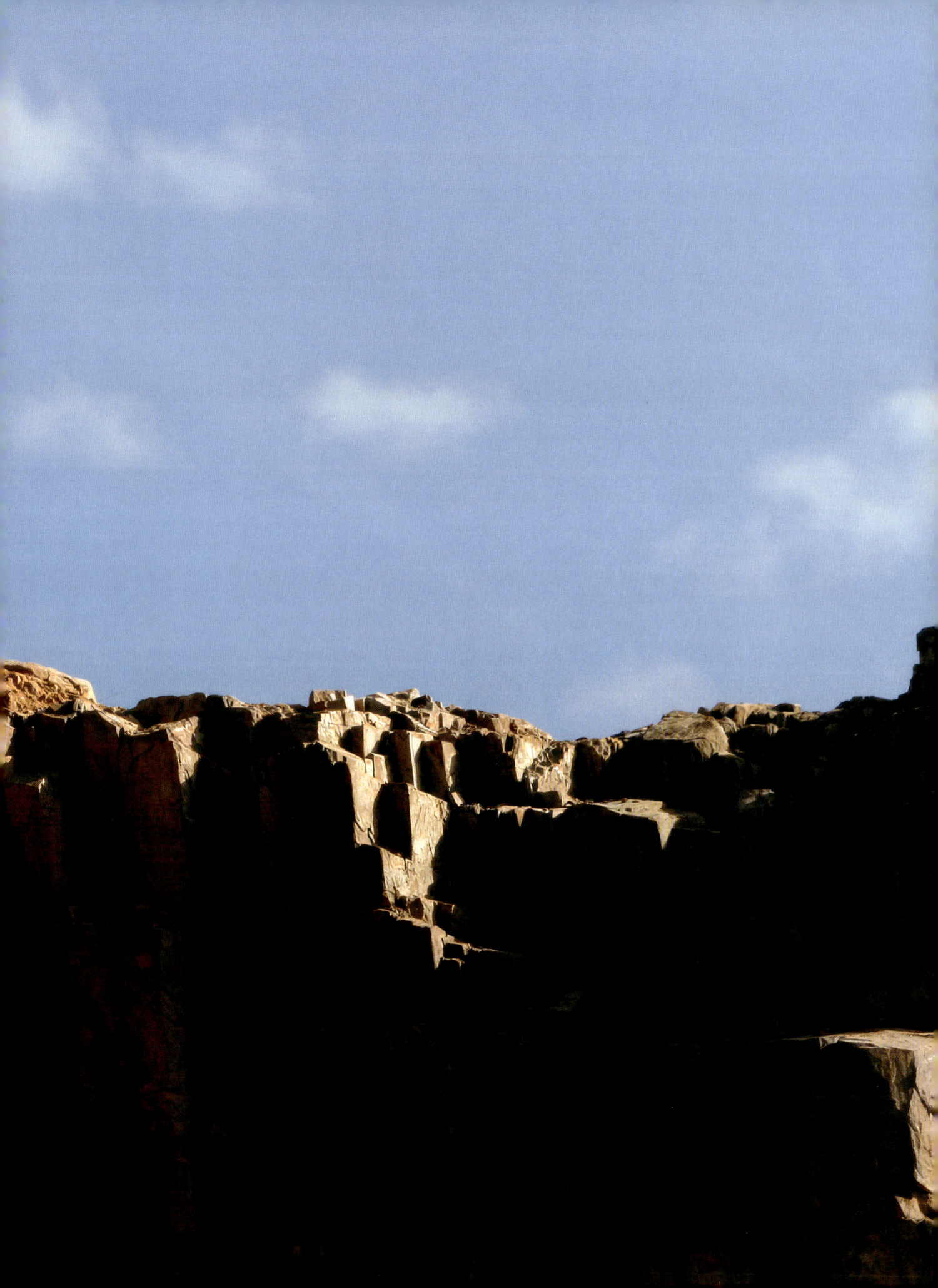

Pumzi (Kenya, 2009)
Director: Wanuri Kahiu

Film synopsis:
After World War III, Earth is no longer habitable, so survivors from the East African Territory now live in the enclosed, self-sufficient, no-waste Maitu community. When Asha, curator at the Virtual Natural History Museum, receives evidence that the world outside could be safe, Maitu's supposedly protective restrictions conflict with her dreams of freedom.

KENYAN FILMMAKER Wanuri Kahiu's short film *Pumzi* is set in the Maitu community, a sand-stricken compound in an East African dystopia ravaged by climate decay. In the postapocalyptic scenario Kahiu presents, the global war over Earth's water reserves limits the community's ability to freely access water and its promises: renewal, cleansing, and movement. Sealed away from the forbidding world, inhabitants live in a self-contained enclave on endless loops of excretion—each person is their own "power generator"—and surveilled sustainability. This high-tech underground city protects its survivors from external climatic threats and keeps them wholly reliant on the order of colonial rule. Community members are forced to medicate themselves with "dream suppressant" pills to prevent dreaming of and imagining futures outside the modes of production in the dystopian present, damning them to a lifetime of exploitation.

At the center of the film is museum worker Asha (Kudzani Moswela), who, in an early pivotal moment of the film, dreams of a lush tree blooming in the desert. As a curator who studies soil's potential to grow life, Asha is concerned with preserving and conserving Earth's former biodiversity in an environment where basic survival remains the chief concern. Her job is to safeguard the future by tending to the roots of the past. When she discovers a fertile, unmarked soil sample at her work, the scanner registers it as unauthorized. Seeing this soil as proof of life beyond the compound, Asha meets with community leaders and attempts to persuade them to grant her an exit visa to the outside world. After her request is denied, she decides to take matters into her own hands.

In an April 2022 conversation titled "Memory Work as Care Work: Black Archives and Archival Practices," archivist Zakiya Collier and her co-panelists assert the essential role Black memory workers—archivists, curators, and librarians—play in testifying to the complexity of how Black life is lived, documented, and remembered.[1] Through acts of care, memory workers can perceive alternative ways of living that remain invisible to others.

Colonialism, as *Pumzi* illustrates, is not satisfied with merely controlling oppressed people's output but must also distort their memory and relationship to the past. In his 1994 essay "Black to the Future," which contains what is thought to be the first use of the term *Afrofuturism*, the writer Mark Dery asked: "Can a community whose past has been deliberately rubbed out, and whose energies have subsequently been consumed by the search for legible traces of its history, imagine possible futures?"[2] *Pumzi* answers yes, by the acts of studying the world and tending to roots. With nourishment and care, the myth of colonialism's inevitability crumbles to dust. From the ashes—and through the creative ways Black futurism challenges the world order—possibility has a chance once again to grow.

—Maya S. Cade

NOTES
1./ "Memory Work as Care Work: Black Archives and Archival Practices," April 12, 2022, Bard Graduate Center, YouTube video, 1:30:14, https://www.youtube.com/watch?v=Mq45rTP3R4I.
2./ Mark Dery, "Black to the Future: Interviews with Samuel R. Delany, Greg Tate, and Tricia Rose," in *Flame Wars: The Discourse of Cyberculture* (Durham, NC: Duke University Press, 1994), 180.

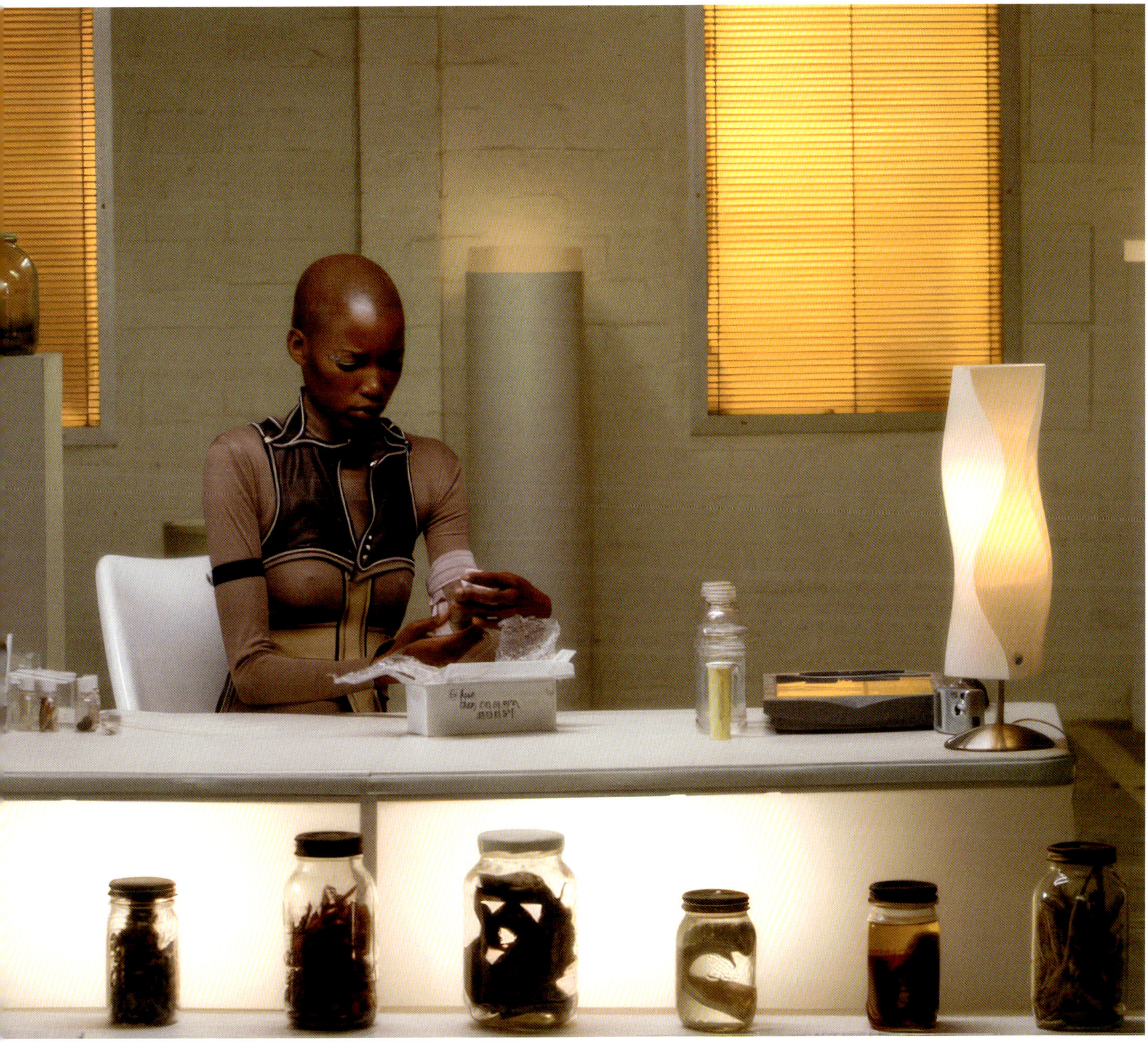

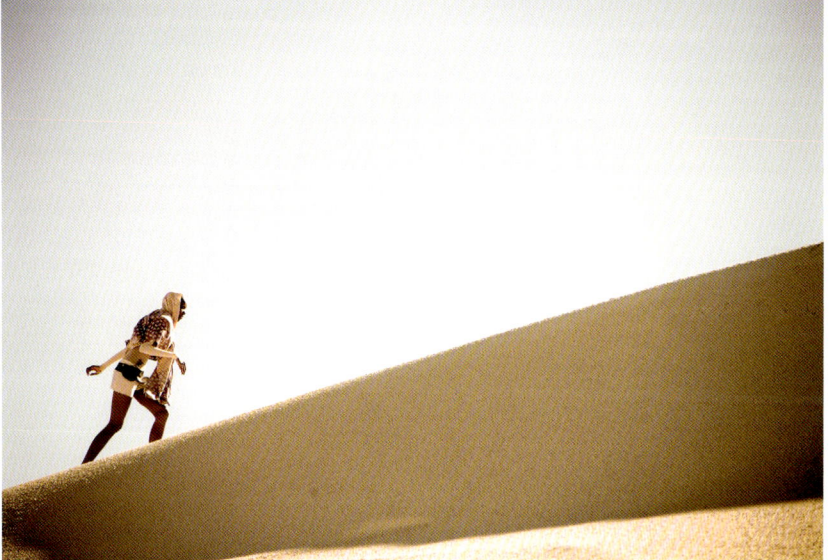

ABOVE, RIGHT, AND PREVIOUS SPREAD:
Kudzani Moswela as Asha

BELOW: Compass that guides Asha through the desert in the film

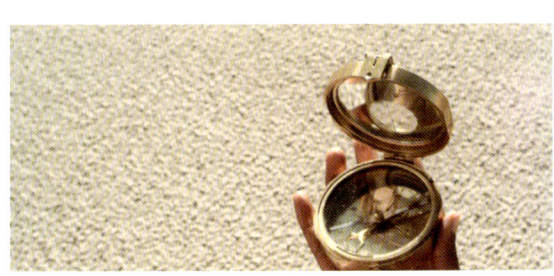

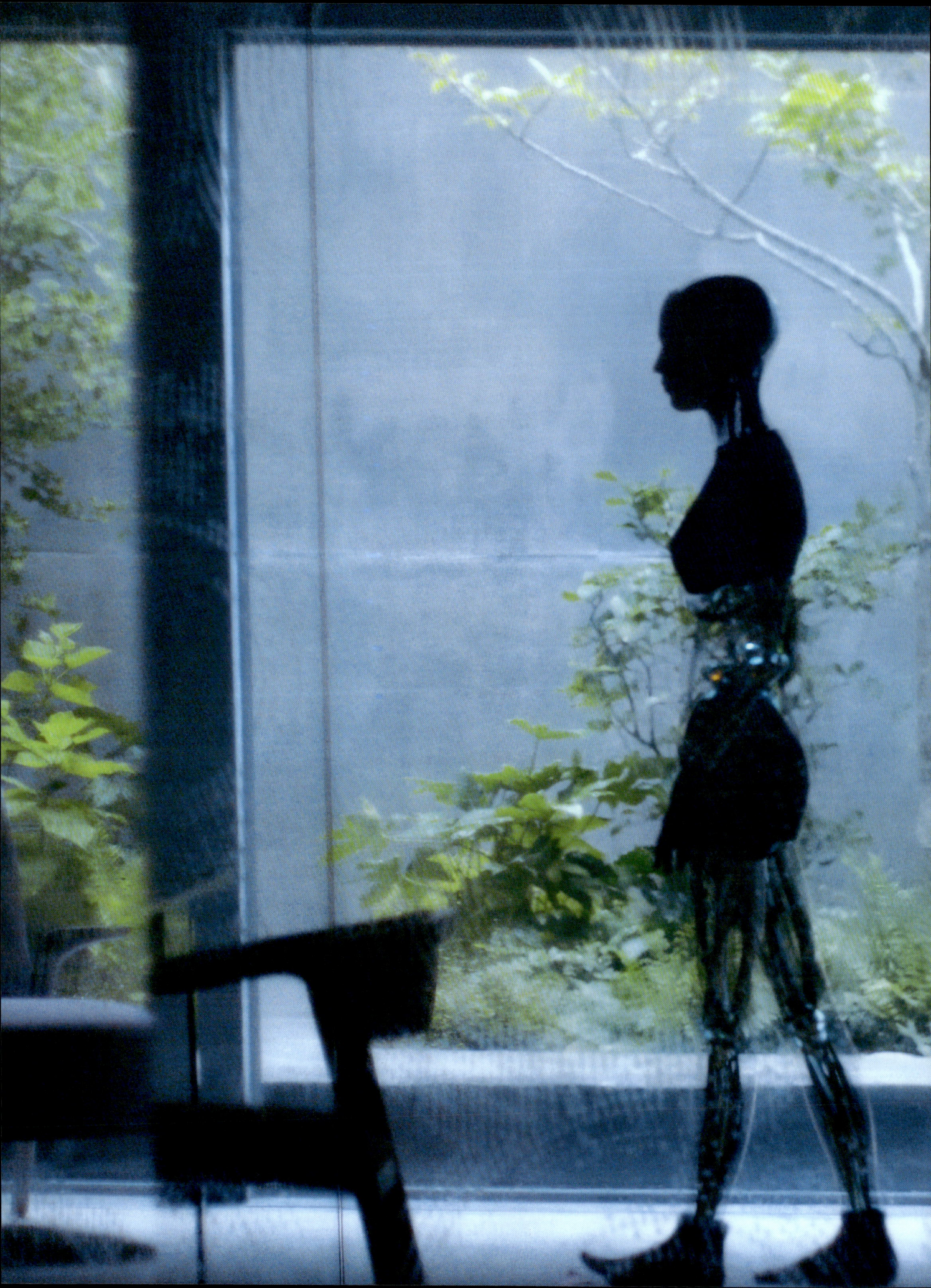

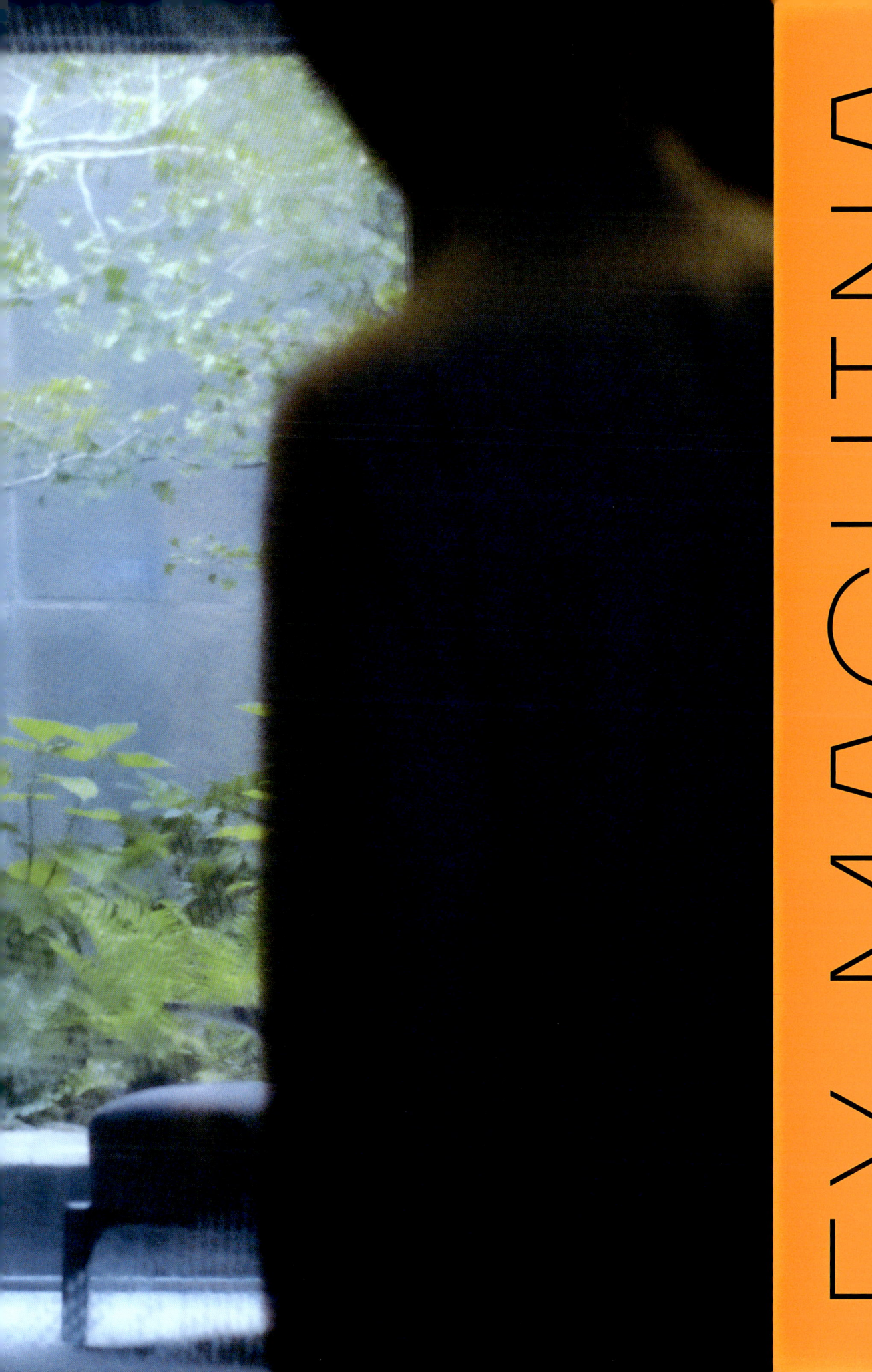

Ex Machina (USA, 2015)
Director: Alex Garland

Film synopsis:
Under the pretense of a random raffle, a computer programmer is invited to the estate of his company's reclusive CEO. Isolated in the CEO's mountain retreat, the programmer performs a Turing test to assess the capabilities of an advanced AI, whose sentience entices and deceives.

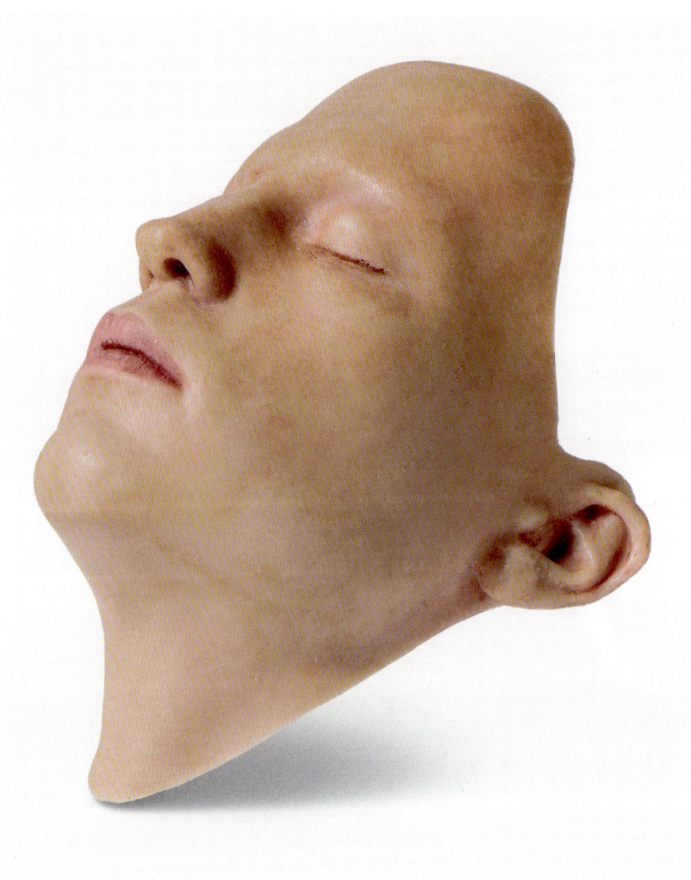

IN 1985 DONNA HARAWAY's "A Manifesto for Cyborgs" suggested the possibility of a cyborg figure that would challenge the oppositional distinctions between human and not-human; as this cyborg called into question the nature of humanity, it would also blur boundaries in other categories, like gender and sexuality.[1] This cyborg, neither human nor machine (and, simultaneously, both human and machine), could embrace new ways of being and, in doing so, highlight the artificial nature of the social systems we've created.

With its frequent use of prosthetics, artificial intelligences, and other cyborg imagery, cyberpunk seemed like the ideal genre in which to demonstrate this radical potential. In practice, however, many filmmakers essentially doubled down on gender, presenting cyborgs as bulked-up masculine power figures, like in James Cameron's *The Terminator* (USA, 1984) and Paul Verhoeven's *RoboCop* (USA, 1987), or as ultra-sexed feminine dolls, such as in Steve De Jarnatt's *Cherry 2000* (USA, 1987) and Duncan Gibbins's *Eve of Destruction* (USA, 1991). Any ability cyborgs might have had to disrupt our understandings of gender or sexual binaries was hidden beneath layers of hulking muscle or curving breasts and slender hips, as though to reassure audiences that these new bodies would pose no real threat to the social order.[2]

Alex Garland's *Ex Machina* more subversively posits cyborg figures who are aware of, and rebel against, their assigned gender roles.[3] To be a cyborg in *Ex Machina* is to be a woman: Ava (Alicia Vikander) and Kyoko (Sonoya Mizuno) are the only female characters in the film.[4] They have both been crafted with female bodies, genitalia, and erogenous zones, and their gendered behaviors come preset: Kyoko has been programmed to serve creator Nathan (Oscar Isaac) both domestically and sexually, while Ava must please Caleb (Domhnall Gleeson), the coder who is testing her. The film's feminism is rooted in gradually unpacking Nathan's and Caleb's expectations that Ava will be submissive, admiring, and heterosexual, and that her personhood can only be granted through a man's evaluation. But while Ava gradually embraces feminine aesthetics in hair, dress, body language,

PREVIOUS SPREAD:
Alicia Vikander as Ava

ABOVE: Ava face prop

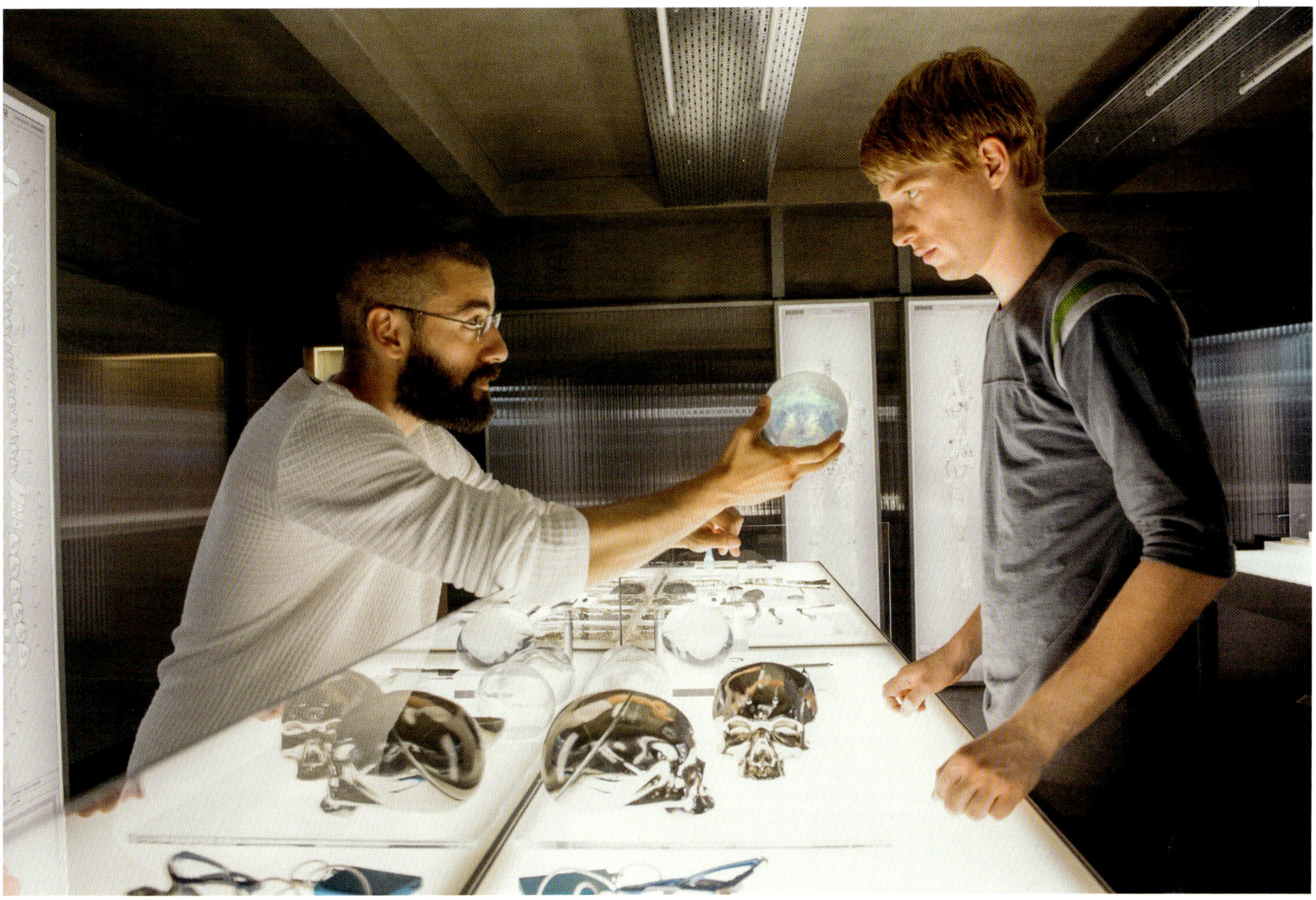

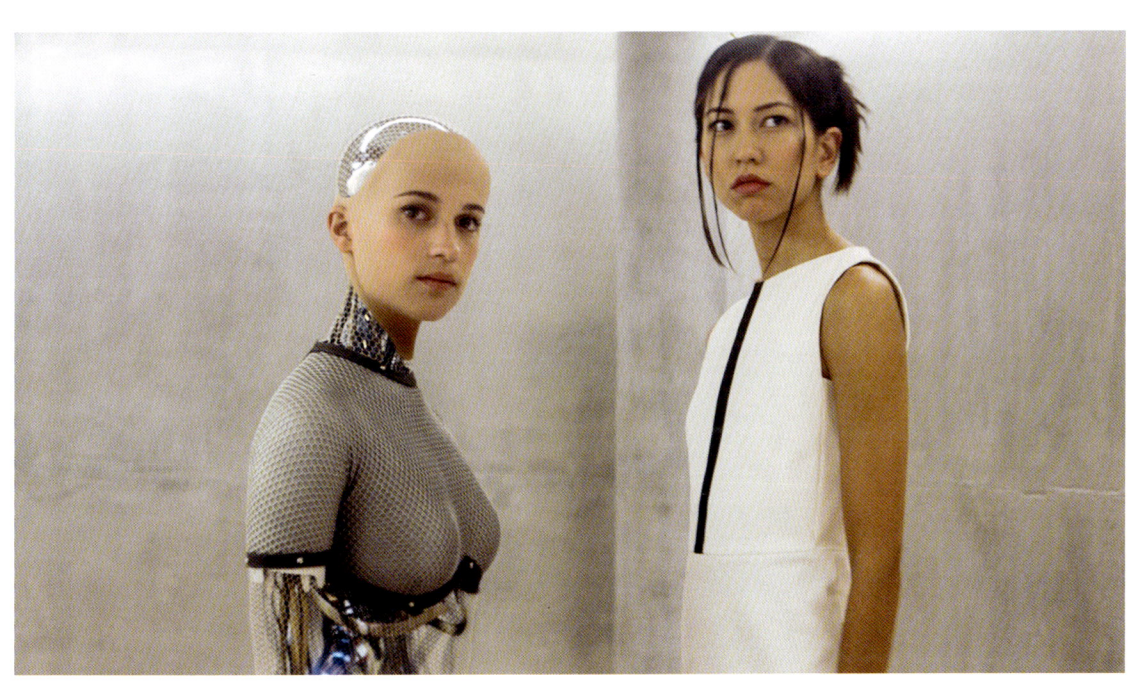

ABOVE: Oscar Isaac as Nathan (left) and Domhnall Gleeson as Caleb

LEFT: Vikander as Ava (left) and Sonoya Mizuno as Kyoko

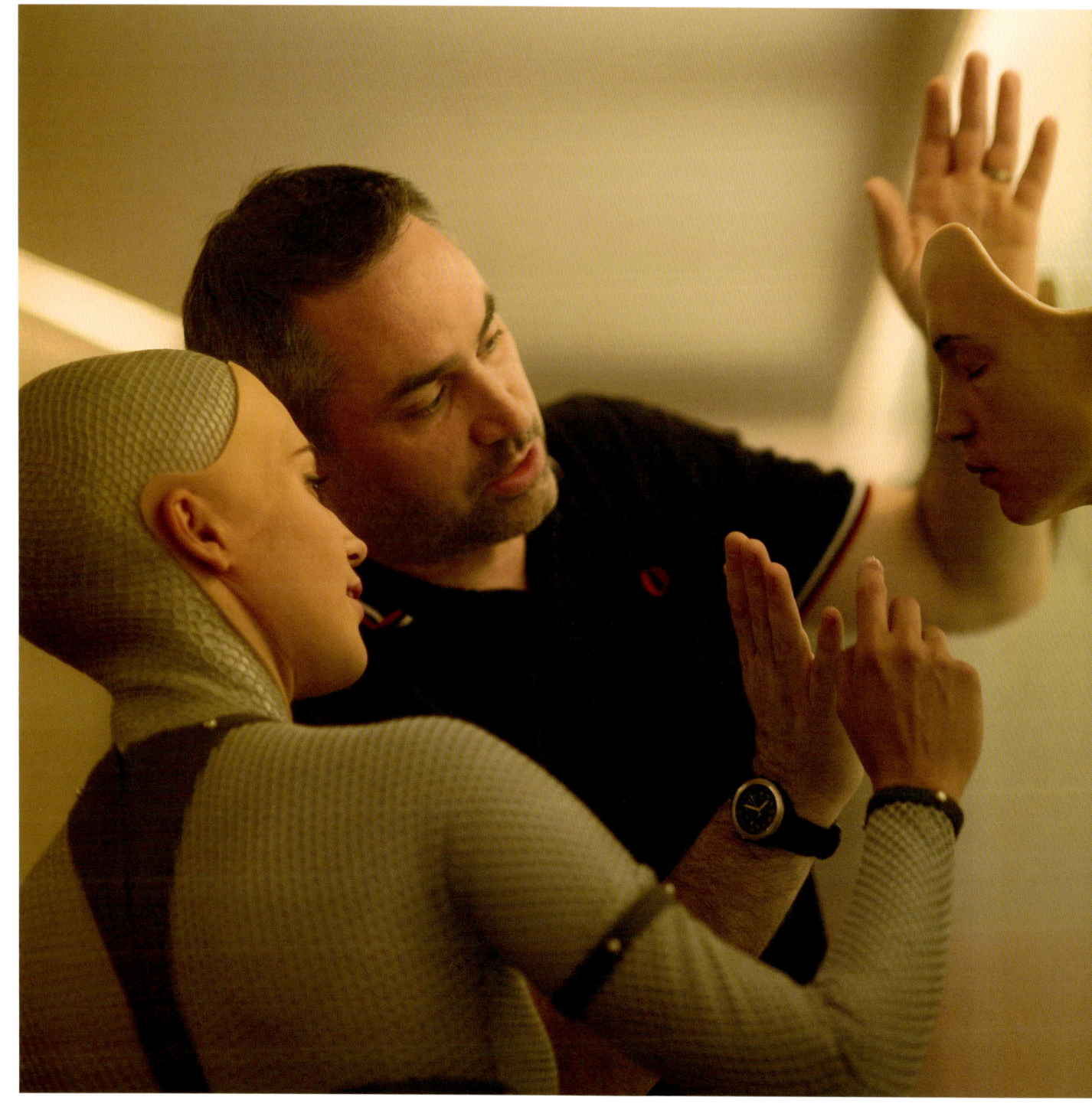

and even outward flesh, she and Kyoko kill Nathan, and she leaves her would-be rescuer, Caleb, trapped, escaping into the world to do as she pleases. The more she claims her feminine appearance, the more she also rejects its implications within a patriarchal social order.

Ex Machina is not a perfect demonstration of Haraway's disruptive cyborg or of feminist politics; rather, the film continues the tradition of hypersexualizing women's bodies through costuming and camera angles as well as the men's objectifying gazes. Further, it fails to challenge racial hierarchies: Kyoko's racialized Japanese body is overtly abused, while Kyoko herself is literally voiceless and dies rather than achieving the same freedom as Ava, who presents as white. Despite these limitations, the film does use cyberpunk's cyborg imagery to call gender into question—specifically, women's assigned roles as subservient pleasure objects, and the degree to

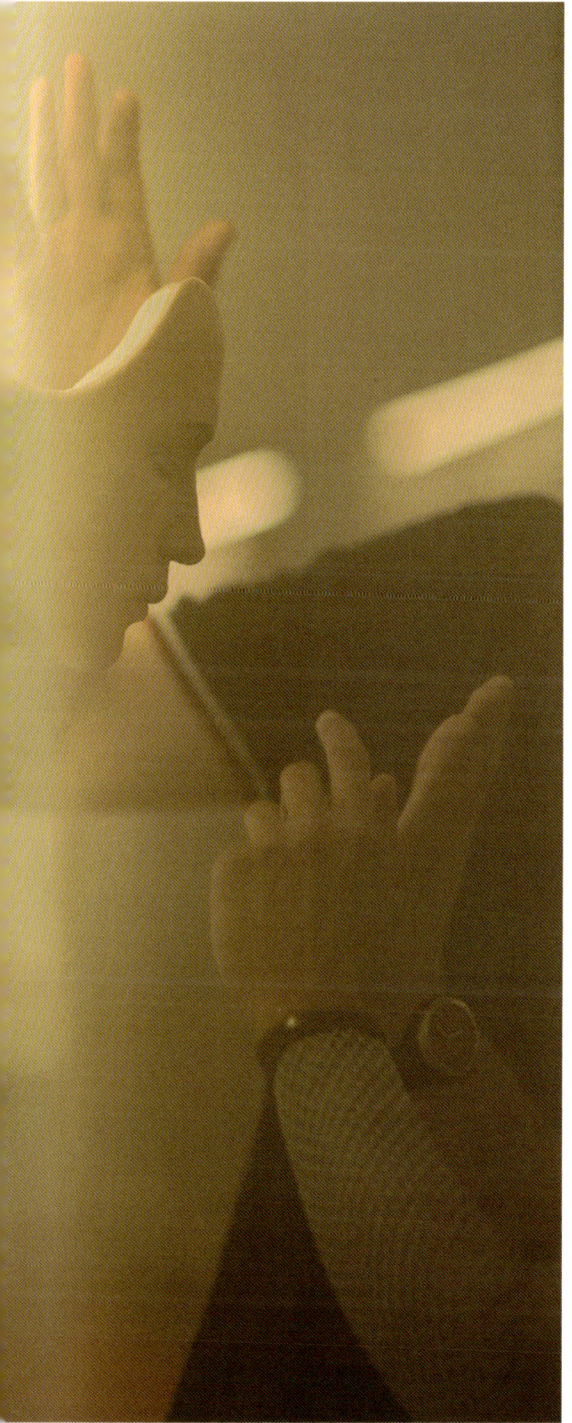

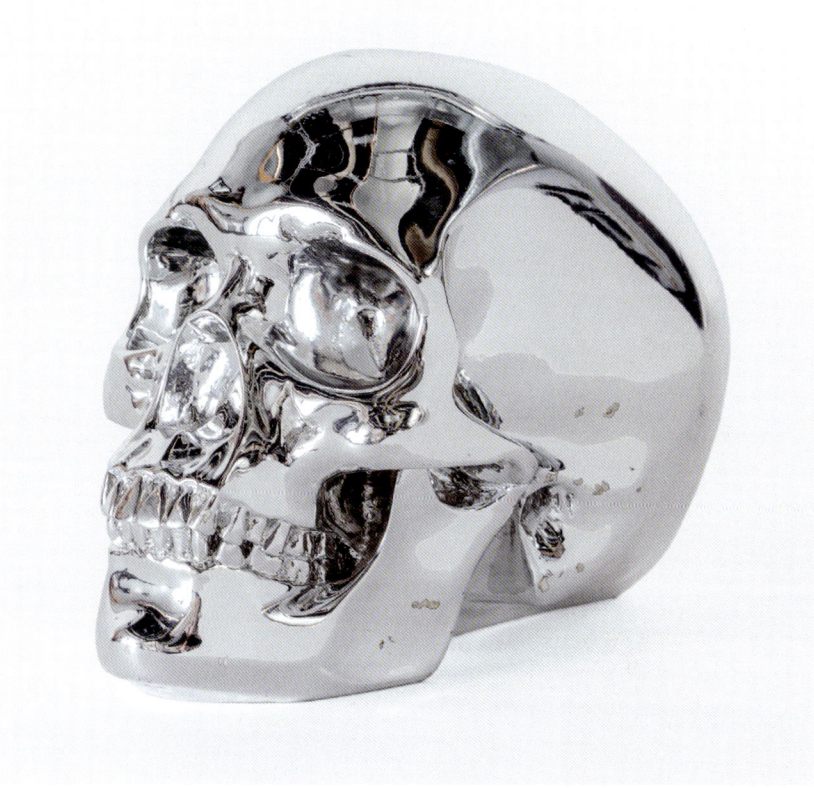

LEFT: Writer-director Alex Garland and Vikander on set

ABOVE: Chrome skull prop

which this behavior is both constructed and imposed by patriarchy. As Ava achieves her dream—people-watching at a traffic intersection—at the end of the film, the viewer is left to speculate on what she, as both woman and machine, might do next.

—Carlen Lavigne

NOTES

1./ Donna J. Haraway, "A Cyborg Manifesto: Science, Technology, and Socialist-Feminism in the Late Twentieth Century," in *Simians, Cyborgs, and Women: The Reinvention of Nature* (New York: Routledge, 1991), chap. 8. First published as "A Manifesto for Cyborgs," *Socialist Review* 80 (1985): 65–108.

2./ Samantha Holland, "Descartes Goes to Hollywood: Mind, Body and Gender in Contemporary Cyborg Cinema," in *Cyberspace/Cyberbodies/Cyberpunk: Cultures of Technological Embodiment*, ed. Mike Featherstone and Roger Burrows (London: Sage Publications, 1995), 157–74.

3./ Similar explorations of cyborgs and gender can be found in cyberpunk literature such as Marge Piercy's *He, She and It* (1991) and Amy Thomson's *Virtual Girl* (1993).

4./ Technically, Ava and Kyoko are embodied artificial intelligences. Many technical distinctions can be made between cyborgs, androids, or robots depending on their blend of technological and organic materials; for purposes of this analysis, Ava has a robot body and her cyborg qualities are not organic but rather anatomical and behavioral.

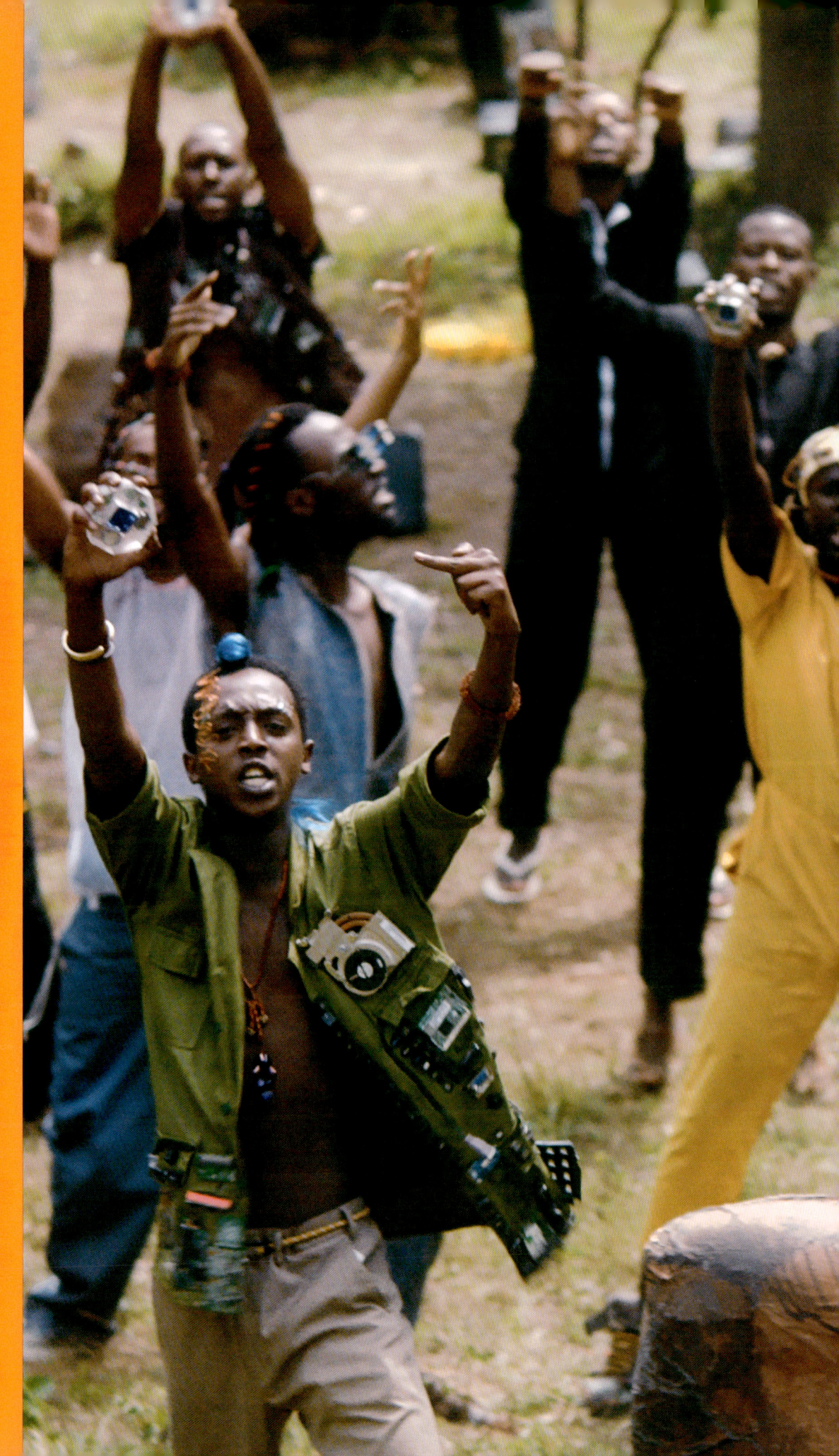

NEPTUNE FROST

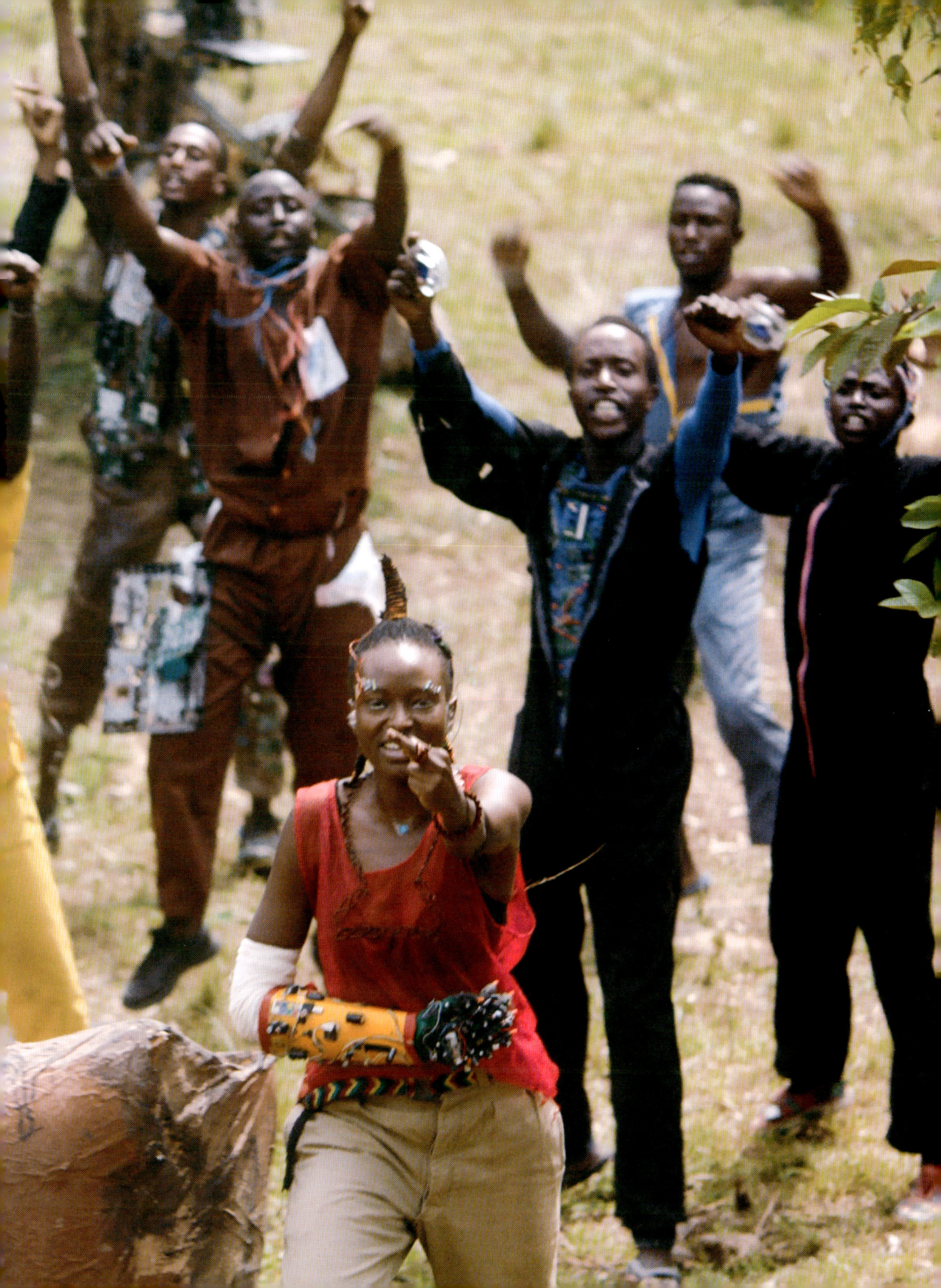

Neptune Frost (Rwanda/USA, 2021)
Directors: Anisia Uzeyman and Saul Williams

Film synopsis:
Set in a futuristic Burundi, this Afrofuturist musical follows the relationship of Neptune, an intersex runaway, and Matalusa, a miner of coltan. Fleeing oppression and violence, they connect with a hacker collective on a compound shaped by recycled tech waste to take on an authoritarian regime that exploits workers and the land.

Each time I watch *Neptune Frost*, I experience an elevation in consciousness—a new height from which to consider my life, the material world, and the technological configurations that bind our society. Even after multiple viewings, I know for certain I will watch again, because this living, breathing poem of a spoken-word musical is a transcendent cinematic experience that operates as an energetic portal to an alternative state of being. *Neptune Frost* pulls me out of the hopeless shadows of overbearing monopolies, holds me inside a space of instinct, and fills me with such a spectrum of sensation that my heart levitates and hacks back into the values that one of the celestial characters in the film says "connect things, that pair things and connect us to cosmic structure … our ancestors."

Neptune Frost calls me home.

The multidimensional homing pigeon, Frost, channels a conversation where a sound man introduces himself to the character Memory (Eliane Umuhire): "Yeah, I'm a sound man. I build systems of sound. I've always felt and built from memory. I dreamt and saw a wheel like Ezekiel. He said, 'Sound holds memory.' I walked here and you arrived, and your name is Memory." She answers, "Yes, the war forced us into other dimensions where the worst had already happened. A new idea blossomed with greater awareness. … Birds fly through portals where pain is the only passport."

Directors Anisia Uzeyman and Saul Williams invented a way to make a film that reconnects all of the pieces of today's technological reality—those visible and those rendered invisible—to paint a

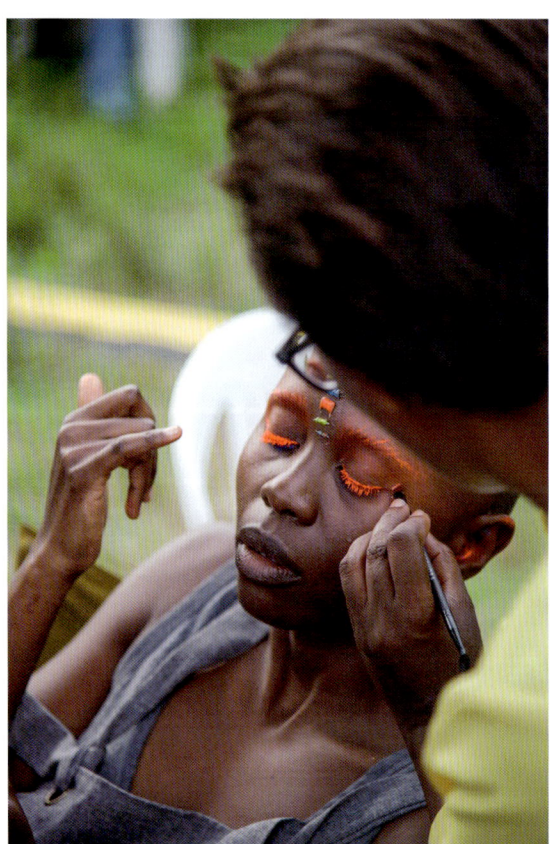

PREVIOUS SPREAD: The hacker collective resistance

LEFT: Actor Eliane Umuhire during makeup application on set

complete picture of our global digital circuitry: how the vibration of colonized African bodies who mine the vibrating rare earth minerals integrate with the devices we hold in our vibrating hands as we tap into invisible waves of electricity and vibration frequencies. And music.

Apple Inc. uses the metallic ore coltan to create smartphones, to harness the power of music to capture human culture. The company's personal device

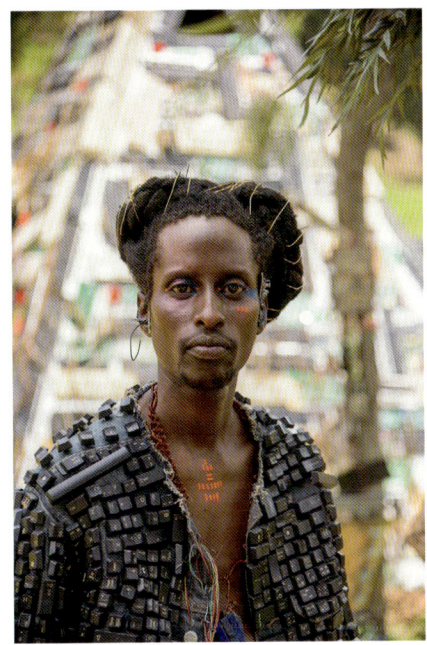

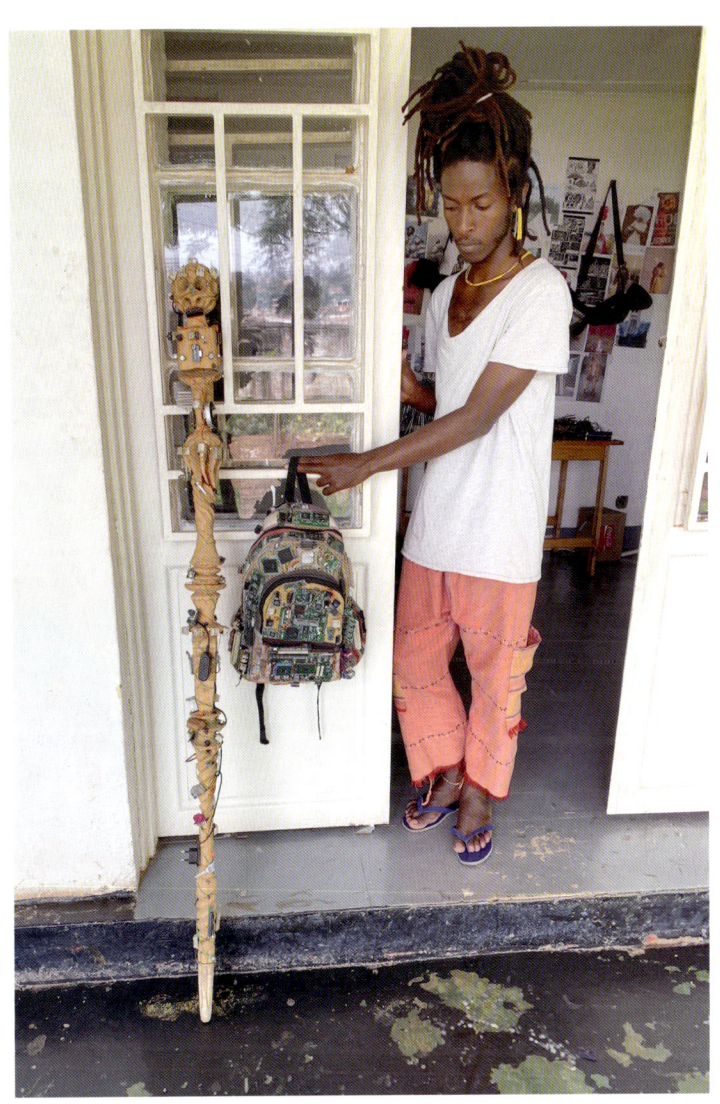

ABOVE: Bertrand Ninteretse as Matalusa

RIGHT: Costume designer Cedric Mizero during production

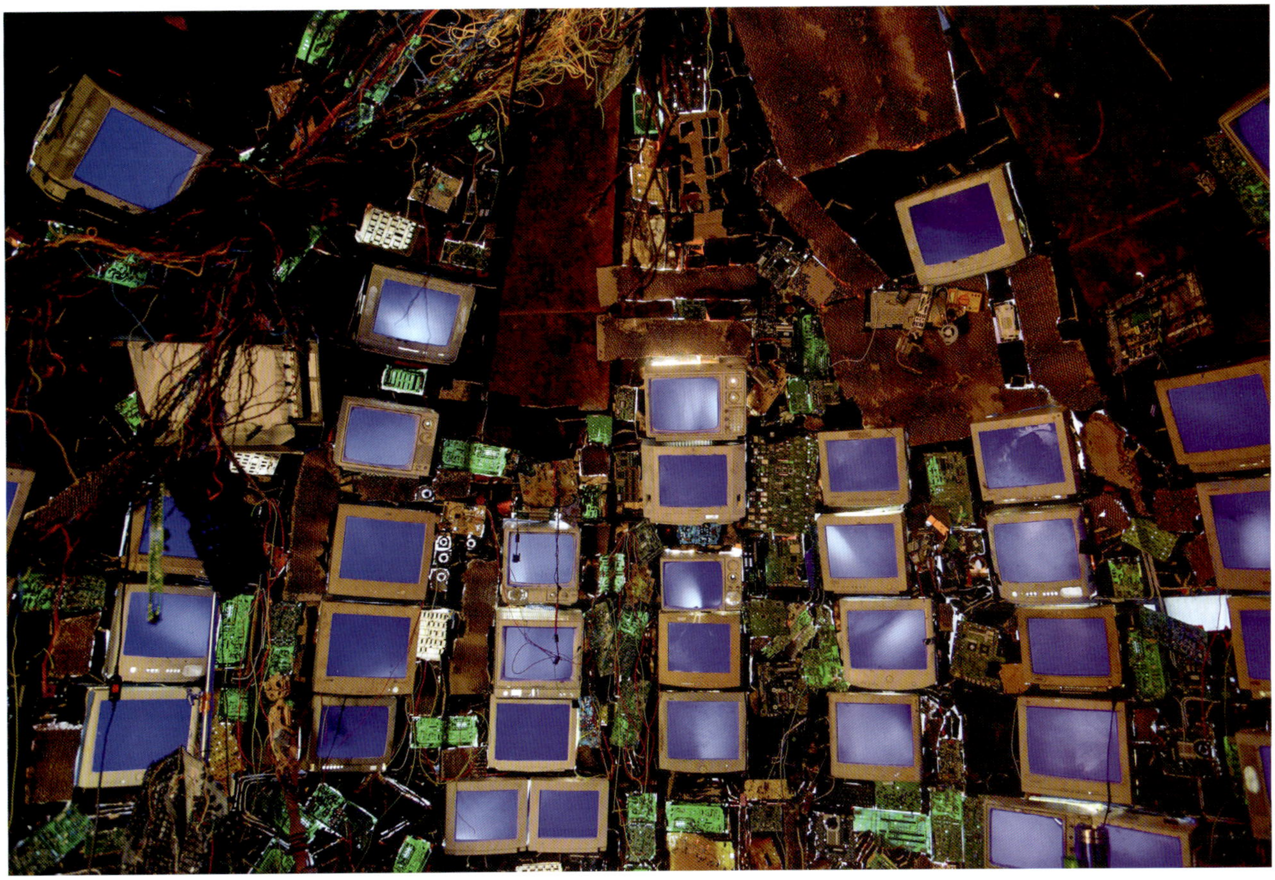

BELOW: Hacker collective base set built of recycled electronic materials

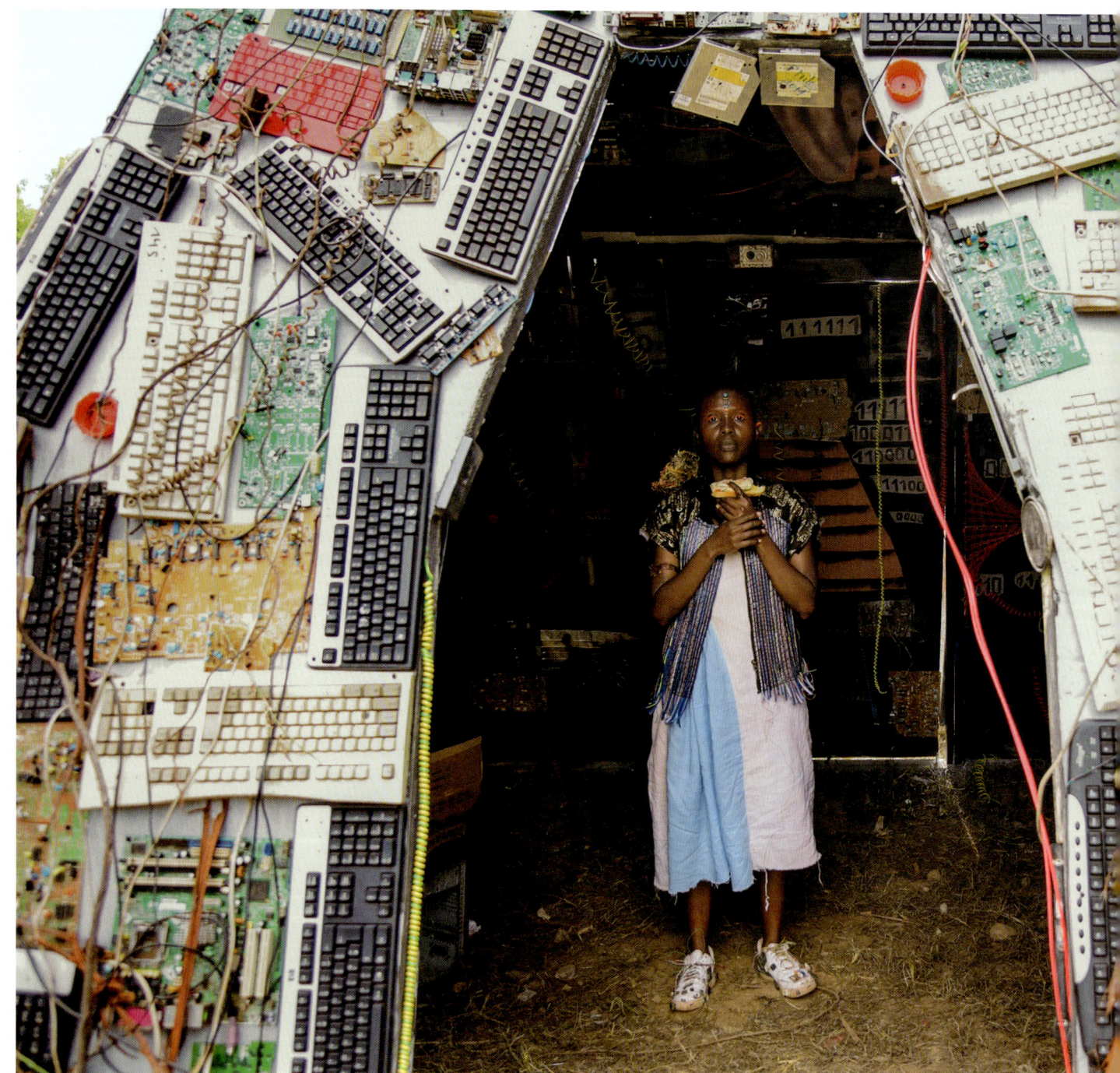

line started using music as a touchpoint to their tech, effecting results so powerful they became the biggest company in the world.

Monopolistic Big Tech continues to attempt to capture human attention while burying our radiant human values behind their story of "The Future" to claim OUR future. But *Neptune Frost* reminds us that our digital circuitry exists beyond Big Data.[1] As elucidated in the film, we live in a delay-tolerant data network of vibrating bodies, sneaker nets,[2] ancestral transmitters, geofrequencies, and energetic firewalls, all of which also connects us to one another through music, a medium that ordinarily, and every minute, transcends time and space.

We do not have to wait for Big Tech's "The Future."

Neptune (a continuously transitioning character played by both cis male actor Elvis "Bobo" Ngabo and cis female actor Cheryl Isheja) is made whole when she penetrates the gender tyranny firewall to traverse into the alternate-geocache-dimension-beyond-war that is Memory's realm. In this radiant domain of

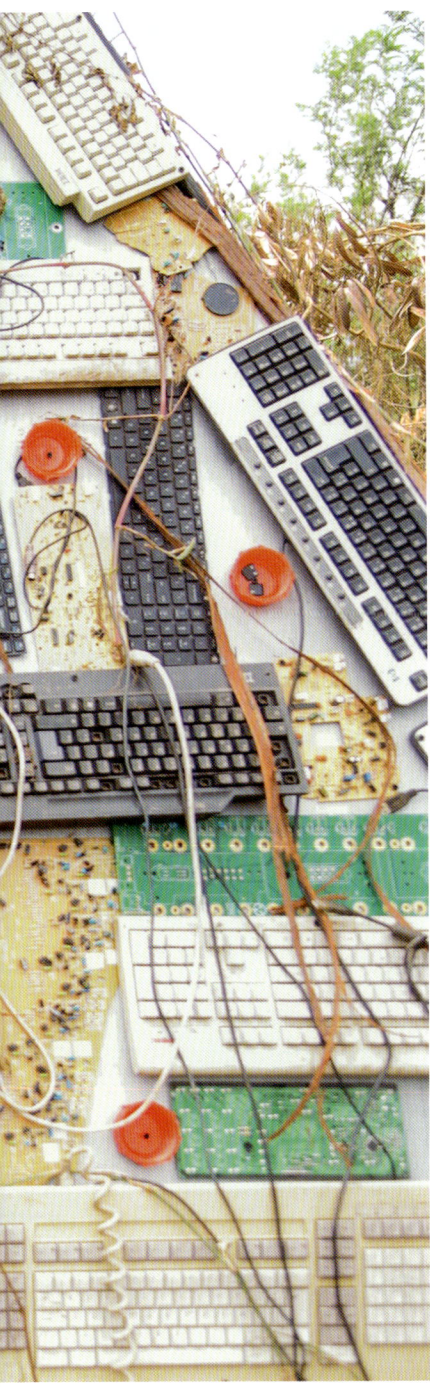

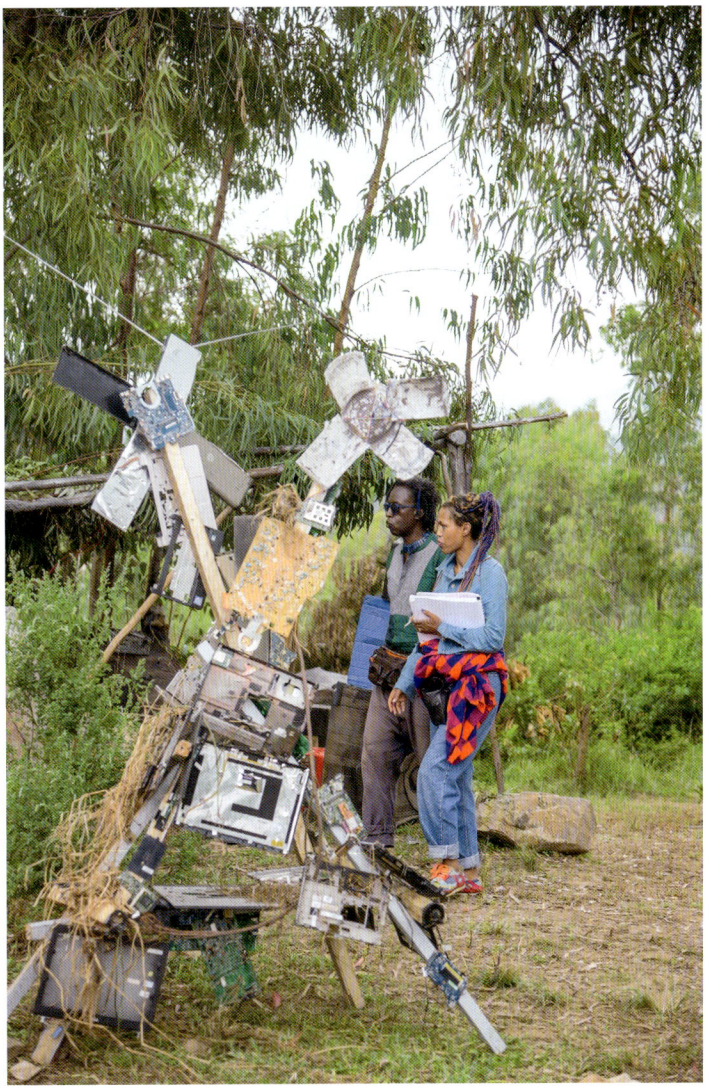

LEFT: Umuhire as Memory

ABOVE: Directors Saul Williams and Anisia Uzeyman on location

presence, Neptune's expansive identities become unified and present as the Motherboard and embody the truth of our global data circuitry, vibrantly illustrated through the costumes by Rwandan fashion designer Cedric Mizero. Inside Memory's realm, Neptune finds love, power, and redemption.

Redemption seekers are so often drawn to the call of love, power, and The Future. I watch this film and feel it coursing through my veins. I know I will find myself, once again, watching, rewinding, and writing lines that break open my mind, reconnect my heart, and enable me to perceive myself and the world around me as wavelengths and rhythms and music, and performance, and visual cadences and painterly patterns that I myself am a part of. It places me squarely on the path to "The Future is now." I will continue to watch this film until I become this film.

I have my passport of pain in hand. I want to be home.

—*Shari Frilot*

NOTES

1./ An Xiao Mina, "The Internet Is Like Water—Global, with Extreme Differences in Access," Medium, April 21, 2015, https://anxiaomina.medium.com/the-internet-is-like-water-global-with-extreme-differences-in-access-68090e53ba7c.

2./ "Sneakernet," Wikipedia, accessed September 10, 2023, https://en.wikipedia.org/wiki/Sneakernet.

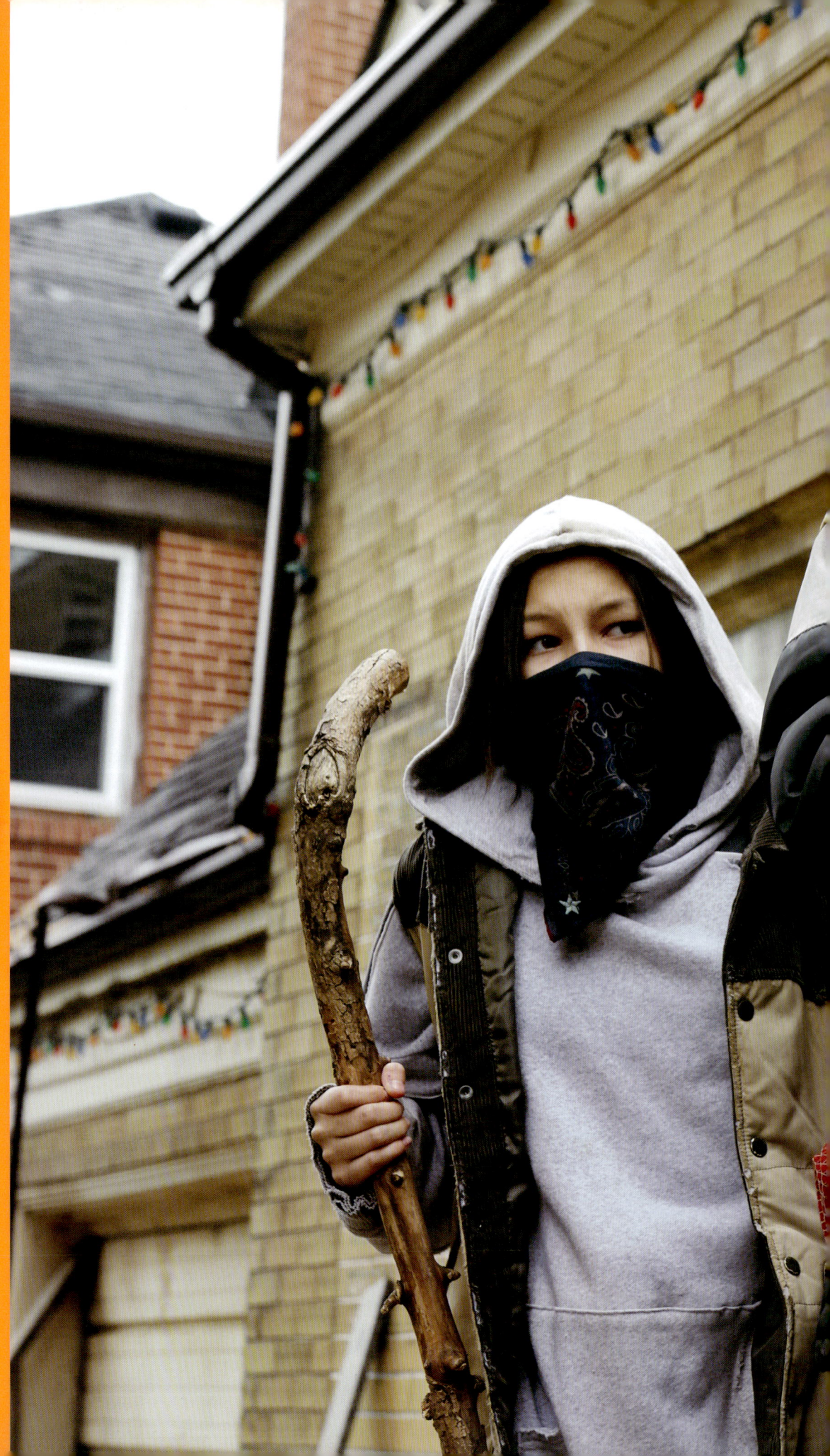

NIGHT RAIDERS

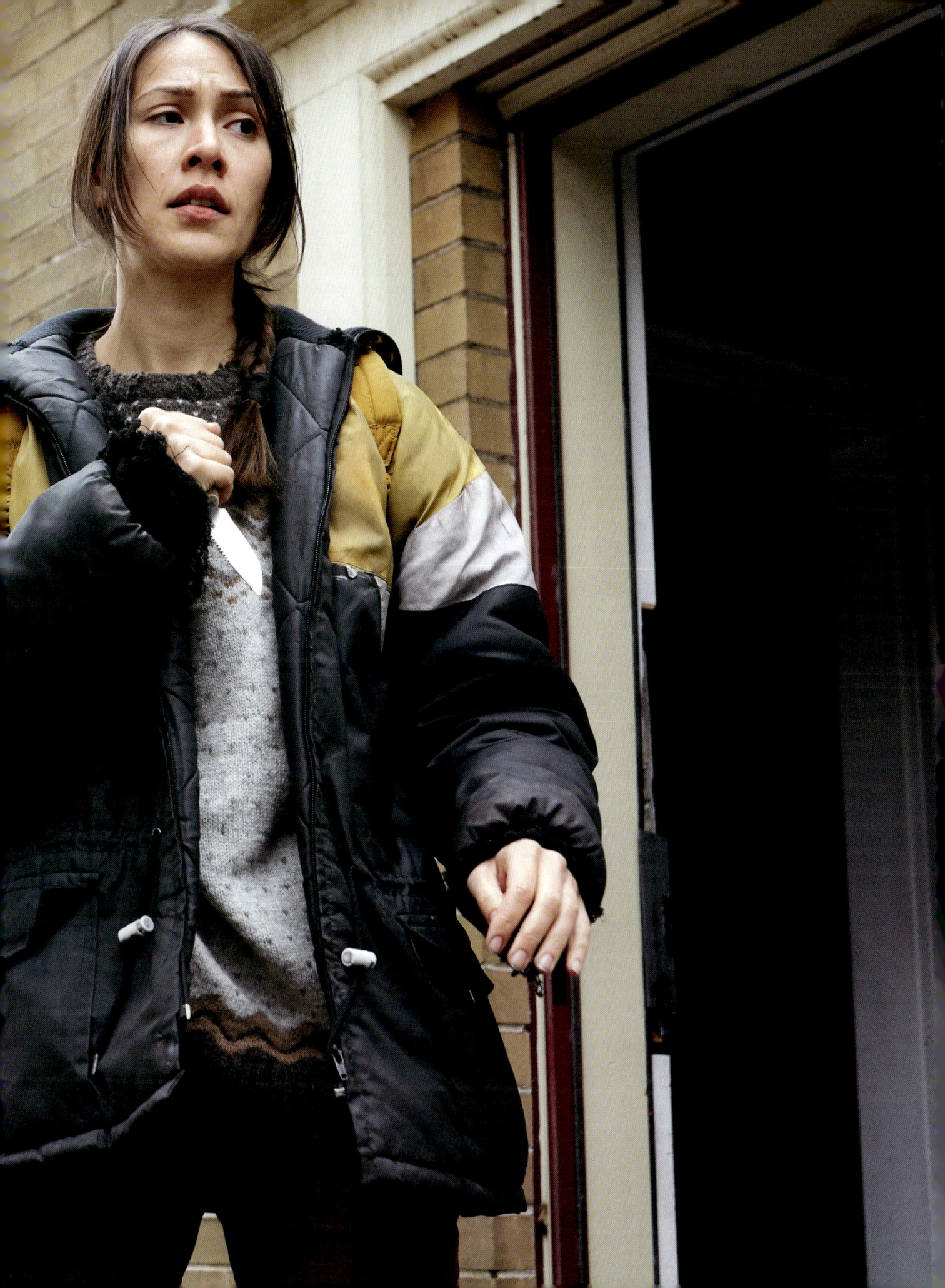

Night Raiders (Canada/New Zealand, 2021)
Director: Danis Goulet

Film synopsis:
In the year 2043, in the aftermath of a civil war, North America is under the control of the Jingos, an authoritarian force that makes children property of the state. Niska, a Cree woman, bands together with a group of First Nations vigilantes to destabilize the military dictatorship and liberate her kidnapped daughter.

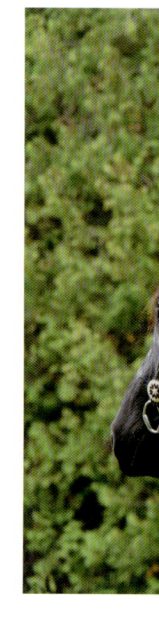

Night Raiders, directed by Cree-Métis filmmaker Danis Goulet, is an Indigenous cyberpunk film that connects the past devastation caused by "Indian boarding schools"[1] of the nineteenth and twentieth centuries to the future survival of Indigenous languages, cultures, and communities. The opening voice-over says, in Cree, "We knew that they would come for us. Like they always had before. We tried to warn the others that they would come for them too. Because we knew how far they would go." The film thus reflects upon its heritage: a fifty-year history of Indigenous science fiction in which alien invasions, apocalyptic plagues, and dystopian plots do not have to be imagined in some kind of distant future but rather represent events that already happened over centuries of European colonization.[2] The opening of *Night Raiders* conveys that these experiences give Indigenous peoples a unique understanding of how to resist, overcome, and thrive in the face of extreme colonial and governmental oppression.

In 2043 postwar North America, all children in the colonized territory are required to attend the Academy, a school of forced assimilation. The colonizers, the Jingos, are also training the children to fight, using them as cannon fodder in their ongoing military subjugation of the continent. The film's first images are of a Cree woman named Niska (Elle-Máijá Tailfeathers) and her daughter Waseese (Brooklyn Letexier-Hart) living off the land in a forest. Despite the idyllic setting, they must still evade flying Jingo drones that patrol for resisters. When Waseese is captured and ends up in the Academy, the film repeatedly cuts between its cold gray buildings and the green forested landscapes of Cree land. Niska reluctantly falls in with a group of Cree-led resisters, and the film contrasts their laughing, warm community circle with the regimented separation and violent competition Waseese experiences in the claustrophobic spaces of the Academy. By focusing on natural space and joyful human interaction, *Night Raiders* balances its dystopian vision with a clear utopian possibility founded in Cree land, culture, and community.

At the end of the film, when Jingo soldiers and their drones come to destroy the Cree-led community and extract its resources, Waseese is revealed as the hacker guardian who was prophesied by Cree elders. Once freed from the Academy, she faces down the drones and speaks to them in Cree. Their response is to break military formation, fly like a flock of birds, and chase off the advancing Jingo soldiers. Goulet's film thus embraces the rich tradition of feminist cyberpunk—embodied by works like Marge Piercy's novel *He, She and It* (1991)—which centers on women hackers and protagonists. It also skillfully traces cyberpunk's dystopian features, such as totalitarian governments and technologies of bodily control, to the enduring impact of European colonialism. The solution to living inside a dystopian nightmare—especially for Indigenous peoples—is decolonization, not assimilation.[3]

—*Patrick B. Sharp*

NOTES
1./ Beginning in the early nineteenth century, hundreds of boarding schools were created in Canada and the United States with the express purpose of removing Indigenous children from their families and cultures to force their assimilation into a white way of living. Many such schools operated until the late twentieth century, using methods that included torture and violence, with thousands of children dying in the process.
2./ For an overview of Indigenous science fiction literature, see Grace L. Dillon, "Imagining Indigenous Futurisms," in *Walking the Clouds: An Anthology of Indigenous Science Fiction*, ed. Grace L. Dillon (Tucson: University of Arizona Press, 2012), 1–12.
3./ Dillon, "Imagining Indigenous Futurisms," 10.

PREVIOUS SPREAD: Elle-Máijá Tailfeathers as Niska (right) and Brooklyn Letexier-Hart as Waseese

BELOW: Tailfeathers as Niska

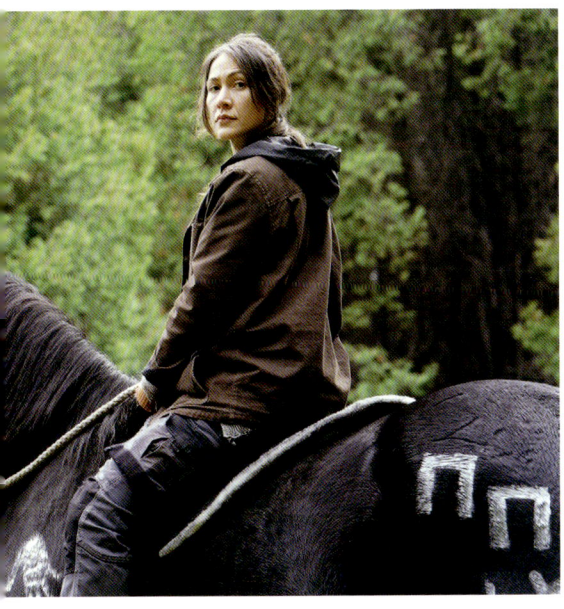

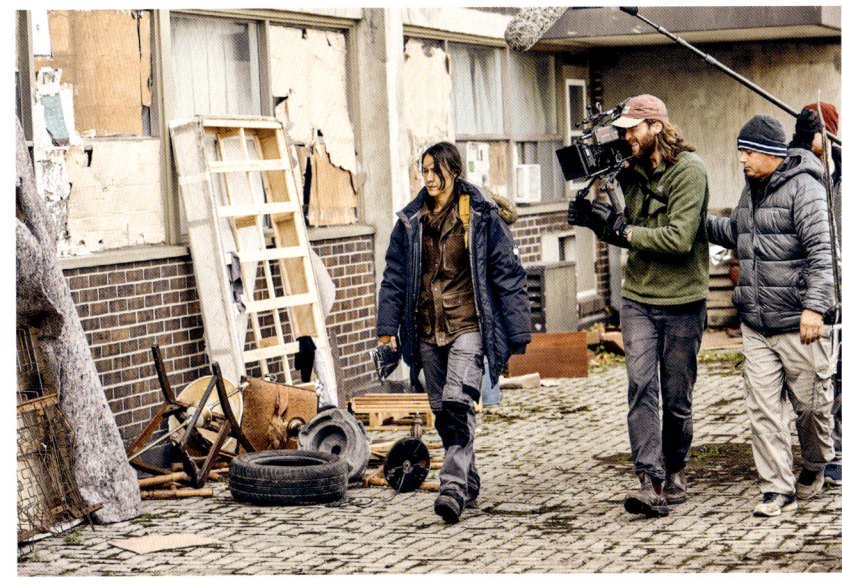

ABOVE: From left: Tailfeathers, cinematographer Daniel Grant, and unidentified crew during production

BELOW: Concept art for the drone

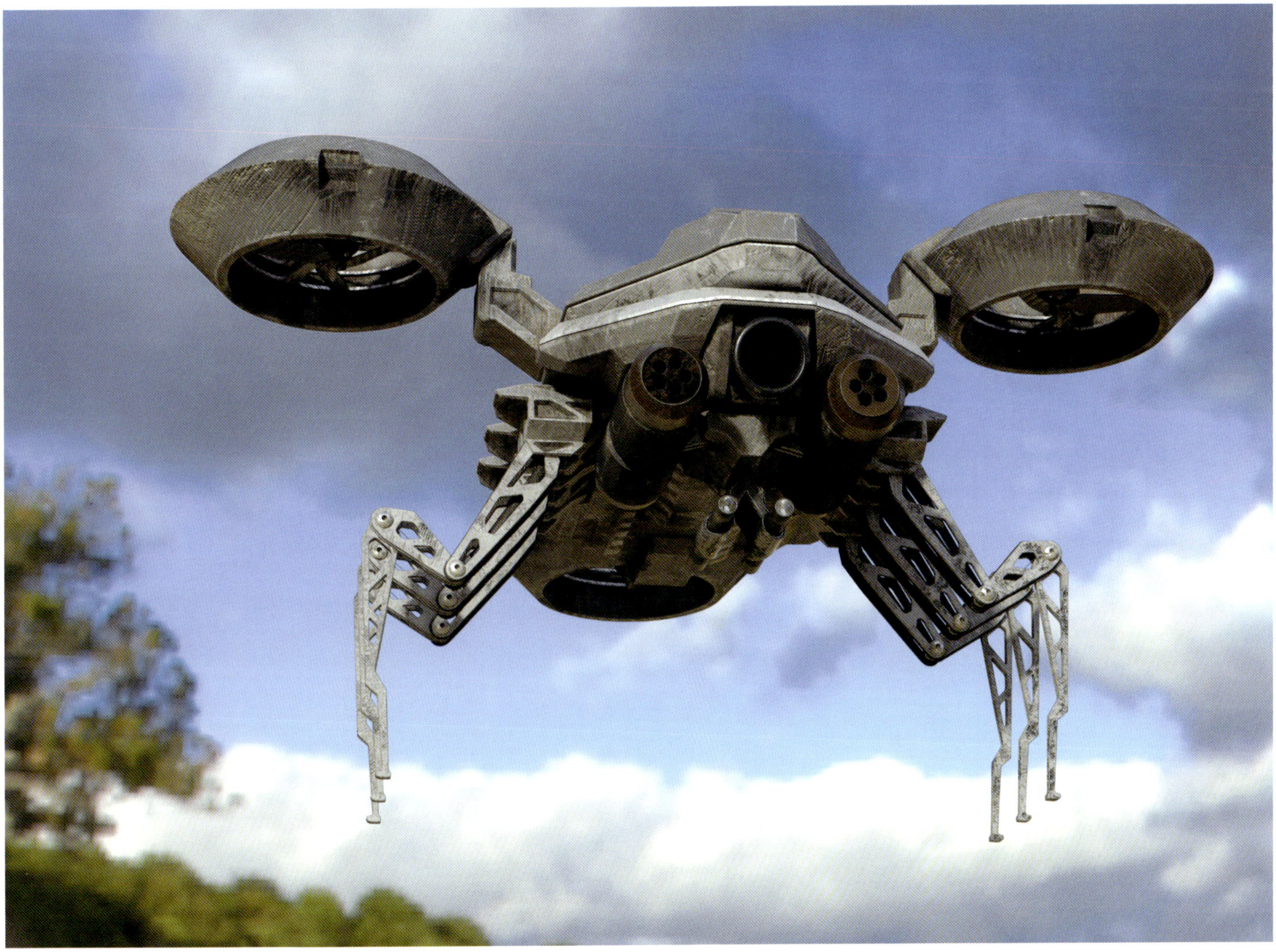

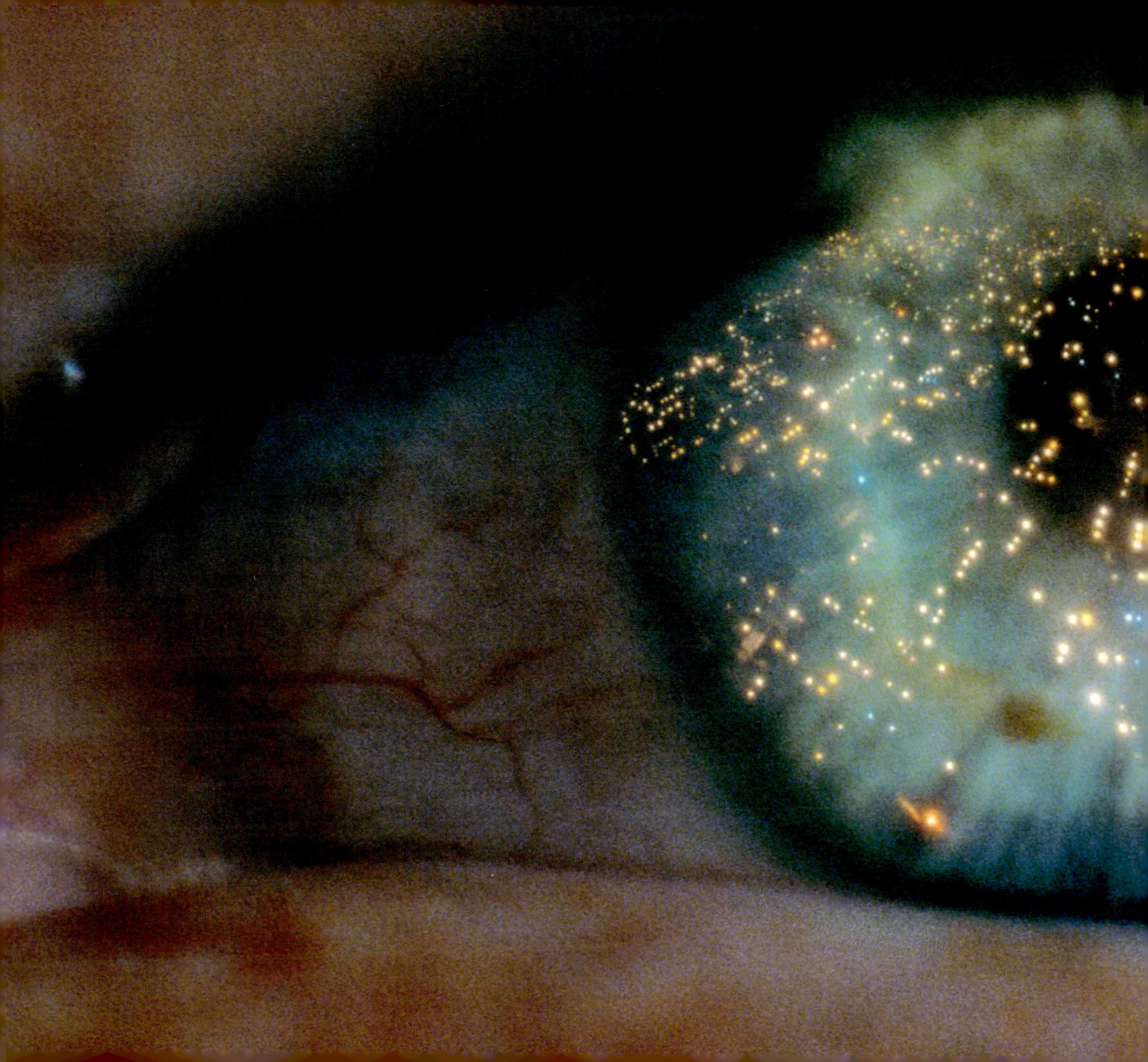

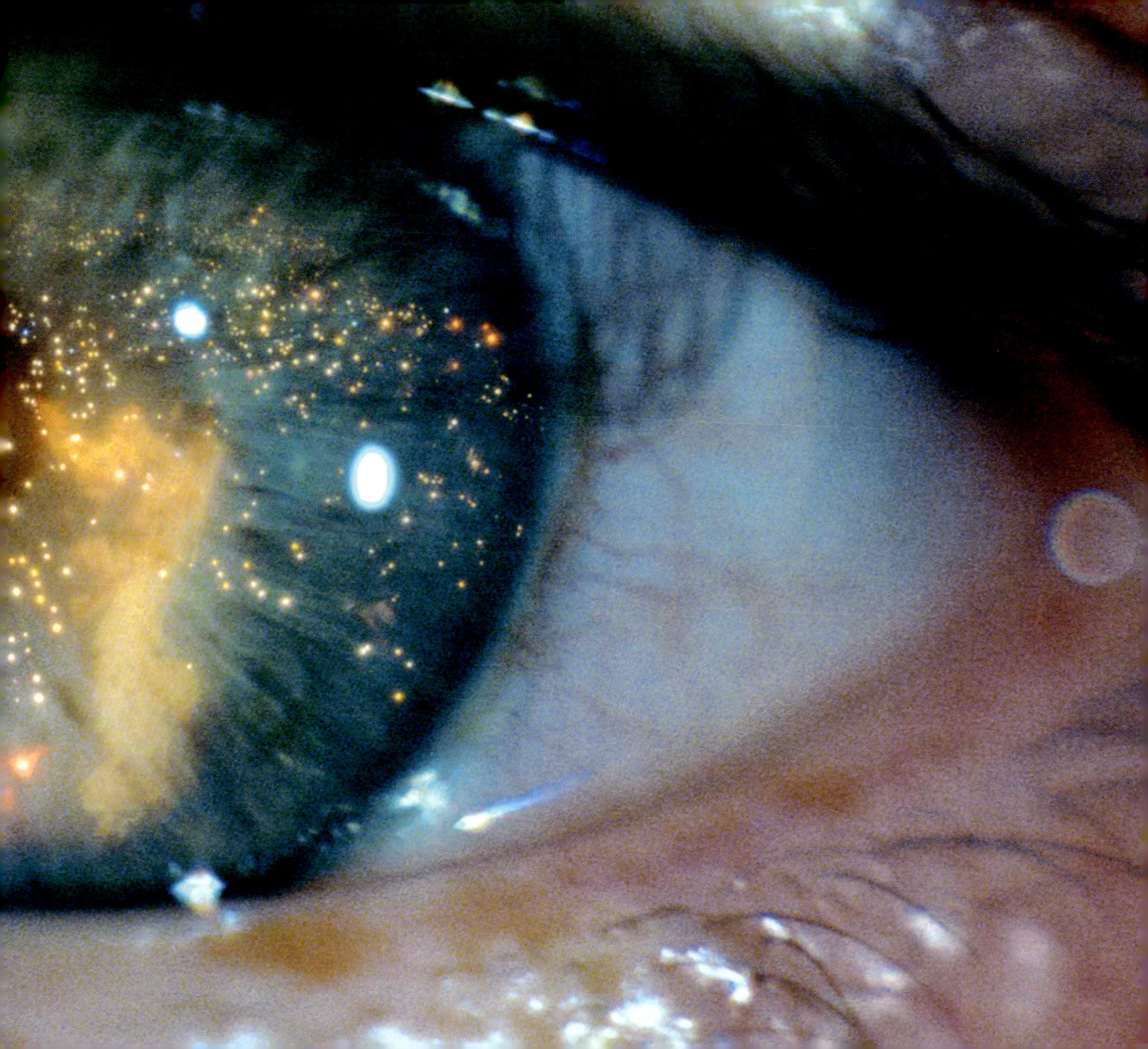

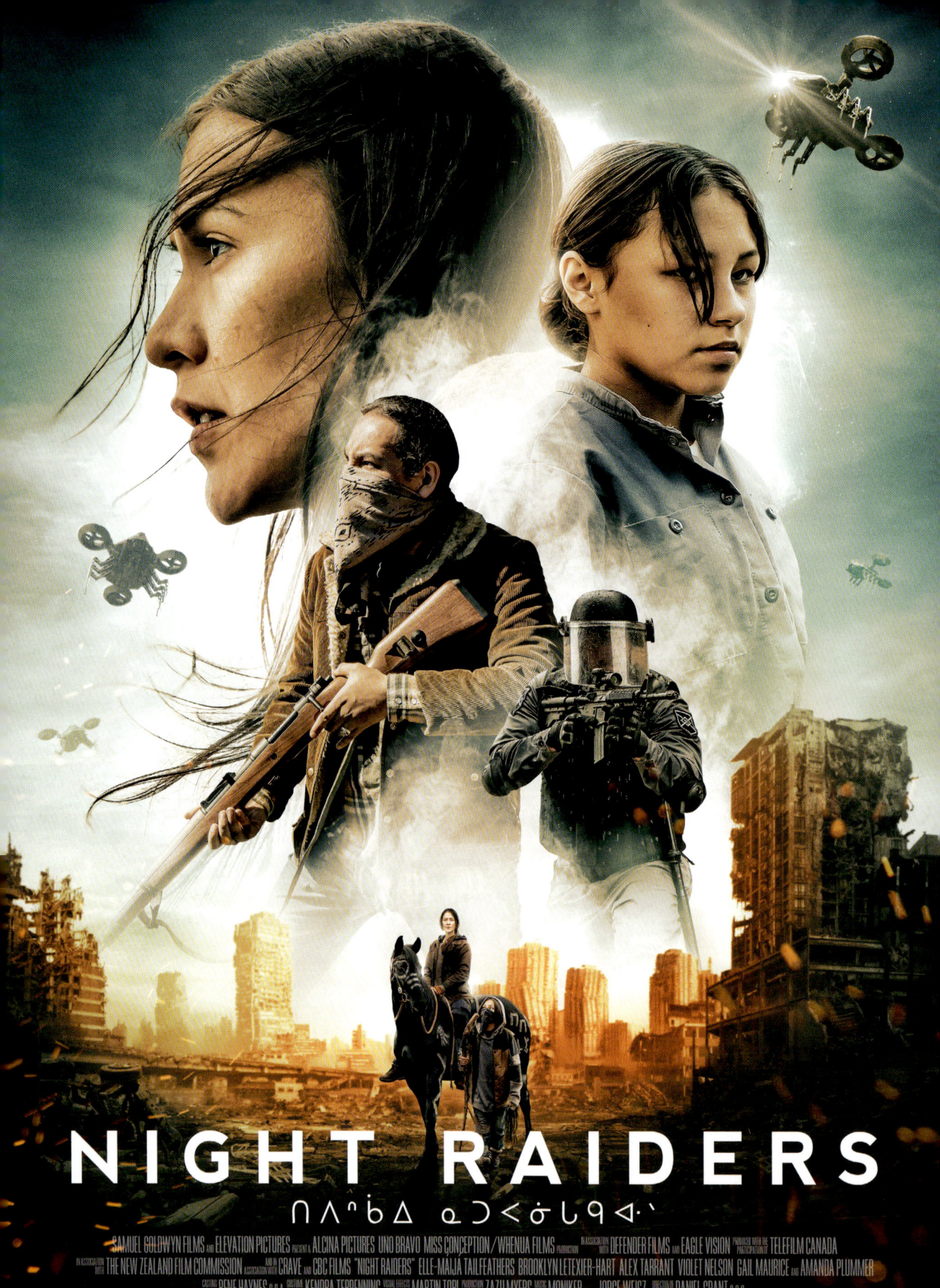

Futurisms: A Conversation with Danis Goulet and Wanuri Kahiu

Doris Berger: Danis and Wanuri, we are so excited to be able to feature your films in this exhibition and to explore Indigenous futurist and Afrofuturist movies in dialogue with cyberpunk cinema. Let's start by discussing your respective approaches to envisioning possible futures in your work. Danis, what motivated you to make the films *Wakening* [Canada, 2013] and *Night Raiders* [Canada/New Zealand, 2021]?

Danis Goulet: I have always been interested in the threads that connect the past, present, and future, and thinking about time in a nonlinear way. One of the things that I had always thought challenging was the idea of taking beings from our oral stories and putting them onscreen. I felt the way these oral traditions were mostly talked about in culture—not in our culture, but in the mainstream culture—was as these quaint folkloric stories from Indigenous people. To me, these are the stories that I grew up with; they were the stories of this land. These stories served a purpose or sometimes functioned as a warning; they were teachings. For *Wakening*, I created a dystopian downtown Toronto where there's an occupation on Canadian land, which is pretty much the situation for Indigenous people in Canada anyway. The film imagines a meeting of Wesakechak and Weetigo, two of the most well-known beings from Cree storytelling. They meet up in a near future where Wesakechak has come to awaken the Weetigo in order for it to turn its hunger on the occupation, as an effort to win the war. The act of placing these characters in the future was a declaration about the fact that they are always going to be here. When we imagine ourselves in the future, it's a very political and hopeful act. North America tried to eradicate Indigenous people through various strategies, which *Night Raiders* gets into more directly. And when you look at that, we weren't supposed to have a future.

It was something I wanted to express because around the time I started developing *Night Raiders* and I made *Wakening*, there was this incredible resistance movement that started on the prairies in the plains of Canada, close to my homelands in Saskatchewan, which is where I am now. This protest, called Idle No More, spread across Canada. Indigenous people did round dances—where people join hands and stand in a circle—in malls at the height of the Christmas shopping season. It was this incredibly powerful intervention.

DB: Wanuri, what inspired you to make *Pumzi* [Kenya, 2009]?

Wanuri Kahiu: The way *Pumzi* came up for me was one day it just hit me that we buy water, and I thought that was such a ridiculous thing. I started making a film about a couple that was going back into the city from the countryside, and they stopped on the side of the road to buy a bottle of fresh air to take back with them. *Pumzi* means *breath*. I realized that the story I was telling was about our responsibility as humans to be mothers of Mother Nature. *Pumzi* is situated thirty-five years after the water wars. Everybody lives inside because the outside is dead. Asha, played by Kudzani Moswela, finds a seed that is supposedly alive, that is sent from the outside, and she plants it, and it starts to grow. I wanted to tell a story about our relationship with natural resources and with the earth because it has to be a relationship of reciprocity, but it seems very often that we continue to take more than we give.

Nicholas Barlow: What is it about science fiction as a genre that you feel is conducive to your practices and thinking?

DG: Science fiction offers a freedom that I didn't realize I was craving; it allowed the future to be created. I was feeling there was a lot of fatigue in Canada when we talked about the history of what

PREVIOUS SPREAD:
Blade Runner (1982)

LEFT: Theatrical poster for *Night Raiders* (2021)

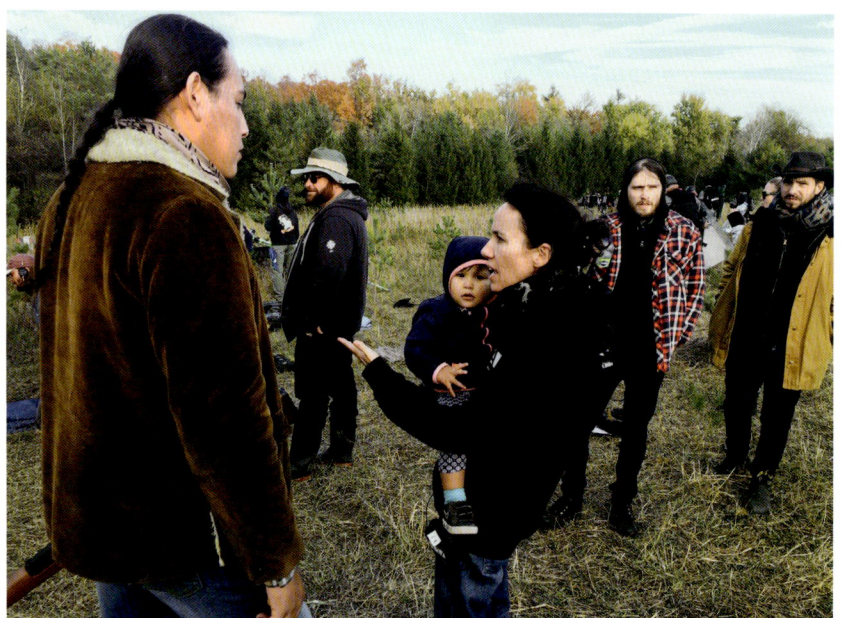

LEFT: Director Danis Goulet (center, holding niece Iskotao) speaks with actor Lindsay Sarazin during the production of *Night Raiders*

happened to Indigenous people. The residential school policy that was inflicted upon Indigenous people was a child-removal policy. *Night Raiders* is based on that history. The same summer we released the film, the Kamloops Indian Residential School started to do ground-penetrating radar, and they discovered the remains of 215 children. That's one school, and there were over one hundred across Canada. It's a horrific situation. I wanted people to be able to imagine what it's like when your children are taken away and you live in a world with no children, so I created a whole world in the future where I imagined a far-right takeover of North America that breaks out into a civil war. *Night Raiders* is in the aftermath of the war. I wanted to invite people in and plunk them in the world where all the circumstances that have already happened to Indigenous people are set up. It was to foster conversation and greater consciousness. I felt that sci-fi offered something that nothing else did.

Everyone has their own interpretation of *The Matrix* [USA, 1999], but mine was colonization—what it is to be a small band of people that are railing against something that feels impossible to fight because it's everywhere. I remember wondering, What would it be like to make that in an Indigenous context? Because so often we are just thought about as victims or in this disempowered way, when we've actually been resisting colonization since the very beginning.

WK: When I started to consider *Pumzi*, I was asked to decide whether I was making a fantasy film or a science fiction film, and it was at that point that it was defined. I knew that I wanted to make a film where science technology was at the heart of it—taking the technology that we currently use and then just pushing it a little further. I hadn't even begun to think that it was African futurist or Afrofuturist or anything, let alone cyberpunk. But the moment I started to create in a space that is supposedly unfamiliar to people who come from my side of the world—i.e., East Africa—the questions became about the genre and not about the film. As if imagination is limited to a zip code. How can an African woman from East Africa even begin to imagine an Afrofuturist world or a science? So the genre itself began to politicize the work that I was doing, when it came very naturally as a story that I was building in the mid-future. And that has now become a really interesting dynamic about accessibility to science and science fiction: who can access it and how we use it. Really, science fiction has always been part of oral history. The use of animals or bugs or using the stars to navigate—there are many African folklore, folktales, and cultural norms that are deeply based in science, so it seems an absurdity not to have science fiction as part of our history and as part of our oral history.

DB: Would you say there's some kind of kinship between Indigenous futurism and Afrofuturism? And what potential do you see in bringing together ancestral imagination and knowledge with speculative fiction?

DG: I think there definitely is a relationship. Indigenous futurism was first talked about in the nineties in the academic and literature space, and it was focused on sci-fi short stories. But it was really building on the legacy and ideas that had

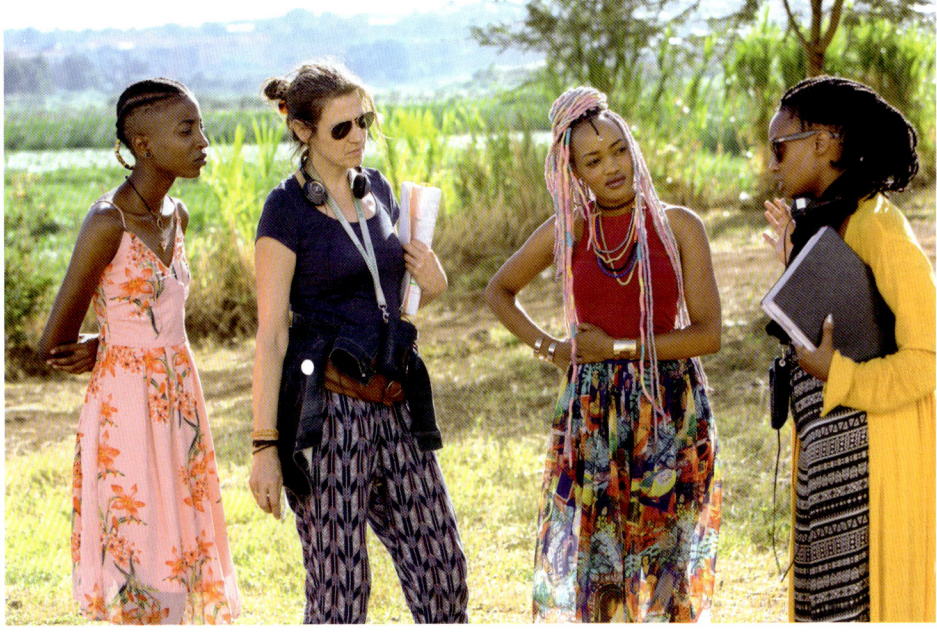

RIGHT: From right: Director Wanuri Kahiu, actor Sheila Munyiva, acting coach Elisabeth Hesemans, and actor Samantha Mugatsia on the set of *Rafiki* (2018)

been established by Afrofuturism. In Indigenous nations across North America, connection to your ancestors and the honoring of ancestral knowledge is prominent; it is the ground we walk on. Language to me contains so much of that knowledge. My dad is a Cree speaker—I grew up hearing it but not speaking it. In the Cree language, there's a complex system of animate and inanimate. You speak about something that's alive in a different way that you speak about something that's nonliving, but it's not a straight-ahead binary. In the Cree language, rocks are considered animate, and so I wondered if drones and technology might also be regarded in the same way in a Cree paradigm. In *Night Raiders*, the young character Waseese, who's grown up around animals and communicates with animals, regards drones as alive in the same way you would regard an animal. Her character's perception of drones as living was a decision that was inspired by the language.

WK: Thinking about ancestral knowledge and speculative fiction: *Pumzi* is based in a world that is run by a council created by women, all different generations. This was to represent a significant part of our culture, which is linked to not only our ancestors but also to our elders. In my culture, you're named after your grandmother, so you become your grandmother. So my father calls me "Mother" because I'm named after his mother. In that very cyclical way, time is not linear, because people repeat themselves—people come back. It was important for me to make sure that, even in the world I created, there was a sense of a constant link to the past and the future, and that that link was continued and unbroken. Even at the end of the film, it feels like a beginning, because time is circular.

NB: I am curious to hear both of your thoughts about placing narratives within utopian versus dystopian worlds, and how you grapple with depictions of oppression, violence, and social and environmental decay in relation to hopeful visions of the future?

DG: Some of the artists that have been a part of the Indigenous futurist movement have talked about the idea that Indigenous people have already lived through the apocalypse. But the hopeful take on that is that you have the skills and the resilience to live through the apocalypse. One of the questions that I wanted to ask is, What does it mean not only to survive but to thrive? Living in a dystopia means that you're in survival mode. It's harder to access joy, connection, love. The beginning of *Night Raiders* finds a character who's very much in survival mode; she's living on the land with her daughter, Waseese, and they're cut off from everything. She then comes upon a camp of Indigenous people who are resisting in spite of the overwhelming oppression that they're surviving. They're creating this beautiful utopian bubble in the midst of dystopia.

WK: I've been investigating this idea of utopian dystopias quite carefully, because I really want to be somebody who builds utopias. I created this idea of Afrobubblegum—fun, fierce, and frivolous images of Africa. It's not based on any framework other than a search for joy, the pursuit of happiness. It's art based on radical hope and awakened curiosity, coming from the African continent. In that sense, *Pumzi* is an Afrobubblegum piece because it is fierce and frivolous in its attempt to say everything and say nothing at the same time. I often try to create spaces

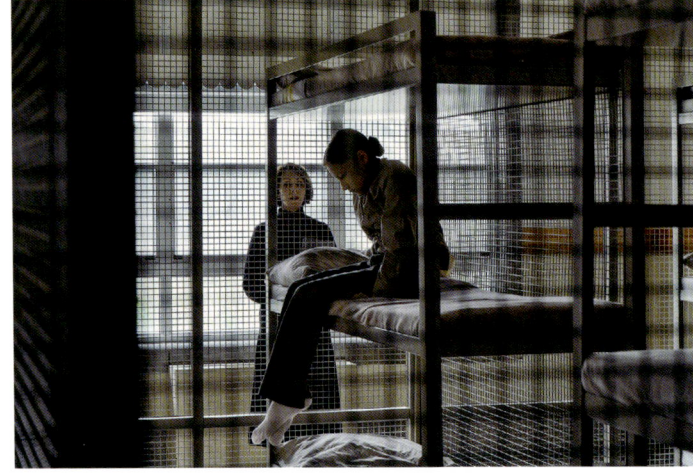 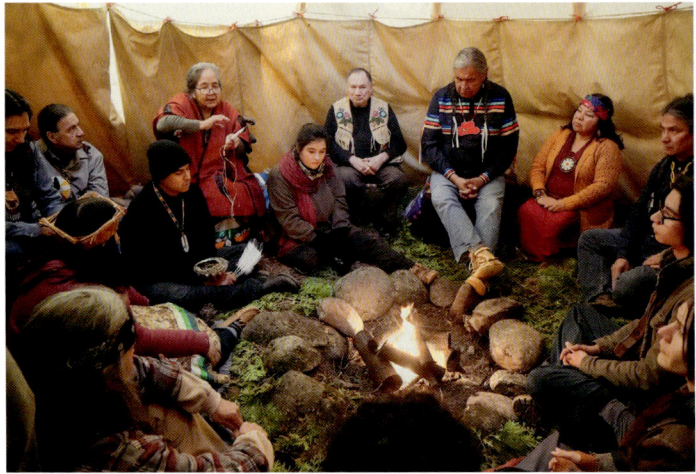

ABOVE: Scenes from *Night Raiders*

free of political oppression in my films and call those utopias.

DB: As independent filmmakers, what are your biggest obstacles in creating speculative worlds?

DG: I worked in casting at first, until I became very disillusioned with what was being made. I was working on a show where there was an Indigenous woman, and at the beginning of the TV show, she walks out in front of a waterfall, stands there stoically and silently, and then sacrifices herself over the waterfall. The value of an Indigenous woman was to be silent and then die, and that's all she did in the show. I watched, one by one, all of these incredible Indigenous actors that had so much to offer walk into this audition and, on repeat, they were silenced and then died, silenced and then died. I just thought, We have to tell our own stories. I looked around and I was like, Who's going to do it? So I quit casting, took a filmmaking workshop, and made my first short film. I also became involved with the imagineNATIVE Film and Media Arts Festival, which was an Indigenous-run festival that was all about Indigenous people as key creatives. I wasn't even dreaming about genre film until I saw the late Jeff Barnaby's early short films *From Cherry English* [Canada, 2004] and *File Under Miscellaneous* [Canada, 2010]. He was doing this really staunch genre work and placing Indigenous experience within genre. It was so new at the time, and there were so many places to go, but the industry was not funding Indigenous film. Canada wasn't even making the distinction between Indigenous content and Indigenous-driven film. So in their minds, if they made *Dances with Wolves* [USA, 1990] or whatever, that was good enough. We had to fight and advocate in so many rooms, and it started in the decades before us—people saying, We deserve funding; we deserve to be behind our stories. It took a lot of advocacy to get to a place where *Night Raiders* could actually get funded at higher budget levels.

WK: There're very few African films that have made money, so it's already a high-risk financial model. It makes it incredibly difficult to get financiers and investors on board, which means that we're very donor and grant dependent, which comes with its own set of ideologies that are not related to the place the film is coming from. Even in the making of my last film, *Rafiki* [Kenya, 2018], there was a conversation about how African the film is—regardless of the fact that I was an African making the film in Africa in an African language—by people who have never been to the country. So the access to funding is very layered, especially when making independent films. It makes it incredibly tricky to start creating work in itself and to get the support for it. We have to realize in a data-minded, data-led world, if you want to see the kind of films you think you deserve—whether it's films made by women, made by Indigenous people, made by minorities, or made from places in the world or the global South that you don't have access to—then make sure that for any device that you're watching it on, you watch films like that. The audiences should know that they matter, and that they are also contributing to the kinds of films that are being made in the world.

RIGHT: Scenes from *Pumzi* (2009)

OVERLEAF: Sketch for *Ghost in the Shell* (1995)

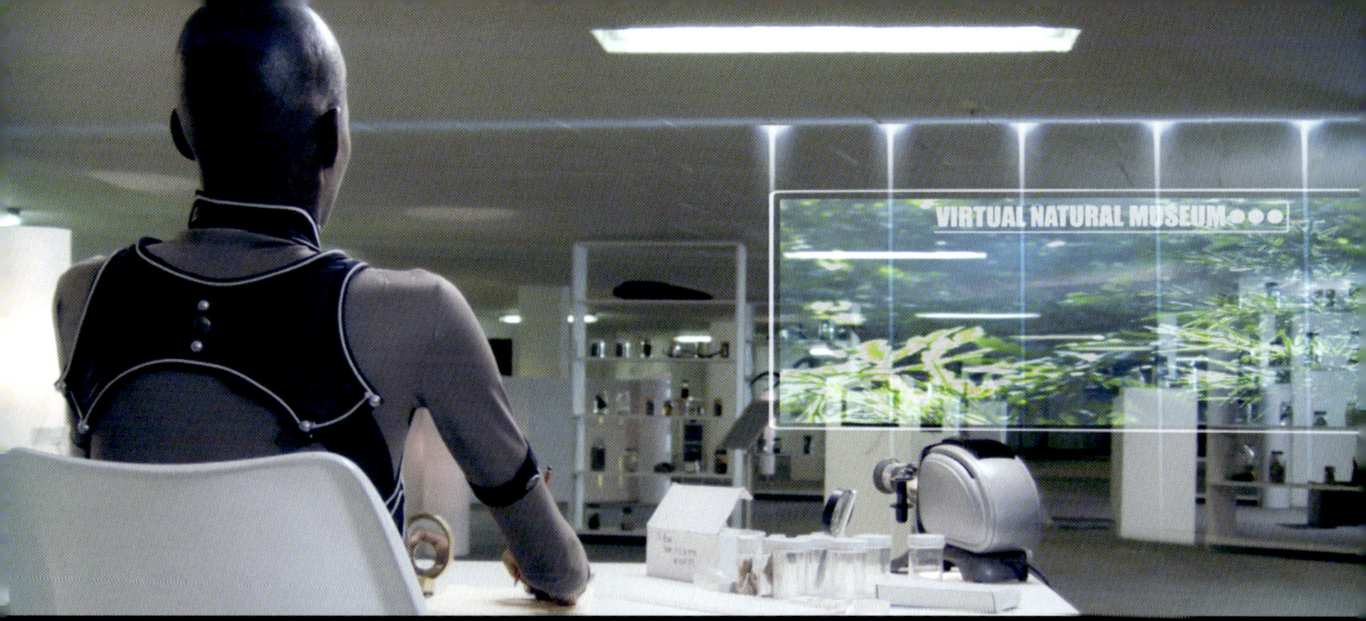

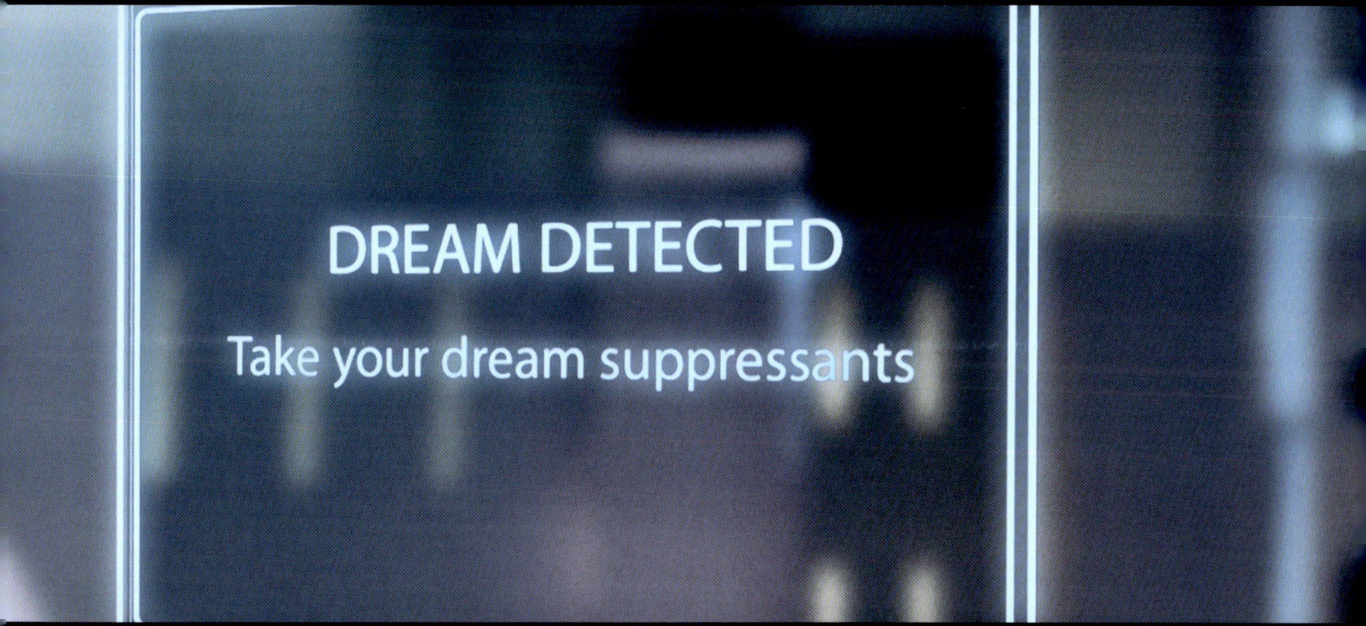

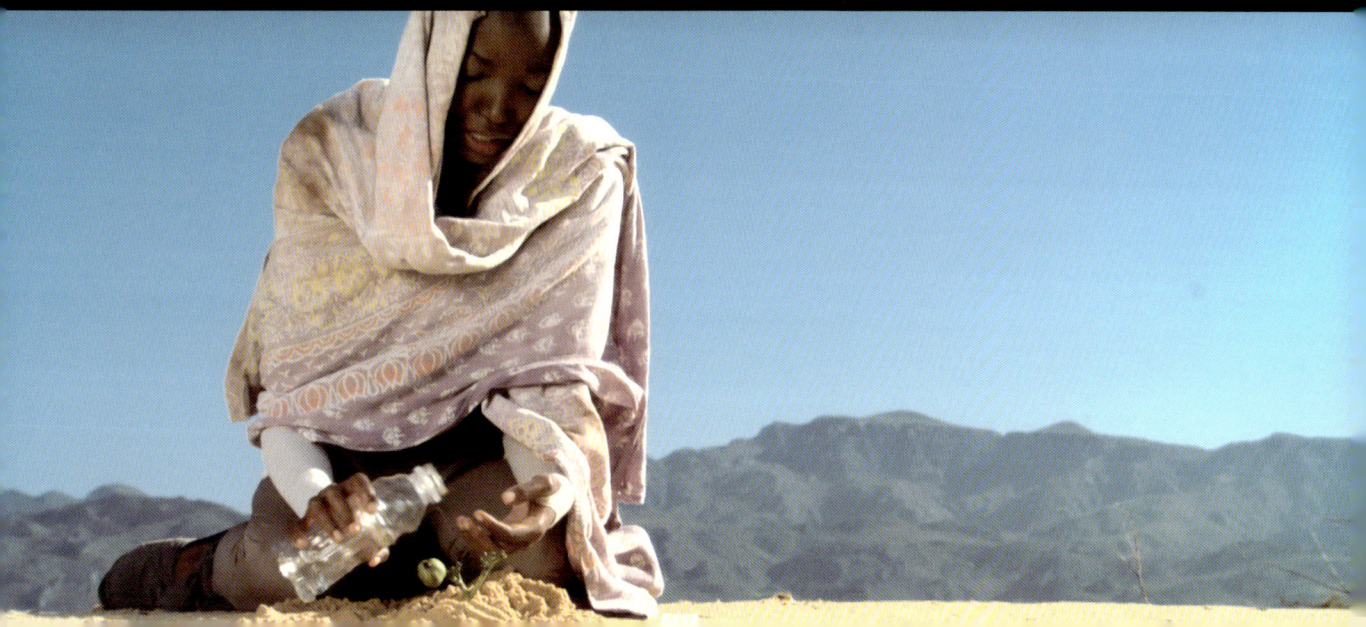

SC-248-L

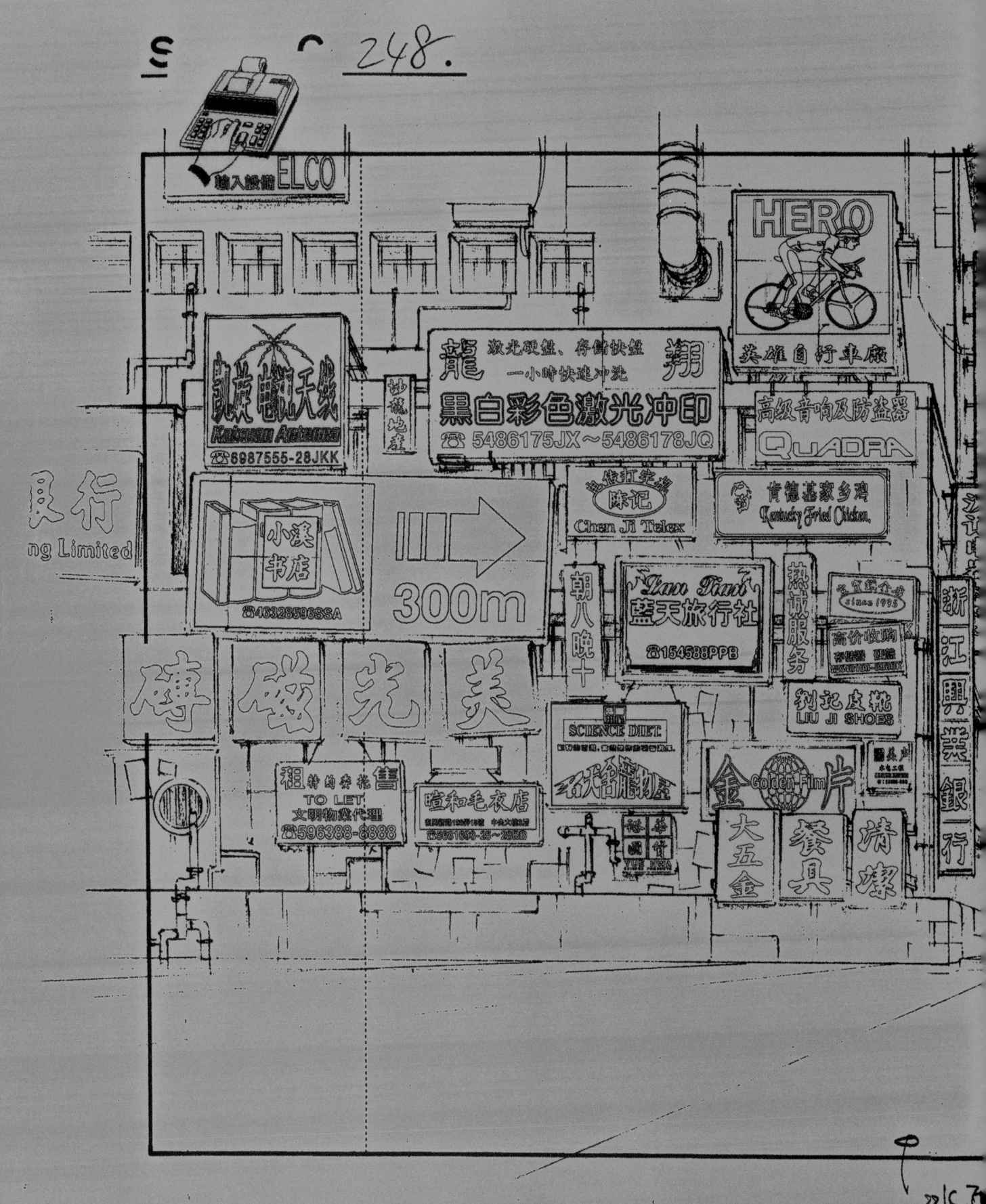

SC-248-R

5+12 秒

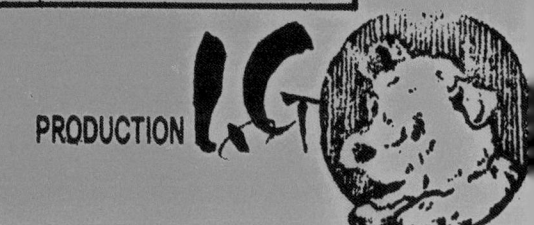

PRODUCTION I.G

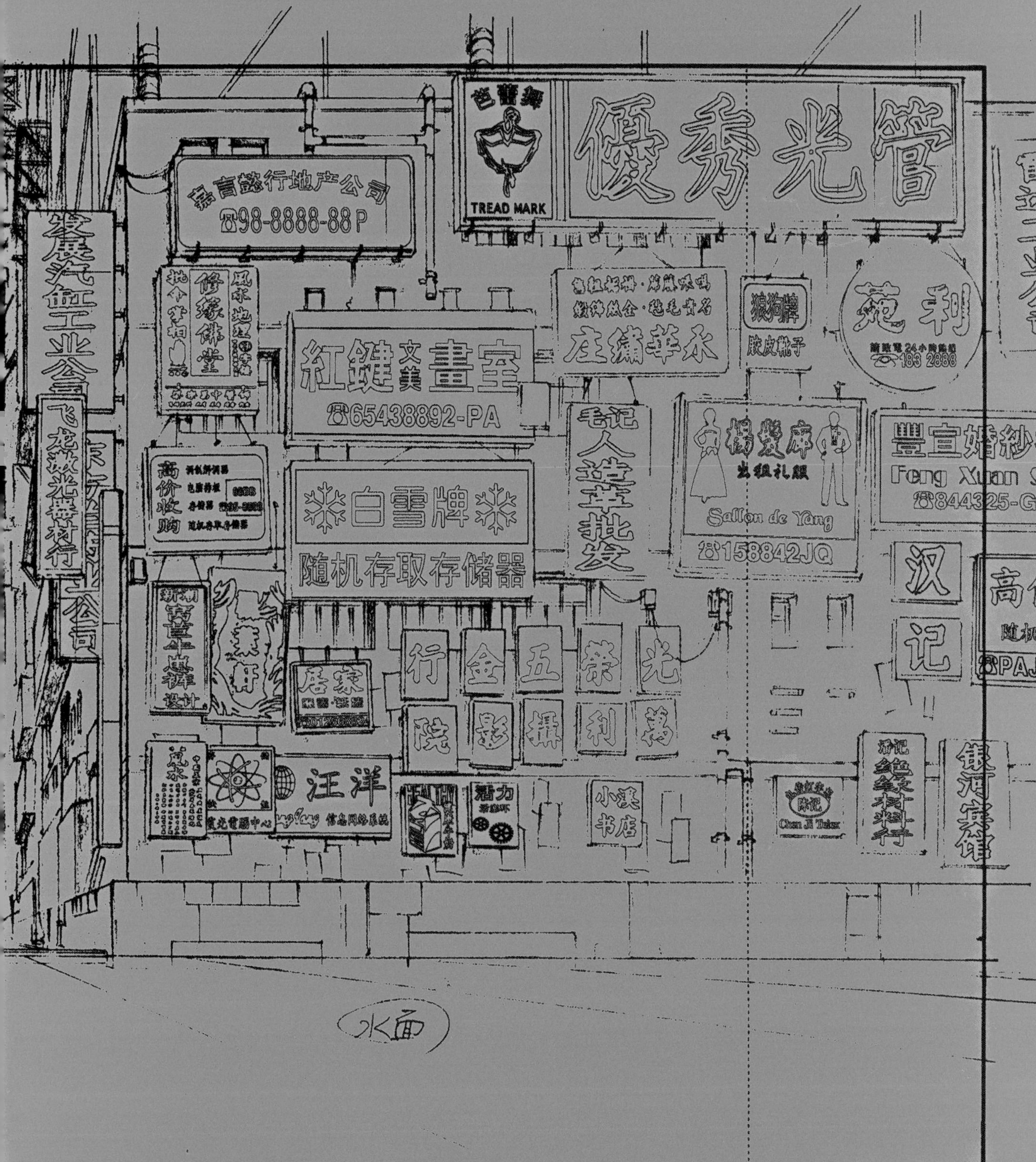

見せない処理にして下さい。
(セルのツゴウジョウ)

Selected Bibliography
Compiled by Emily Rauber Rodriguez

Allen, Kathryn, ed. *Disability in Science Fiction: Representations of Technology as Cure.* London: Palgrave, 2013.

Armstrong, Tim. *Modernism, Technology, and the Body: A Cultural Study.* New York: Cambridge University Press, 1998.

Attebery, Stina. "Indigenous Posthumans: Cyberpunk Surgeries and Biotech Boarding Schools in *File Under Miscellaneous* and SyFy's *Helix*." *Extrapolation* 57, nos. 1–2 (Spring/Summer 2016): 95–116.

Attebery, Stina, and Josh Pearson. "'Today's Cyborg is Stylish': The Humanity Cost of Posthuman Fashion in Cyberpunk 2020." In *Cyberpunk and Visual Culture*, edited by Graham J. Murphy and Lars Schmeink, 55–79. New York: Routledge, 2018.

Bainbridge, William S. *Goals in Space: American Values and the Future of Technology.* Albany: State University of New York Press, 1991.

Balsamo, Anne. *Technologies of the Gendered Body: Reading Cyborg Women.* Durham, NC: Duke University Press, 1996.

Barnett, P. Chad. "Reviving Cyberpunk: (Re)Constructing the Subject and Mapping Cyberspace in the Wachowski Brothers' Film *The Matrix*." *Extrapolation* 41, no. 4 (Winter 2000): 359–74.

Barr, Marleen S., ed. *Future Females, the Next Generation.* Lanham, MD: Rowman & Littlefield, 2000.

Baudemann, Kristina. "Indigenous Futurist Film: Speculation and Resistance in Jeff Barnaby's *Rhymes for Young Ghouls* and *File Under Miscellaneous*." In *Canadian Science Fiction, Fantasy, and Horror: Bridging the Solitudes*, edited by Amy J. Ransom and Dominick M. Grace, 151–65. New York: Palgrave Macmillan, 2019.

Baudrillard, Jean. "Simulacra and Simulations." In *Jean Baudrillard: Selected Writings*, edited by Mark Poster, 166–84. Cambridge: Polity Press, 2001.

Bell, David, and Barbara M. Kennedy, eds. *The Cybercultures Reader.* New York: Routledge, 2000.

Booth, Austin. "Women's Cyberfiction: An Introduction." In *Reload: Rethinking Women and Cyberculture*, edited by Mary Flanagan and Austin Booth, 25–41. Cambridge, MA: MIT Press, 2002.

Bould, Mark, Andrew M. Butler, Adam Roberts, and Sherryl Vint, eds. *The Routledge Companion to Science Fiction.* New York: Routledge, 2009.

Braidotti, Rosi. "Cyberfeminism with a Difference." In *Feminisms*, edited by Sandra Kemp and Judith Squires, 520–29. Oxford: Oxford University Press, 1997.

———. "Post-Human, All Too Human, Towards a New Process Ontology." *Theory, Culture & Society* 23, nos. 7–8 (December 2006): 197–208.

Brown, Stephen P. "Before the Lights Came On: Observations of a Synergy." In *Storming the Reality Studio*, edited by Larry McCaffery, 173–77. Durham, NC: Duke University Press, 1991.

Brown, Steven T. *Tokyo Cyberpunk: Posthumanism in Japanese Visual Culture.* London: Palgrave Macmillan, 2010.

Bryant, Levi R. *Onto-Cartography: An Ontology of Machines and Media.* Edinburgh: University of Edinburgh Press, 2014.

Bukatman, Scott. *Terminal Identity: The Virtual Subject in Postmodern Science Fiction.* Durham, NC: Duke University Press, 1993.

Butler, Andrew M. *Cyberpunk.* London: Pocket Essentials, 2000.

———. "Early Cyberpunk Film." In *The Routledge Companion to Cyberpunk Culture*, edited by Anna McFarlane, Graham J. Murphy, and Lars Schmeink, 119–27. New York: Routledge, 2020.

Byers, Thomas B. "Terminating the Postmodern: Masculinity and Pomophobia." *Modern Fiction Studies* 41, no. 1 (Spring 1995): 5–34.

Cadigan, Pat. "Foreword: Virtual Reality: As Real as You Want It to Be." In *Virtual Reality: Applications and Explorations*, edited by Alan Wexelblat, xi–xii. Cambridge, MA: Academic Press, 1993.

Cadora, Karen. "Feminist Cyberpunk." *Science Fiction Studies* 22, no. 3 (November 1995): 357–72.

Calvert, Bronwen, and Sue Walsh. "Speaking the Body: The Embodiment of 'Feminist' Cyberpunk." In *Speaking Science Fiction: Dialogues and Interpretations*, edited by Andy Sawyer and David Seed, 96–108. Liverpool: Liverpool University Press, 2002.

Capetola, Christine. "Cyberpunk and the Future Sounds of Janelle Monáe." In *The Routledge Companion to Cyberpunk Culture*, edited by Anna McFarlane, Graham J. Murphy, and Lars Schmeink, 245–51. New York: Routledge, 2020.

Carbonell, Curtis. "*Schismatrix* and the Posthuman: *Hyper-embodied Representation*." *Fafnir-Nordic Journal of Science Fiction and Fantasy Research* 3, no. 2 (2016): 7–16.

Castells, Manuel. "Communication, Power and Counter-power in the Network Society." *International Journal of Communication* 1 (2007): 238–66.

Cavallaro, Dani. *Cyberpunk and Cyberculture: Science Fiction and the Work of William Gibson.* London: Athlone Press, 2000.

Chu, Seo-Young. *Do Metaphors Dream of Literal Sleep? A Science-Fictional Theory of Representation.* Cambridge, MA: Harvard University Press, 2010.

Clynes, Manfred E., and Nathan S. Kline. "Cyborgs and Space." *Astronautics* 5, no. 9 (September 1960): 26–27, 74–76.

Condry, Ian. *The Soul of Anime: Collaborative Creativity and Japan's Media Success Story.* Durham, NC: Duke University Press, 2013.

Corn, Joseph J., and Brian Horrigan. *Yesterday's Tomorrows: Past Visions of the American Future.* Baltimore: Johns Hopkins University Press, 1996.

Cox, Ryan J. "Kusanagi's Body: Dualism and the Performance of Identity in *Ghost in the Shell* and *Stand Alone Complex*." In *Cyberpunk and Visual Culture*, edited by Graham J. Murphy and Lars Schmeink, 127–38. New York: Routledge, 2018.

DeCook, Julia R. "A [White] Cyborg's Manifesto: The Overwhelmingly Western Ideology Driving Technofeminist Theory." *Media, Culture & Society* 43, no. 6 (September 2021): 1158–67.

Delany, Samuel R. *Silent Interviews: On Language, Race, Sex, Science Fiction, and Some Comics.* Middletown, CT: Wesleyan University Press, 1994.

Denison, Rayna. *Anime: A Critical Introduction.* London: Bloomsbury, 2015.

Dery, Mark. "Black to the Future: Interviews with Samuel R. Delany, Greg Tate, and Tricia Rose." *South Atlantic Quarterly* 92, no. 4 (Fall 1993): 735–78.

———. *Escape Velocity: Cyberculture at the End of the Century.* New York: Grove Press, 1996.

Dery, Mark, ed. *Flame Wars: The Discourse of Cyberculture.* Durham, NC: Duke University Press, 1994.

Dillon, Grace L. "Indigenous Scientific Literacies in Nalo Hopkinson's Ceremonial Worlds." *Journal of the Fantastic in the Arts* 18, no. 1 (Winter 2007): 23–41.

———. "Introduction: Indigenous Futurisms, *Bimaashi Biidaas Mose, Flying* and *Walking* towards You." *Extrapolation* 57, nos. 1–2 (2016): 1–6.

Easterbrook, Neil. "The Arc of Our Destruction: Reversal and Erasure in Cyberpunk." *Science Fiction Studies* 19, no. 3 (November 1992): 378–94.

English, Daylanne K., and Alvin Kim. "Now We Want Our Funk Cut: Janelle Monáe's Neo-Afrofuturism." *American Studies* 52, no. 4 (January 2013): 217–30.

Eshun, Kodwo. "Further Considerations on Afrofuturism." *New Centennial Review* 3, no. 2 (Summer 2003): 287–302.

Featherstone, Mike, and Roger Burrows, eds. *Cyberspace/Cyberbodies/Cyberpunk: Cultures of Technological Embodiment*. London: Sage Publications, 1995.

Fernández, María. "Cyberfeminism, Racism, Embodiment." In *Domain Errors!: Cyberfeminist Practices*, edited by María Fernández, Faith Wilding, and Michelle M. Wright, 29–44. Brooklyn, NY: Autonomedia, 2003.

Flanagan, Mary, and Austin Booth, eds. *Reload: Rethinking Women and Cyberculture*. Cambridge, MA: MIT Press, 2002.

Flisfeder, Matthew. *Postmodern Theory and Blade Runner*. London: Bloomsbury, 2017.

Foster, Thomas. *The Souls of Cyberfolk: Posthumanism as Vernacular Theory*. Minneapolis: University of Minnesota Press, 2005.

Freedman, Carl. *Critical Theory and Science Fiction*. Middletown, CT: Wesleyan University Press, 2000.

———. "Marxism, Cinema and Some Dialectics of Science Fiction and Film Noir." In *Red Planets: Marxism and Science Fiction*, edited by Mark Bould and China Miéville, 66–82. Middletown, CT: Wesleyan University Press, 2009.

Gibson, William. "The Future Perfect: How Did Japan Become the Favored Default Setting for So Many Cyberpunk Writers?" *Time*, April 30, 2001.

———. *Neuromancer*. New York: Ace Books, 1984.

Gillis, Stacy, ed. *The Matrix Trilogy: Cyberpunk Reloaded*. London: Wallflower Press, 2005.

Gilroy, Paul. *The Black Atlantic: Modernity and Double Consciousness*. Cambridge, MA: Harvard University Press, 1993.

Goicoechea, María. "The Posthuman Ethos in Cyberpunk Science Fiction." *CLCWeb: Comparative Literature and Culture* 10, no. 4 (2008).

Graham, Elaine. "Cyborgs or Goddesses? Becoming Divine in a Cyberfeminist Age." *Information, Communication & Society* 2, no. 4 (1999): 419–38.

Gray, Chris Hables. *Cyborg Citizen: Politics in the Posthuman Age*. New York: Routledge, 2001.

Gray, Kishonna L. "Race, Gender, and Virtual Inequality: Exploring the Liberatory Potential of Black Cyberfeminist Theory." In *Producing Theory in a Digital World: The Intersection of Audiences and Production in Contemporary Theory*, edited by Rebecca Ann Lind, 175–92. Lausanne, Switzerland: Peter Lang, 2012.

Haraway, Donna. "A Cyborg Manifesto: Science, Technology, and Socialist-Feminism in the Late Twentieth Century." In *Simians, Cyborgs and Women: The Reinvention of Nature*, 149–81. New York: Routledge, 1991.

Harper, Mary Catherine. "Incurably Alien Other: A Case for Feminist Cyborg Writers." *Science Fiction Studies* 22, no. 3 (November 1995): 399–420.

Hassler-Forest, Dan. *Science Fiction, Fantasy, and Politics: Transmedia World-Building Beyond Capitalism*. Lanham, MD: Rowman & Littlefield, 2016.

Hayles, N. Katherine. "How Cyberspace Signifies: Taking Immortality Literally." In *Bridges to Science Fiction and Fantasy: Outstanding Essays from the J. Lloyd Eaton Conferences*, edited by Gregory Benford, Gary Westfahl, Howard V. Hendrix, and Joseph D. Miller, 151–60. Jefferson, NC: McFarland, 2018.

———. *How We Became Posthuman: Virtual Bodies in Cybernetics, Literature, and Informatics*. Chicago: University of Chicago Press, 1999.

Heuser, Sabine. *Virtual Geographies: Cyberpunk at the Intersection of the Postmodern and Science Fiction*. Amsterdam: Rodopi, 2003.

Holland, Samantha. "Descartes Goes to Hollywood: Mind, Body and Gender in Contemporary Cyborg Cinema." In *Cyberspace/Cyberbodies/Cyberpunk: Cultures of Technological Embodiment*, edited by Mike Featherstone and Roger Burrows, 157–74. London: Sage Publications, 1995.

Hollinger, Veronica. "Cybernetic Deconstructions: Cyberpunk and Postmodernism." *Mosaic: An Interdisciplinary Critical Journal* 23, no. 2 (Spring 1990): 29–44.

———. "Posthumanism and Cyborg Theory." In *The Routledge Companion to Science Fiction*, edited by Mark Bould, Andrew M. Butler, Adam Roberts, and Sherryl Vint, 267–78. New York: Routledge, 2009.

Hopkins, Patrick D., ed. *Sex/Machine: Readings in Culture, Gender, and Technology*. Bloomington: Indiana University Press, 1999.

Jameson, Fredric. "Postmodernism, or The Cultural Logic of Late Capitalism." *New Left Review* 1, no. 146 (July/August 1984): 53–92.

———. "Progress Versus Utopia; or, Can We Imagine the Future?" *Science Fiction Studies* 9, no. 2 (July 1982): 147–58.

Jones, Gwyneth. "Trouble (Living in the Machine)." In *Deconstructing the Starships: Science, Fiction and Reality*, 91–98. Liverpool: Liverpool University Press, 1999.

Kafer, Alison. "The Cyborg and the Crip: Critical Encounters." In *Feminist, Queer, Crip*, 103–28. Bloomington: Indiana University Press, 2013.

Kakoudaki, Despina. "Pinup and Cyborg: Exaggerated Gender and Artificial Intelligence." In *Future Females, the Next Generation*, edited by Marleen S. Barr, 165–95. Lanham, MD: Rowman & Littlefield, 2000.

Kelly, James Patrick. "Who Owns Cyberpunk?" In *Strange Divisions and Alien Territories: The Sub-Genres of Science Fiction*, edited by Keith Brooke, 144–55. London: Palgrave Macmillan, 2012.

Kelly, James Patrick, and John Kessel. "Introduction: Hacking Cyberpunk." In *Rewired: The Post-Cyberpunk Anthology*, edited by James Patrick Kelly and John Kessel, vii–xv. San Francisco: Tachyon, 2007.

Kelly, James Patrick, and John Kessel, eds. *Rewired: The Post-Cyberpunk Anthology*. San Francisco: Tachyon, 2007.

Kilgore, DeWitt Douglas. *Astrofuturism: Science, Race, and Visions of Utopia in Space*. Philadelphia: University of Pennsylvania Press, 2003.

King, C. Richard, and David J. Leonard. "'Is Neo White?' Reading Race, Watching the Trilogy." In *Jacking In to the Matrix Franchise: Cultural Reception and Interpretation*, edited by Matthew Kapell and William G. Doty, 32–47. New York: Continuum Press, 2004.

Kirby, David A. "The Future Is Now: Diegetic Prototypes and the Role of Popular Films in Generating Real-World Technological

Development." *Social Studies of Science* 40, no. 1 (February 2010): 41–70.

———. *Lab Coats in Hollywood: Science, Scientists, and Cinema*. Cambridge, MA: MIT Press, 2011.

Lai, Larissa. "Future Asians: Migrant Speculations, Repressed History and Cyborg Hope." *West Coast Line* 38, no. 2 (Fall 2004): 168–75.

Latham, Rob, ed. *Science Fiction Criticism: An Anthology of Essential Writings*. London: Bloomsbury Publishing, 2017.

Lavender, Isiah, III. *Afrofuturism Rising: The Literary Prehistory of a Movement*. Columbus: Ohio State University Press, 2019.

Lavender, Isiah, III, ed. *Black and Brown Planets: The Politics of Race in Science Fiction*. Jackson: University Press of Mississippi, 2014.

Lavender, Isiah, III, and Graham J. Murphy. "Afrofuturism." In *The Routledge Companion to Cyberpunk Culture*, edited by Anna McFarlane, Graham J. Murphy, and Lars Schmeink, 353–61. New York: Routledge, 2020.

Lavigne, Carlen. *Cyberpunk Women, Feminism and Science Fiction*. Jefferson, NC: McFarland, 2013.

Leary, Timothy. "The Cyberpunk: The Individual as Reality Pilot." In *Storming the Reality Studio*, edited by Larry McCaffery, 245–58. Durham, NC: Duke University Press, 1991.

Leblanc, Lauraine. "Razor Girls: Genre and Gender in Cyberpunk Fiction." *Women and Language* 20, no. 1 (Spring 1997): 71–76.

Le Guin, Ursula K. *The Language of the Night: Essays on Fantasy and Science Fiction*. Brooklyn, NY: Ultramarine Press, 1979.

Lenhardt, Corinna. "Cyberpunk and Indigenous Futurisms." In *The Routledge Companion to Cyberpunk Culture*, edited by Anna McFarlane, Graham J. Murphy, and Lars Schmeink, 344–52. New York: Routledge, 2020.

Lévy, Pierre. *Cyberculture*. Minneapolis: University of Minnesota Press, 2001.

Lippit, Akira Mizuta. *Atomic Light (Shadow Optics)*. Minneapolis: University of Minnesota Press, 2005.

Luckhurst, Roger. *Science Fiction*. Cambridge: Polity Press, 2005.

Martinez, Dolores. "Bodies of Future Memories: The Japanese Body in Science Fiction Anime." *Contemporary Japan* 27, no. 1 (2015): 71–88.

McCaffery, Larry, ed. *Storming the Reality Studio*. Durham, NC: Duke University Press, 1991.

McFarlane, Anna. "Cyberpunk and 'Science Fiction Realism' in Kathryn Bigelow's *Strange Days* and *Zero Dark Thirty*." In *Cyberpunk and Visual Culture*, edited by Graham J. Murphy and Lars Schmeink, 235–52. New York: Routledge, 2018.

McFarlane, Anna, Graham J. Murphy, and Lars Schmeink, eds. *The Routledge Companion to Cyberpunk Culture*. New York: Routledge, 2020.

McHale, Brian. "Elements of a Poetics of Cyberpunk." *Critique: Studies in Contemporary Fiction* 33, no. 3 (Spring 1992): 149–75.

Meehan, Paul. *Tech-Noir: The Fusion of Science Fiction and Film Noir*. Jefferson, NC: McFarland, 2008.

Mes, Tom. *Iron Man: The Cinema of Shinya Tsukamoto*. Godalming, UK: FAB Press, 2005.

Millar, Melanie Stewart. *Cracking the Gender Code: Who Rules the Wired World?* Toronto: Second Story Press, 1998.

Moynagh, Maureen. "Speculative Pasts and Afro-Futures: Nalo Hopkinson's Trans-American Imaginary." *African American Review* 51, no. 3 (Fall 2018): 211–22.

Murphy, Graham J., and Lars Schmeink, eds. *Cyberpunk and Visual Culture*. New York: Routledge, 2018.

Murphy, Graham J., and Sherryl Vint, eds. *Beyond Cyberpunk: New Critical Perspectives*. New York: Routledge, 2010.

Nama, Adilifu. *Black Space: Imagining Race in Science Fiction Film*. Austin: University of Texas Press, 2008.

Nayar, Pramod K. *Posthumanism*. Cambridge: Polity, 2014.

Nilges, Mathias. "The Realism of Speculation: Contemporary Speculative Fiction as Immanent Critique of Finance Capitalism." In *Speculative Finance / Speculative Fiction*, edited by David M. Higgins and Hugh C. O'Connell. Special issue, *CR: The New Centennial Review* 19, no. 1 (Spring 2019): 37–60.

Nixon, Nicola. "Cyberpunk: Preparing the Ground for Revolution or Keeping the Boys Satisfied?" *Science Fiction Studies* 19, no. 2 (July 1992): 219–35.

Novotny, Patrick. "No Future! Cyberpunk, Industrial Music, and the Aesthetics of Postmodern Disintegration." In *Political Science Fiction*, edited by Donald M. Hassler and Clyde Wilcox, 99–123. Columbia: University of South Carolina Press, 1997.

O'Donnell, Patrick, Stephen J. Burn, and Lesley Larkin, eds. *The Encyclopedia of Contemporary American Fiction: 1980–2020*. 2 vols. Hoboken, NJ: Wiley, 2022.

Orbaugh, Sharalyn. "The Genealogy of the Cyborg in Japanese Popular Culture." In *World Weavers, Globalization, Science Fiction, and Cybernetic Revolution*, edited by Wong Kin Yuen, Gary Westfahl, and Amy Kit-sze Chan, 55–72. Hong Kong: Hong Kong University Press, 2005.

———. "Sex and the Single Cyborg: Japanese Popular Culture Experiments in Subjectivity." In *Robot Ghosts and Wired Dreams: Japanese Science Fiction from Origins to Anime*, edited by Christopher Bolton, Istvan Csicsery-Ronay, and Takayuki Tatsumi, 172–92. Minneapolis: University of Minnesota Press, 2007.

Orr, Jackie. "Materializing a Cyborg's Manifesto." *Women's Studies Quarterly* 40, nos. 1–2 (Spring/Summer 2012): 273–80.

Paffrath, James D., and Stelarc, eds. *Obsolete Body: Suspensions: Stelarc*. Davis, CA: J.P. Publications, 1984.

Pfiel, Fred. "These Disintegrations I'm Looking Forward to: Science Fiction from the New Wave to New Age." In *Another Tale to Tell: Politics and Narrative in Postmodern Culture*, 83–94. New York: Verso, 1990.

Pilsch, Andrew. *Transhumanism: Evolutionary Futurism and the Human Technologies of Utopia*. Minneapolis: University of Minnesota Press, 2017.

Plant, Sadie. "On the Matrix: Cyberfeminist Simulations." In *The Cybercultures Reader*, edited by David Bell and Barbara M. Kennedy, 325–36. New York: Routledge, 2000.

Raulerson, Joshua. *Singularities: Technoculture, Transhumanism, and Science Fiction in the Twenty-First Century*. Liverpool: University of Liverpool Press, 2013.

Rhee, Jennifer. *The Robotic Imaginary: The Human & The Price of Dehumanized Labor*. Minneapolis: University of Minnesota Press, 2018.

Rivera, Lysa. "Chicana/o Cyberpunk after el Movimiento." *Aztlán: A Journal of Chicano Studies* 40, no. 2 (Fall 2015): 187–202.

Robins, Kevin. "Cyberspace and the World We Live In." In *Cyberspace/Cyberbodies/Cyberpunk: Cultures of Technological Embodiment*, edited by Mike Featherstone and Roger Burrows, 135–56. London: Sage Publications, 1995.

Rodriguez, Francisco Collado. "Fear of the Flesh, Fear of the Borg: Narratives of Bodily Transgression in Contemporary U.S. Culture." In *Beyond Borders: Re-defining Generic and Ontological Boundaries*, edited by Ramón Plo-Alastrué and María Jesús Martínez-Alfaro, 67–80. Heidelberg, Germany: Universitätsverlag C. Winter, 2002.

Roh, David S., Betsy Huang, and Greta A. Niu, eds. *Techno-Orientalism: Imagining Asia in Speculative Fiction, History, and Media*. New Brunswick, NJ: Rutgers University Press, 2015.

Rucker, Rudy, R. U. Sirius [Ken Goffman], and Queen Mu [Alison Bailey Kennedy]. *Mondo 2000: A User's Guide to the New Edge*. New York: Harper Perennial, 1992.

Saito, Kumiko. "Anime." In *The Routledge Companion to Cyberpunk Culture*, edited by Anna McFarlane, Graham J. Murphy, and Lars Schmeink, 151–61. New York: Routledge, 2020.

Sandoval, Chela. "Cyborg Feminism and the Methodology of the Oppressed." In *Feminist and Queer Information Studies Reader*, edited by Patrick Keilty and Rebecca Dean, 117–36. Sacramento, CA: Litwin Books, 2012.

Schallegger, René. "Homo Ex Machina? – Cyber-Renaissance and Transhumanism in *Deus Ex: Human Revolution*." In *Early Modernity and Video Games*, edited by Tobias Winnerling and Florian Kerschbaumer, 52–63. Cambridge: Cambridge Scholars, 2014.

Schaub, Joseph Christopher. "Kusanagi's Body: Gender and Technology in Mecha-Anime." *Asian Journal of Communication* 11, no. 2 (2001): 79–100.

Schmeink, Lars. *Biopunk Dystopias: Genetic Engineering, Society, and Science Fiction*. Liverpool: Liverpool University Press, 2016.

Seu, Mindy. *Cyberfeminism Index*. Los Angeles: Inventory Press, 2022.

Sharon, Tamar. "A Cartography of the Posthuman: Humanist, Non-Humanist and Mediated Perspectives on Emerging Biotechnologies." *Krisis: Journal for Contemporary Philosophy* 2 (2012): 4–19.

Sharp, Patrick B. *Darwinian Feminism and Early Science Fiction: Angels, Amazons and Women*. Cardiff: University of Wales Press, 2018.

Shiner, Lewis. "Confessions of an Ex-Cyberpunk." *New York Times*, January 7, 1991.

Short, Sue. *Cyborg Cinema and Contemporary Subjectivity*. New York: Palgrave Macmillan, 2005.

Silvio, Carl. "Refiguring the Radical Cyborg in Mamoru Oshii's *Ghost in the Shell*." *Science Fiction Studies* 26, no. 1 (March 1999): 54–72.

Slusser, George, and Tom Shippey, eds. *Fiction 2000: Cyberpunk and the Future of Narrative*. Athens: University of Georgia Press, 1992.

Sobchack, Vivian. *Screening Space: The American Science Fiction Film*. New Brunswick, NJ: Rutgers University Press, 1987.

Springer, Claudia. "Psycho-cybernetics in Films of the 1990s." In *Alien Zone II: The Spaces of Science Fiction Cinema*, edited by Annette Kuhn, 203–18. New York: Verso, 1999.

Sterling, Bruce, ed. *Mirrorshades: The Cyberpunk Anthology*. New York: Arbor House, 1986.

Stockton, Sharon. "'The Self Regained': Cyberpunk's Retreat to the Imperium." *Contemporary Literature* 36, no. 4 (Winter 1995): 588–612.

Strait, Kevin M., and Kinshasa Holman Conwill, eds. *Afrofuturism: A History of Black Futures*. Washington, DC: Smithsonian Books, 2023.

Tatsumi, Takayuki. *Full Metal Apache: Transactions between Cyberpunk Japan and Avant-Pop America*. Durham, NC: Duke University Press, 2006.

———. "Generations and Controversies: An Overview of Japanese Science Fiction, 1957–1997." *Science Fiction Studies* 27, no. 1 (March 2000): 105–14.

———. "Transpacific Cyberpunk: Transgeneric Interactions between Prose, Cinema, and Manga." In *Cyberpunk in a Transnational Context*, edited by Takayuki Tatsumi. Special issue, *Arts* 7, no. 1 (March 2018).

Taylor, Paul A. "Hackers: Cyberpunks or Microserfs?" *Information, Communication & Society* 1, no. 4 (1998): 401–19.

Thomas, Susan. "Between the Boys and Their Toys: The Science Fiction Film." In *Where No Man Has Gone Before: Women and Science Fiction*, edited by Lucie Armitt, 109–22. New York: Routledge, 1991.

Turkle, Sherry. "Looking Toward Cyberspace: Beyond Grounded Sociology—Cyberspace and Identity." *Contemporary Sociology* 28, no. 6 (November 1999): 643–48.

Vint, Sherryl. *Bodies of Tomorrow: Technology, Subjectivity, Science Fiction*. Toronto: University of Toronto Press, 2007.

———. "Coding of Race in Science Fiction: What's Wrong with the Obvious?" In *Worlds of Wonder: Readings in Canadian Science Fiction and Fantasy Literature*, edited by Jean-Francois Leroux and Camille R. LaBossière, 119–30. Ottawa: University of Ottawa Press, 2004.

———. "Cyberwar: The Convergence of Virtual and Material Battlefields in Cyberpunk Cinema." In *Cyberpunk and Visual Culture*, edited by Graham J. Murphy and Lars Schmeink, 253–75. New York: Routledge, 2018.

VNS Matrix. "A Cyberfeminist Manifesto for the 21st Century." VNS Matrix: Merchants of Slime, 1991. vnsmatrix.net/the-cyber-feminist-manifesto-for-the-21st-century.

Whalen, Terence. "The Future of a Commodity: Notes Toward a Critique of Cyberpunk and the Information Age." *Science Fiction Studies* 19 (March 1992): 75–88.

Wohlsen, Marcus. *Biopunk: DIY Scientists Hack the Software of Life*. New York: Current, 2011.

Wolmark, Jenny, ed. *Cybersexualities: A Reader on Feminist Theory, Cyborgs, and Cyberspace*. Edinburgh: Edinburgh University Press, 1999.

Yaszek, Lisa. "Feminist Cyberpunk." In *The Routledge Companion to Cyberpunk Culture*, edited by Anna McFarlane, Graham J. Murphy, and Lars Schmeink, 32–40. New York: Routledge, 2020.

Yaszek, Lisa, Sonja Fritzsche, Keren Omry, and Wendy Gay Pearson, eds. *The Routledge Companion to Gender and Science Fiction*. New York: Routledge, 2023.

Yoshimoto, Mitsuhiro. "The Postmodern and Mass Images in Japan." *Public Culture* 1, no. 2 (Spring 1989): 8–25.

Yu, Timothy. "Oriental Cities, Postmodern Futures: *Naked Lunch*, *Blade Runner*, and *Neuromancer*." *MELUS* 33, no. 4 (Winter 2008): 45–71.

Contributors

NICHOLAS BARLOW is an assistant curator at the Academy Museum of Motion Pictures. In his previous position as a curatorial assistant at the Hammer Museum, Los Angeles, he served as lead curator on *Cruel Youth Diary: Chinese Photography and Video from the Haudenschild Collection* (2023) and assisted with the exhibitions *Tishan Hsu: Liquid Circuit* (2020), *Paul McCarthy: Head Space, Drawings 1963–2019* (2020), and *Lifes* (2022). From 2015 to 2018, he was a curatorial assistant at the Los Angeles County Museum of Art.

CRAIG BARRON is creative director at Magnopus as well as an educator and author, focusing on cinema's evolution across the digital age. He formerly worked at Industrial Light & Magic, where he contributed to iconic films such as *Raiders of the Lost Ark* (1981) and *E.T. the Extra-Terrestrial* (1982). Through his VFX studio, Matte World Digital, he served as a VFX supervisor on *Zodiac* (2007) and *Hugo* (2011). He won an Oscar for Visual Effects for *The Curious Case of Benjamin Button* (2008).

DORIS BERGER is vice president of curatorial affairs at the Academy Museum of Motion Pictures. She co-curated the museum's exhibitions *Stories of Cinema* (2021), *Backdrop: An Invisible Art* (2021), and *Regeneration: Black Cinema, 1898–1971* (2022), and curated *Isaac Julien: Baltimore* (2022). She previously worked as director of the Kunstverein Wolfsburg, Germany, had a postdoctoral fellowship at the Getty Research Institute, and was a curator at the Skirball Cultural Center, Los Angeles. She is the author of *Projected Art History: Biopics, Celebrity Culture, and the Popularizing of American Art* (2014) and the editor of *Light & Noir: Exiles and Émigrés in Hollywood, 1933–1950* (2015), among other books.

DEFORREST BROWN JR. is an Alabama-raised, ex-American rhythmanalyst, writer, and curator. He has released three albums as Speaker Music: *Of Desire, Longing* (2019), *Black Nationalist Sonic Weaponry* (2020), and *Techxodus* (2023). His written work explores the links between the Black experience in industrialized labor systems and Black innovation in electronic music. His debut book, *Assembling a Black Counter Culture*, was published in 2022.

MAYA S. CADE is a Brooklyn-based writer and film programmer, and the award-winning creator and curator of Black Film Archive. She is a scholar-in-residence at the Library of Congress. She proudly hails from New Orleans, Louisiana.

ASHLEY CLARK is the curatorial director at the Criterion Collection. He previously worked as director of film programming at the Brooklyn Academy of Music, and has curated film series at the Museum of Modern Art, New York; the Smithsonian National Museum of African American History & Culture, Washington, DC; TIFF Bell Lightbox, and BFI Southbank, among other venues. His writing has appeared in the *New York Times*, *Vulture*, and *Sight & Sound*. He is the author of the book *Facing Blackness: Media and Minstrelsy in Spike Lee's* Bamboozled (2015).

MILLIE DE CHIRICO is a film programmer, writer, and the former curator of TCM Underground, a late-night cult movie franchise on Turner Classic Movies that ran from 2006 to 2022. Her book *TCM Underground: 50 Must-See Films from the World of Classic Cult and Late-Night Cinema* was published in 2022. She currently co-hosts the weekly film podcast *I Saw What You Did* on the Exactly Right network and teaches film in Atlanta.

SHARI FRILOT is senior programmer and chief curator of New Frontier at Sundance Film Festival. She is the founder and driving creative force behind New Frontier at Sundance, a showcase of storytelling at the intersection of film, art, and new media technology, which world premiered the prototype of the Oculus Rift VR headset. Shari has programmed features for Sundance since 1998 and has garnered a Webby, multiple Emmy awards, and is the inaugural winner of the Peabody Visionary award.

DAVID A. KIRBY is chair of the Department of Interdisciplinary Studies in the Liberal Arts at Cal Poly University, San Luis Obispo. He studies how the fictional stories we tell about science impact our perceptions of science as a social, cultural, and political force. His book *Lab Coats in Hollywood: Science, Scientists, and Cinema* (2011) examines the collaborations between scientists and the entertainment industry. His "diegetic prototype" concept provided a foundation for creative approaches to technological development, including design fiction.

NORMAN M. KLEIN is a critic, urban and media historian, novelist, and faculty in the School of Critical Studies at California Institute of the Arts. His books include *Seven Minutes: The Life and Death of the American Animated Cartoon* (1993), *The History of Forgetting: Los Angeles and the Erasure of Memory* (1997) and *The Vatican to Vegas: The History of Special Effects* (2004). His work explores the relationship between collective memory and power in urban spaces; the thin line between fact and fiction; and erasure, forgetting, scripted spaces, and the social imaginary.

CARLEN LAVIGNE is the author of *Cyberpunk Women, Feminism and Science Fiction* (2013) and *Post-Apocalyptic Patriarchy: American Television and Gendered Visions of Survival* (2018). Her work has appeared in publications such as *MOSF Journal of Science Fiction*, *Journal of Gaming and Virtual Worlds*, and *The Routledge Companion to Gender and Science Fiction* (2023). She is head of communications studies at Red Deer Polytechnic, Alberta. She holds a PhD in communications from McGill University.

AKIRA MIZUTA LIPPIT teaches film and literature at the University of Southern California, Los Angeles. He is the author of *Electric Animal: Toward a Rhetoric of Wildlife* (2000), *Atomic Light (Shadow Optics)* (2005), *Ex-Cinema: From a Theory of Experimental Film and Video* (2012), and *Cinema without Reflection: Jacques Derrida's Echopoiesis and Narcissism Adrift* (2016). He is currently working on books about the nonexistence of Japanese cinema and David Lynch's baroque alphabetics.

EMILY RAUBER RODRIGUEZ is a curatorial assistant at the Academy Museum of Motion Pictures, where she contributed to the exhibitions *Regeneration: Black Cinema, 1898–1971* (2022) and *John Waters: Pope of Trash* (2023). She holds an MA and a PhD in cinema and media studies as well as a graduate certificate in cinematic arts archiving and preservation from the University of Southern California. Her scholarly work focuses on race and ethnicity in speculative fiction.

K.J. RELTH-MILLER is director of the Film Programs department at the Academy Museum of Motion Pictures, which she joined in 2022 after having worked as a programmer for the UCLA Film & Television Archive, the Slamdance Film Festival, AFI FEST, and the Cinefamily. Since 2018, she has been an adjunct professor in the Film/Video department at CalArts. She holds an MA in media studies and film from the New School.

PATRICK B. SHARP is professor of liberal studies at California State University, Los Angeles. His scholarship explores the complex relationships between colonization, race, gender, and evolutionary narrative. His publications include *Savage Perils: Racial Frontiers and Nuclear Apocalypse in American Culture* (2007), *Darwinian Feminism and Early Science Fiction: Angels, Amazons and Women* (2018), and the anthology *Sisters of Tomorrow: The First Women of Science Fiction* (2016), which he co-edited.

Image Credits

The images in this book are reproduced with permission. All reasonable efforts have been made to contact the rights holders. Any errors or omissions will be corrected in subsequent editions.

©20th Century Studios, Inc.: 29, 42–43 top row, 44–45 bottom row, 126, 127 left and top right
Courtesy A24 Films: 34 top, 158–59
©ANM (1991) XXXIII Limited Partnership, courtesy TriStar Pictures: 21 top, 48–49 fourth row, 118–21, 123
©Academy Museum Foundation, photo by Joshua White/JWPictures.com: 78 left, 100 bottom (matte painting by Syd Dutton), 160, 163
©Black Audio Films, courtesy Smoking Dogs Films: 36–37 bottom row, 38–39 top row, 132–35
©Disney: 40–41 top and third rows, 45 middle
©Doubleday: 26 left
Courtesy Futuro Films: 40–41 second row, 153 bottom (concept art: Miguel Ángel Álvarez)
Courtesy Futuro Films, photo by Luis Aguilar: 4–5, 16–17, 30 right, 148–153 top
Courtesy Danis Goulet, photo by Kona Goulet: 178
©Guardian Trust Company, courtesy Universal Studios Licensing: 42 bottom, 80–81, 84–85
Courtesy Inspired Minority: 21 bottom, 157 bottom left, 181
Courtesy Inspired Minority, photo by Mark Wessels: 154–55, 157 top, 157 bottom right, 179
©Kaijyu Theater: 40–41 bottom row, 48–49 third row
©Kino Lorber: 38–39 third row
©Kino Lorber, photo by Chris Schwagga: 6–7, 18 right, 31–33, 164–69, back cover
Courtesy Gene Kozicki, photo by Virgil Mirano: 44 middle, 67 bottom left
Photo by Alwin Kuchlar: 128–31
Courtesy Lions Gate Films, Inc.: 38–39 second row, 48–49 top and bottom row, 67 bottom right
Courtesy MGM Media Licensing: 20–21 top middle, 26 right, 28 left, 44–45 top row, 48–49 second row, 86–87, 89–90, 91 top right, 92–94, 97
Courtesy of Margaret Herrick Library, Academy of Motion Picture Arts and Sciences, cover, 2–3, frontispiece, 19 right, 19 left (production design drawing: Jack T. Collis), 26 center, 27, 28 right, 30 left, 43 bottom, 46–47, 52–57, 67 bottom left (costume design drawing: Stephen Loomis), 70–71, 72 left, 72 right (costume design drawing: Michael Kaplan), 73–77, 79 top, 88, 91 top left and bottom, 95–96, 101 (production design drawing: Jack T. Collis), 117 (poster by Killian Eng), 124–25, 142–145, 146 and 147 bottom (storyboard by Tani Kunitake), 162
Courtesy Margaret Herrick Library, Academy of Motion Picture Arts and Sciences, photo by Jasin Boland: 147 top

Courtesy Margaret Herrick Library, Academy of Motion Picture Arts and Sciences, photo by Kim Gottlieb-Walker: 64–65, 67 top
Courtesy Margaret Herrick Library, Academy of Motion Picture Arts and Sciences, photo by Takashi Seida: 122
©Shirow Masamune/Kodansha·Bandai Visual· Manga Entertainment: 48–49 top and bottom row, 112–114, 115 (background by Hiromasa Ogura), 116 right (background by Shuichi Kusamori), 116 left, 182–83
©Mashroom/AKIRA Committee: 20 bottom
©Mashroom/AKIRA Committee, courtesy of Margaret Herrick Library: 102–5
©Syd Mead Inc., artist: Syd Mead: 68–69, 79 bottom, 127 bottom right
Moviestore Collection via Alamy: 78 right
©Night Raiders East Inc.: 36–37 top row, 173 bottom (concept art: Goran Delic), 176
©Night Raiders East Inc., photo by Ramona Diaconescu: 173 top left, 180 right
©Night Raiders East Inc., photo by Christos Kalohoridis: 173 top right, 180 left
©Night Raiders East Inc., photo by Ian Watson: 170–71
Courtesy Paramount Pictures: 98–99, 100 top
Courtesy Paramount Pictures, photo by Ava V. Gerlitz: 136–37, 140 bottom, 141 top
©Popular Library: 18 left
Synthescape Art Imaging: 82–83, 140 top, 141 bottom
Synthescape Art Imaging, photo by Ava V. Gerlitz: 138–39
©Shinya Tsukamoto/Kaijyu Theater: half title, 106–11
©Universal, Film4, and DNA Films, courtesy Universal Studios Licensing: 22–23, 34 middle and bottom, 35, 161
©Warner Bros. Entertainment Inc.: 20 top, 24–25, 36–37 middle row, 38–39 bottom row, 42–43 middle row, 174–75
Westdeutscher Rundfunk: 58–63

I, Cyberpunk, pp. 32–53

32–33: *Neptune Frost*; 34–35: *Ex Machina*; 36–37 by row, from top: *Night Raiders*, *Blade Runner*, *The Last Angel of History*; 38–39 by row, from top: *The Last Angel of History*, *Escape from New York*, *Neptune Frost*, *The Matrix*; 40–41 by row, from top: *Tron*, *Sleep Dealer*, *Tron*, *Tetsuo: The Iron Man*; 42–43: *Alita: Battle Angel* (top row), *Blade Runner* (middle row; bottom right), *Videodrome* (bottom left); 44–45: *RoboCop* (top row), *Blade Runner* (middle left), *Tron* (middle right), *Alita: Battle Angel* (bottom row); 46–47: *RoboCop*; 48–49 by row, from top: *Ghost in the Shell*, *The Terminator*, *Tetsuo: The Iron Man*, *Johnny Mnemonic*, *Ghost in the Shell*; 52–53: *The Matrix*

Academy Museum of Motion Pictures
Board of Trustees

Ted Sarandos, *Chair*
Miky Lee, *Vice Chair*
Kimberly Steward, *Secretary*
Jim Gianopulos, *Treasurer*

Patricia Bellinger Balzer
Howard Berger
Jason Blum
Arnaud Boetsch
Effie T. Brown*
David Dolby
Tom Duffield
Sidonie Seydoux Dumas
Eric Esrailian
Sid Ganis*
Olivier de Givenchy
Julia S. Gouw
Ray Halbritter
Tom Hanks
Travis Knight
Bill Kramer
Eva Longoria
Ryan Murphy
Dominic Ng
Katherine L. Oliver
Alejandro Ramírez Magaña
Shira Ruderman
Regina K. Scully
Jacqueline Stewart
Emma Thomas
Janet Yang
Kevin Yeaman

* Honorary Trustee

Ex Officio

Jacqueline Stewart
Academy Museum Director and President

Bill Kramer
Academy and Academy Foundation CEO

Janet Yang
Academy President and Academy Foundation Trustee

Howard Berger
Academy Vice President and Academy Foundation President

Tom Duffield
Academy and Academy Foundation Treasurer

This publication accompanies the exhibition *Cyberpunk: Envisioning Possible Futures Through Cinema*, curated by Doris Berger with Nicholas Barlow and Emily Rauber Rodriguez and presented at the Academy Museum of Motion Pictures, Los Angeles, October 6, 2024–April 12, 2026.

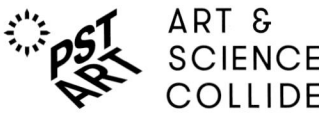

Cyberpunk: Envisioning Possible Futures Through Cinema is among more than sixty exhibitions and programs presented as part of PST ART. Returning in September 2024 with its latest edition, PST ART: *Art & Science Collide*, this landmark regional event explores the intersections of art and science, both past and present. PST ART is presented by Getty. For more information about PST ART: *Art & Science Collide*, please visit pst.art

Generous support also provided by the Alfred P. Sloan Foundation Program in Public Understanding of Science and Technology and the Los Angeles County Board of Supervisors through the Los Angeles County Department of Arts and Culture.

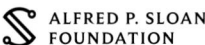

Academy Museum Digital Engagement Platform sponsored by Bloomberg Philanthropies.

Bloomberg Philanthropies

Published in 2024 by the Academy Museum of Motion Pictures and DelMonico Books • D.A.P.

Academy Museum of Motion Pictures
6067 Wilshire Boulevard
Los Angeles, California 90036
academymuseum.org

DelMonico Books available through:
ARTBOOK | D.A.P.
75 Broad Street, Suite 630
New York, NY 10004
artbook.com
delmonicobooks.com

© 2024 Academy Museum Foundation, Los Angeles

All texts © 2024 Academy Museum Foundation and the authors

All rights reserved. No part of this book may be reproduced or transmitted in any form or by any means, electronic or mechanical, including photocopy, recording, or any other information storage and retrieval system, or otherwise without written permission from the publishers. The ©Oscar® statuette is the registered design mark and copyrighted property of the Academy of Motion Picture Arts and Sciences.

Design by Michael Worthington, Counterspace
Editing by Nikki Bazar
Proofreading by Susan Richmond

Academy Museum of Motion Pictures
Director of Publications: Stacey Allan
Senior Editor: Chelsea Bingham
Editorial Manager: Madeleine Heppermann
Senior Publications Coordinator: Lars Eckstrom

DelMonico Books
Publisher: Mary DelMonico
Director of Production: Karen Farquhar

Color separations by Echelon, Los Angeles
Printed and bound in China

ISBN: 978-1-63681-131-4
LCCN: 2024936781

Front cover: Daryl Hannah as Pris in *Blade Runner* (1982)
Half title: Tomorowo Taguchi as the Salaryman in *Tetsuo: The Iron Man* (1989)
pp. 2–3: Special makeup effects crew during production of *The Matrix* (1999)
pp. 4–5: Node bar scene in *Sleep Dealer* (2008)
pp. 6–7: Rebecca Mucyo as Elohel and Bertrand Ninteretse as Matalusa in *Neptune Frost* (2021)
Frontispiece: Harrison Ford as Rick Deckard in *Blade Runner*
Back cover: Yannick Kamanzi as a member of the hacker resistance in *Neptune Frost* (2021)